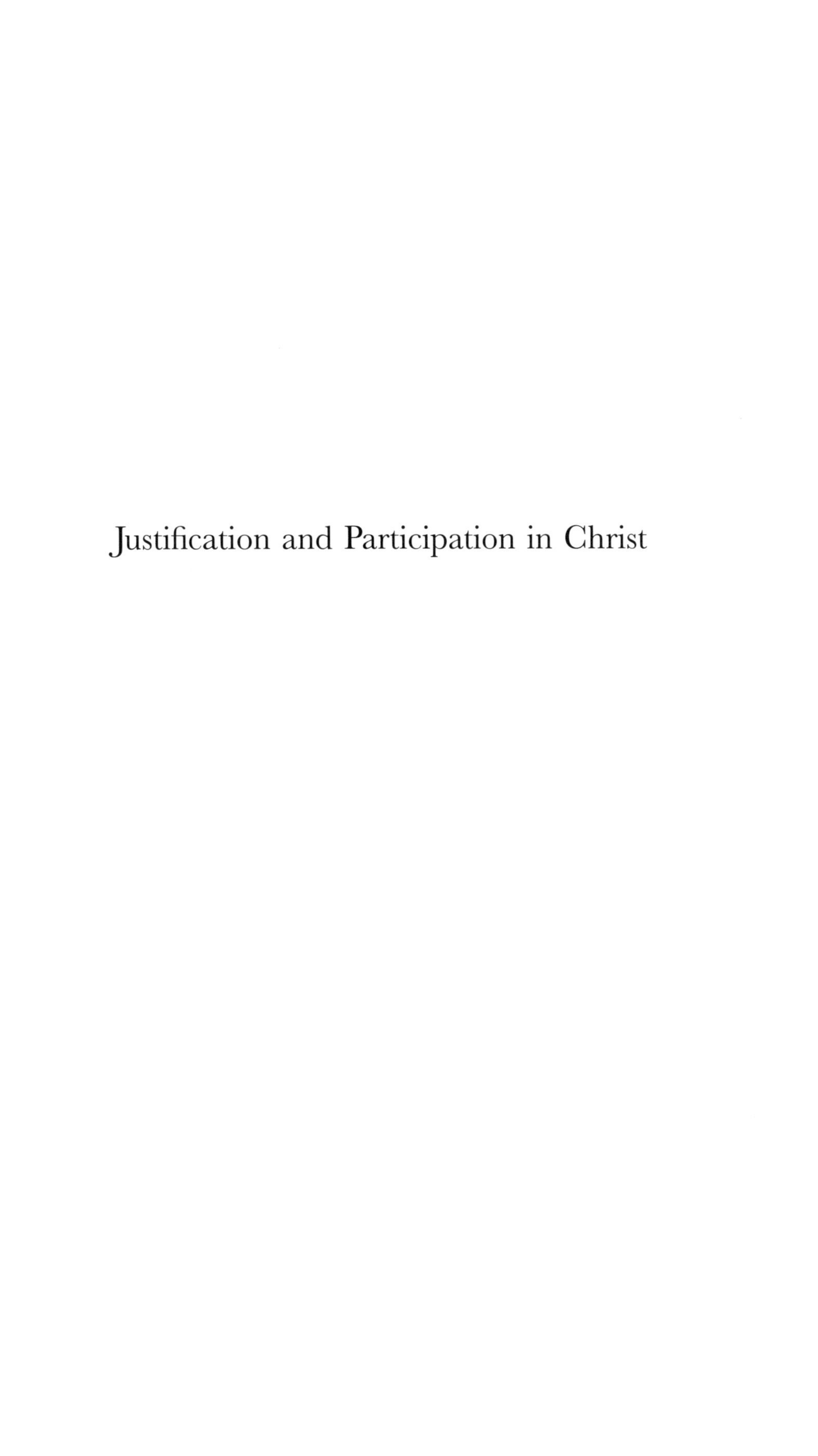

Justification and Participation in Christ

Studies in Medieval and Reformation Traditions

VOLUME 130

Justification and Participation in Christ

The Development of the Lutheran Doctrine of Justification from Luther to the Formula of Concord (1580)

By

Olli-Pekka Vainio

BRILL

LEIDEN • BOSTON
2008

On the cover: Richard Meier, Jubilee Church Dio Padre Misericordioso (Roma, Italia). Photo: Kuorikoski, Arto @

This book is printed on acid-free paper.

Library of Congress Cataloging-in-Publication Data

Vainio, Olli-Pekka.
Justification and participation in Christ: the development of the Lutheran doctrine of justification from Luther to the Formula of concord (1580) / by Olli-Pekka Vainio.
p. cm. — (Studies in medieval and Reformation traditions ; v. 130)
Includes bibliographical references (p.) and index.
ISBN 978-90-04-16526-7 (hardback : alk. paper) 1. Justification (Christian theology)—History of doctrines—16th century. 2. Lutheran Church—Doctrines—History—16th century. I. Title. II. Series.

BT764.3.V36 2008
234.'70882841—dc22

2007048081

ISSN 1573-4188
ISBN 978 90 04 16526 7

PRINTED IN THE NETHERLANDS

CONTENTS

ACKNOWLEDGEMENTS

First of all, I am deeply obliged to Prof. Emeritus Tuomo Mannermaa, who encouraged the young undergraduate to immerse himself in the world of the 16th century theology. Even after his retirement he has offered help and guidance for which I am deeply grateful. While he was the person to set the wheels in motion, his successor Prof. Risto Saarinen and Dr. Sammeli Juntunen kept them running. Dr. Simo Peura and Dr. Juhani Forsberg acted as examiners of the manuscript and helped me to improve the analysis a great deal. Other scholars who have commented or helped otherwise me in my studies are Prof. Irene Dingel, Prof. Bengt Hägglund, Dr. Rudolf Keller, Prof. Robert Kolb, lic. theol., MA, Timo Nisula, lic. theol. Simo Kiviranta (†), Dr. Pekka Kärkkäinen, Prof. Antti Raunio and Dr. Martti Vaahtoranta. I am grateful to the staff and all my fellow colleagues at the Department of Systematic Theology for the possibility of working in such a scholarly atmosphere.

The original and longer (some footnotes and a chapter on Regensburg Diet and interims have been omitted here) Finnish version was published by the Finnish Theological Literary Society (2004). My research has been financially supported by the Finnish Cultural Foundation, the Finnish Graduate School of Theology, the Theological Institute of Finland, the Lutheran Church Research Institute and the Department of International Relations of the Ev. Luth. Church of Finland and Martin-Luther-Bund (Erlangen).

Olli-Pekka Vainio
Riihimäki, May 2007

Fides enim apprehendit Christum et habet eum praesentem includitque eum ut annulus gemmam, Et qui fuerit inventus cum tali fide apprehensi Christi in corde, illum reputat Deus iustum.
— *Martin Luther*

Aber Christus Jhesus (mit welchem ich vereinigett / uñ eun ding mit ym worden bin / durch den glauben in in) ist nit amechtig / sonder starck genüg / ist nicht ein sünder / sond die ewig gerechtigkeit / deñ er ist das lamm gottes / das auff sich nimpt die sünde der welt / der ist uns geben von got dem vater / das er sey unser weysheit / gerechtigkeit / erlösung und das ewig leben.
— *Johannes Bugenhagen*

Sic et Christus propagat bonum suum in omnes homines, sed ex ipso renatos et regeneratos. Renascimur autem tantum per fidem, igitur per fidem tantum efficimur participes Christi.
— *Johannes Brenz*

Salvabo vos non in arcu, sed in Domino vestro, id est, in Filio, qui vere est Emanuel, vere adest in credentibus, cum voce Evangelii sustentantur, et simul dat Spiritum sanctum: Sic. 1. Joh. 4. dicitur: in hoc sciamus, quod in ipso maneamus, et ipso in nobis, quia de Spiritu suo dat nobis.
— *Philip Melanchthon*

Nicht von wegen der grossen wirdigkeit oder ansehens des Glaubens selbs. X. Sondern in person Christi. XI. Doch nicht ausser uns. XII. Sondern umb scinct willen / wie er uns geschenkt / angetragen / zugeeignet / und durch den vereinigt ist.
— *Joachim Mörlin*

Neque enim virtus, gratia, efficacia, merita & beneficia Christi, extra ipsius personam, & sine ea, etiamsi ipse non adsit, credentibus communicantur, imo sicut Aduersarij ipsi satentur, Christum ipsum ante omnia nobis donari, & nostrum fieri, nobis adesse, ac nobiscum coniunci oportet, ut ita ex ipso, in ipso, & per ipsum, impleamur in omnem plenitudinem Dei, Eph.3.
— *Martin Chemnitz*

Das also alle die so durch ein rechten / waren / lebendigen Glauben (der ein Werck des Heiligen Geists ist / in uns) Christum ergreiffen / volkommene verzeihung unnd vergebung aller irer Sünden haben.
— *Jacob Andreae*

Formam & ἐνδελέχειαν, seu animam & vitam fidei impertit Christus mediator, quem fides, velut annulus gemmam, complectitur.
— *David Chytraeus*

Iustos nos esse non propter qualitatis dignitatem, sed propter Filium Dei, quem fides agnoscit, intuetur, apprehendit, & in eo acquiescit, & veluti annulus preciosam gemmam, eum complectitur. Christus enim est endelechia fidei, & fides Christum apprehendit.
— *Nicolaus Selnecker*

Gleich wie ein Ring / darin ein Köstlicher Edler stein gefalt / hoch und theuer / etlich hundert Cronen werd mag geschetsst werden / so erdoch am Gold gering ist / Aber von wegen des Edlen steins / das Schmaragds und Rubins: Also wird der Glaube gerhümpt / unnd die gerechtigkeit uns seligkeit im zugerechnet / nicht seiner würdigkeit halben / sondern das er in sich / den Edlen bewerten Edelstein Jesum Christum / mit seinem ganzen reich uñ allen wolthaten fasset. Dann Christus Jesus ist unnd bleibt unsere gerechtigkeit / heiligung / weissheit und erlösung / bis an unsere ende.
— *Tilemann Hesshus*

Inhabitatio Dei in renatis, est gratiosa Dei actio, qua Deus essentialiter inhabitat in renatos, seu timente Deum in sua Ecclesia, eos suis donis replens, vivificans, & salvans.
— *Johannes Wigand*

Fides viva est, quae Christum, qui est vita, & in se credentes vivificat, vere apprehendit.
— *Jacob Heerbrand*

CHAPTER ONE

INTRODUCTION

1.1. *Doctrina stantis et cadentis ecclesiae*

> In the evangelical theology, there's no consensus on the speciality and meaning concerning the doctrine of justification. There is no single evangelical doctrine of justification, much less one single Lutheran doctrine of justification. There are at least a dozen of them.[1]

These words of Wolfhart Pannenberg naturally shock the churches, which have treasured the doctrine of justification as their most precious jewel. Pannenberg uttered this after the Joint Declaration on the Doctrine of Justification (JDDJ, 1999), which established agreement between the Lutheran World Federation and the Roman Catholic Church on central Soteriological themes. According to Pannenberg, the convoluted history of Lutheranism has produced a number of different interpretations of justification.[2]

Generally, the doctrine of justification has been the core of all Lutheran theology. Martin Luther (1483–1546) teaches in his Schmalkaldic Articles (SA) that: "On this article stands all that we teach and practice against the pope, the devil, and the world. Therefore we must be quite certain and have no doubt about it. Otherwise everything is lost, and the pope and the devil and whatever opposes us will gain victory and be proved right."[3] In the Apology of the Augsburg Confession (*Apologia Confessionis Augustanae*, AC) Philip Melanchthon (1497–1560) calls the doctrine of justification "the most important topic of Christian teaching."[4] The same emphasis is apparent in the texts of the other

---

[1] Wolfhart Pannenberg, *Hintergründe des Streites um die Rechtfertigungslehre in der evangelischen Theologie* (München: Verlag der Bayerischen Akademie der Wissenschaften 2000), p. 3.

[2] Moreover, the disagreement between Lutheran theologians goes back to the approaches, which have been burdened by powerful philosophical assumptions. See Risto Saarinen, *Gottes Wirken auf uns. Die transzendentale Deutung des Gegenwart-Christi-Motivs in der Lutherforschung* (Stuttgart: Franz Steiner Verlag Wiesbaden GmbH. 1988).

[3] *BSELK SA* II, 5.

[4] *BSELK AC* IV, 2.

prominent Reformation theologians as well. For example, Martin Chemnitz (1522–1586), the major contributor to the Formula of Concord (*Formula Concordiae*, FC), claimed that "Indeed, this locus is the pinnacle and chief bulwark of all teaching and of the Christian religion itself; if this is obscured, adultered, or subverted, it is impossible to retain purity of doctrine in the other loci."[5] The self-understanding of the Reformers evidently was that the doctrine of justification was the one by which the Church stands or falls (*doctrina stantis et cadentis ecclesiae*);[6] in other words, the Lutheran Church is not genuine Church if it does not have genuine teaching on justification.[7]

Given these prestigious statements it may seem inconceivable that there has never been such a thing as a singular Lutheran doctrine of justification. Researchers, however, have long claimed that since the first half of the 16th century there have been different interpretations of justification. The best-known claim is probably that Luther and Melanchthon differed on the matter. Without a clear picture of it history, Lutheran theology lacks the integrity needed for both ecumenical practices and spirituality. Present-day Lutheranism has to identify and articulate its doctrine of justification with greater clarity.

[5] Chemnitz, *Loci* II, 200–201 (443). The emphasis on justification does not mean downplaying other doctrines. Trinitarian doctrines and christology, for example, are intimately connected with the doctrine of justification. On the notion of *doctrina* in Luther, see Eeva Martikainen, *Doctrina: Studien zu Luthers Begriff der Lehre* (Helsinki: Luther-Agricola-Gesellschaft 1992). On the connection between christology and justification, see August Kimme, *Rechtfertigung und Heiligung in christologischer sicht, Eine dogmatische Untersuchung* (Erlangen: Martin-Luther-Verlag 1989), p. 10. On ecclesiology and justification, see Jürgen Lutz, *Unio und communio. Zum Verhältnis von Rechtfertigungslehre und Kirchenverständnis bei Martin Luther. Eine Untersuchung zu ekklesiologischen relevanten Texten der Jahre* 1519–1528 (Paderborn: Bonifatius 1990). Christian dogma is not a collection of separate ideas, but a coherent system where every doctrine is either prerequisite for or consequence of the doctrine of justification. See, for example, Luther's statement in *WA* 40 II, 46, 18–47, 19. On justification as a criterion, see Thomas Kaufman, *Die "Kriteriologische funktion" der Rechtfertigungslehre in den lutherischen Bekenntnisschriften*, ZThK Beiheft 10 (1998), pp. 47–64; Risto Saarinen, "Die Rechtfertigungslehre als Kriterium," *Kerygma und Dogma* 44 (1998/2).

[6] The adage, however, appears first at the beginning of the 17th century. See Theodor Mahlmann, "Zur Geschichte der Formel 'Articulus stantis et cadentis ecclesiae,'" *Lutherische Theologie und Kirche* 17 (1993), pp. 187–194; Alister McGrath, *Iustitia Dei. A History of the Christian Doctrine of Justification*, 2nd ed. (Cambridge: Cambridge University Press 1998), p. 188.

[7] On similar ideas on other theologians, see, e.g., Andreae, *Ein christliche Predig*, Eiii2; Bugenhagen, *Von dem Christlichen Glauben*, Gviii; Chytraeus, *Catechesis*, B2; Heerbrand, *Disputationes*, 57–88.

1.2. *Justification, Ecumenism, and Spirituality*

Tuomo Mannermaa engages with this lack of consensus, suggesting that Luther's idea of Christ's presence in faith should be regarded as the genuine evangelical doctrine of justification, which would have both historical integrity and value for ecumenical utility. According to Mannermaa, *unio cum Christo* means the union of the sinner and Christ in justification, which produces 'salutary exhange' (*commercium admirabile*); the sinner receives the righteousness of Christ, and Christ receives the sins of the sinner. If *unio cum Christo* constitutes justification, participation in Christ means participation in the divine nature as well. Consequently, this enables conjunction with divine love, which is the essence of God. The free and spontaneous love of God, therefore, is given in faith to the believer; this love is no human endeavor but a work of God in the human person. The presence of divine love could function as a joint theme for ecumenical discussion, and enable dialogue with Roman Catholic and Orthodox Churches.[8] In his book *Christ Present in Faith*, Mannermaa introduces the *unio cum Christo* theme as the intersection between Lutheran and Orthodox theologies.[9]

However, problems arise when Mannermaa claims that utilizing the *unio cum Christo* theme requires downplaying the forensic understanding of justification defined in FC, since they are mutually exclusive. Luther regards participation in the human-divine person of Christ as the central part of justification, while FC identifies God's indwelling

[8] Tuomo Mannermaa, "Einig in Sachen Rechtfertigung? Eine lutherische und eine katholische Stellungnahme zu Jörg Baur," *Theologische Rundschau* 55 (1990).

[9] Tuomo Mannermaa, *Christ Present in Faith. Luther's View of Justification* (Minneapolis: Fortress Press 2005). Mannermaa's thinking had a major influence on the content of JDDJ. See Juhani Forsberg, "Der finnische Beitrag zum Dokument Gemeinsame Erklärung zur Rechtfertigungslehre," in *Caritas Dei. Beiträge zum Verständnis Luthers und der gegenwärtige Ökumene*, Festschrift für Tuomo Mannermaa zum 60. Geburtstag (Helsinki: Luther-Agricola-Gesellschaft 1997). Mannermaa (*Christ Present in Faith*, 46) has claimed that Luther's doctrine of justification could be interpreted as deification (*theopoiesis, deificatio*). This would enable common ground for discussion between churches with a strong patristic emphasis. Among others, Albrecht Beutel has remarked that Luther seldom, if ever, uses such terms in relation to justification. See Beutel, "Antwort und Wort," in *Luther und Ontologie. Das Sein Christi im Glauben als Strukturiendes Prinzip der Theologie Luthers* (Helsinki: Schriften der Luther-Agricola-Gesellschaft 1993), 73–77. According to Risto Saarinen ("Die Teilhabe an Gott bei Luther und in der finnischen Lutherforschung," in *op. cit.*, pp. 176–178) the use of the terms can be argued on the grounds that they thematically equate to Luther's ideas, although the exact terms are rarely used.

as the consequence of justification.[10] Although Mannermaa's model is ecumenically helpful, it raises suspicions if the utilization of the model requires juxtaposition of the documents of the Book of Concord (BC).[11] Hence, the interpretation of justification has an effect on ecumenical practice. In addition, Friederike Nüssel has shown how the different interpretations effect spirituality in practice; his works serves to illustrate how a particular theoretical emphasis effects practice. Nüssel uses as examples the birth of faith, the relation between justification and renewal, and the doctrine of baptism. Without considering possible flaws in Nüssel's historical analysis, the problematic aspects of these areas are presented in the following.[12]

Faith. Lutheran theology has always emphasized how the Holy Spirit effects the inception of faith through the Word and Sacraments; thus, the inception of faith is not within human power. Faith is an instrument (*instrumentum*), which receives Christ's merit. The meritoriousness of human deeds is delimited by the emphasis on the efficacy of the Sacraments and the reality of original sin.

Still, we must ask what faith is in its essence. While it is clear that faith is in the believing person, and is actualized through the movements of the mind (*motus animae*),[13] how is it possible to adhere to the forensic ideal if faith as internal reality is the prerequisite for justification? According to Nüssel, Lutheran theologians have regarded change as consequent on, not antecedent to, justification—and especially not a part of justification. This, however, leaves the ontological status of faith outside description. The primarily divine and justifying aspect of faith has been removed. If faith is essentially a non-divine entity, is it then reckoned to be something it is not? In other words, if justifying faith

---

[10] Tuomo Mannermaa, "Hat Luther eine trinitarische Ontologie?," in *Luther und Ontologie*, p. 329.

[11] Mannermaa's interpretation of Luther has attracted criticism claiming that his thinking is synergistic or legalistic. See for example Ken Schurb, "The New Finnish School of Luther Research and Philip Melanchton," *Logia* XII/3 (2003): pp. 31–36. Gottfried Martens, however, considers Mannermaa's thinking useful for confessional Lutheranism as well. See Martens, "Christusgemeinschaft als Erkenntnisgrund. Anmerkungen zu einem bemerkenswerten Tagungsbericht," *Lutherische Theologie und Kirche* 19 (1995), p. 177.

[12] Friederike Nüssel, *Allein aus Glauben. Zur Entwicklung der Rechtfertigungslehre in der konkordistischen und frühen nachkonkordistischen Theologie* (Göttingen: Vandenhoeck & Ruprecht 2000).

[13] E.g., Wigand (*Syntagma*, 224) states: "Ubi sit [fides]. Esse fidem in mente & corde motus quosdam, hoc est, noticiam verbi Dei & Messiae, ac in corde assensum atque; fiduciam in Christum..."

is not a divine entity, it must be a human deed, a virtue, or perhaps an infused habit (*habitus*).[14] To avoid synergism we must answer that faith (the heart of soteriology), which is reckoned as worth eternal life, is something other than minimal achievement. This closely resembles the Roman Catholic idea of *meritum de congruo*, which is an inevitable consequence if participation in Christ is removed from justification.[15]

Sanctification. If the present aspects of salvation, such as regeneration, renewal, and sanctification, were regarded as either logically,[16] or even temporally, antecedent or consequent to justification, is justification then not something that needs augmentation to become more than a wholly extrinsic and abstract act: has it no noticeable effects on the individual? If so, can justification remain the regulative core of dogma? Moreover, if sanctification is regarded as the consequent work of the Spirit, does this not detach sanctification from grace as well as Christ's merit? In this scenario sanctification is the responsibility of the individual, in synergy with God.[17] Christ changes the *state* of the individual *coram Deo*, but is the change in the *nature* of the person dependent on the person?

Baptism. Generally, Lutherans held to the main tenets of Luther's baptismal theology. Namely, that baptism is not a mere sign or promise, but the effective means of grace, which frees one from condemnation and regenerates. The affectiveness of baptism was maintained for baptized children. However, what happened to the baptized adults was unclear, and the subject was avoided. Luther's teaching on conversion as the return to baptismal grace and other pastoral uses of baptism were seldomly used.[18]

According to Nüssel, the deficiencies in baptismal theology were a result of the notion of forensic justification in which salvation was understood only as imputation. Uniting baptismal regeneration with

---

[14] These problems are apparent in *Lutherans and Catholics in Dialogue VII: Justification by Faith*. E.g., John Johnson ("Justification According to the Apology of the Augsburg Confession and the Formula of Concord," in *op. cit.*, pp. 198–199) attempts to present the doctrines of CA and FC using their common features. Faith is reckoned as righteousness but God's essential righteousness has nothing to with this. In this case, the definition of faith without human deeds becomes impossible. The opposition of synergism turns out to be a defense of synergism.

[15] Friederike Nüssel, *Allein aus Glauben*, pp. 148–150, 176–177, 337–340.

[16] Logical difference means causal order of things, which does not indicate temporal difference.

[17] Nüssel, *Allein aus Glauben*, pp. 169–170. See also Wolfhart Pannenberg, *Systematische Theologie*, Bd. 3 (Göttingen: Vandenhoeck & Ruprecht 1993), pp. 246–247.

[18] Nüssel, *Allein aus Glauben*, pp. 160–165.

forensic justification was problematic since regeneration is an effective transformation, which was set apart from justification. It was impossible to join baptism, faith, justification, and regeneration together if the forensic and effective aspects of justification were separated.[19] Nüssel demonstrates thus how deviation from Luther affects the spiritual practice and claims that FC was the culmination point of this digression.

1.3. *Earlier Studies: Different Approaches to the Doctrinal Development of Lutheranism*

The question of the genuine nature of the doctrine of justification is affected by different approaches to the doctrinal development of Lutheranism. The studies on this development usually employ one of three possible interpretative traditions: harmonization, separation, or the progressive tradition.[20]

First, some studies emphasize the doctrinal unity of Lutheranism and the forensic interpretation of justification with the presupposition that Lutheranism is a relatively monolithic phenomenon. Certain unquestioned premises determine the analysis, which inevitably leads to a harmonized reading. Harmonization does not necessarily mean a forced interpretation; rather it can mean exhibiting justification with common features of various thinkers without taking into account a general analysis of their theologies or the problems various theologies create.

One exemplar of this tradition is Robert Preus, who claims four common features of Lutheran theology in the 16th and 17th centuries. First, the centrality of justification. Second, justification is the forensic imputation of Christ's alien righteousness (*iustitia aliena*). Third, this imputation occurs through faith alone. Additionally, the union of Christ and the sinner is the consequence of justification. The object

[19] Nüssel, *Allein aus Glauben*, pp. 167–168. Nüssel's study does not give an exact account of how baptismal theology developed after Luther. For detailed analysis of the subject, see Juha Pihkala, *Gnadenmittel oder Gnadenangebot? Auslegungsgeschichte des Passus per baptismum offeratur gratia Dei im Taufartikel der Confessio Augustana im zietraum von* 1530–1930, Studien zur systematischen Theologie und Ethik 34 (Münster: Lit. Verlag 2003).

[20] Some studies and scholars fit into more categories than one. The distinction here is more pedagogical than analytical, seeking only to exemplify different approaches to the issue.

of justifying faith is not Christ in us (*Christus in nobis*) but Christ for us (*Christus pro nobis*).[21]

Lowell Green attempts to demonstrate how both Luther and Melanchthon had similar teaching on justification. However, he claims that their thinking developed over the course of their lives. Initially Luther had 'Catholic remnants' in his theology, which resulted in an emphasis on the presence of Christ in the believer. Melanchthon, however, pushed Luther in a different direction, and by about 1530 he concurred fully with Melanchthon's theology. The mature theology of the Reformer focuses on Christ's sufferings, not His indwelling in faith.[22]

Along with the afore-mentioned American theologians some German theologians share the same features, albeit with a somewhat different tone. They emphasize the unity of Lutheran theology and imputation but try to find a way to combine union with Christ with justification.

According to Jörg Baur, for Luther justification means forgiveness of sins and the imputation of alien righteousness. God's creative Word causes this, and the justified person is completely dependent on the works of God. Christ is the place of salvation (*Heils-Ort*), which means that an individual does not try to find salvation in himself or herself, but from outside in Christ. In faith the person is in Christ (*Insein in Christus*), which also causes renewal. Since God's word is creative by nature, it does not need anything human to accomplish salvation of an individual. Thus, the inchoate new righteousness cannot be grounds for salvation. The characteristics of Luther's thinking remain intact in later Lutheranism, which Baur finds exemplified in Johannes Gerhard and Johannes Quenstedt.[23]

Gottfried Martens sees the distinction between the Law and Gospel as the central feature of Lutheran theology. The Gospel-effected faith is not a fiction but an actual change in the sinner. This change is demonstrated in the distinctive movement of the mind; faith is effective and alters the reality of life (*Lebensgeschichte*). As the process of sanctification starts the creative works of the Spirit (*das schöpferische Wirken des heiligen*

[21] Robert Preus, *Justification as Taught by Post-Reformation Lutheran Theologians* (Fort Wayne: Concordia Theological Seminary 1982).

[22] Lowell Green, *How Melanchthon helped Luther find the Gospel. The Doctrine of Justification in the Reformation* (Greenwood: The Attic Press Inc 1980), pp. 147–149, 185.

[23] Jörg Baur, *Salus Christiana. Die Rechtfertigungslehre in der Geschichte des christlichen Heilsverständnisses*, Bd. 1 (Gütersloh: Gütersloher Verlagshaus Gerhard Mohn 1968), pp. 54–74.

Geistes) evoke obedience, good works, and proliferation of inherent righteousness (*iustitia inhaerens*). In spite of this renewal, salvation is based on imputation (*Imputationshandeln Gottes*).[24]

According to Edmund Schlink, as a principle justification is depicted similarly everywhere in BC. Justification causes inchoate renewal but salvation is not dependent on this change. This is more apparent with regard to CA, AC, and SA. However, in FC the efficiency is attenuated. Schlink, however, interprets FC to mean that the affectiveness appears in the antecendent and consequent themes. Justification thus also has an effective context in FC.[25]

Gunther Wenz claims that externality (*Exzentrinizität*) and internality (*Innesein*) belong together in BC, and are not at odds with each other, since they represent different sides of the same coin. Although Luther and Melanchthon use different terminology, no substantial difference existed (*Grundsatzdifferenz*) between them. *Unio cum Christo* means the presence of Christ in conscience, which takes place through the Spirit (*Geistgegenwärtigkeit*) and causes renewal. Renewal, of course, is not a prerequisite for justification.[26]

According to Martin Greschat, Luther concurred with Melanchthon's forensic interpretation around 1531. For Greschat, justification is a momentary 'word-event' (*Wortgeschehen*), which is sharply separated from renewal. Greschat interprets *unio cum Christo* not as christological union but as an anthropological category, which creates the context for imputation.[27]

According to Reinhardt Flogaus, both Luther and Melanchthon understood justification as effective reality. After 1532 Luther gave prece-

---

[24] Gottfried Martens, *Die Rechtfertigung des Sünders—Rettungshandeln Gotter oder historisches Interpretament? Grundentscheidungen lutherischer Theologie und Kirche bei der Behandlung des Themas 'Rechtfertigung' im ökumenischen Kontext* (Göttingen: Vandenhoeck & Ruprecht 1992), pp. 97–108.

[25] Edmund Schlink, *Theologie der Lutherischen Bekenntnischriften* (München: Evangelischer Verlag Albert Lempp 1940), pp. 154–198.

[26] Günther Wenz, "Unio. Zur Differenzierung einer Leitkategorie finnischer Lutherforschung im Anschluss an CA I–VI," in *Unio. Gott und Mensch in der nachreformatorischen Theologie*, hrsgb. Matti Repo und Rainer Vinke (Helsinki: Schriften der Luther-Agricola-Gesellshaft 1996), pp. 339, 376–377, 380; *Theologie der Bekenntnischriften der evangelisch-lutherischen Kirche. Eine historische und systematische Einführung in das Konkordienbuch*, Bd. 2 (Berlin: Walter de Gruyter 1998), pp. 48–51.

[27] Martin Greschat, *Melanchthon neben Luther. Studien zur Gestalt der Rechtfertigungslehre zwischen* 1528 *und* 1537, Untersuchungen zur Kirchengeschichte, Bd. 1 (Witten: Luther-Verlag 1965), pp. 83–84, 100, 245.

dence to forgiveness of sin over the gift of the Spirit. The late Melanchthon, however, considered these simultaneous (*simul*), although he gave forgiveness higher existential meaning. FC is consistent with Luther's view that the gift of divine presence is consequent on justification.[28]

German scholarship has taken the change involved in justification seriously but has not interpreted the change from the viewpoint of christological union; *unio cum Christo* is an existential, not christological, category. The change is understood as an external causal influence. Consequently, there is nothing in the person which could determine the essence of faith. The simultaneously present renewal is identified by a new quality which the Spirit creates. This quality has no positive role in justification since it is only a causally created *quality*. Only a perfect and momentary declaration of forgiveness of sins justifies, not inchoate renewal, which is carried out until death.

The separating tradition stands opposite the harmonizing tradition; it attempts to demonstrate that Melanchthon's forensic interpretation deviated from Luther.[29] Hence, BC contains different interpretations of justification; CA and SA especially are considered at odds.[30]

---

[28] Reinhard Flogaus, "Luther versus Melanchthon? Zur Frage der Einheit der Wittenberger Reformation in der Rechtfertigungslehre," *Archiv für Reformationsgeschichte* Vol. 91 (2000).

[29] It is clear that Luther's followers did not follow all his teachings. For example, Melanchthon, Chytraeus, Selnecker, and Wigand considered Luther's teaching on the bondage of the will too severe. Luther argued against free will by appealing to the necessity (*necessitas*) which God as the omniscient being causes: since God knows everything, there is no such thing as free will. This was too deterministic an argument for many. See Robert Kolb, "'A Hammer of God against Free Choice'. Johannes Wigand's Interpretation of Luther's *De servo arbitrio*," in *Vanha ja nuori*, Juhlakirja Simo Heinisen täyttäessä 60 vuotta, eds. Kaisamari Hintikka et al, Studia missiologica et oecumenica Fennica 60 (Helsinki: Luther-Agricola-Gesellschaft 2003), pp. 142–143. On the diverse notions of Law in Luther and Melanchthon, see Antti Raunio, "Divine and Natural Law in Luther and Melanchthon," in *Lutheran Reformation and Law*, ed. Virpi Mäkinen, Studies in Medieval and Reformation Traditions CXII (Leiden: Brill 2006). Additionally, the era between Luther's death and undersigning of FC was an age of controversy and debate on the legitimate interpretation of Luther's theology. Against this background, the separating tradition has the warrant of historical fact. James Estes has, however, demonstrated substantial correlation between Luther's and Melanchthon's political thought. It is obvious that simplifications will not do justice to the multifaceted history of Lutheran theology. See Estes, *Peace, Order and the Glory of God. Secular Authority and the Church in the Thought of Luther and Melanchthon* 1518–1559, Studies in Medieval and Reformation Traditions CXI (Leiden: Brill 2005).

[30] Such a dualistic attitude is found in Albrecht Ritschl and Adolf Harnack as well. But then again it must be remembered that FC has been in dispute since its inception. Irene Dingel has demonstrated that several pamphlets were published for and against

Finnish Luther scholarship has usually regarded later Lutheranism as a monolithic entity: the later generations primarily followed the thinking of Melanchthon and thus digressed from Luther. A major influence on this tradition has been Lauri Haikola's analysis of the differences between Luther's and Melanchthon's theories of satisfaction.[31] According to Haikola, Melanchthon principally utilized the Anselmian theory of vicarious satisfaction in which Christ's merit consists of perfect obedience to the divine Law. Salvation means imputation of the juridical merit. Haikola claims that Luther's theory of satisfaction requires a more profound christological basis. For Luther, redemption includes everything Christ does beginning from His incarnation. Reconciliation is not reduced to simply acquiring juridical merit. The work of Christ is not separated from His person; His merit is situated in His person and is donated to sinners in connection with this person.[32]

Mannermaa also claims that there were two fundamentally different doctrines of justification in early Lutheranism: the doctrine of Luther and the doctrine of FC, the later based on the theology of Melanchthon. In FC, justification is only 'favor' or 'grace' (*favor*), i.e., reception of the forgiveness of sins for the sake of Christ. The 'gift' (*donum*) or God's divine indwelling is an independent entity which logically follows the forgiveness. In Luther's theology, however, both *favor* and *donum* are understood christologically. Since Christ is both *favor* and *donum*, justification and sanctification are inseparable. These differences lead

FC between 1580 and 1600. What is of great importance is that the controversy centered on the method of FC and on christological issues. The doctrine of justification did not cause much debate. See Dingel, *Concordia controversa. Die öffentlichen Diskussionen um das lutherische Konkordienwerk am Ende des* 16. *Jahrhunderts*, Quellen und Forschungen zur Reformationsgeschichte 63 (Gütersloh: Gütersloher Verlagshaus 1996).

[31] Lauri Haikola, "A comparison of Melanchthon's and Luther's doctrine of Justification," *Dialog* 2 (1963), pp. 32–39. On the differences between Luther and Melanchthon, see also Karl Holl, *Gesammelte Aufsätze zur Kirchengeschichte*, Band 1 (Tübingen: Mohr 1932), p. 128; Emanuel Hirsch, *Die Theologie des Andreas Osiander und ihre geschichtlichen Voraussetzungen* (Göttingen: Vandenhoeck & Ruprecht 1919), p. 228; *Hilfsbuch zum Studium der Dogmatik* (Berlin: Walter der Gryuter 1937), p. 160; Michael Rogness, *Philip Melanchthon. Reformer without Honor* (Minneapolis: Augsburg 1969), pp. 65–121; Jaroslav Pelikan, *From Luther to Kierkegaard. A Study in the History of Theology* (St. Louis: Concordia 1950), pp. 44–45.

[32] Haikola, "A comparison"; See also Haikola, *Studien zu Luther und Luthertum* (Wiesbaden: Otto Harrassowitz 1958), pp. 56–68, 125–155.

Mannermaa to suggest that in ecumenical dialogue we must choose between Luther and FC, since the two are mutually exclusive.[33]

The separating tradition regarding Luther and Melanchthon also includes Alister McGrath's lengthy presentation on the development on the doctrine of justification in western theology. According to McGrath, Luther understood justification as a sanative process while Melanchthon limited justification to imputation from CA onwards.[34] McGrath claims that Luther's doctrine of justification eventually disappears from the Lutheran theological tradition.[35]

Fundamentally, the differences culminate in the role of christology in justification: does the person of Christ have any other meaning than acquiring merit? Within the separating tradition, the forensic view is interpreted as disengagement of the person of Christ from the work of Christ. The merit of Christ could be apprehended without His person.

On the one hand, the separating tradition has raised suspicions because it is ecumenically applicable, which has been perceived as compromising the purity of the Lutheran doctrine. On the other hand, the

[33] Tuomo Mannermaa, "Einig in Sachen Rechtfertigung? Eine lutherische und eine katholische Stellungnahme zu Jörg Baur," *Theologische Rundschau* 55 (1990), p. 329. The relation between imputation and renewal has played a major role in Lutheran-Catholic dialogue. For example, Karl Lehmann's and Wolfhart Pannenberg's ecumenical consultation *Lehrverurteilungen—kirchentrennend?* claims that the genuine Lutheran doctrine of justification includes both the favor and the gift. Melanchthon's theology, however, influenced reduction of justification to favor only, which was followed by the gift. Luther's distinction between favor and grace illustrates how "external" (*äussere*) favor determines the life of the believer; the gift effects actual change in the believer and the Spirit starts to purify the sinful flesh. See Karl Lehmann & Wolfhart Pannenberg, *Lehrverurteilungen—Kirchentrennend? Rechtfertigung, Sakramente und Amt im Zeitalter der Reformation und heute* (Freiburg im Breisgau: Herder 1986), pp. 54–55. See also Horst Pöhlmann, *Rechtfertigung. Die gegenwärtige kontroverstheologische Problematik der Rechtfertigungslehre zwischen der evangelisch-lutherischen und der römisch-katholischen Kirche* (Gütersloh: Gütersloher Verlagshaus 1971), pp. 324–328; Edmund Schlink, *Ökumenische Dogmatik. Grundzüge* (Göttingen: Vandenhoeck & Ruprecht 1983), pp. 430–433. The consultation has been criticized for mixing justification with sanctification. For example, Jörg Baur has claimed that Luther joins justification with renewal but this renewing gift does not justify. Mannermaa ("Einig in sachen Rechfertigung") has agreed with Baur's criticism that sanctification does not save. However, this does not exclude the fact that Luther thinks that the gift, i.e., Christ, is the foundation of grace. On Luther's view, see *StA* 2, 493, 9–10; 494, 10–12 (*Rationis Latomianae*). *Unio cum Christo* consists of union with both the favor and the gift. When Luther says that the gift justifies, he does not mean the effects of the gift but the gift itself, i.e., Christ. Thus, the central question is how the presence of Christ in the believer is the foundation of justifying faith.

[34] McGrath, *Iustitia Dei*, pp. 200–205, 212. McGrath, however, claims that Melanchthon also uses sanative notions later on in his theology.

[35] McGrath, *Iustitia Dei*, p. 219.

differing philosophical preconditions have raised suspicions as well. German scholarship has been linked with anti-metaphysical Neokantianism, and from this point of view the idea of the real presence of Christ has resembled too closely the substance metaphysics of Roman Catholicism.[36]

---

[36] Risto Saarinen, *Gottes Wirken*, pp. 185–204. The Finnish Luther School has tended to use words such as "ontology" or "ontic" in relation to justification. These terms, however, are rather ambiguous. In this study, they simply mean "concerned with the nature and relations of being" and do not refer to any particular type of ontology, such as "substance ontology" or "relational ontology". The latter has been utilized by German neoprotestantism (such as Ritschl and Wilhelm Herrmann), and has been understood as union with Christ through causal influence (known as *transzendentales Wirkungsdenken*). Union means the effects which are evoked in the believer by faith. The substance of God and the sinner are not actually united; rather the sinner is redirected according to the nature of God while remaining separate from God. The Finnish Luther School has been criticized on the grounds of relational ontology. See Karsten Lehmkühler, *Inhabitatio. Die Einwohnung Gottes im Menschen*, Forschungen zur systematischen und ökumenischen theologie 104 (Göttingen: Vandenhoeck & Ruprecht 2004), pp. 238–286. First, scholars have thought that Christian dogmatics can deal only with subjects, which are capable of being felt and known (*Erkennbar*). Thus, *unio* can mean only a description of psychological phenomena. On this, see Saarinen, *Gottes Wirken*, 83. It is not, however, clear why this case should be so if even the biblical *kerygma* is not limited to things which can be known. Second, the relational ontology attempts to oppose mysticism, according to which God can be encountered without means. This is clearly opposed to Luther's intentions since he binds union with Christ with the Word, Sacraments, and the historical facts of Christ's incarnation, suffering, etc. Third, relational ontology tries to oppose substance metaphysics since it resembles Catholic theology. Deification (*Vergöttlichung*) can be identified with substantial, or habitual, grace (*"Verdinglichung" der Gnade*). This is obviously a poor argument since it interprets the texts using an external and anachronistic category. Additionally, Finnish scholars do not use *unio cum Christo* within classical Aristotelian metaphysical theory. Aristotelian substance metaphysics suggests that grace is either substance or accidence. Neither of these is in accordance with Luther since he denies both interpretations. Because of his denial, the proponents of relational ontology have tried to read Luther so that he disassociates himself completely from the concept of substance and replaces it with the category of external influence. While it is true that Luther disassociates himself from Aristotle, he does not, however, replace it with something even worse. Luther uses the christological dogma that Christ has two natures but only one person. Since something analogous takes place in union with Christ, not just the Word, but the present person of Christ also constitutes the relation of God and the believer. Compare Wilfred Joest, *Ontologie der Person bei Luther* (Göttingen: Vandenhoeck & Ruprecht 1967), pp. 32–34. Union does not simply mean participation in God's attributes only, since God's essence and attributes are inseparable. The Lutherans attempt to illustrate that the relation between God and human kind utilizes neither substance metaphysics nor relational ontology. In the 16th century, the Lutherans generally oppose Catholic substance ontology but the replacement solutions vary. This study does not attempt to pin down the theological ontologies of the theologians but merely to describe the Trinitarian, or *theo*-logical, foundations of *unio cum Deo*. These solutions are naturally based on a deeper, usually

Moreover, Finnish scholarship has been accused of limiting the material of analysis to the texts of the younger Luther.[37]

More recent scholarship, however, has demonstrated that the doctrinal development within the two previous traditions is more complicated than has usually been portrayed. Those scholars who try to expand the results of the previous traditions, and create detailed accounts of individual theologians and the lines of development, belong within the progressive tradition (still, this tradition does not represent a monolithic school of thought). One important discovery has been that *unio cum Christo* joins the different aspects of justification, not only in Luther, but in the theologies of later Lutheran theologians as well. This challenges both the standard notion of forensic justification and the theory of deviation after Luther.

For example, Reinhardt Flogaus, Leif Erikson and Bengt Hägglund have claimed that Melanchthon's doctrine of justification has an effective aspect as well. Erikson and Hägglund claim that the theory that Luther and Melanchthon differ in terms of effectiveness is flawed.[38]

Friederike Nüssel's comprehensive history of the Lutheran doctrine of justification analyzes theologians from Luther onwards until the end the 17th century. With regard to Luther and Melanchthon, however, she takes advantage of the studies produced within the separating tradition.[39] For this reason, her analysis of the end of the 16th century lacks some detail.[40] The greatest merit of Nüssel's work is the demonstration of the severe problems the doctrine of justification faced due to the

---

unspoken, conception of reality. Mannermaa ("Hat Luther eine trinitarische Ontologie?") has attempted to define Luther's theological ontology.

[37] See, e.g., Flogaus, "Luther versus Melanchthon?", pp. 36–42. Flogaus wonders why the Finnish Luther scholars are generally critical of Karl Holl's Neokantian Luther interpretations but never criticize his interpretation of Melanchthon. On the typical criticisms of the Finnish Luther School, see Saarinen, "Die Teilhabe an Gott", pp. 167–170.

[38] Leif Erikson, *Inhabitatio—illuminatio—unio. En studie i Luthers och den äldre lutherdomens teologi* (Åbo: Åbo akademi 1986); Bengt Hägglund, "Rechtfertigung—Wiedergeburt—Erneuerung in der nachreformatorischen Theologie," *Kerygma und Dogma* (1959).

[39] Nüssel, *Allein aus Glauben*. Nüssel uses Martin Greschat's work.

[40] Nüssel (*Allein aus Glauben*) omits the theological development of the late Melanchthon and analyses the theologies of the formulators of FC, such as Martin Chemnitz, only perfunctorily.

formulations of FC in the 17th century, when the influence of Johann Arndt and Valentin Weigel created the need for additional clarification of the doctrine of justification and union. Theologians tried to resolve the crisis by inventing additional unitive categories along with God's indwelling to keep their theology consistent. For example, a union which precedes justification (*unio fidei formalis*) had been invented to prevent the detachment of soteriology from christology. *Unio fidei formalis* is consequently followed by *inhabitatio Dei*, which causes good works. Hence, the orthodox Lutheran theology tries to go back to Luther's teachings on the importance of Christ's presence in faith.

Martti Vaahtoranta's thorough study of Johan Gerhard (1582–1637) demonstrates Gerhard's employment of the *unio fidei formalis* theme. Justification takes place in union with Christ (*unio/induitio Christi*), which is followed by sanctifying *inhabitatio Dei*. *Unio Christi* is not only an extrinsic causal influence of God but also an ontological salutary exchange.[41]

Theodor Mahlmann's substantial article on the uses of the *unio cum Christo* in the 16th century claims that justification and union with Christ cohere. Not only Luther but also the theologians of Lutheran orthodoxy teach the simultaneity of justification and union. However, along the lines of David Hollazius (1648–1713) Mahlmann emphasizes that two different unions must be distinguished within justification: the formal-relational union and the sanctifying mystical union. This makes it possible to obliterate the notion that renewal is the basis for justification.[42]

1.4. *The Aim of this Study*

The relation between Luther and later Lutheran generations is still ambiguous. The analysis of the late 16th century theologians has been insufficient, making the context of FC obscure. The theological posi-

[41] Martti Vaahtoranta, *Restauratio imaginis divinae. Die Vereinigung von Gott und Mensch ihre Voraussetzungen und Implikationen bei Johann Gerhard* (Helsinki: Luther-Agricola-Gesellshaft 1998), pp. 243–244, 249–267, 268–275.

[42] Theodor Mahlmann, "Die Stellung der unio cum Christo in der lutherischen Theologie des 17. Jahrhunderts," in *Unio. Gott und Mensch in der nachreformatorischen Theologie*, hrsgb. Matti Repo und Rainer Vinke (Helsinki: Luther-Agricola-Gesellshaft 1996).

tions developed in this period are key in understanding the nature of the Lutheran doctrine of justification. The existing research does not provide enough precise analysis of the development of the doctrine of justification immediately after the death of Luther and before the signing of FC. The aim of this study is to analyze the development of the doctrine of justification from Luther to FC from the point of view of union with Christ. Special attention will be paid to the relation between the forensic and effective aspects of justification.

Lutherans have traditionally described justification with concepts such as 'forensic' and 'effective'. The classical juxtaposition is as follows. The forensic view of justification means a declaration or imputation (*imputatio/reputatio*), which occurs outside the individual in the heavenly forum (*in foro coeli*) for the sake of Christ's merit. The effective view means that this imputation is based on something intrinsic. Although these terms are used widely, they are not fixed. It is problematic that almost all 16th-century Lutherans thought that justification had something to do with participation in Christ, and that justification also meant a change that was depicted through the metaphor of a bad tree changing into a good one (Matth. 7:17–18). Imputation is joined with effective change, although the qualitative change is not the foundation of imputation.

In such a construct renewal (*renovatio*) of the sinner can appear in two different contexts. First, it may be the part of justification which enables the birth of justifying faith. Second, renewal can mean the good works of the regenerate person and the processual sanctification which results from justification. For clarity, I will coin the term $renovatio_1$ to refer to the renewal which enables justification, while the term $renovatio_2$ refers to good works and sanctification. The concept of *renovatio* appears in the texts of the Reformers but its meaning is not usually explicated in detail. My distinction attempts to illustrate existing but often-unarticulated differences in the use of the term.

Generally, Lutherans agree on the nature of $renovatio_2$; the Spirit causes the renewal and it grows to the extent that the Spirit receives more room in the soul. The Reformers, however, use different systems to illustrate the nature of $renovatio_1$. The comparison of these systems reveal the most crucial differences among theologians.

German scholars use the terms 'external' and 'internal' generally to describe the nature of justification. This distinction, however, is as ambiguous as the rest. Still, it can be used to demonstrate the extent to which justification occurs outside or inside the individual. Externality usually refers to the free nature of justification; some interpret externality as spatial, some deny this.[43] Internality refers to the nature of the internal renewal (both *renovatio*$_1$ and *renovatio*$_2$).

From the point of view of the justified sinner, these aspects can be illustrated in the following figure. Effective justification is preceded by anticipatory external inclination. Faith, however, is already something internal to the person: the will of the sinner is renewed and consequently wants to believe in Christ. Faith receives forgiveness of sins and produces good works. Justification is punctual and as such perfect. Additionally, it starts the process of sanctification.

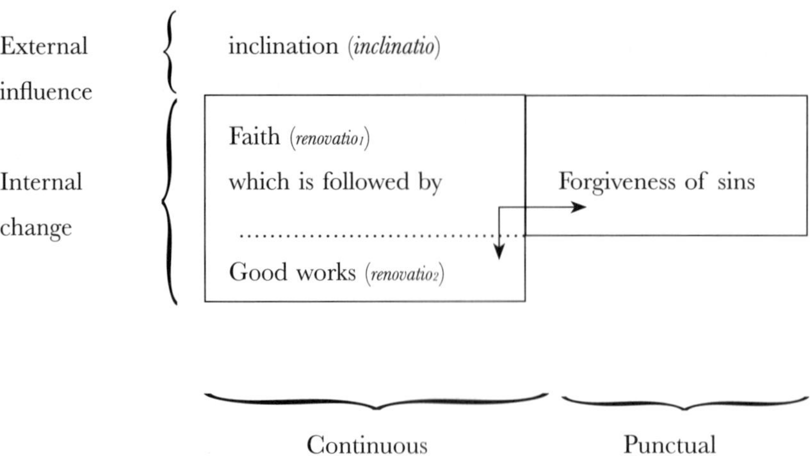

This study in historical theology uses a method of close reading and conceptual analysis. However, the study is not genetic; it does not seek to explain the causal connections between different theologies or the thinking of individual theologians. The analysis focuses on the internal coherence of the most prominent theologians of the 16th century,[44] who are then compared with each other in terms of their inclusiveness and exclusiveness.

The second chapter discusses three prominent first-generation Reformers: Luther, Johannes Bugenhagen, and Johannes Brenz. Their

[43] For example, Luther (*CR* 2, 502) denies the spatial interpretation of *extra nos*. According to Luther "[Christ] does not say: I give you the way, the truth and the life—as if He worked in me while being placed outside of me (quasi extra me positus operetur in me)." See section 3.3.

[44] For the sake of brevity, individual works are not listed here.

doctrines of justification are quite similar: justification takes place in union with Christ. *Unio cum Christo* has been the structuring principle for original Lutheran theology.

The third chapter analyzes the development of Melanchthon's thought. Although Melanchthon introduced forensic terms into Lutheran theology, he did not abandon the unitive aspect of justification. Justification was for him both forensic and effective, but his description of the nature of the union with God was different than Luther's.

The fourth chapter focuses on the Osiandrian controversy. After Luther's death, Andreas Osiander argued against Melanchthon's forensic soteriology, claiming that Melanchthon had corrupted Luther's teaching with his "frigid imaginations" of imputed righteousness. Both Gnesiolutherans and Philippists condemned Osiander's interpretation of Luther. One of the most important opponents of Osiander was Matthias Flacius Illyricus, who furthered the forensic style of Melanchthon. However, Flacius occupied the other extreme position, and his doctrine of justification was in danger of becoming mere fiction.

The fifth chapter concentrates mainly on Martin Chemnitz's view on justification. The analysis begins with Chemnitz's close friend and colleague, Joachim Mörlin. Since justification has an incarnatory foundation for them—the merit of Christ being inseparable from His person—justification requires participation in Christ. Chemnitz is studied in more detail than his contemporaries because he has been regarded as the leading theologian of second-generation Lutheranism.

The sixth chapter analyses Jacob Andreae, David Chytraeus, and Nicolaus Selnecker, the other second-generation Reformers and formulators of FC. Although their views concur with the christological thinking of Luther and Chemnitz they also use language typical of Melanchthon and Flacius. I will also briefly discuss three other well-known theologians of lesser influence.

The seventh chapter analyses FC's doctrine of justification. The analysis of the contemporary theologians offers a hermeneutic background for possible contemporary interpretations of FC. In the concluding chapter, I will construct five basic models of justification and assess their compatibility. In doing so this study will respond to the question of what the evangelical doctrine of justification is and suggest how it might function both in the spirituality of the church and in ecumenical practice.

CHAPTER TWO

THE BEGINNING OF THE LUTHERAN REFORMATION: JUSTIFICATION AS PARTICIPATION IN CHRIST

The first Reformers typically understood salvation as the communion of the sinner and Christ. This is apparent not only in the texts of Luther, but also in the theology of other prominent first-generation reformers such as Johannes Bugenhagen and Johannes Brenz.

2.1. *Martin Luther*

2.1.1. *Christ as the Form of Faith*

Luther's *Commentary on Galatians* (1531/1535)[1] is one of his most important texts on justification.[2] First, it is his answer to *Papal Confutation*, which was written by Roman Catholic theologians in reply to the

[1] *Weimarer Ausgabe* contains a short, but original text of Luther (1531) and comprehensive annotation of Luther's actual lectures by Rörer and Cruciger (1535). The annotation, however, presents some problems of textual criticism. As *Beutel* ("Antwort und Wort" in *Luther und Ontologie*, p. 437) points out it occasionally uses melanchthonian terminology. In any case, Luther gave his approval to the annotation. See Luther's preface to the 1535 edition in *WA* 40 I, 33.

[2] For the more detailed studies on the younger Luther's doctrine of justification, see Simo Peura, *Mehr als ein Mensch? Die Vergöttlichung als Thema der Theologie Martin Luthers von* 1513–1519 (Stuttgart: Franz Steiner Verlag Wiesbaden GmbH 1994); Sammeli Juntunen, *Der Begriff des Nichts bei Luther in den Jahren von* 1510 *bis* 1523 (Helsinki: Luther-Agricola-Gesellschaft 1996), pp. 238–253, 378–403; Lutz, *Unio und communio*, pp. 35–81; Asger Højlund, *Ved gaven helbreder han naturen. Helbredelsetanken i Luthers retfaerdiggørelselaere* (Århus: Menighedsfakultetets Videnskabelige Serie 4. 1992), pp. 21–218; Walther von Loewenich, *Duplex iustitia. Luthers stellung zu einer unionsformel des* 16. Jahrhunderts (Wiesbaden: Franz Steiner Verlag GmbH 1972). On the interpretations of the *Commentary on Galatians* especially, see Karin Bornkamm, *Luthers Auslegung des Galaterbriefs von* 1519 *und* 1531 (Berlin: Walter de Gruyter 1963); Greschat, *Melanchthon neben Luther*, pp. 80–109; Hermann Kleinknecht, *Gemeinschaft ihne Bedingungen: Kirche und Rechtfertigung in Luthers grosser Galaterbrief-Vorlesung von* 1531 (Stuttgart: Calwer Verlag 1981); Martin Lienhard, *Martin Luthers christologisches Zeugnis* (Berlin: Evangelische Verlanganstalt. 1980); Mannermaa, *Christ present in faith*; Peter Manns, "Fides absoluta—fides incarnata" in *Reformata reformanda*, Teil 1, Festgabe für Hubert Jedin zum 17. Juni 1965, hrsgb. Erwin Iserloh & Konrad Repgen (Münster: Aschendorff 1965), 265–312. I have also used Simo Peura's unpublished presentation, which was held in Luther Congress in Copenhagen (2002).

Augsburg Confession.[3] Secondly, FC's article on justification ends in a passage in which Luther's *Commentary* is recommended as a more profound explanation of justification.

> For any further, necessary explanation of this lofty and sublime article on justification before God, upon which the salvation of our souls depends, we wish to recommend to everyone the wonderful, magnificent exposition by Dr. Luther of St. Paul's Epistle to Galatians, and for the sake of brevity we refer to it at this point.[4]

Hence, BC exalts this particular text of Luther more than any other confessional text. This leads to the important hermeneutic conclusion that Luther's texts should not be read in terms of FC (or any other document), but be given permission to speak on their own behalf. In the following I will note briefly Luther's central ideas on justification as they are represented his *Commentary on Galatians*.

Luther argued that the righteousness of faith that avails *coram Deo* is based on participation in Christ's own righteousness.[5] This participation is depicted through the formulation 'apprehending Christ' (*apprehendere Christum*).[6] Understanding the meaning of the verb *apprehendo* is of great importance in illuminating Luther's view of justification. In some studies, Luther's notion of faith is abbreviated to the formula 'faith that apprehends Christ' (*fides apprehensiva Christi*).[7]

The word *apprehendere* was widely used in the scholastic philosophy of mind. According to Thomas Aquinas, there are appetitive (*appetitivus*) and apprehensive (*apprehensivus*) faculties in the human

---

[3] Wenz, *Theologie der Bekenntnischriften*, p. 47.

[4] *BSELK SD* III, 67.

[5] *WA* 40 I, 541, 17–20: "Quare Evangelice Christum induere non est legem et opera, sed inaestimabile donum induere, scilicet remissionem peccatorum, iustitiam, pacem, consolationem, laetitiam in Spiritu sancto, salutem, vitam et Christum ipsum." See also *WA* 40 I, 42, 7–43, 5; 46, 7–47, 2; 46, 19–20, 28–30; 48, 29–33; 50, 17–23.

[6] See, e.g., *WA* 40 I, 164, 18–21: "Verum autem Evangelium est, quod opera aut charitas non est ornatus seu perfectio fidei, Sed quod fides per se donum Dei et opus divinum in corde, quod ideo iustificat, quia apprehendit ipsum Christum Salvatorem." The verb *apprehendo* appears in the *Commentary* over 300 times.

[7] Luther uses this formulation in *WA* 39 I, 45, 21–22: "Haec est autem fides apprehensiva (ut dicimus) Christi, pro peccatis nostris morientis, et pro iustitia nostra resurgentis." For more on this formulation, see Seils, *Glaube*, p. 54; Gerhard Ebeling, *Disputatio de homine. Dritter Teil. Die Theologische Definition des Menschen. Kommentar zu These* 20–40, (Tübingen: J. C. B. Mohr 1989), p. 450; Eero Huovinen, *Fides infantium. Martin Luthers Lehre vom Kinderglauben*, Veröffentlichungen des Instituts für europäische Geschichte 159, (Mainz: Philipp von Zabern 1991), pp. 157–170.

soul.[8] Appetitive faculties include those involved in the acts of will, whereas apprehensive faculties are involved with knowledge and understanding. For Luther as well, *apprehendo* means intellectual apprehension when seen in terms of understanding and comprehension. The term has deeper meaning when the object of knowledge becomes the property of a knowing subject.[9] Luther gives the term a special interpretation, which helps to fathom his understanding of justification.

Luther's understanding of apprehension can be characterized as follows. The Gospel is the proclamation about God, who shows His mercy to the fallen human race by sending His Son to live a human life. The incarnation of Christ is a medium of communication through which God reveals something of himself.[10] The human being is naturally unaware of such a merciful attitude.[11] Hence, the Holy Spirit declares this mercy to the sinner through the proclamation of the gospel; the Holy Spirit reveals God to the sinner, not as an angry tyrant but as a loving and forgiving father.[12] The intellectual and cognitive apprehension

---

[8] Thomas Aquinas, *Summa*, I, 79–80. On Gabriel Biel, see Leif Grane, *Contra Gabrielem. Luthers Auseinandersetzung mit Gabriel Biel in der Disputatio Contra Scholasticam Theologiam* 1517 (Gyldendal: Acta theologica Danica IV, 1962), pp. 98–113. Naturally, Luther was aware of such distinctions and their meanings. See *WA* 4, 308, 1–9 (Dictata super Psalterium 1513–16); *WA* 59, 40 (Eigenhändige Randbemerkungen zu Gabriel Biels Collectorium und Canonis Misse Expositio. Seit 1516/17).

[9] Huovinen (*Fides infantium*) has demonstrated how the notion of "infused faith" (*fides infusa*) forms a pair with "apprehending faith" (*fides apprehensiva Christi*). *Fides infusa* depicts the actual effects of God in the human being, while *fides apprehensiva* is disposed towards the object of faith. Luther states that intellectual perception is the means of apprehending Christ in faith. *WA* 40 I, 447, 15–28: "Apprehenditur autem Christum non lege, non operibus, sed ratione seu intellectu, illuminato fide."

[10] *WA* 40 I, 224, 8–225, 2: "...si salvari vis, non per opera, sed filium dei, missus in carnem qui tulit peccata tua. Ibi ante iustitiam mera mors, ira, peccatum; lex humiliat tantum. Tum venit et revelat se vere, ut agnoscas eum, sic: Ego sum deus tuus, ego volo te salvare, donare tibi volo, non mereri debes, i. e. donat sua opera bona gratis ad hanc divinitatem, non propter verecundiam, impedientibus monachis. Si dico: hoc facio etc. i. e. volo te deum esse, i. e. volo a te experiri misericordiam, bonitatem, das heist ex deo kretzmer deus non venit ad gloriam gratiae suae, nisi prius lex nos nidderschlag, ut donet divinitatem."

[11] *WA* 40 I, 607, 5–10, 26–32. The natural knowledge of God drives the individual only to love God with his or her own powers. This, however, is only righteousness of works. See *WA* 40 I, 603, 1–609, 6; 603, 14–609, 20.

[12] *WA* 40 I, 602, 5–603, 2; 602, 18–603, 13. The Gospel is a proclamation of Christ, who forgives sins, donates grace and makes the believer the sharer of eternal life. See *WA* 40 I, 232, 16–20; 259, 9–260, 2; 259, 33–260, 14; 262, 2–5, 20–23. The Gospel soothes the accusing conscience. *WA* 40 I, 342, 2–4, 20–22. The proclamation of the Gospel is spreading the knowledge of Christ (*propagare cognitionem Christi*). *WA* 40 I, 387, 1–388, 10; 387, 21–30.

of God means knowing Him as God who gives Himself to and on behalf of sinners.

Nevertheless, the incarnation of the Son does not have simply intellectual content since the second person of the Trinity becomes an actual human being. Luther states:

> When the merciful Father saw that we were being oppressed through the Law, that we were being held under a curse, and that we could not be liberated from it by anything, He sent His Son into the world, heaped all the sins of all people upon him, and said to Him: "Be Peter the denier, Paul the persecutor, blasphemer and assaulter; David the adulterer; the sinner who ate the apple in paradise; the thief on the cross. In short, be the person of all men, the one who has committed the sins of all men".[13]

In summary, Christ took the place of sinners and is slain on their behalf. The assumption of humanity in incarnation is described through the classical teaching of personal union (*unio personalis*) of the two natures in Christ. Christ is one person who is at the same time both human and divine. The communication of attributes (*communicatio idiomatum*) takes place in the person of Christ, between the two natures.[14] Christ, who is holy in His own person, takes on Himself the sins of the world through incarnation.[15] Hence, Christ becomes a sinner in the eyes of God; He is now the greatest and only sinner (*maximus et solus peccator*)

---

[13] *WA* 40 I, 437, 18–438, 18: "Ista est iucundissima omnium doctrinarum et consolationis plenissima quae docet habere nos hanc ineffabilem et inaestimabilem misericordiam et charitatem Dei, scilicet: cum videret misericors Pater per legem nos opprimi et sub maledicto teneri nec ulla re nos posse ab eo liberari, quod miserit in mundum filium suum in quem omnia omnium peccata coniecit et dixit ad eum: Tu sis Petrus ille negator, Paulus ille persecutor, blasphemus et violentus, David ille adulter, peccator ille qui comedit pomum in Paradiso, Latro ille in Cruce, In Summa, tu sis omnium hominum persona qui feceris omnium hominum peccata, tu ergo cogita, ut solvas et pro eis satisfacias. Ibi Lex venit et dicit: Invenio illum peccatorem suscipientem omnium hominum peccata in se et nullum praeterea peccatum video nisi in illo, Ergo moriatur in cruce. Atque ita invadit eum et occidit. Hoc facto totus mundus purgatus et expiatus est ab omnibus peccatis, Ergo etiam liberatus a morte et omnibus malis. Sublatis vero peccato et morte per unum illum hominem Deus nihil aliud videret amplius in toto mundo, praesertim si crederet, quam meram purgationem et iustitiam. Et si quae peccati reliquiae remanerent, tamen prae illo Sole, Christo, Deus eas non cerneret."

[14] While Luther does not use this term in the *Commentary*, the notion is clearly present. *WA* 40 I, 415, 8–416, 5; 416, 9–17. *Communicatio idiomatum* is described in detail in section 5.2.2.

[15] *WA* 40 I, 91, 1–4, 9–15; 443, 23–24.

because he has taken to his account the sins of Paul, Peter, David, and everybody else's.[16]

Personal union and the communication of the attributes is the prerequisite for the salvation of the human being. As the true God, Christ has the power to destroy the powers that keep creation and humanity captive. Sin, death, and God's wrath are nullified in the person of Christ. This annihilation (*annihilare*) is the act of God which is contrary to the act of creation (*creare*). The destruction of the opposing powers and the

---

[16] *WA* 40 I, 433, 3–434, 4: "Das sind cavillationes rationis humanae. Quomodo potest Christus dici maledictus dei, qui suspensus in ligno, cum non fuerit latro? Paulus bene munivit sua verba: factum maledictum non pro se, sed nobis. Emphasis in: 'Nobis.' Christus innocens. Omnis latro debet suspendi. ergo Christus, quia gerit personam omnium latronum. Ego debeo mori et damnari; hoc facit Christus; ideo oportet Christum facere latronem etc. Hoc viderunt prophetae, quod Christus futurus omnium maximus latro, blasphemus, sacrilegus, fur, quia non iam gerit personam suam. Non est natus Christus in divinitate e virgine, sed peccator, qui fecit, commisit omnia peccata nostra; non quod ipse, sed commiserit in suum corpus. Et sic comprehenditur ut aliquis, qui inter latrones, si etiam innocens. Quantomagis si sponte sua et patris voluntate voluit communicare corpus et sanguinem eorum, qui erant latrones, peccatores. Ideo submersus in omnia." See also 433, 17–434, 20; 437, 5–438, 11; 437, 18–438, 13; 438, 24–28; 448, 2–7, 17–26. According to Luther, the reality of assumption is underlined by his interpretation of Ps. 40:13, 41:5, 69:6, where a sinner prays for his sins. Luther interprets these words as those of Christ. *WA* 40 I, 435, 1–36, 7; 435, 21–436, 16. On Christ as the greatest sinner, see *WA* 40 I, 273, 2–8, 17–25; 434, 2–4, 21–24; 434, 34–435, 12; 437, 1–438, 2; 437, 10–14; 442, 9–443, 2; 442, 31–443, 15; 448, 8–449, 12; 448, 27–449, 19; 449, 30–32. Mannermaa (*Christ present in faith*, 13–16) claims that Christ has assumed a sinful human nature in incarnation; to carry the burden of sins, He must actually own them in Himself. This does not mean that Christ had committed sins, or that He had personal guilt, since Christ is innocent in His person. Luther, however distinguishes between incarnation and *kenosis*. Christ does not assume sin in incarnation but in *kenosis*. See, e.g., *WA* 5, 603: 5–8, 624: 33–36 (*Operationes in Psalmos* 1519–1521); 10 III, 331:4–11 (*Predigten des Jahres* 1522); 17 II, 288:17–289:1 (*Fastenpostille* 1525); 36, 143:15–144:1 (*Predigten des Jahres* 1532); 41, 629: 18–26, 231:23–26 (*Predigten des Jahres* 1536); 44, 311 12–39 (*Vorlesungen über 1. Mose* 1535–1545); 46, 136:4–13 (*Predigten des Jahres* 1538). I am indebted to Sammeli Juntunen for showing me these passages. In his *Commentary on Genesis* Luther teaches that in incarnation Christ purifies the sinful flesh He has received from St. Mary and makes it holy. In spite of this purification, "death" remains in the assumed nature. *WA* 44, 311, 13–35: "In illo autem puncto conceptionis virginalis Spiritus sanctus purgavit et sanctificavit massam peccati, et extersit venenum Diaboli et mortis, quod est peccatum. Etsi mansit mors in ea carne propter nos, tamen fermentum peccati expurgatum est, et facta est purissima caro per Spiritum sanctum purificata, et unita cum divina natura in una persona." This seems to be the standard understanding of assumption among Lutherans. Selnecker claims the same in Paedagogia 2, 187: "Spiritus Sanctus est Spiritus sanctificationis, & ex sanquine virginis, quam purificaverat, Christi corpus aedificavit & sanctificavit, ut esset mundum, & immune ab omni peccato, ut alibi prolixius ostenditur." On Chemnitz's similar views, see section 5.2.2.

creation of the new righteousness are acts that can be attributed to God alone.[17] The saving power is thus in the divine nature of Christ.[18]

The sin assumed from humanity and God's essential righteousness clash now in the person of Christ. When sin encounters the divinity of Christ it is exposed to divine righteousness and life—divine attributes which destroy the tormenting powers.[19] From this it follows that righteousness is now bound to the person of the incarnated and risen Christ.

---

[17] *WA* 40 I, 441, 1–11: "Ista sunt capitalia nostrae theologiae, quae obscuraverunt Sophistae. Et hic vides, quam necesse sit articulus: filium Dei Christum. Ubi quem negavit Arius, necesse cadere ab articulo redemptionis. Nam 'vincere peccatum in seipso' gehort her zu, quando 'homo'. ergo oportet sit verus deus. Lex, mors, ira ut destruerentur, mus divina potentia sein; dare vitam in seipso, das mus divinitas; Annihilare et creare est divinae maiestatis. Cum ergo dicat scriptura, quod destruxerit mortem, peccatum in seipso et dederit vitam. Ergo qui incipiunt negare divinitatem Christi, postea amittunt totum Christianismum, facti Turcae. Ideo saepe dixi, ut bene discatis articulum iustificationis. Interim donec docemus per Christum iustificari, cogimur ostendere Christum verum dei filium." See also *WA* 40 I, 442, 3–7, 21–24.

[18] Christ as the Son of God acts like His Father. In other words, Christ shares the same nature with the Father, who is also the Creator. See *WA* 40 I, 80, 8–82, 1: "Ideo oportet eos constanter concipiamus. er ficht fidem weidlich [1. Joh. 5,4] an, quia scit 'esse victoriam'. Sententia notanda, quod Christus deus, quia Paulus eadem ei tribuit quae patri: pacem, ipsam gratiam, vitam, victoriam mortis, peccati, inferi equaliter cum patre. Hoc nullo modo liceret et esset sacrilegium, nisi deus esset Christus, quia is sol nicht pacem geben qui non hat. Et non affert Christus pacem ut Apostoli praedicando sed donando. pater dat, facit remissionem peccatorum et pacem. Haec eadem dat Christus etc. Dare autem gratiam et remissionem peccatorum et vivificationem, iustificationem, liberationem a morte, peccatis non sunt opera creaturae sed unius, solius maiestatis. Angeli non possunt iustificare, liberare a morte, peccatis me, remittere ea. Ea omnia pertinent ad gloriam summae maiestatis, creatricis, et tamen Christus habet eadem dare et creare, ergo oportet hunc esse verum deum. Multa argumenta in Iohanne quibus attribuit Christo divinitatem. Non est alia res quam a patre habemus, quam a filio; alioqui aliter dixisset Paulus, sed coniungit duo simul, gratiam et pacem. Ideo hoc dico, quia periculum est, ne in tot erroribus succedant haeretici, Ariani, Eunomiani, Macedoniani." See also *WA* 40 I, 80, 25–81, 28. Salvation is incomprehensible without human nature. God can be known only in His incarnate form. *WA* 40 I, 78, 3–79, 6; 78, 24–26. The righteousness of Christ is based on His incarnation, suffering, and resurrection. *WA* 40 I, 64, 22–65, 18.

[19] *WA* 40 I, 278, 2–10: "Mors mea ligat me, venit alia quae est vita, quae vivificat in Christo, et illa vita quae liberat a funibus mortis. Tum mors quae me ligabat, iam ligata, quae me occidit, iam occisa per ipsam mortem i. e. vitam. Sic Christus dulcissimis vocabulis vocatur mea mors, peccatum contra peccatum, quia occidit ideo peccatum, ut me iustificet. Tum peccatum est vita, tum lex est libertas, tum mors est vita, quia eo ipso, quod me iustificavit, est etc. Sic est venenum veneni et [Röm. 7, 23] iustificat. Das sind fein speculationes et phrases Pauli: 'Legem mentis meae' Ro. 7. est consolatoria phrasis etc. 'Ego sum per legem legi mortuus.'" See also 20–29; 279, 7–10, 23–29; 438, 9–440, 12; 438, 32–440, 35; 565, 2–567, 10; 565, 18–567, 22.

> Therefore Christ the power of God, righteousness, blessing, grace and life, overcometh these monsters and destroys them, even sin, death, and the curse, without war or weapons, in His own body, and in Himself...[20]

This theory of atonement has traditionally been termed the *Christus Victor* theory, because Christ wins (*vincit*) through a confrontation with the tormenting powers. In addition to this motive, Luther speaks about how Christ has come under the law and willingly suffered as sentenced by the law on behalf of human kind.[21] Later Lutheran generations in particular structured Christ's relation to the law through the concept of obedience (*oboedientia*). Christ has suffered the punishment of the law (*oboedientia passiva*) but also fulfilled the law when humans were incapable of this (*oboedientia activa*). Luther does not use these concepts, although he does mention how Christ has submitted Himself to the law in the passive sense of obedience.[22] Christ has also actively fulfilled the law and everything that is missing from the divine and perfect righteousness.[23]

---

[20] *WA* 40 I, 440, 21–23: "Ideo Christus, divina virtus, iustitia, benedictio, gratia et vita, vincit et tollit illa monstra: Peccatum, Mortem et Maledictionem, sine armis et proelio, in suo corpore et Semetipso."

[21] *WA* 40 I, 564, 26–568, 24.

[22] *WA* 40 I, 297, 18–22.

[23] *WA* 40 II, 42, 29–32: "In tempore vero tribulationis non audiam neque admittam nisi Christum donum, qui pro peccatis meis mortuus impertiit mihi suam iusticiam et hoc, [Röm. 10, 4] quod mihi deest in vita, pro me fecit et implevit. Ipse 'enim est finis legis ad iustitiam omni credenti'." The annotation uses the concept of "obedience", which does not appear in Luther's own text. E.g., *WA* 40 I, 568, 15–16: "Non factus est Magister legis, sed discipulus obediens legi, ut hac sua obedientia redimeret eos, qui sub lege erant." Gustaf Aulén has claimed that Luther primarily understands redemption in terms of the *Christus Victor* theory of satisfaction. See Aulén, *Den kristna försoningstanken: huvudtyper och brytningar* (Stockholm: Svenska kyrkans diakonistyrelse 1931, pp. 121–122). This is not true; the theory of *satisfactio vicaria* also has a substantial position in Luther's soteriology. See, e.g., *WA* 17 I, 316 (*Predigten des Jahres* 1525); *WA* 10 I, 121; 684, 719 (*Predigten des Jahres* 1522); 31 II, 339. On the critique of Aulén's views, see Osmo Tiililä, *Das Strafleiden Christi. Beitrag zur Diskussion über die Typeneinteilung der Versöhnungsmotive* (Helsinki: Annales Academiae Scientiarum Fennicae B XLVIII 1941), 227–228; Højlund, "Forsoningen i Luthers teologi" in *Forsoningen. Udvalget for Konvent for Kirke og Theologi* 1995; Lars Koen, *The Saving Passion. Incarnational and Soteriological Thought in Cyril of Alexandria's Commentary on the Gospel according to St.John* (Uppsala: Acta Universitas Upsaliensis 31 1991), pp. 127–131; John Montgomery, *Chytraeus on Sacrifice. A Reformation treatise in Biblical Theology* (*St. Louis: Concordia Publishing House* 1962), pp. 139–146. According to Robert Letham (*The Work of Christ* (Downer's Grove: IVP 1993), pp. 174–175), the classical theories of satisfaction are complementary but not exclusive. On philosophical problems of satisfaction, see Tommi Lehtonen, *Punishment, Atonement and Merit in modern Philosophy of Religion* (Helsinki: Luther-Agricola-Gesellshaft 44, 1999), pp. 189–244. When Luther (*WA* 40 I, 568, 21–22) states that Christ is not disposed towards the Law actively (*active*), but passively (*passive*), he resists the idea of Christ as the new lawgiver but does not deny *obodientia activa*.

Luther binds this view of vicarious atonement to the person of Christ. Atonement cannot be separated from the person Christ, and only in communication with Him is salvation of the individual possible.

> Therefore I have vanquished the law by double right and authority: firstly, as the Son of God, and Lord of the Law; secondly, in your person (*in persona vestra*); which is as much as if you had yourselves overcome the law; for my victory is yours.[24]

According to Luther, sin and death no longer exist in believers, only righteousness and life. This is so because Christ has fulfilled the law, and through His suffering and death destroyed sin and death in his person.[25] The Christian still feels the effects of sin in his own life, but God no longer imputes the guilt to him.[26] The reason for this non-imputation is union with Christ that takes place in faith and in which the salutary exchange (*commercium admirabile*) occurs. The parties to this participation are mutually entangled with each other's attributes:[27] the Christians's sin, damnation, death and all the evil is transferred to Christ, and the righteousness of Christ is transferred to the Christian.[28]

Hence, salvation is now bound ontologically to the person of Christ. In other words, Christ *himself* is the righteousness of the Christian. When a Christian believes in Christ, he participates in the person of Christ and His merits. The proclamation of the gospel thus delivers both the intellectual and cognitively understood information about what Christ has done for human beings (*favor*) and Christ himself, i.e., the gift

---

[24] *WA* 40 I, 566, 14–17: "Ideo duplici iure legem vici, prostravi, trucidavi: Primum ut filius Dei, Dominus legis, Deinde in persona vestra, quod tantundem est, ac si vosipsi legem vicissetis."

[25] *WA* 40 I, 443, 1–12: "...getretten et mich auff sein hals genomen et dixit: ego feci peccatum, quod fecit Martinus,—Ipse ergo est vere maledictus secundum legem, sed non pro se. Si me non suscepisset, nihil lex in eum; pro sua persona erat liber, non potuisset maledici, mori; sed quia susceperat libere peccatum meum, non pro sua persona sed mea. Ideo dedit suam personam mihi, quae est innocens; ideo per ipsum liberor a maledicto legis. Das ist maximum. Ego sum benedictus, humanitate et divinitate, nihil egeo, sed inanibo me et larva tua ambulabo. Sic ergo comprehensus, cum gestaret peccatum meum, et sic crucifixus. et tamen non potuit mori. Ideo resurrexit et iam non invenitur in eo peccatum, mors, nec larva mea; nulla mors videtur. In illam imaginem mus man hinsehen. Qui hoc credit, habet."

[26] *WA* 40 I, 273, 2–9, 19–29; 274, 6–11, 23–34; 278, 5–9, 20–29; 438, 1–4, 13–18; 439, 33–440, 14; 440, 7–12, 26–33; 441, 1–11, 16–27; 445, 2–11, 19–22; 566, 14–17; 569, 3–7, 14–21.

[27] The union naturally has a sacramental foundation. Baptism, for example, is not just an external sign but effective clothing with Christ's righteousness. *WA* 40 I, 540, 1–9; 540, 33–541, 35.

[28] *WA* 40 I, 454, 9–455, 6; 454, 19–455, 30.

(*donum*). Cognitive understanding of the mercy of God and possession of the gift form one indivisible entity, since mercy becomes effective only through the gift, Christ's real presence. Mercy here means the objective foundation of salvation: Christ's salvific acts and, through them, earned forgiveness of sins. The gift means Christ's effective, salvific, and vivifying presence in human kind.[29]

Luther characterizes this presence by saying that Christ is the form of faith.[30] In order to understand this correctly we must examine the scholastic backround of the term. The sophists,[31] Luther's theological opponents, claimed that the natural faculties of the human soul had not been totally corrupted since the fall. Human love still follows the order of love laid down in creation (*ordo caritatis*), whereby human love always inclined towards the greater and better object.[32] The highest good (*summum bonum*), i.e., God, is at the top of this order. Even after the fall, the human being still has the right disposition towards good, which can be used to evoke the love for God. The human being can love God more than anything else and thus fullfil the first commandment. If a greedy person can love money, which is good as such, surely he or she is capable of loving God who is greater good.[33] When a person

[29] *WA* 40 I, 236, 15: "...donum habet in corde, sed parvitas huius doni et pretii quod in fide tenet maior est coelo et terra, quia Christus maior est qui hoc donum est." *WA* 40 I, 72, 28–29: "Et haec duo vocabula, Gratia et Pax, complectuntur universum Christianismum. Gratia remittit peccatum, Pax quietat conscientiam."

[30] Luther refers to the Aristotelian distinction between matter (*materia*) and form (*forma*). Matter means an entity, which without the form is in a state of chaos. It is not the matter, but the form that makes the thing what it is. The Latin phrase *causa formalis* means the cause, which gives form to matter.

[31] 'Sophist' means a theologian who does theology using Aristotelian metaphysics, such as St. Thomas Aquinas. Luther also mentions Ockham and Scotus in this respect. *WA* 40 I, 226, 20. On Luther's criticism of scholastic theology, see Grane, *Contra Gabrielem*, 57–82. In scholastic theology there was no one theory of justification since the issue was continuously in dispute. What unites different scholastic theories of justification is an attempt to interpret justification in terms of some general theory of human behavior. Luther's own view is critical of such action, but he is still dependent on these theories himself.

[32] On Luther's critique of ordo caritatis, see Antti Raunio, *Summe des Christlichen Lebens. Die "Goldene Regel" als Gesetz der Liebe in der Theologie Martin Luthers von* 1510 *bis* 1527 (Mainz: von Sabern 2001), pp. 57–59, 76–87, 121, 123.

[33] *WA* 40 I, 226, 20–27; 228, 18–21; 231, 15–19; 291, 15–20; 459, 31–460, 21. For example, St. Aquinas claims that the human being naturally desires salvation while being unable to reach it by natural means. Despite this, people have the faculty of love, although it is deficient. See Aquinas, *Summa*, I–II, 8.

does everything that is in himself (*facere quod in se est*) the law is fulfilled and God infuses his grace into this person.[34]

The grace infused in the believer is a quality or habitus which is connected to the person as accidence. This grace or love is the form which gives new divine being to the matter (*materia*) of faith, which is needed because faith as such is incapable of attaining to God.[35] The human being can then fulfill the law because the habitus infused in him raises human love to the new level where it can attain God. According to Luther, this means that the human being is saved because of the co-operation between natural love and the assisting habitual divine love.[36]

This co-operation is impossible in Luther's view since he thinks that as a sinner the human being does not have the faculties required for coming into contact with God. *Ordo caritatis* does not function properly in the fallen state. The human intellect and will are blackened (*tenebrae*) and perverted (*perversitas*) in spiritual matters.[37] It is impossible to act according the principle *facere quod in se est*, since human endeavors to love do not lead towards loving God according to *ordo caritatis*. Human love thus cannot be the way to God; if anything, love in itself is a way that leads away from God, or even worse, *against* God (*contra Deum*). In keeping with this, only a superficial or accidental change in the human

---

[34] On *facere quod in se est* principle in scholastic theology, see McGrath, *Iustitia Dei*, pp. 83–91, 112. According to Luther, *facere quod in se est* means that a person could fulfill the Law with his or her own powers, and is thus able to acquire *meritum de congruo*. This provides grace, which makes the person worthy of eternal life (*gratia gratum faciens*), and eventually leads to reception of *meritum de condigno*. See, e.g., *WA* 40 I, 220, 4–10, 13–16, 22–29; 227, 21–25; 228, 18–21; 230, 19–20; 291, 16–20.

[35] *WA* 40 I, 225, 25–30: "Vides ergo, quod Christiana iustitia non est inhaerens forma, ut ipsi loquuntur. Dicunt enim: quando homo facit aliquod bonum opus, hoc Deus acceptat et pro illo opere infundit ei charitatem. hanc infusam charitatem dicunt esse qualitatem haerentem in corde eamque vocant formalem iustitiam (Expedit vobis scire istum modum loquendi). Nihilque minus audire possunt, quam istam qualitatem, informantem cor ut albedo parietem, non esse iustitiam." See also *WA* 40 I, 226, 13–230, 22; 302, 32–303, 20; 422, 14–16. Scholastic theology had multiple interpretations of the roles of the Holy Spirit and love as infused habits. According to Petrus Lombardus, infused love is the Spirit. Melanchthon especially appreciated Lombard's view. See Saarinen, "Ipsa dilectio Deus est. Zur Wirkungsgeschichte von. 1. Sent. dist. 17 des Petrus Lombardus bei Martin Luther," in *Thesaurus Lutheri*, hrsgb. Tuomo Mannermaa et al. (Helsinki: Veröffentlichungen der Finnischen Theologischen Literaturgesellschaft 153, 1987). However, both Luther (*WA* 39 1, 319, 14–320, 18) and Chemnitz (*Loci* II, 245b (553)) criticise Lombard for not distinguishing created and uncreated love. Uncreated love, i.e., God, justifies while created love as a human quality does not.

[36] *WA* 40 I, 230, 28–30.

[37] *WA* 40 I, 293, 18–294, 22.

faculties of the soul and their new direction is not enough. People are in need of a more profound change.[38] Another problem in the requirement of the individual doing everything in himself is that it obviates faith and Christ's salvific work. Faith is less important than love, which gives form to faith and makes it live (known as *fides charitate formata*). Thus the central doctrine is the Law, not faith.[39]

Against this background Luther describes his own understanding of Christ as the form of faith (*fides Christo formata*). In opposition to the 'sophists', Luther claimed that the true formal righteousness (*iustitia formalis*) is not love, but faith or Christ himself.[40]

> But we substitute that love for faith, and while they say that faith is the 'monogram', mere initial letters, but love is its living colors and completion, we say in opposition that faith takes hold of Christ and that He is the form that adorns and informs faith as color does the wall. Therefore Christian faith is not an idle quality or an empty husk in the heart, which may exist in a state of mortal sin until love comes along to make it alive. But if it is true faith, it is a sure trust (*fiducia*) and firm acceptance (*assensus*) in the heart, which takes hold of Christ. Christ is the object of faith, or rather not the object but, so to speak, the One who is present in the faith itself (*in ipsa fide Christus adest*). Thus faith is a sort of knowledge (*cognitio*) or darkness that nothing can see. Yet the Christ whom faith takes hold of is sitting in this darkness as God sat in the midst of darkness on Sinai and in the temple. Therefore our actual 'formal righteousness' (*formalis iustitia*) is not a love that informs faith; but is faith itself, a cloud in our hearts, that is, trust in a thing we do not see, in Christ, who is present although he cannot be seen at all.
>
> Therefore faith justifies because it takes hold of and possesses this treasure, the present Christ. But how He is present—this is beyond our thought; for there is darkness, as I have said. Where the confidence of

---

38 *WA* 40 I, 461, 16–24. See also McGrath, *Iustitia Dei*, pp. 190–197; Mannermaa, *Christ present in faith*, pp. 34–37.

39 *WA* 40 I, 164, 15–19; 422, 14–22.

40 *WA* 40 I, 197, 7–198, 2; 229, 2–13; 369, 1–6; 363, 8–364, 2; 370, 6–11; 371, 1–4; 372, 8–12. Luther can use the expressions 'Christ' and 'faith' as mutually interchangeable concepts. See and compare *WA* 40 I, 229, 2, 13, 18, 25; 232, 24; 363, 9; 364, 12; 368, 31; 369, 24; 408, 7. Both faith and Christ are formal causes of righteousness, based on the following line of thought. Luther merges the relational and ontological aspects together. The relational aspects mean that the human intellect is disposed out of the person to an outward object. Intellect is now defined by the object and in relation to the object. The ontological aspect means that the form of the object now becomes the form of the observer as well. Consequently, it is possible to describe what the presence of Christ in faith means; God is both the object and the subject of faith. Epistemologically, the act of knowing and the object of knowing are one and the same. For a more detailed explanation, see Mannermaa, "Hat Luther eine trinitarische Ontologie?".

> the heart is present, therefore, there Christ is present, in that very cloud and faith. This is the actual, formal righteousness on account of which a man is justified; it is not on account of love, as the sophists say. In short, just as the sophists say that love forms and fulfills faith, so we say that it is Christ who forms and fulfills faith or who is the form (*actus*; *Seinswirklichkeit*) of faith. Therefore the Christ who is grasped by faith and who lives in the heart is the true Christian righteousness, on account of which God counts (*reputat*) us righteous and grants us eternal life. Here there is no work of the law, no love; but there is an entirely different kind of righteousness, a new world above and beyond the Law. For Christ or faith is neither the Law nor the work of the Law.[41]

However, before Christ can be the form and *Seinswirklichkeit* of faith, the sin dwelling in humanity must be annihilated (*redigere in nihilum*).[42]

---

[41] *WA* 40 I, 228, 28–229, 30: "Nos autem loco charitatis istius ponimus fidem, Et sicut ipsi dicunt fidem monogramma et charitatem vivos colores et plenitudinem ipsam, ita nos e contra dicimus fidem apprehendere Christum qui est forma, quae fidem ornat et informat, ut color parietem. Quare fides Christiana non est otiosa qualitas vel vacua siliqua in corde quae possit exsistere in peccato mortali, donec charitas accedat et eam vivificet, Sed si est vera fides, est quaedam certa fiducia cordis et firmus assensus quo Christus apprehenditur, Sic ut Christus sit obiectum fidei, imo non obiectum, sed, ut ita dicam, in ipsa fide Christus adest. Fides ergo est cognitio quaedam vel tenebra quae nihil videt, Et tamen in istis tenebris Christus fide apprehensus sedet, Quemadmodum Deus in Sinai et in Templo sedebat in medio tenebrarum. Est ergo formalis nostra iustitia non charitas informans fidem, sed ipsa fides et nebula cordis, hoc est, fiducia in rem quam non videmus, hoc est, in Christum qui, ut maxime non videatur, tamen praesens est. Iustificat ergo fides, quia apprehendit et possidet istum thesaurum, scilicet Christum praesentem. Sed quo modo praesens sit, non est cogitabile, quia sunt tenebra, ut dixi. Ubi ergo vera fiducia cordis est, ibi adest Christus in ipsa nebula et fide. Eaque est formalis iustitia propter quam homo iustificatur, non propter charitatem, ut Sophistae loquuntur. Summa: sicut Sophistae dicunt charitatem formare et imbuere fidem vel formam esse fidei. Ergo fide apprehensus et in corde habitans Christus est iustitia Christiana propter quam Deus nos reputat iustos et donat vitam aeternam."

[42] Christ as the form of faith makes faith actual. To make this happen, the naturally sinful form must be annihilated. *WA* 40 I, 488, 15–19: "Nam Deus est Deus humilium, miserorum, afflictorum, oppressorum, desperatorum et eorum qui prorsus in nihilum redacti sunt; Estque Dei natura exaltare humiles, cibare esurientes, illuminare caecos, miseros et afflictos consolari, peccatores iustificare, mortuos vivificare, desperatos et damnatos salvare etc. Est enim Creator omnipotens ex nihilo faciens omnia." *WA* 40 I, 512, 17–26: "Post istas ergo confutationes et argumentationes satis prolixe et pulchre docet Paulus legem nihil aliud esse, si verum et optimum eius usum perspexeris, quam Paedagogian quandam ad iustitiam. Humiliat enim homines et capaces iustitiae Christi reddit, cum suum proprium officium facit, id est, cum eos reos agit, terret, redigit in cognitionem peccati, irae, mortis, inferni. Hoc enim facto perit opinio institiae et sanctitatis propriae et incipit dulcescere Christus cum suis beneficiis. Quare lex non est contra promissa Dei, sed potius pro illis. Quanquam autem non implet promissionem et non affert iustitiam, tamen suo officio et usu humiliat nos atque ita reddit capaces gratiae et beneficii Christi." See also *WA* 40 I, 488, 12–15; 508, 30–36; 509,

This annihilation begins with the Law. The Law shows that mankind is entirely sinful and drives the sinner to confess his or her blindness and separation from God.[43] Until now, the human being has not been interested in the gospel. When the sinner realizes that he or she has not fulfilled the requirements of the Law, God's wrath and hell start to terrify him or her. The Law thus breaks human self-righteousness and makes way for the acceptance of Christ.[44] By giving up his or her own righteousness, the sinner confesses that only God is truly righteous and in His mercy gives righteousness as a gift.[45]

The proclamation of the Gospel evokes faith in the sinner. This faith grasps and possesses (*apprehendit*) Christ. The mode of this apprehension is to be understood in terms of Aristotelian epistemology, which Luther uses when he speaks about Christ as the form of faith. Aristotle claimed that in the act of knowing, the form of the object of knowledge is transferred into the knower.[46]

In the middle ages debate concerning the mode of transference was extremely contentious. Although Aristotle was considered a great authority, there was no consensus on how to interpret his particular

17–28. See also Theodor Dieter, *Der Junge Luther und Aristoteles. Eine historisch-systematische Untersuchung zum Verhältnis von Theologie und Philosophie* (Berlin: Walter der Gruyter 2001), pp. 257–275.

[43] *WA* 40 I, 505, 17–27; 506, 20–28; 506, 34–507, 14.

[44] *WA* 40 I, 224, 20–25: "Altera pars: si vis salvus fieri, salus non contingit per opera, Sed Deus misit unigenitum filium suum in mundum, ut nos per eum vivamus. Is crucifixus, mortuus est pro te et obtulit peccata tua in corpore suo. Ibi nulla est congruitas aut opus ante gratiam, sed mera ira, peccatum, pavor, mors. Itaque Lex ostendit tantum peccatum, perterrefacit et humiliat atque hoc modo praeparat ad iustificationem et impellit ad Christum." The Law is *praeparatrix ad gratiam* (*WA* 40 I, 487, 30–488, 14; 508, 30–36.) and *paedagogian ad iustitiam*. (*WA* 40 I, 512, 17–19).

[45] *WA* 40 I, 224, 20–29.

[46] According to Aristotle, when we think about horses, for example, we think of actual horses as they are comprehended in reality. This means that the object of the intellect is the form (*eidos, forma*) as the form is actualized in individual objects (e.g., in horses). This kind of thinking, however, requires that the same form be actualized in the observer's mind (without the matter). In perception, we perceive objects which are outside the mind, although the form of the object is in the mind at the same time. See Leen Spruit, *Species Intelligibilis: From Perception to Knowledge. I. Classical Roots and Medieval Discussions* (Leiden: Brill 1994), pp. 37–38, 45–46: "[For Aristotle] Perceiving is a special sort of change in the perceiver: the objects of perception, acting via some medium, causally affect the perceptual apparatus; and the apparatus changes inasmuch as it receives the form of the object without its matter." "Thus, the identity of the intellect with its objects means that the rational structure of the world is re-enacted in human thought." See Aristotle, *De anima*, 424a17.

notions.[47] It was generally held that the human intellect becomes somehow identical with the object, though it does not convey its own form to the intellect. In the latter case, the object would cease to be what it is; objects are what they are only because of their particular form. Theologians thus supposed the existence of a particular intelligible species (*species intelligibilis*), which is identical with the form of the object but remained distinct from it.[48] In the German humanism of the 16th century the idea that such a species existed was commonly held.[49] For example, Jodocus Trutvetter, Luther's teacher at the university of Erfurt, thought that in the act of knowing the object of knowing or 'the picture', a natural likeness, (*naturalis similitudo*) was transferred into the knower.[50]

Luther's conception of the act of knowing is not based directly on any previous theory since he forms a quite independent interpretation of Aristotle.[51] According to Luther, when the human intellect focuses

---

[47] Spruit, *Species intelligibilis* I, pp. 397–398, 404. The internal tension in Aristotle's thought resulted in widespread controversy in the Middle Ages. Aristotle's texts do not make it clear what the actual mode of presence of the form in the intellect is.

[48] Spruit, *Species intelligibilis* I, p. 47: "Aristotle's integrated theory of perception and intellectual thought is the framework of the Scholastic doctrines of the species in medio and the species intelligibiles. In the interaction between the actualized medium and sense organs, the senses do not receive the form itself or a physical similitude: they merely become identical in form to the external objects."

[49] Spruit, *Species Intelligibilis: From Perception to Knowledge. II. Renaissance Controversies, Later Scholasticism, and The Elimination of the Intelligible Species in Modern Philosophy* (Leiden: Brill 1995), pp. 128–129.

[50] Jodocus Trutvetter, *Summa* VIII, Ff.

[51] Luther's application of Aristotle's theory is original, interpreting Aristotle in very ontologically realistic terms to mean that Christ is not present in the mind simply in the sense of *species intelligibilis* but as the actual form. A good example of Luther's realism is his view on theological language; the words refer not only to the objects but carry them within. See ReijoTyörinoja, "Nova vocabula et nova lingua. Luther's conception of Doctrinal Formulas," in *Thesaurus Lutheri*; Eeva Martikainen, *Doctrina: Studien zu Luthers Begriff der Lehre* (Helsinki: Luther-Agricola-Gesellschaft 26, 1992). Although Luther criticized Aristotle on many points, in this regard he considered his views correct. See *WA* 1, 29, 15–31 (*Sermo Lutheri in natali Christi* 1515). See also Dieter, *Der Junge Luther*, p. 260. Ockham's thinking has probably also influenced Luther. Ockham claimed that the form of the object is not transferred into the perceiver. Using this notion he criticizes some branches of the scholastic theory of perception, which requires the special notion of *species intelligibilis*. Although Luther is not an Ockhamist, they share the same criticism of mediating species. Both deny the mediating species while Luther thinks that (in theological perception) the form (and not its substitute) is actually present. On Ockham's theory of perception, see Vesa Hirvonen, *Passions in William Ockhams's philosophocal psychology* (Dordrecht: Kluwer Academic Publishers Boston 2004), pp. 67–69; Spruit, *Species intelligibilis I*, pp. 291–298. Luther criticizes the scholastic theories of perception, which deny the actual presence of form in the mind. The

on Christ in the gospel, it apprehends and owns Christ. Hence, Christ is made the form of the human intellect. In faith, the believer not only possesses the intelligible species of Christ, but Christ himself. The believer is not only transformed into the natural likeness of Christ, but Christ himself is present in him or her.

Based on this, justification does not consist of redirection of the human faculties of the soul, gone astray because of sin.[52] Christ himself must become the Life of the sinner; the apprehended Christ has taken over the human being and He now becomes the new will of the sinner. It can be stated that in faith the appetitive and apprehensive faculties merge.[53] The Christian believes in Christ because Christ himself is both object of faith and subject of faith.[54] The faith that saves is a new divine reality in the human being: Christ, who takes over the intellect and other faculties of the soul.[55] This also means that human faculties as *materia*

scholastic criticism of such a theory was as follows. The disposition of faith towards its object belongs to the faculty of the intellect, which assents to its object, although it is beyond rational knowledge. Since the intellect receives knowledge through assimilation of *species intelligibilis* of the object of the perception, the species becomes the form of the subject. In order to receive knowledge, the knower and the known must become one. However, it was considered not possible to know God through knowledge since this would suggest that the individual and God become one, which was deemed impossible. Thus faith, as intellect, cannot be the foundation of the relationship with God. Consequently, 'the sophists' claimed that the appetitive faculty of the soul, i.e., the will and love, is the primary organ of religious life since they obtain their object without assimilating it. See also *WA* 40 I, 245, 12–246, 2; 246, 14–18; 261, 2–9, 19–28; 297, 30–33; 423, 7–11, 23–29; 443, 12–444, 2; 443, 35–444, 18; 447, 2–5, 15–23.

[52] According to Mannermaa ("Über die Unmöglichkeit, gegen die texte Luthers zu sysmatisieren. Antwort an Gunther Wenz," in *Unio*, p. 390), entities such as 'life' and 'bliss' are not anthropological or psychological entities inherent in the soul since they are divine attributes, which are shared through the Spirit. The believer participates in the divine life since Christ as a divine person is present in the heart.

[53] This is apparent in *WA* 40 I, 282–288, where Luther explains Gal. 2:20 (I live; yet not I, but Christ lives in me). Intellect precedes the will in salvation. The justifying faith, however, includes the mortification and renewal of the will. Before this, intellect must renounce its inability to know God. Thus, the will is renewed as well, which makes a person capable of faith. According to Bernhard Lohse, the distinction between the functions of the faculties of the soul was not soteriologically significant since Luther tends to speak about the human being as a whole (*totus homo*). See Lohse, *Ratio und Fides. Eine Untersuchung über die RATIO in der Theologie Luthers* (Göttingen: Vandenhoeck & Ruprecht 1958), pp. 90–92. See also Petri Järveläinen, *A Study on Religious Emotions* (Helsinki: Schriften der Luther-Agricola-Gesellshaft 47, 2000), pp. 100–104.

[54] *WA* 40 I, 545–546; 610; *WA* 40 II, 178–179.

[55] Christ's status as the form of the faith means that the mind of the believer and the mind of Christ share the same form. Ks. *WA* 40 I, 650, 21–32. "...per omnia de Deo cogitant, ut in corde affectus est, habent eandem formam in animo quam Deus vel Christus."

are nothing when compared to *forma*, because it is the form that gives matter its essence. Thus the change that takes place in conversion has no merit. The form, Christ, is primary, not matter.[56]

Faith is no human deed but God's gift, is primary received through the gospel.[57] Reception is *passio*, being the object of the influence and thus being affected.[58] In order to benefit from the imputation of Christ's righteousness (*reputatio*), Christ has to take His place in the person's heart.

> Here it is to be noted that these three things, faith, Christ, acceptation, or imputation, must be joined together. Faith takes hold of Christ, and has Him present, and holds Him enclosed, as the ring does the precious stone. And whoever shall be found having this confidence in Christ apprehended in the heart, him will God accept as righteous.[59]

Since it is the person of Christ that has become the righteousness of the sinner through His death and resurrection, there is no way to imagine that the only present reality in the human being is a new consciousness.[60]

---

[56] Mannermaa, *Christ present in faith*, pp. 23–31; Juntunen, *Der Begriff des Nichts*, pp. 347–353.

[57] *WA* 40 I, 130, 1–3: "Ideo semper docemus: Es ist fides et cognitio simpliciter donum Dei qui hoc creat in nobis et conservat per verbum. 1. Donat per illud, auget et conservat." *WA* 40 II, 36, 2–4.

[58] *WA* 40 I, 42, 7–43, 2: "Sed iusticia quae ex nobis sit, non est Christiana iusticia, non simus per eam probi. Christiana iusticia est mere contraria, passiva, quam tantum recipimus, ubi nihil operamur sed patimur alium [1. Kor. 2, 7] operari in nobis scilicet deum."

[59] *WA* 40 I, 233, 16–24: "Est et hic notandum, quod ista tria, Fides, Christus, Acceptio vel Reputatio, coniuncta sunt. Fides enim apprehendit Christum et habet eum praesentem includitque eum ut anulus gemmam, Et qui fuerit inventus cum tali fide apprehensi Christi in corde, illum reputat Deus iustum."

[60] Among others, Eberhard Jüngel and Albrecht Beutel have interpreted Luther this way. See Jüngel, *Das Evangelium von der Rechtfertigung des Gottlosen als Zentrum des christlichen Glaubens: eine theologische Studie in ökumenischer Absicht* (Tübingen: Mohr 1998), p. 181; Beutel, "Antwort und Wort," pp. 90–91. See also Karl Holl, Gesammelte Aufsätze zur Kirchengeschichte, Band 1. (Tübingen: Mohr Siebeck 1932), pp. 35–37. The crucial question remains: if Christ is more than new conscience, what do we mean? The basic difference between Finnish Luther scholars and these scholars is the idea of whether some new internal entity is needed for the emergence of new consciousness and justification. The German interpretation is that justification occurs as an outward influence, where nothing is given into the person. The Finns have claimed that Christ has to be an internal and efficient reality to enable imputation. The forgiveness of sins is based only on the apprehension of Christ, not on inchoate righteousness or the efficiency of the presence of Christ. Dennis Bielfeldt ("Ontology of Deification," in *Caritas Dei. Beiträge zum Verständnis Luthers und der gegenwärtige Ökumene*, Festschrift für Tuomo Mannermaa zum 60. Geburtstag, eds. Oswald Bayer et al. [Helsinki: Schriften der Luther-Agricola-Gesellshaft 39, 1997]) has attempted to create ontological models that could illustrate the presence of Christ in faith philosophically.

More than apprehension of cognitive knowledge and mental assent of Christ and his deeds, the Christian and Christ must become one person (analogous to the way Christ is one, other than the fact that He has two natures). The parties to this conjunction participate in each other's attributes without changing or losing their own essence. Luther states that the Christian and Christ are like one person (*quasi una persona*). The relation between Christ and the believer must be examined according to the rules of christology.[61]

Luther often emphasized that the Christian cannot separate himself or herself from the person of Christ, even as they remain distinct identities. Otherwise the human being is still in the grip of sin and death.[62] Through faith the believer is in Christ and Christ is in him.[63]

---

[61] *WA* 40 I, 285, 24–286, 21: "Verum recte docenda est fides, quod per eam sic conglutineris Christo, ut ex te et ipso fiat quasi una persona quae non possit segregari sed perpetuo adhaerescat ei et dicat: Ego sum ut Christus, et vicissim Christus dicat: Ego sum ut ille peccator, quia adhaeret mihi, et ego illi; Coniuncti enim sumus per fidem in unam carnem et os, Eph. 5.: 'Membra sumus corporis Christi, de carne eius et de ossibus eius.' Ita, ut haec fides Christum et me arctius copulet, quam maritus est uxori copulatus. Ergo fides illa non est otiosa qualitas, sed tanta est eius magnitudo, ut obscuret et prorsus tollat ista stultissima somnia doctrinae Sophisticae de fictione fidei formatae et charitatis, de meritis, de dignitate aut qualitate nostra etc." See also *WA* 40 I, 285, 5–286, 1. Although the union with Christ is real, the substances are not absorbed into one another and lose their original identity. See Peura, "Der Vergöttlichungsgedanke in Luthers Theologie 1518–1519" in *Thesaurus Lutheri*, pp. 179–180. See also Gerhard Ebeling, *Disputatio de homine*, pp. 175–177. *WA TR* 4 665, 16–19. (19. Juni 1540) "Ego interrogavi; [2. Petri 1, 4] Doctor tum: Non loquitur, quod nos simus futuri dei naturaliter, sed participatione. Christus enim inhabitat in nobis. Ut autem aliquis participat ex mea pecunia, sic nos ex Christo."

[62] *WA* 40 I, 285, 2–286, 3; 285, 8–23: "Paulus suam peculiarem phrasin habet, non humanam, sed divinam et coelestem, qua Evangelistae et caeteri Apostoli (praeter unicum Ioannem qui interdum etiam sic loqui solet) non sunt usi. Et nisi Paulus hac forma loquendi prior usus fuisset ac eam nobis conceptis verbis praescripsisset, nemo etiam ex sanctis ausus fuisses ea uti. Est enim plane insolens et inaudita, Ut: 'Vivo', 'non vivo'; 'mortuus sum', non mortuus sum; sum peccator, non sum peccator; habeo legem, non habeo legem. Sed ista phrasis vera est in Christo et per Christum. Quare si in causa iustificationis discernis personam Christi et tuam, tum es in lege, manes in ea et vivis in te, quod est mortuum esse apud Deum et damnari a lege, Quia fidem habes, ut Sophistae nugantur, informatam charitate. Sic exempli causa loquor. Nullus enim est qui talem fidem habet. Ideo quae Sophistae de fide informata Charitate docuerunt, mera ludibria Satanae sunt. Sed concedamus reperiri posse hominem qui talem fidem habeat, tamen eam habens esset vere mortuus, quia tantum haberet historicam fidem de Christo quam etiam Diabolus et omnes impii habent."

[63] *WA* 40 I, 284, 20–28: "Interim foris quidem manet vetus homo, subiectus legi; sed quantum attinet ad iustificationem, oportet Christum et me esse coniunctissimos, ut ipse in me vivat et ego in illo (Mirabilis est haec loquendi ratio). Quia vero in me vivit, ideo, quidquid in me est gratiae, iustitiae, vitae, pacis, salutis, est ipsius Christi, et tamen illud ipsum meum est per conglutinationem et inhaesionem quae est per fidem, per quam efficimur quasi unum corpus in spiritu. Quia ergo vivit in me Christum,

Participation in Christ in faith generates participation in the Trinity as well (2. Pet. 1:4).[64] Luther's *Commentary on Galatians* does not describe justification only in forensic terms if forensic justification is defined as an act that happens *completely and ontologically* outside of the person.[65] Justification means becoming connected with a new reality: Christ is the form and *Seinswirklichkeit* of the sinner. Christ's victory over sin and death are granted to the believer through the real presence of Christ, which is the prerequisite of justification.[66]

> Christ living in me abolishes the Law, condemns the sin, and mortifies the death. These must vanish wherever He is present since Christ is eternal peace, consolation, righteousness, and life, which takes place of the terrors of the Law, the sadness of the soul, sin, Hell, and death.[67]

This inevitably raises questions about the connection between imputation and the acquisition of righteous. What does Luther actually mean when he says that the present reality in the individual is the prerequisite for the imputation of Christ's righteousness?

2.1.2. *Justification as Imputation and Regeneration*

The perfection of justification is based on God's mercy and favor, which is given to the sinner through imputation. However, this imputation can take place only if Christ is present in the individual through faith.[68] According to Luther, justifying righteousness involves the apprehension of Christ in faith, not merely imputation (*pura reputatio*).[69] Thus Luther

---

necesse est simul cum eo adesse gratiam, iustitiam, vitam ac salutem aeternam et abesse legem, peccatum mortem." See also *WA* 40 I, 282, 3–283, 9; 284, 4–8.

[64] *WA* 40 I, 182, 4–5, 15–16.

[65] See also Lienhard, *Martin Luthers christologisches Zeugnis*, pp. 103–108.

[66] Luther does not use the concept *inhabitatio* in the *Commentary* to illustrate Christ's indwelling, employing concepts such as "to live" (*vivit*), "to stay within" (*in me manet*) and "to be joined together" (*conglutinatus*). See, e.g., *WA* 40 I, 283–284.

[67] *WA* 40 I, 283, 34–284, 28: "Vivens autem in me Christus abolet legem, peccatum damnat, mortem mortificat, quia ad praesentiam ipsius illa non possunt non evanescere. Est enim Christus aeterna pax, consolatio, iustitia et vita; His autem cedere oportet terrorem legis, moerorem animi, peccatum, Infernum, mortem."

[68] *WA* 40 I, 233, 1–5: "Das heist ein gros ding, fide apprehendere Christum portantem peccata mundi. Da von 3. Ro.: Reputantur. Omnis Christianus die 3 schlies ynneinander: fides quae includat Christum et habeat eum praesentem ut in einer Zang ein edlenstein. Qui fuerit inventus tali fide apprehensi Christi, illum reputat deus iustum."

[69] *WA* 40 I 372, 8–11: "Non est pura reputatio, sed involvit ipsam fidem et apprehensionem Christi passi pro nobis, quae non levis res. Sic vides, quod sine operibus

distances himself from the strictest interpretations of forensic justification. The individual also becomes one with the apprehended Christ. But what is the relation between apprehending Christ and becoming righteous?

Justification is connected with becoming righteous since it involves 'being formed'. Justifying faith changes something in the person. If it does not produce change it is not real faith.[70] Justification means being born again as a new creature (*nova creatura*). All of this takes place without human merit, similar to natural birth.

> There is no work or merit that brings him his inheritance, except his birth only; and so in obtaining the inheritance he is a mere patient, and not an agent (*patientia et passione*): simply to be born is that which makes him an heir. So we obtain eternal gifts, namely, the forgiveness of sins, righteousness, the glory of the resurrection, and everlasting life, not as agents, but as patients, that is, not by doing, but by receiving...So faith only makes (*efficit*) us sons of God, born of the Word, which is the womb of God, wherein we are conceived, carried, born and nourished up. By this birth, then, we are made new creatures: formed (*fieri et formari*) by faith in the word; we are made Christians, children, and heirs of God...[71]

---

propter peccata manentia et peccata oportet illam habere reputationem quae fit propter Christum, in quem credimus." The phrase *non est pura reputatio* is omitted in the annotation. See also *WA* 40 I, 366, 6–367, 10; 371, 2–373, 2; 576, 1–577, 10. Luther juxtaposes verbal (*verbaliter*) and actual (*realiter*) change. Verbal change implies only outward transformation while actual change transforms the mind and the will as well. See *WA* 40 II, 179.

[70] *WA* 40 I, 421, 21–28: "Ficta est quae audit de Deo, Christo et omnibus mysteriis incarnationis et redemptionis et apprehendit illas res auditas et pulcherrime de eis novit loqui, et tamen mera opinio et inanis auditus manet qui tantum relinquit bombum in corde de Evangelio, de quo multa garrit, re vera autem non est fides, quia non renovat nec immutat cor, non generat novum hominem, sed relinquit eum in priori sua opinione et conversatione. Estque haec fides valde perniciosa, quam satius esset non habere. Et Philosophus moralis melior est tali Hypocrita qui hanc fidem habet." *WA* 40 I, 265, 30–36: "Postquam vero homo fide iustificatus est et iam Christum fide possidet et novit eum esse iustitiam et vitam suam, certe non erit otiosus sed ut bona arbor proferet bonos fructus, Quia credens habet Spiritum sanctum; ubi is est, non sinit hominem esse otiosum, sed impellit eum ad omnia exercitia pietatis, ad dilectionem Dei, ad patientiam in afflictionibus, Ad invocationem, gratiarum actionem, ad exhibendam charitatem erga omnes." In other words, justification transforms the person into a good tree, which bears good fruit.

[71] *WA* 40 I, 597, 19–29: "Nihil enim facit ad hoc, ut nascatur, sed tantum patitur. Itaque passive, non active pervenimus ad ista aeterna bona, remissionem peccatorum, iustitiam, resurrectionis gloriam et ad vitam aeternam. Nihil prorsus hic intercedit, sola fides apprehendit oblatam promissionem. Sic hic sola fides efficit filios Dei, natos ex verbo, quod est uterus divinus, in quo concipimur, gestamur, nascimur, educamur etc. Hac ergo nativitate, hac patientia seu passione, qua simus Christiani, simus etiam filii

On the other hand, while Luther stresses the reality of change, he also stresses the distinct nature of justification, good works, faith and love.

> Therefore this must be avoided as infernal poison. We must conclude with Paul that we are justified through mere faith, not through 'faith formed by love'. The faculty of justification does not belong any 'form', which makes someone accepted since the faculty of justification belongs to faith itself. It is faith which apprehends Christ the Saviour in the heart. This faith justifies without love and before any occurrence of love.[72]
>
> The fact that Christ gives commandments and teaches, or actually interprets the law in the Gospels does not belong to the locus of justification but in the locus of Good Works.[73]

Although justification and processual renewal cannot be separated, Luther considered it of great importance to distinguish between the two, otherwise the inner consistency of the doctrine of justification is endangered.[74] Both aspects exist at the same time because Christ is the source of both, being both the favor and the gift. The righteousness present in the Christian consists of two parts: first, imputed righteousness and second, renewal begun in the Christian through the presence of Christ. But what exactly is the relation between justification and renewal, and what are the implications for the certainty of salvation?[75] Where should a terrified sinner look for the certainty of God's forgiveness?

Two types of renewal appear in Luther's *Commentary on Galatians*. First, the renewing union with Christ takes place in faith, which is followed by the renewing union with the Holy Spirit, which causes good works.[76]

---

et haeredes. Existentes autem haeredes liberi sumus a morte, diabolo etc. et habemus iustitiam et vitam aeternam. Verum ista mere passive nobis obvenit, nihil enim facimus, sed patimur nos fieri et formari novam creaturam per fidem in verbum." See also *WA* 40 I, 596, 12–597, 13; 599, 8–600, 4; 597, 14–23; 600, 16–20.

[72] *WA* 40 I, 239, 30–240, 16: "Ideo vitanda est ut venenum infernale Et concludendum cum Paulo: Sola fide, non fide formata charitate, nos iustificari. Quare non isti formae gratificanti tribuenda est vis iustificandi, sed fidei quae apprehendit et possidet in corde ipsum Christum Salvatorem. Haec fides sine et ante charitatem iustificat."

[73] *WA* 40 I, 568, 25–27: "Quod autem Christus in Evangelio praecepta tradit et legem docet seu potius interpretatur, hoc non ad locum de iustificatione, sed ad locum de bonis operibus pertinet."

[74] In *Von den Conciliis und Kirchen* 1539 (*WA* 50, 599–600) Luther emphasises against the antinomians that Christ must be both *gratia* and *donum*. Removing *donum* from the heart of soteriology leads to a make-believe Christian life, in which grace is spoken about but the person keeps on sinning.

[75] On the certainty of salvation, see *WA* 40 I, 299, 29–35; 578, 25–33.

[76] On the same distinction in Luther's earlier texts, see Pekka Kärkkäinen, *Luther trinitarische Theologie des Heiliges Geistes* (Mainz: von Zabern 2005), pp. 148–149.

> This word of promise given to Abraham brings us Christ, and when He has been apprehended in faith, the Holy Spirit is immediately (*mox*) donated for the sake of Christ. Then God and one's neighbor is loved, and the cross is carried.[77]

Union with Christ renews the person in the sense of *renovatio*$_1$. In other words, he is made capable of believing in Christ, which is naturally impossible for man.[78] *Renovatio*$_1$ renewal takes place through union with the person, attributes, and deeds of Christ. The new life and renewal are here understood as Christ's life and gifts in the individual.[79] In this sense, there is no separation, or even distinction, between justification and renewal (*renovatio*$_1$). Luther uses the metaphor of the bad tree that is made good in this case. When the nature of the tree is changed, it can now bear good fruit according to its new nature. Accordingly, a Christian who has been justified and renewed (*renovatio*$_1$) can now perform deeds that are good in God's sight (*renovatio*$_2$).[80] In this sense justification is connected with becoming righteous, though justification is based on the presence of the Gift, Christ, in the sinner, not only on this change as such. Justification as imputation of alien righteousness is needed until death since the Christian, although in a state of renewal, is still sinful.[81]

The nature of the subject has to be changed so that it can produce truly good acts. Accordingly, it is necessary that a good tree actually bear good fruit.[82] Justification is a beginning for life-long renewal. The Holy Spirit illuminates and renews (*renovatio*$_2$) the Christian day by day

---

[77] *WA* 40 I, 401, 16–19: "Huic credendum est; ea vox promissionis Abrahae affert Christum, quo fide apprehenso mox donatur Spiritus sanctus propter Christum. Tum diligitur Deus et proximus, bona opera fiunt, fertur crux." Luther has several illustrations of the order of salvation. On the one hand, the Holy Spirit is given immediately in faith. See *WA* 40 I, 330, 20–25. On the other hand, the person first believes in Christ, and is forgiven. Only after this is the Spirit given to renew the person. See *WA* 40 I, 408, 29–32; 579, 14–16.

[78] *WA* 40 I, 312, 31–313,13: "Multa quidem purgantur, praecipue autem ipsum caput serpentis, hoc est incredulitas et ignorantia Dei, praeciditur et conteritur, sed squamosum corpus et reliquiae peccati manent in nobis."

[79] *WA* 40 I, 283, 19–290, 31.

[80] *WA* 40 I, 265, 29–36; 287, 2–5, 19–23; 402, 1–11, 13–17; 404, 1–6, 17–18; *WA* 40 II, 66, 1–6, 14–22, 30–32.

[81] *WA* 40 I, 233, 8–234, 5; 235, 1–236, 2. See also *WA* 40 I, 233, 25–234, 23; 235, 15–236, 16; 236, 26–32; 40 II, 86, 4–8, 13–19.

[82] *WA* 40 I, 219, 29–30; 234, 6–8, 18–23; 239, 11–240, 10; 240, 16–26; 265, 3–9; 252, 14–253, 6; 252, 29–253, 21. The tree is made good in order to bear good fruit. Love thus belongs within Christian righteousness. See Manns, "Fides absoluta-fides incarnata", 296–297.

so that it becomes easier to love God and one's neighbor.[83] Since this renewal remains imperfect until death, the Christian needs justification as an imputation of Christ's righteousness in order to maintain the certainty of salvation.

The conjunction between *renovatio*$_1$ renewal and justification does not lead to righteousness of works and an attempt to find the certainty of salvation within the believer. The argument for this can be summarized in the four following points.

First, the *renovatio*$_1$ renewal that enables justifying faith is not the same thing as the *renovatio*$_2$ renewal that follows justification. Renewal in the first sense means apprehending Christ Himself and his merits. This is required because without renewal a sinner is unable to have faith in Christ. The Holy Spirit is then poured into the heart and this causes good works.

Second, Luther rejects the possibility of renewal and indwelling being available to the senses. Christ certainly dwells in the believer but He is in the cloud. The believer may perceive the movements in the soul: such as cognition, assent, and trust, but faith is still a darkness that does not actually show anything.[84] The believer looks to the crucified Christ outside of himself and this salutary looking gives the believer the inner certainty that Christ is not far from him but *intimio interior meo.*[85]

Third, the inner renewal and the new life caused by the indwelling of Christ is Christ's own life, not ours.[86] Luther formulates this through the concept of form (*forma*). Christ, as the form of faith, gives human

---

[83] *WA* 40 I, 400, 31–402, 22; 40 II 168, 15–17. The regenerates have the form of Christ (*forma Christi*). *WA* 40 I, 649, 19–30; 650, 13–651, 15. See also *WA* 40 II, 177, 4–178, 5; 178, 16–19; 179, 33–35; 180, 22–30. This means actual renewal in the believer. New skills of evaluation (*iudicium*), new will, new mind, new movements of the mind (*motus animi*), new affects of love and the faculty to do outward good works result from this renewal. The Spirit infuses these new affects in the mind of the believer. *WA* 40 I, 572, 2–11; 574, 2–13; 578, 11–579, 6; 572, 16–31; 574, 23–575, 12; 578, 34–579, 17; *WA* 40 II, 124, 27–30; 177, 4–178, 5; 178, 16–179, 23.

[84] *WA* 40 I, 228, 28–229, 30: "Fides ergo est cognitio quaedam vel tenebra quae nihil videt, Et tamen in istis tenebris Christus fide apprehensus sedet, Quemadmodum Deus in Sinai et in Templo sedebat in medio tenebrarum. Est ergo formalis nostra iustitia non charitas informans fidem, sed ipsa fides et nebula cordis, hoc est, fiducia in rem quam non videmus, hoc est, in Christum qui, ut maxime non videatur, tamen praesens est. Iustificat ergo fides, quia apprehendit et possidet istum thesaurum, scilicet Christum praesentem. Sed quo modo praesens sit, non est cogitabile, quia sunt tenebra, ut dixi. Ubi ergo vera fiducia cordis est, ibi adest Christus in ipsa nebula et fide".

[85] On the importance of Christ's real presence for the certainty of salvation, see, e.g., *WA* 33, 234, 19–235, 7 (*Sermons on John* 1531).

[86] *WA* 40 I, 197, 25–198, 14.

faculties of soul a new essence. A believer lives no longer as himself but Christ lives in him. Now it is Christ who looks through the believer's eyes.[87] All the works of the believer are now perfect in God's sight, not *simpliciter*, but because the believer is diffused (*diffusa*) by faith.[88] Thus the believer cannot refer to his works before God, because they are not his works but Christ's.[89]

Fourth, since Christ is the *forma* of faith, He alone is decisive. When we look at objects, we make judgments about them according to their form. When we see a house, we recognize it as one because it has the form of a house. Similarly, when God looks at the believer, He sees Christ as the form of the believer. The *materia* (renewal, good works, or love) of the believer does not avail *coram Deo*. This is Luther's explanation in his *Commentary on Galatians* on the passages in the Bible where it seems that deeds are meritorious (e.g., Gen. 4:3–).[90] This way of speaking is, according to Luther, possible because faith truly makes a person's deeds righteous. The special example of this is Abraham, who is diffused by faith so that the deeds are no longer done by the sinner, but the righteous person. Faith is like divine nature in the person of Christ: the whole is made truly holy because of the participation in divinity (*genus apotelesmaticum*). Faith and deeds together form a composition (*compositio*). It is thus possible to say that deeds are salvific, although they are salvific only because of the faith that makes them so.[91]

---

[87] See especially the *Commentary on Gal.* 2:20. *WA* 40 I, 282–288.

[88] *WA* 40 I, 417, 1–8; 417, 12–418, 11.

[89] *WA* 40 II, 170–173. Here also is a link with the Theology of the Cross. The believer boasts, according to Luther, because of being stupid, weak and a sinner. God's power is efficient in these opposites according to 2. Cor. 12:9.

[90] *WA* 40 I, 412–419.

[91] *WA* 40 I, 417, 1–8; 417, 12–418, 11: "Permittamus igitur Spiritui sancto, ut loquatur in Scripturis vel de fide abstracta, nuda, simplici, vel de concreta, composita, incarnata; Omnia sunt fidei quae operibus tribuuntur. Non enim moraliter, sed Theologice et fideliter sunt opera inspicienda. Sit ergo in Theologia fides perpetuo divinitas operum et sic perfusa per opera, ut divinitas per humanitatem in Christo. Qui in ferro ignito attingit ignem, ferrum attingit. Ita qui tetigit cutem Christi, vere Deum tetigit. Est ergo fides Fac totum (ut ita loquar) in operibus; Ut Abraham dicitur fidelis, quia fides diffusa est in totum Abraham, ut inspiciens eum operantem nihil videam Abrahae carnalis vel operantis, sed tantum credentis. Ista ideo tam diligenter inculco, ut clare tradam fidei doctrinam, deinde ut ad obiecta adversariorum qui commiscent Philosophiam et Theologiam et ex moralibus operibus Theologica faciunt, recte et facile respondere possitis. Theologicum opus est fidele opus. Sic homo Theologicus est fidelis, item ratio recta, voluntas bona est fidelis ratio et voluntas, Ut fides in universum sit divinitas in opere, persona et membris, ut unica causa iustificationis quae postea etiam tribuitur materiae propter formam, hoc est, operi propter fidem. Ut regnum divinitatis traditur Christo homini non propter humanitatem sed divinitatem. Sola enim

Luther considers this teaching a specialty. This is, however, a way to answer the scholastic theologians who claim that only love gives form to faith and perfects it. Luther insists *vice versa* that faith gives form to love; thus, faith makes love perfect.[92] Consequently, deeds justify only because of faith—and because of Christ, who is present in faith.

2.1.3. *Did Luther alter his Views on Justification?*

However, some scholars have tried to show that Luther changed his thinking dramatically long after 1531.[93] Clearly this is not the case. Luther never abandons the union of extrinsic and intrinsic aspects of justification although his concepts gain deeper meanings. Even if Luther had changed his views, the Formula of Concord refers to his *Commentary on Galatians* as an authoritative source for right understanding of justification. However, the question is not trivial. The possible change of course in Luther's way of thinking is of vital importance for Lutheran identity.

Luther's disputations from the late 1530s in particular have raised suspicions that he may have corrected his views. These disputations, however, contain at least two serious problems. First, there are various texts. It is precarious to put too much weight on them because one may ultimately be quoting an editor's interpretation instead of Luther's own view. The textual variants differ in several points and contain comments from other authors. In principle, Luther himself wrote the theses at the beginning of the disputations.

---

divinitas creavit omnia humanitate nihil cooperante; Sicut neque peccatum et mortem humanitas vicit, sed hamus qui latebat sub vermiculo, in quem diabolus impegit, vicit et devoravit diabolum qui erat devoraturus vermiculum. Itaque sola humanitas nihil effecisset, sed divinitas humanitati coniuncta sola fecit et humanitas propter divinitatem. Sic hic sola fides iustificat et facit omnia; Et tamen operibus idem tribuitur propter fidem." See also *WA* 40 I, 418, 7–9; 418, 25–33; 427, 3–5, 11–14, 22–24. See also Manns 1965, 299–300, 311.

[92] In a late disputation, Luther calls faith "*form*", "*entelekheia*" and "*actus primus*" of love. See *WA* 39 I, 318 (*Die Zirkulardisputation de veste nuptiali*). All these terms are synonymous; they mean actualization, which give form to a subject.

[93] Flogaus, "Luther vs. Melanchthon?", p. 37: "Doch nach 1531 ist das Gegenwart-Christi-Motiv und der fröhliche wechsel kein bestimmendes Motiv seiner Rechfertigungslehre mehr." See also Ulrich Asendorf, "Rechtfertigung und Vergottung als Thema in Luthers Theologie und als Brücke zur Orthodoxie," *Ökumenische Rundschau* 41 (1992), p. 186; Green, *How Melanchthon helped Luther*, pp. 61–85, 184–185; Erich Seeberg, *Luthers Theologie in ihren Grundzügen* (Stuttgart 1950), p. 118.

Second, disputations were written in a certain format: first, claims were presented based on pre-determined theses. Next, the claims were answered briefly. Every question concentrated on one clearly demarcated issue. The answers did not contain everything that the respondent had to say about the issue; they were usually very concise and sometimes rather obscure and simplifying. In the following, I will analyze some of Luther's disputations.

In the *Promotion disputation of Hieronymus Weller and Nicholas Medler* (1535) justification is defined only (*tantum*) as forgiveness of sins. Luther answers a question posed by Melanchthon, who is interested in the role of obedience (*obedientia*) in justification. Luther answers briefly that since only forgiveness of sins justifies, the new obedience is not a part of justification.[94]

In the *Promotiondisputation of Palladius and Tilemann* (1537) the formal cause of justification is pardon, imputation and divine acceptation (*miseratio, imputatio et acceptatio divina*). The Christian's renewal and obedience is, however, only death and damnation (*mors et damnatio*).[95] Here Luther opposes the view that renewal (*novitas*) is the formal cause of justification. According to him, the formal cause can only be the acceptation on God's part.

In the *Promotiondisputation of Joachim Mörlin* (1540) Luther argues that justification means relational and not qualitative change. Qualitatively, the Christian will always remain full of sin (*plenus peccato*). Relationally, the Christian is holy (as an angel) since God does not ascribe sins to him or her. Here Luther only repeats what Melanchthon has said before, although it is unclear to what extent Luther actually follows Melanchthon. It is obvious that 'relation' is a term which Luther uses to oppose justification as a qualitative change. In this case, qualitative

[94] *WA* 39 I, 58, 29–32 (*Die Doktorpromotion von Hieronymus Weller und Nikolaus Medler* 1535): "Iustificatio tantum significat remissionem peccatorum. Nihil interest inter obedientiam, quia Paulo remittuntur peccata ante obedientiam. Paulus non est aliter iustus nisi illa remissione peccatorum." Flogaus ("Luther versus Melanchthon?"), among others, does not take the context into account.

[95] *WA* 39 1, 228, 7–10 (*Die Promotionsdisputation von Palladius und Tilemann* 1537): "Causa formalis iustificationis et salutis nostra est miseratio, imputatio et acceptatio divina. Hac remota nostra novitas seu obedientia nova non consistit coram Deo, non placet Deo, imo est mors et damnatio." These notions appear in all available manuscripts. See also *WA* 39 1, 230, 15–20; 234, 19–235, 12.

would mean accidental infusion of new habits. Clearly, justification cannot be based on human qualities but on a new relation to God.[96]

In several disputations Luther distinguishes between the two ways of purification from sin.[97] A good examples can be found in the *Second disputation against Antinomians* (1538).

> Sin ceases in two ways in Christians. First (*primo modo*), it ceases so that it is not reckoned (*imputative*). When I receive forgiveness of sins through faith in Christ, I am freed from sin as if it never existed, and as if we already were in heaven. Through Christ, sin is removed from its office, as Isaiah says: "the yoke of his burden and the rod of his oppressor" (Isaiah 9:3), i.e., from the requirements of the law, which drives all us sinners. Thus, sin will be abolished and truly ceases to exist in us because we have Christ (*qui Christum habemus*), who swallows the sin in his own body and takes away the rod of the oppressor. However, it ceases so that it is not reckoned, not as if that we had merited the grace. Sin then (*deinde*)

---

[96] *WA* 39 II, 141, 1–6 (*Die Promotionsdisputation von Joachim Mörlin* 1540.): "R. [M. L.] ad antecedens: Christianus est dupliciter considerandus, in praedicamento relationis et qualitatis. Si consideratur in relatione, tam sanctus est, quam angelus, id est, imputatione per Christum, quia Deus dicit, se non videre peccatum propter filium suum unigenitum, qui est velamen Mosi, id est, legis. Sed christianus consideratus in qualitate est plenus peccato." The existing manuscripts differ, which makes it hard to determine Luther's original intention. A similar distinction appears in the *Promotiondisputation of Macchabäus Scotus* (1542). Here Luther responds only to the claim that faith is not righteousness since it is knowledge (*notitia*). Christian righteousness is not qualititative or accidental in this sense, since faith is righteousness because God reckons faith as such. See *WA* 39 II, 151, 11–12.

[97] Similar distinctions appear in other disputations as well. See *WA* 39 1, 99, 25–31 (*Die Disputation de Justificatione* 1536): "Primum enim purificat imputative, deinde dat spiritum sanctum, per quem etiam substantialiter purgamur. Fides purgat per remissionem peccatorum, spiritus sanctus purgat per effectum. Haec est mundificatio et purificatio divina, quae de coelo demittitur, sed per fidem et spiritum sanctum. Haec est theologia spiritualis, quam philosophi non intelligunt, cum vocent iustitiam qualitatem. Summa: Gentium corda sunt realiter immunda, sed Deus reputat ea munda." The series of theses dating from the same year, however, identifies apprehending Christ and the donation of the Spirit. See *WA* 39 I, 83, 26–27 (*Die* 3. *Thesenreihe über Römer* 3, 28 1536). The third disputation against the antinomians also uses the order *primo-imputative-secundo-formaliter* but here Luther simply refers to general ways in which the Church is holy. See *WA* 39 1, 493, 24–494, 3 (*Die dritte Disputation gegen die Antinomer* 1538): "Sancta et ecclesia propter partem, quae est in ea, per synecdochen, ut diximus, et nos etiam sumus puri et sancti, sed primo per imputationem, quia non imputatur nobis peccatum. Secundo sumus etiam formaliter iusti, ut quando per istas primitias et Spiritum sanctum mihi datum de coelo per fidem incipio luctare et pugnare cum peccato et blasphemia." On other similar passages, see *WA* 39 1, 434, 1–12; 436–437; 472, 13–15 (*Die zweite Disputation gegen die Antinomer*). *WA* 39 1, 491, 15–492, 5; 492, 20–493, 9; 521, 3–522, 3; 563, 7–564, 7 (*Die dritte Disputation gegen die Antinomer*). *WA* 40 II, 432b, 30–33 (*Vorlesungen über die Psalmen* 2. 1532). In the disputations against the antinomians, Luther attempts to emphasize the presence of Christ as an effective gift. For this reason, the texts contain distinctions between different ways of purification.

> ceases in us in another way, namely formally (*formaliter*). Namely, while some remnants (*reliquae*) of all kinds of sins against both the first and the second table... still cling to us, we ask for deliverance in prayer from God the Father through Jesus Christ... This way sin is won truly, and I actually become pure (*formaliter et expurgative*), since from day to day I increasingly purify myself and mortify the sin, which still clings to my flesh, until all this, which belongs to the old man is defeated and destroyed.[98]

Here Luther uses arguments similar to those in his *Commentary on Galatians* where imputation, faith, and apprehending Christ are merged. Imputation is based on grasping and possessing Christ. It takes place only, "because we have Christ". This apprehension is clearly an effective and renewing (*renovatio*$_1$) act since Luther speaks of the relics (*reliquae*) of sin, which are the object of the follow-up purification (*renovatio*$_2$).[99]

While Luther uses more specified terminology in his disputations than he uses in other texts, there is absolutely no reason to claim that the order of Christ's presence and imputation has changed. Luther still obviously holds on to his previous stand: faith means becoming one with Christ.[100] In the *Promotiondisputation of Hieronymus Weller and Nikolaus*

---

[98] *WA* 39 1, 431, 10–432, 11 (*Die zweite Disputation gegen die Antinomer* 1538): "Porro dupliciter cessat apud christianos. Primo modo imputative. Cum ego propter fidem in Christum accipio remissionem peccatorum, et prorsus liberor a peccato, ac si nullum esset, ac si iam essemus in coelo. Tollitur enim per Christum, ut ait Esaias: Iugum oneris et sceptrum exactoris, seu illa exactio legis, qua omnes rei agimur. Ita peccatum in nobis, qui Christum habemus devorantem in suo corpore peccatum nostrum et sceptrum exactoris auferentem, prorsus tollitur et vere cessat, sed imputative, non quod nos hoc sic meruimus. Deinde etiam secundo modo cessat in nobis peccatum formaliter, quia, cum haereant in nobis adhuc quaedam reliquae omnis generis peccatorum et contra primam et secundam tabulam, ut diffidentiae, vanitatis, timoris et dubitationis erga Deum, desperationis, item irae, concupiscentiae, odii et inimicitiae etc., pro istis interpellamus apud Deum patrem per Christum Iesum dicentes sive orantes: Remitte nobis, o pater, in coelis debita nostra, et remittit ille peccata petentibus iuxta hoc Ioan.: Si confiteamur invicem peccata nostra, fidelis est Deus et iustus, ut remittat nobis peccata nostra. Atque hoc modo formaliter et expurgative tollitur peccatum, quia hic de die in diem magis ac magis expurgo et mortifico peccatum adhuc haerens in carne mea, donec hoc tandem totum, quod est veteris hominis, tollatur et consumatur et evadat purus et clarificatus homo absque omni macula ac labe."

[99] The same idea is stated in Luther's response to Latomus in 1521. E.g., *StA* 2, 493, 33–34: "Remissa sunt omnia per gratiam, sed nondum omnia sanata per donum. Donum etiam infusum est. Fermentum mixtum est." The gift appears as a prerequisite for favor since the Christian in *StA* 2, 494, 11–12: "non placet nec habet gratiam, nisi ob donum hoc modo peccatum expurgare laborans."

[100] See also Seils, *Glaube*, 53: "Man kann also nach dem, was in den Disputationen vorgetragen wird, nicht ohne weiteres von dem Gedanken an die Einheit von Gott und Mensch in Christus und den dabei rechtfertigenden "fröhlichen Wechsel" von Sünde und Gerechtigkeit übergehen." See also Ebeling, *Disputatio de homine*, 175.

Medler (1535) Luther sets the scholastic faith (*fides acquisita seu Historica*) and the receiving faith (*fides apprehensiva*) which makes Christ effective in us (*in nobis efficacem*) against each other.[101] After justification the person is able to do good works, i.e., be like a good tree. If not, this means that Christ does not dwell in the person's heart, and he or she has only *fides acquisita*, since Christian faith exists only where Christ renews the heart through his indwelling. Christ's inhabitation in the heart of the believer is not only related to sanctification and good works but also to justifying faith itself.[102]

It is obvious that *renovatio$_1$* is also a part of justification in Luther's disputations. Through faith in Christ a person becomes a good tree. After justification a person does good because he or she *is* good and righteous, not in order to *become* good and righteous.[103] The good that

---

[101] *WA* 39 I, 45, 16–17 (*Die Thesen für die Promotionsdisputation von Weller und Medler* 1535): "Oportet igitur de alia fide quadam eum loqui, quae faciat Christum in nobis efficacem contra mortem, peccatum et legem." This faith is *vere infusa* since it is not available through human powers. The Spirit donates (*donat et servat*) this faith to the hearts of believers through the Word of the Gospel. *WA* 39 I, 27–30.

[102] In the *Second Disputation against the Antinomians*, the imputation takes place "...qui Christum habemus devorantem in suo corpore peccatum nostrum..." *WA* 39 1, 431, 10–432,11. (*Die zweite Disputation gegen die Antinomer* 1538). *WA* 39 I, 46, 20–30: "Quod si opera non sequuntur, certum est, fidem hanc Christi in corde nostro non habitare, Sed mortuam illam, scilicet acquisitam fidem." Luther quotes the Song of Songs (2:16) in the same disputation. True faith receives Christ with open arms and says "My beloved is mine and I am his". *WA* 39 I, 46, 3–4: "Dilectus meus mihi et ego illi". The bride and groom terminology appears a couple of times in the disputations. See *WA* 39 I, 498, 17; 575, 8; 580, 1 (Die dritte Disputation gegen die Antinomer). According to *Seils* (1996, 45, 53), Luther's earlier use of bridal mysticism is replaced in the late disputations by more technical terminology such as "*misericordia*" and "*reputatio*". See, e.g., *WA* 39 I, 97, 21; 109, 27 (*Disputatio de iustificatione*); 222, 14–19 (*Die Promotionsdisputation von Palladius und Tilemann* 1537); 304, 2–7 (*Die Zirkulärdisputation de veste nuptiali*); 482, 15; 504, 25; 506, 6; 521, 12; 527, 8 (*Die dritte Disputation gegen die Antinomer*).

[103] Luther juxtaposes his own view with Aristotle's (*Nicomachean ethics* II, 1103a) according to which the person becomes virtuous by practicing virtues. See *WA* 39 1, 69, 16–29. (*Die Disputation über Daniel* 4, 24 1535): "Persona est prior opere. Aristoteles id fatetur, quod ante actum secundum necessario praesupponatur actus primus, sicut in grammatica opus est primo nominativo, post desideratur appositum cum adverbiis. Qui non habeat primum actum, id est, vitam, huic non praecipio, ut agat. Quale nam opus, ubi non est persona operans? In omni propositione oportet existere rem praesentem. Verbum non praedicatur, nisi de nomine, nec est segregatum a nomine. Os et oculus Dei videndus in scriptura, sicut loquitur ista intelligi debet. Loquitur secundum cor, non tractat res prophanas et obscuras vel mirabiles. Rex ille, de quo supra dictum est, faciens bona multa non placet Deo, quia persona mala est. Et ideo sunt ipsa opera plane impia, abiecta et adversa. At non est in usu, inquiunt, dato praecepto exigi et intelligi fidem. Bene, oportet novam discere grammaticam, novas linguas, sicuti Apostoli loquebantur novis linguis." *WA* 39 I, 282, 11–14 (*Die Zirkulärdisputation de veste nuptiali*): "Nam hic iustus non fit iuste agendo, sed iustus factus iuste et bene operatur et est

is performed after justification is not meritorious because its source is Christ who is present in the believer.[104] Renewal in any sense is not a human deed because it is rooted in Christ: a process of change from the state of sin towards the likeness of Christ.[105]

The idea of union with Christ appears in other texts of Luther from the same period, in addition to disputations. For example, in the Schmalcald Articles (1537) Luther denies that he has changed his mind concerning justification.

> I cannot change at all what I have consistently taught about this until now, namely, that "through faith" (as St. Peter says) we receive a different, new, clean heart and that, for the sake of Christ our mediator, God will and does regard us as completely righteous and holy. Although sin in the flesh is still not completely gone or dead, God will nevertheless not count it or consider it.
>
> Good works follow such faith, renewal, and forgiveness of sin, and whatever in these works is still sinful or imperfect should not even be counted as sin or imperfection, precisely for the sake of Christ.... Furthermore, we also say that if good works do not follow, then faith is false and not true.[106]

---

et manet persona iusta, sancta et pia per solam fidem in Christum, antequam iuste, pie et bene operatur per misericordiam Dei." Luther uses the formulation "Fides facit personam" in the same context (*WA* 39 I, 282, 16). The relation between the apprehension of Christ and renewal is apparent in the late disputations as well. See also *WA* 39 II, 236, 12–23. (*Die Promotionsdisputation von Hieronymus Nopp und Friedrich Bachofen* 1543.): "13. Post vero iustificatam personam efficax est per charitatem erga alios, id est, Deum et proximum." See also *WA* 39 2, 243. 16–21, where Luther claims that in order for faith to be living and true, it must apprehend Christ.

[104] *WA* 39 I, 46, 18–19 (*Thesen de fide* 1535): "Iustificati autem sic gratis, tum faciamus opera, imo Christus ipse in nobis facit omnia."

[105] *WA* 39 I, 204, 12–13 (*Die Promotionsdisputation von Palladius und Tilemann* 1537): "Formatur enim Christus in nobis continue, et nos formamur ad imaginem ipsius, dum hic vivimus."

[106] *BSELK SA* XIII: "Quod de justificatione hactenus semper et assidue docui, mutare nec minimo possum, videlicet nosper fidem (ut Petrus loquitur) aliud novum et mundum cor acquirere et Deum propter Christum, mediatorem nostrum, nos justos et sanctos reputare. Et etsi peccatum in carne nondum plane ablatum et mortuum est, tamen Deus illud nobis non vult imputare nec meminisse. Hanc fidem, renovationem et remissionem peccatorum sequuntur bona opera. Et quod in illis pollutum et imperfectum est, pro peccato et defectu non censetur idque etiam propter Christum atque ita totus homo, cum quoad opera sua iustos homo, cum quoad personam suam, tum quoad opera sua justus et sanctus est et nominatur ex mera gratia et misericordia in Christo super nos effusa, expansa et amplificata. Quare gloriari ob merita et opera non possumus, cum absque gratia et misericordia adspiciuntur, sed, ut scriptum est 1. Cor. 1.: "Qui gloriatur, in Domino glorietur", quod scilicet habeat Deum propitium. Sic enim omnia bene se habent. Dicimus praeterea, ubi non sequuntur bona opera, ibi fidem esse falsam et non veram."

In the Schmalcald Articles justification also involves an effective and intrinsic aspect. One receives "a new, clean heart". In order for faith to be real, it has to be actualized in good works. At that, Luther describes the order of salvific events in a manner that unites faith, renewal, and forgiveness, but separates love from these. Since these three are one, renewal is not a consequence of imputation. However, renewal here clearly means not the capability to do works that are good in God's sight, i.e., good works.[107]

On this point Luther is very concise. He does not mention the actual presence of divinity in faith, which he does so often elsewhere. He uses similar language in a sermon dating from the same period, stressing that Christ is God's Gift (*geschenk und Gabe*) who is received through faith. This faith causes the renewal of the heart. Renewal is thus not a good work or merit, but participation in Christ's righteousness.[108]

In the sermons on John (1538) Luther reiterates the same thing as he did in 1535: Christ has merited righteousness for sinners outside of them (*ausser*) but it becomes their own through the gift.

> This is the wonderful righteousness that we are called righteous or such that we have righteousness. This is no deed or thought or anything in us, rather it is wholly outside of us in Christ, and it is truly ours through

[107] A typical misreading of the Schmalkald Articles is found in *Greschat* (*Melancththon neben Luther*, pp. 206–207), who claims that justification and renewal are one entity but that there is a logical difference between them. This is obviously an interpretation that does not arise from the text, according to which the logical difference is mentioned only between justification-renewal and good works.

[108] *WA* 47, 97, 22–37 (*Reihenpredigten über Johannes* 3–4 1538): "Wird also diess geschenck und Gabe, nemlich, der Sohn des vaters, mit keiner Hand, finger oder fusse ergriffen, auch nicht in einem kloster oder Munchskleide gefunden noch sonst irgends in ein gefesse auffgefangen, sondern allein mit dem hertzen und glauben ergrieffen. Und wen diese gabe in dein hertz kompt, das du von hertzen an Christum gleubest, so bleibestu kein alter mensch, als ein Dieb, Ehebrecher oder morder, sondern wirst ein neuer mensch, dan du hast das liecht in deinem hertzen. Derhalben so wil unser herrgott erstlich grundlich das hertz haben, das mus allein gleuben. Unser herrgott nimpt das aller beste, als den inwendigsten menschen, nicht den mund oder die hand, sondern das hertz, das du von inwendig from sejest. Do gehets den wohl zu, das, wen du gleubest an Christum, so wird das hertz rein, wie S. Petrus [Apg. 15, 9] Actorum am 15. capittel saget: Durch den glauben werden die hertzen gereiniget, und derselbige glaube lest dich dan nicht hoffertig noch stoltz sein. Den wen das hertz gereiniget ist, so sind die hende, augen, fusse und alle andere glieder auch rein, thun andere werck den zuvorn. Der glaub lest dich dan nicht einen Sunder, Hurer oder Ehebrecher sein, sonder, wie das hertz ist, also folget auch hernach das gantze leben."

His favor and gift. And it is ours just as if we ourselves had achieved and acquired it.[109]

Naturally, Christ has acquired the merit outside of the sinner and without any cooperation. Yet, in justification the merit does not stay outside the person; merit is actualized both in the favor and the gift, and thus the merit becomes an attribute of the sinner, a new internal reality.[110]

The idea of salutary exchange appears in several sermons from the end of the 1530s onwards.[111] In Sermons on John (1538) Luther explains how the Christian congregation is one body (*ein Leib*) with Christ. Now, Christ as the Groom donates all His goods (*aller seiner gueter*) i.e., righteousness, holiness, and salvation to the bride, i.e., the congregation.[112] In a sermon from 1539 Luther teaches how a Christian has become a

---

[109] *WA* 46, 44, 34–38 (*Reihenpredigten über Johannes* 1–2 1538): "Das ist jhe eine Wunderliche Gerechtigkeit, das wir sollen gerecht heissen oder Gerechtigkeit haben, welche doch kein werck, kein gedancken und kurtz gar nichts in uns, sondern gar ausser uns in Christo ist und doch warhafftig Unser wird durch sein gnade und geschenck, Und so gar unser eigen, als were sie durch uns selbs erlangt und erworben." Mörlin uses the same passage to oppose Osiander. See Mörlin, *Historia*, Eiiii.

[110] The same idea appears in *Tabletalks*. The passage does not include a precise date, but the annotation began in 1530. *WA TR* 6 71, 17–22: "Christliche Gerechtigkeit ist nicht eine solche Gerechtigkeit, die in uns ist und klebet, wie sonst eine Qualitas und Tugend, das ist, das man bei uns findet oder das wir fühlen; sondern ist eine fremde Gerechtigkeit gar außer uns, nehmlich Christus selber ist unsere formalis Iustitia, vollkommene Gerechtigkeit und das [1. Kor. 1, 30] ganze Wesen."

[111] On the other hand, later Luther preached sermons in which he sets the favor before the *donum*. E.g., Flogaus ("Luther vs. Melancththon?", p. 38) has referred to the following sources: *WA* 40 II, 353, 2–11; 357, 15–358, 1; 357, 35–358, 20; 420, 10; 421, 21–422, 18; 421, 5–422, 5. (*Vorlesung über Ps* 51); *WA* 45, 149, 33–145, 3. (*Predigt vom* 30.9.1537); *WA* 21, 458, 23–37. (*Crucigers Sommerpostille* 1544). In these passages, however, since *donum* is identified with the renewal of the Holy Spirit and good works, it is not synonymous with the christological *donum* used elsewhere. Moreover, these passages define favor as efficient reality and as the actualization of God's presence. In this case, donum is preceded by God's presence. Luther uses the notion "*donum*" in at least two different senses. First, it can appear as a pair *gratia-donum*, when it means actualization of God's grace (*gratia*) in the believer. Accordingly, *donum* may refer either to Christ or faith. Second, *donum* may refer to the gift of the Spirit, which is identified with actual consequences of justification, such as good works. According to Kärkkäinen (*Luthers trinitarische Theologie*, pp. 107–108), Luther can speak about the donation of the Spirit such that the Spirit is given continuously. Thus, giving of the Spirit does not necessarily mean that the spirit is not already present.

[112] *WA* 46, 712, 30–39 (*Reihenpredigten über Johannes* 1–2 1538): "Und haben gehoert, das dis die meinung sey, das die rechtschaffene Christliche Kirche sey mit Christo ein leib im Glauben und das sie Christi Braut sey, und er jr Breutigam und Heubt, sie aber sein eigenthum, und wil der Breutigam, das die Braut aller seiner gueter, als der ewigen Gerechtigkeit, Heiligkeit und Seligkeit durch den Glauben an jn teilhaftig sey, derhalben so hat er sie auch mit Himlischer weisheit und stercke gezieret und geschmuecket, das sie fuer Gott herrlich und gros sey. Wo nu die Christliche Kirche ist und

sharer (*teilhafftig*) of the Spirit through Christ, who redeems the believer from the Law and judgment.[113]

In a crucial point of history Luther and Bugenhagen wrote a letter to Elector Johann Friedrich (1541) as a response to the Regensburg Diet. In their letter they opposed the doctrine of *Liber Ratisbonensis* by appealing to the ambiguities contained in the article of justification. Then they presented the true evangelical doctrine of justification.

> For God avails nothing else than His beloved Son who is wholly pure and holy in His eyes. Where the Son is, the Father sees Him and in Him He is pleased. Now the Son is apprehended not through works, but through faith only, without deeds and placed in the heart. Thus says God: The heart is holy because of my Son, who dwells there through faith.[114]

In his *Explanation of Isaiah* 53 (1544) Luther refers to Christ's ascension to the right hand of the Father. Christ does not remain idle but pours out the gift of the Spirit (*effudit donum Spiritus sancti*). Through this gift Christ's suffering is made efficient on earth, setting people free from sin. This liberation takes place through both the favor and the gift. God's favor cleanses a person imputatively and forgives sins. God's gift transfers the person from the power of sin to righteousness and prepares him or her to walk according to God's will. Both the favor

das Goettliche Wort rein geprediget und die Sacrament gehandelt werden mit trewem vleis aus dem Wort Gottes, es auch gehoeret und mit gleubigem hertzen."

[113] *WA* 47, 196, 27–38 (*Predigten* 1539): "...aber wer an Christum gleubet, der wird teilhafftig dieser unmesslichen freiheit, do der Geist spricht: Du bist nicht allein vom Gesetze Mosi frej, sondern auch von aller seiner anklage und verdammung. Derhalben so haben wir nun einen prediger, der alles hat, den andern hat ehrs mitt massen gegeben. Wir, so da gleuben, kriegen aus demselbigen unmessigem geiste auch, genissen seines auch als des Heubtguttes durch den glauben. Darnach machet ehr Christum ihme gleich, und so gross als ehr ist, als Joan: 14. Cap. auch gesaget wirdt. Aber wir sind von ihme und nicht von uns selbst, wir sind frej nach dem gewissen von allen Gesetzen und schrecken, aber in ihme. So nun in Christo der Geist volkomlich ist, so haben wir durch ihnen den Geist auch. Wir haben einen solchen prediger, da wir aus der unausprechlichen fulle zu schoepffen haben. Da trincken wir aus und werden sath an ihme, an leib und seel."

[114] *WA BR* 9, 408, 56–61: "Gott gilt nichts, denn blos vnd allein sein lieber son Jhesus Christus, der ist gantz rein vnd heilig fur yhm. Wo der ist, da sihet er hin vnd hat seinen wolgefallen an yhm Luce 3.13 Nu wird der son nicht durch werck, sondern allein durch den glauben, on alle werck ergriffen vnd ym hertzen gefasset. Da spricht denn Gott: Das hertz ist heilig vmb meines sons willen, der drinnen wonet durch den glauben."

and the gift are connected so that their efficiency is tied with the giving of the Holy Spirit.[115]

In the *Lectures on Genesis* (1535–1545) as well, the inhabitation of Christ is prior to the application of His merit. Luther opposes the view that grace is given a greater significance than the gift. Justification consists of both the grace and the gift,[116] but this does not mean that real change in a believer is the ground for justification; instead, Christ himself is the *iustitia formalis* of the person justified. Christ is not only *causa efficiens*

---

[115] *WA* 40 III, 726, 17–727, 20 (*Vorlesungen über Jesaja* 9 *und* 53 1543/44): "Ad quid ergo, quae causa finalis proprie huius regni? 'propter transgressionem populi mei, quae erat plaga ipsorum'. Sedet in regno suo non ociosus, nec propter se, sed ad dextram Dei exaltatus [Joh. 16, 7] iudicans mundum et 'effudit donum Spiritus sancti'. 'Si abiero', inquit, 'mittam, si non abiero, non veniet ad vos'. Ergo raptus et excisus est e terra, ut exerceret vim et efficaciam istius suae passionis, ut, scilicet, liberaret nos, non tantum secundum gratiam, sed et secundum donum [Eph. 4, 8] ad renovationem naturae, ut dicitur: 'ascendisti in altum et accepisti dona pro hominibus'. Ideo sedet ad dextram Dei, aeterni patris, misso Spiritu sancto, non tantum, ut sanet nos imputatione, donata remissione peccatorum propter ipsius mortem, sed ut etiam efficax sit in nobis et transferat nos a peccato in iusticiam, sanet corpus et animam, non tantum remisso peccato, sed prorsus expurgato et sublato, ut puri sine omnium peccatorum pavore, motu et ardore Deo serviamus in omni pietate et sanctitate vitae; positus est in aliam vitam, ut nos sanaret a peccatis et transgressione illa, quae erat 'plaga nostra'.... meruit Filius Dei, Dominus ac redemptor noster Iesus Christus, non solum remissionem peccatorum sua passione et reconciliationem, [Joh. 1, 17] Sed etiam 'donum', quia per Christum non tantum 'data gratia', sed 'et veritas facta', Ioan. 1. Non fucus est in Christo, ut tantum sit impetrata gratia; Imo peccatum etiam expurgatur." See also Lienhard, *Martin Luthers christologisches Zeugnis*, pp. 265, 271–2.

[116] *WA* 44, 374, 5–19: "CHESED, hoc est, beneficium, donum, gratia, misericordia. Non est [1. Tim. 6, 2] Chanan, sed Chesid, unde Chasid. Paulus exponit beneficium. 1. Timothei 6. qui beneficii participes sunt. Non solum favorem aut gratiam significat, sed etiam donum spiritus sancti, Gratia enim sola non sentitur, sed oportet accedere donum. Dedit ei Christus spiritum sanctum in carcere, spiritum veritatis, qui eum sustentavit in morte, turpitudine et confusione, et inspiravit ipsi hunc sensum: Noli timere, confortetur cor tuum, sustine Dominum. Haec est totalis et maxima consolatio, quod Deus respicit et inclinat ad ipsum donum suum, hoc est, inspirat spiritum fortitudinis, consilii, Macht ein festen, starcken, lebendigen heyligen auß jm, Vivificat enim in media morte, mortificat in ipsa damnatione, ut cor eius possit statuere: Utut saeviat in me herus, tamen non moriar, virtus et fama mea non peribit. Haec loquitur Chesed sive spiritus in cor eius, ut non habeat cogitationes inferni aut mortis, sed vitae et tranquillitatis." Imputation is here understood as *making* righteous. *WA* 42, 569, 6–11. "Paulus a semine carnali ad credentes ex gentibus promissionem transfert: quia enim tota res in eo consistit, quod Abraham Deo credidit, et reputatum est ei ad iusticiam, hoc est, quod credendo factus est iustus et haeres aeterni regni, universalem hanc inde extruit, quod omnis, qui promissioni credit sicut Abraham, sit haeres aeterni regni et iustus, sive sit carnale Abrahae semen, sive non." See also Juhani Forsberg, *Das Abrahambild in der Theologie Luthers. Pater Fidei Sanctissimus*, Veröffentlichungen des Instituts für Europäische Geschichte Mainz 117, (Stuttgart. Franz Steiner Verlag Wiesbaden GmbH 1984), pp. 68–73.

of justification, but also *causa formalis*.[117] Justification is explicitly related to the inhabitation of Christ.[118]

It is thus problematic to argue that Luther changes his view of justification.[119] Christ's real presence in the person joins together both justification and renewal. Luther always understood justification as an act that actually changes the object. This is obvious in both his early and later texts. Below are three quotations from Luther which illustrate his teaching from different periods. The excerpts are from *Antilatomus* (1521), *Commentary on Galatians* (1535) and the letter to Johann Friedrich (1541).

> ...but the person is not acceptable, and he does not own the favor otherwise than because of the gift, which effects the purification from sin.[120]

---

[117] *WA* 43, 249, 25–29, 36–39: "Neque solum est causa efficiens, sed et formalis, hoc est, benedictio ipsa. Ex ipso enim et in ipso sumus benedicti, Christi et uncti, et de hoc singuli possumus gloriari. Christus est mea formalis benedictio, unctio, vita, salus, quia ei adhaereo per fidem, et ab hoc benedicente denominor Benedictus, meque ipsum benedictum nuncupo...Neque enim in meis meritis aut operibus haeret promissio: Sed in semine Abrahae, ab illo benedicor, cum id fide apprehendo, et vicissim mihi adhaerescit benedictio, et diffunditur per totum corpus et animam, ut et ipsum corpus vivificetur et salvetur per idem semen."

[118] *WA* 43, 256, 19–20: "Econtra vera iustificatio est quanto certus sum per fidem, semen benedictum habitare in me, per quod me benedico." See also *WA* 40 III, 726, 17–727, 20 (*Vorlesungen über Jesaja* 9 *und* 53 1543/44.) "Ad quid ergo, quae causa finalis proprie huius regni? 'propter transgressionem populi mei, quae erat plaga ipsorum'. Sedet in regno suo non ociosus, nec propter se, sed ad dextram Dei exaltatus [Joh. 16, 7] iudicans mundum et 'effudit donum Spiritus sancti'. 'Si abiero', inquit, 'mittam, si non abiero, non veniet ad vos'. Ergo raptus et excisus est e terra, ut exerceret vim et efficaciam istius suae passionis, ut, scilicet, liberaret nos, non tantum secundum gratiam, sed et secundum donum [Eph. 4, 8] ad renovationem naturae, ut dicitur: 'ascendisti in altum et accepisti dona pro hominibus'. Ideo sedet ad dextram Dei, aeterni patris, misso Spiritu sancto, non tantum, ut sanet nos imputatione, donata remissione peccatorum propter ipsius mortem, sed ut etiam efficax sit in nobis et transferat nos a peccato in iusticiam, sanet corpus et animam, non tantum remisso peccato, sed prorsus expurgato et sublato, ut puri sine omnium peccatorum pavore, motu et ardore Deo serviamus in omni pietate et sanctitate vitae; positus est in aliam vitam, ut nos sanaret a peccatis et transgressione illa, quae erat 'plaga nostra'...meruit Filius Dei, Dominus ac redemptor noster Iesus Christus, non solum remissionem peccatorum sua passione et reconciliationem, [Joh. 1, 17] Sed etiam 'donum', quia per Christum non tantum 'data gratia', sed 'et veritas facta', Ioan. 1. Non fucus est in Christo, ut tantum sit impetrata gratia; Imo peccatum etiam expurgatur."

[119] The claim that Luther gives up the participatory language later in his life is not justified. Flogaus ("Luther vs. Melancththon?"), however, is correct when he points out that imputation has precedence over the effects of renewal. See also Seils, *Glaube*, p. 89. It is not possible to analyze Luther's later texts further within this study. A more profound answer would require a study of its own.

[120] *StA* 2, 494, 11–12.

> Faith is really righteousness, but it is not enough. Also, in faith there still are remnants of sin in our flesh.... Hence it is necessary that righteousness also has an other aspect, which makes it perfect; namely, that God reckons faith as righteousness.[121]

> It is a different thing to become and to do (*fieri & agere*), to be and to make (*esse & facere*)... Undoubtedly, the one who has become righteous cannot be without good works as a tree cannot be without fruit. For God avails nothing else than His beloved Son who is wholly pure and holy in His eyes. Where the Son is, the Father sees Him and in Him He is pleased. Now the Son is apprehended not through works, but through faith only, without deeds and placed in the heart. Thus says God: The heart is holy because of my Son, who dwells there through faith.[122]

For the later Luther justification was also an effective and unitive act, but he still consistently emphasized the imputation of Christ's righteousness. As stated, this imputation is always based on Christ's presence in faith. Thus, the intrinsic aspect, *donum*, is always an essential part of Luther's understanding of justification.

However, it remains problematic that Luther never articulated the nature of *renovatio*$_1$ with precision.[123] The notion is always present but often in unarticulated, though necessary, form. This complicated the reception of Luther's thinking in the next generation, when the central problem in justification was the relation between justification and renewal.[124] The relation of *donum* and *renovatio*$_1$ was particularly problematic for students of Luther, even for Melanchthon. In the following, I shall examine the theologies of two prominent first-generation Reformers, whose thinking concurred with Luther on the most important points.

---

[121] *WA* 40 I, 364.

[122] *WA BR* 9, 407, 41, 46–408, 56–61.

[123] On the other hand, the reason may also be unwillingness. Luther may have thought that a thorough explanation based on some rationalistic model would have harmed the mystery of salvation. For example, the metaphor of the ring and jewel pictures something that mere reason is unable to reach while giving a sufficient account of the matter.

[124] I have already referred to the idea of annihilation, according to which the Christian is always nothing in relation to God. By employing this notion, Luther maintains the consistency of his system of thought. The mystical type of speech is hard to follow, however. How can one speak about new affects but at the same say that they are "nothing"? After Luther, the theme of annihilation in the context of justification appears rarely, if ever.

2.2. *Johannes Bugenhagen*

A central figure in the first generation of reformers was Johannes Bugenhagen (1485–1558).[125] Bugenhagen's theology is in accordance with Luther in the main points. His best-known theological work, *Von dem Christlichen Glauben und rechten guten wercken* (1526),[126] follows Luther's tract *On the Freedom of a Christian*[127] in both content and method of presentation.

Bugenhagen based his doctrine of justification firmly on christology and incarnation. Through the incarnation Christ takes the place of the sinner and frees her from the power of the devil. Likewise Bugenhagen stressed the meaning of Christ's sufferings: Christ has died and risen from the dead for the sins of the world.[128] The effects of Christ's work

---

[125] Bugenhagen was best known as the author of the church orders. However, his theology had a great influence on succeeding Lutheran generations. See Ralf Kötter, *Johannes Bugenhagens Rechtfertigungslehre und der Römische Katholizismus. Studien zum Sendbrief an die Hamburger* (Göttingen: Vandenhoeck & Ruprecht 1994), p. 11.

[126] Kötter, *Johannes Bugenhagens Rechtfertigungslehre*, p. 12. On justification in the early works, see Kötter, *op. cit.*, 17–69. Compare Hans Holfelder, *Tentatio et consolatio. Studien zu Bugenhagens "Interpretatio in librorum Psalmorum"*, Arbeiten zur Kirchengeschichte 45 (Berlin/New York 1974). According to Kötter (*op. cit.*, pp. 48–50, 52–53, 67), unio cum Christo is a central feature in the commentary on Psalms (1524) as well. E.g., "...Sumus ergo cum Christo unum, quia sponsa sumus, ergo et reges et sacerdotes...Hae filiae regum, et hae virgines, quae pertinent ad sponsam ad Christum, trahuntur bono odore, qui undiquaque effluit à vestimentis eius, quod est verbum gratiae, et plenitudo, ex qua omnes accepimus..." Cited in Kötter, *op. cit.*, p. 53.

[127] Kötter (*Johannes Bugenhagens Rechtfertigungslehre*, pp. 262–301) has compared both books. Bugenhagen copies the distinction between faith and love from Luther. See also Holfelder 1981, 42–55. Kötter (*op. cit.*, p. 287) claims that Bugenhagen's theology of the word is not as christologically structured as it is for Luther. The preached word primarily has a cognitive meaning and its effects are explained pneumatologically. See also Holfelder, *Solus Christus. Die Ausbildung von Bugenhagens Rechtfertigungslehre in der Paulusauslegung* (1524/25) *und ihre Bedeutung für die theologische Argumentation im Sendbrief "Von dem Christlichen Glauben"* (1526). *Eine Untersuchung zur Genese von Bugenhagens Theologie* (Tübingen: J. C. B. Mohr Siebeck 1981), p. 75. On the other hand, Bugenhagen may only be trying to build a coherent Trinitarian system, in which every person of the Trinity works according to their nature. See, e.g., *Confessio fidei*, Ciiv–Ciii, where Bugenhagen explains the third article of the Creed to mean that the Spirit is the creator of communication (*gemeynschafft*). Although Bugenhagen uses cognitive notions, he does not employ a similar theory to Melanchthon, according to whom Christ is not the object of ontological participation. On Melanchthon, see chapter 3.

[128] Bugenhagen, *Von dem Christlichen Glauben*, Aiiii[v]–Biii, Bvii[v], Diii. See also Bugenhagen, *Confessio fidei*, Ci[v]–v: "De salvatore nostro Iesu Christo. Docemus omnis misericordiae patrem, optime ac multo melius quam plenum nos, miserabilem adeo ac calamitatis plenum nostrum interitum peruidisse, quodque liberari ex illo, proprii neque cõsilii esset, neque opis. Misisse itaque ac dono eum dedisse praeter omnia merita nostra (imo contrarium nos merueramus) unigenitum filium suum, humana carne indutum.

are pictured using terminology that was very dear to him,—words such as 'father' and 'child'—borrowed from Romans 8:14–17.[129] God the Father sent Christ the Son into the world in order to make the sons of the devil into sons of God. God is no longer to be conceived as a strict judge (*strenger richter*) but as a friendly father (*freundtlicher vater*). This new relationship is made possible through faith, which unites the believer to Christ.[130]

Faith is a new free and effective reality that cleanses the heart.[131] It is a new way of being that gives the sinner an internal certainty, which gives her the courage to stand in the front of God without fear.[132] The *unio cum Christo* theme serves the purposes of pastoral counseling and certainty of salvation. It is not limited to sanctification, or simply a consequence

---

Hunc pro nobis mortuum resurrexisse, nosque a peccatis nostris, quibus operti eramus, suo sanguine, si id fide apprehendamus, id est, si in hoc ex animo unice confidamus ac speremus coram Deo, lauisse ac mundauisse, spiritumque sanctum hoc suo merito nobis demeritu esse, per quem in Christum ex Evangelii predicatione credamus, per quem filij ac haeredes Dei simus, per quem detur propter Christum flagitare quicquid libitum fuerit a dilecto nostro patre per orationem, & nihil eum relinquere non ex auditum. Esse itaque hoc pacto Deum, si quando in Christum spem nostram collocamus, dilectum nobis patrem, qui nos foveat, ac nostri curam agat, cum aliorum hominum feuerus sit iudex. Docemus eum qui gloriatur de suis operibus, sanctitate, cruce, non vere adhuc didicisse quid sit in Domino gloriari, coram Dei in unum Christum spem omnem reponere, id quod vera demum est, germana & Christo digna fides, quae iustos ex iniustis, filios Dei ex filijs Satanae facit. Haec concio peculiaris Eungeliij concio est de domino nostro Iesu Christo, quae aeternam tribuit vitam omni credenti. Ac praeter unicam hanc nulla est in terris salus, ut Petri, Acto.4. inquit." This is the locus of justification in its entirety as it appears in *Confessio fidei et doctrinae*.

[129] Kötter, *Johannes Bugenhagens Rechtfertigungslehre*, pp. 191–192.

[130] Bugenhagen, *Von dem Christlichen Glauben*, Bii^{v}–Biii: "Also weñ wir in Christum glauben / so ist Christus unser aygen / mit aller seyner gerechtigkeit / mit himel und erde / uñ allem das darinen ist. Da Gott der Vater ist durch den selbigen Christum unser aigen / dyeweil er umb seynes suns willen / den wir haben durch den glauben angenommen / ist nit mer wyder uns ein strenger richter / sondern ein freundtlicher vater / des wir kinder durch glawben an Jhesum Christum geworden sind / Alls geschriben steet Johannis. 1." Bugenhagen can even say that God makes believers "Gods" through the adoption that occurs in faith (*Götzer*). See Kötter, *Johannes Bugenhagens Rechtfertigungslehre*, p. 191.

[131] Bugenhagen, *Von dem Christlichen Glauben*, Svi^{v}: "Aber eyn solch rain Herz hat niemand, deñ Gott gebe es, Gott aber rainigt das Herz durch eingegossenen glauben. Act 15." Thus, Bugenhagen can speak about faith as infused reality. The term, however, appears in the work only once to illustrate the faith that is not meritorious. Kötter, *Johannes Bugenhagens Rechtfertigungslehre*, p. 179.

[132] Bugenhagen, *Von dem Christlichen Glauben*, D: "Die weil das diser rechte glaube (on welchen niemandt kan selig werdenn) gottes krafft ist / so stercket er die menschen / des die (wenn die not heran kommet) unerschrocken sein / vor Gottes gericht / vor sünden / vor teuffel etc." The notion of *Gerechtigkeit Gottes* is similar to Luther; God's righteousness means that God makes believers righteous. See Bugenhagen, *Von dem Christlichen Glauben*, Bviii^{v}.

of justification, but is a part of it, as is apparent in Bugenhagen's advice to a sinner terrified by the accusations of the devil.

> When the devil says: how have you poor sinner become so defiant? When have you done enough for your sins, or are you even able to do so? Or how have you received such great righteousness? Then my answer is: I know well that I'm poor and a sinner. But Jesus Christ (with whom I have united and become one through the faith in Him) is not poor, but strong enough; He is not a sinner but eternal righteousness because He is the Lamb of God who takes away the sin of the world. If you can do something to Christ—then bring it on! He is mine and I'm His and God is through Him my beloved Father. With the righteousness (that Christ Himself is) I can well stand before God.[133]

Bugenhagen did not distinguish between justification and renewal. He emphasized how the heart cleansed through faith gladly submits itself to God's commandments and obeys them.[134] Christ has become present in faith and sins are forgiven. Now, the present Christ rules the heart in which he dwells through faith.[135] Hence, faith involves an effective

---

[133] Bugenhagen, *Von dem Christlichen Glauben*, Cii–Ciii: "Darumb künden die allaine in Christum glauben / in allen nötté bestebdig klich bleiben / dess sie nit umb der sünde willen verzweifle / sondern sicher sein des ewigen lebens / weñ auch schon alle sünden `vhanden weren / uñ die teuffel mitt der gantzen helle / die sich also / wie yetz und gesagt ist / uff Christum / der stercker deñ teuffel ist / verlassen. Deñ sy sind in Christo / uñ Christus in in (johanis. 6.)...Wenn denn der Teuffel sprech / Wo von bistu amechtiger armer sünder so trotzig worden? Wenn hastu deñ gnüg gethan / oder kanstu gnüg thün / für deine sünde? Oder woher hast du so grosse gerechtigkeit als durhümest? So antwort ich. Ich wayswol / dass ich amechtig unnd ein sünder bin / Aber Christus Jhesus (mit welchem ich vereinigett / uñ eun ding mit ym worden bin / durch den glauben in in) ist nit amechtig / sonder starck genug / ist nicht ein sünder / sond die ewig gerechtigkeit / deñ er ist das lamm gottes / das auff sich nimpt die sünde der welt / der ist uns geben von got dem vater / das er sey unser weysheit / gerechtigkeit / erlösung und d3 ewig leben. Kanst du etwas wider den Christum aussrichten / so beweyss dein kunst / der ist mein / so bin ich sein / uñ Got ist durch in mein lieber vater. Mit der gerechtigkeit (die Christus selbst ist) werd ich wol besteen für got..."

[134] Bugenhagen, *Von dem Christlichen Glauben*, Gviii^{v}: "Denn durch den glauben in Christum werden uns alle sünde vergeben / uñ werden kinder Gottes unnd fromm gemacht / das wir nu mit gereinigetem hertzen / lust haben zü Gottes gebotten / uñ ayn unlust / wider alles das gottes gebot nit leyden künden..."

[135] Bugenhagen, *Sechs Predigten*, 10: "Qui credit et assumit sic Christum, habet remissionem peccatorum, ascendit ad caelos, sedet ad dextram, ut nos regat et dominetur in cordibus nostris, ut haberemus spiritum, quo possimus resistere omnibus inimicis nostris. Ideo ascendit, ut semper et ubique regnet. Hic legi satisfactum est pro omnibus credentibus, quod ego non compleo, ipse complevit, quod hinfurder pecco, non imputatur, quia interpellat pro me, ne decidam et vincar, facit Christus, qui regit corda vostra sedens ad dextram patris etc. Ne a peccato vocamur, sacerdos est et rex." Compared to the later views of Melanchthon (see section 3.5) on the relation between the

change. In faith, the sinner becomes a good tree, and the works produced are pleasant in the eyes of God. The works are pleasant only because of present faith.[136] This change effected by faith is, however, different than good works, which follow faith.[137] Bugenhagen's view is not strictly forensic since he holds Christ's person and works together. Therefore, forgiveness of sins is an effective event (*renovatio*$_1$) which takes place as salutary exchange.[138]

2.3. *Johannes Brenz*

Johannes Brenz, a reformer from Württemberg, is known through his involvement in the debates on Christ's presence in the Holy Supper and consequent opposition to Melanchthon's theology. Christ's real presence in the bread and the wine was the basis for Brenz's thinking, which drove a wedge between himself and Melanchthon.[139]

Brenz's view on justification was also based on real communion with Christ. The doctrine of justification in the early thinking of Brenz can be characterized as follows. When a person receives the Word in faith he consequently participates in Christ, as well as the Trinity.[140] Hence,

human being and the Holy Spirit, it is interesting how Bugenhagen defines the analogy of the human spirit and the Holy Spirit. The relationship between person and God is based on the human spirit being "*habitaculum verbi Dei*". Kötter, *Johannes Bugenhagens Rechtfertigungslehre*, p. 223.

[136] Bugenhagen, *Von dem Christlichen Glauben*, Hiiii–Hiiiiv: "Allein diser glaube macht auss uns güte beume / das ist / rechtfertigt und frey võ den sünden. Darumb künden wir auch güte frucht bringen / dass ist / alle unsere werck sind gut in dem glauben."

[137] E.g., Bugenhagen, *Von dem Christlichen Glauben*, Bviii, Hii–J.

[138] See also Kötter, *Johannes Bugenhagens Rechtfertigungslehre*, pp. 195, 205, 240–241: "Der präsentische Aspekt ist dabei sowohl forensisch als auch effektiv dimensiert: In der gläubigen Vereinigung mit Christus erfährt der Sünder die Sündenvergebung und die Zusprechung der iustitia aliena Christi; es kommt zum heilsamen Austausch der Qualitäten. Glauben bedeutet dann gegenwärtibe überwindung der Anfechtung; dem Gläubigen eignet zu dem schon jetzt als Kind Gottes und Bruder Christi die Anteilhabe am ewigen Reich Gottes. Bugenhagens rechtfertigungslehre erweist sich somit als konsequent christologisch konzipiert: Christi menschwerdung bildet die Grundlage für die Ermöglichung des Heils, die gläubige Vereinigung mit dem gegenwärtigen Christus stellt die konkrete Aneignung der perfektischen Heilstatt in der Gegenwart dar."

[139] On Brenz's and Melanchthon's differences on Christ's presence in the Holy Supper, see Hans Christian Brandy, *Die späte Christologie des Johannes Brenz* (Tübingen: J. C. B. Mohr 1992), pp. 28–32, 41–44. Brandy (*op. cit.*, pp. 267–270) has also shown how Brenz's detailed christology serves soteriology and pastoral theology first and foremost, not intellectual ambitions.

[140] Martin Brecht, *Die Frühe Theologie des Johannes Brenz* (Tübingen: J. C. B. Mohr Siebeck 1966), pp. 214–216.

justification is not only a forensic act but also an effective change. The forgiveness of sins, inchoate purifying of corrupted nature, and the change from unholiness to righteousness all take place in the one act of justification. Justification involves more than imputation, which gives new life in Christ.[141] In spite of this, Brenz made a distinction between justification and good works. Good works are not done in order to merit salvation but simply because new life is a necessary consequence of justification.[142] More than simply noetic or historical faith, justifying faith is trust in Christ, which causes good fruits.[143] In 1531 Brenz corresponded with Melanchthon on justification.[144] Although Brenz reconsidered some parts of his teaching—such as the role of imputation in justification—communion with Christ was still the basis for imputation.[145]

For example, in his *Explicatio Epistolae Pauli ad Romanos* (1538) Brenz defined justification as imputation.[146] However, justifying faith is defined as unitive, in which case faith means participation (*conferatio/comparatio*) with God.[147] This union and Christ's presence makes imputation possible. First Christ is apprehended in faith and then his righteousness is reputed as righteousness that avails *coram Deo*.[148] Where Christ is, there

---

[141] Brecht, *Die Frühe Theologie*, pp. 225–237.

[142] Brecht, *Die Frühe Theologie*, 237: "'Prius enim iustificari nos oportet, deinde operari, ut prius vivificari nos oportet, quam pro vita animae operemur.' Die guten Werke der Liebe sind für uns vorbereitet 'post iustificationem, non ut ex eis iustificemur sed ut in eis ambulemus cum gratiarum actione. Omnia enim opera charitatis gratiarum actio sunt iustificationis, non ipsa iustificatio, quae est per fidem.'"

[143] Brecht, *Die Frühe Theologie*, 239: "Die zugehörigkeit der Liebe mit ihren Werken zum Glauben aber hat Brenz sehr deutlich, gelegentlich fast gewagt, ausgesprochen: "Non enim ideo iusti sumus, quia verbum audimus et Christus venit, sed quia credimus et iuxta fidem operamur." Der Sinn ist der: nicht ein noetischer oder nur historischer Glaube rechtfertigt, sondern der Glaube, der sich Christus anvertraut und dann auch gute Werke tut."

[144] This will be examined in more detail in section 3.3.

[145] Brecht, *Die Frühe Theologie*, p. 247.

[146] Brenz, *ad Romanos*, 99, 6–7: "...homines iustificari seu iustos reputari tantum gratia Dei propter Christum per fidem."

[147] Brenz, *ad Romanos*, 141, 19–20: "Fides enim eam habet naturam, quam habet Dominus Deus noster, ut recte pro sua ratione conferatur Deo." Brenz has a note in the margins, which says "Fides Deo comparatur." Brenz, *ad Romanos*, 243, 27–28: "Christus autem habitat in nobis per fidem in Christum ipsum." Brenz, *ad Romanos*, 241–243.

[148] Brenz, *ad Romanos*, 231, 32–36: "Et Deus cum invenit in nobis Christum, imputat eciam nobis iusticiam et perfectionem Christi. Ut enim in corpore membra fruuntur dignitate capitis, ita in Christo credentes fruuntur iusticia eius, quia Christus caput est credentium, credentes autem sunt membra eius." Brenz, *ad Romanos*, 152, 1–7: "Hic epilogus est eius argumentationis, in qua Paulus evidentissimis argumentis probavit, quod iusticia contingat nobis per solam fidem, hoc est quod sola fides sit organon illud,

is also forgiveness of sins and salvation. Brenz used different metaphors to depict this presence. For example, he spoke of the way believers are set in Christ through faith (*insiti Christo per fidem*).[149] The head and body metaphor is also used often. Because Christ died and was raised in his own body, the same thing happens to believers, who are the members of the body of which Christ is the head (*membra Christi*).[150] Christ is "the treasury of all goods" (*thezaurus omnium bonorum*). The sharer of Christ also shares in all his goods: righteousness, victory over death and hell, and eternal glory.[151] Justification means real participation in Christ's person. Faith in Christ evokes both imputation, regeneration, and vivification.

Melanchthon wrote in his letter that he had interpreted Brenz's teaching to mean that faith justifies because it is the root (*radix*) of good works. Although Brenz reconsidered his teaching, he still uses the term in his *Commentary to Romans*. Faith really is the *radix* and fountain (*fons*) of good works. Brenz uses the following metaphors to illustrate this. The human soul produces not only life but also actions. Light produces not only colors but also brightness. The root of the tree causes not only potential but actual fruit. In the same manner faith produces good works.[152] The sinner is, nevertheless, justified through

---

quo suscipitur Christus, propter quem solum reputamur coram Deo iusti et evadimus in tribunali Dei horribili illud perpetuae condemnationis iuditium." The same order (*inhabitatio-iustificatio*) appears everywhere in the book. See, e.g., Brenz, *ad Romanos*, 32, 19–21; 101, 30; 108, 30–109, 7; 125, 6–10; 183, 13–15; 218, 24–30; 231, 25–30; 243, 21–30.

[149] Brenz, *ad Romanos*, 227, 14–19: "Primum enim pii sunt insiti Christo per fidem. Ubi autem Christu est, ibi est remissio peccatorum et salus. Quare pii nihil habent comdemnationis, eciamsi adhuc gestent secum peccatum. Impii autem non sunt inserti Christo per fidem, sed contemnunt Christum et abiiciunt eum. Ubi autem non est Christus, ibi non est remissio peccatorum. Itaque in impiis est peccatum et condemnatio" Brenz uses also words such as *complantatio, incorporatio, transplantatio* and *mutatio.* See Brenz, *ad Romanos*, 180, 6–181, 26.

[150] Brenz, *ad Romanos*, 183, 11–15: "Haec ut rectius intelligamus, observandum erit duplicem esse potentiam mortis et resurrectionis Christi. Altera est quam mors et resurrectio exercent in persona Christi, altera quam exercent in nobis aut nostra persona, qui sumus membra Christi."

[151] Brenz, *ad Romanos*, 283, 4–10: "Quid autem habet filius Dei? Primum habet iusticiam; deinde habet victoriam super omnes afflictiones, mortem et horrores inferni; postremo habet summam et perpetuam foelicitatem. Innumera sunt bona, quae habet filius Dei, thezaurus est omnium bonorum. Quare cum Deus nobis filium donaverit, cum eo eciam simul donabit omnia bona eius ac praesertim liberationem ex omnibus afflictionibus."

[152] Brenz, *ad Romanos*, 31, 27–32, 3: "Nam necessario sunt facienda, quia fides, quae justificat, non potest quiescere, quin secum afferat exercitium bonorum operum: ut anima non solum affert homini vitam, sed eciam opera vitae; ut lumen non solum

Christ apprehended in faith, not through Christ's inchoate effects in human nature even if they are necessarily present.[153]

Brenz's teaching of Christ's real presence in faith surfaced in the Osiandrian controversy, when Brenz and Jacob Andreae tried to find a peaceful solution to the dilemma and refused to condemn Osiander as a heretic.[154] A solution was offered according to which the imputation of Christ's righteousness holds within it the essential righteousness of Christ. Brenz was not satisfied with this but was unable to offer anything better. As a consequence, the mainstream decided to oppose Osiander by emphasizing imputation over inhabitation.[155]

2.4. *Conclusion*

Luther, Bugenhagen, and Brenz held a similar view of justification. A precondition of salvation is the incarnation and satisfactory death of Christ. The meaning of Christ's work is depicted through various theories of satisfaction. Christ has destroyed the powers of death and hell in himself and fulfilled the demands of divine law. Both incarnatory and forensic theories of satisfaction are used in a complementary way. The ontological and real participation in Christ enables the salutary exchange of attributes, the sinner receivies the righteousness of Christ and Christ receives the sins of the sinner. The union that takes place in justification must be understood through a christological framework, not through Aristotelian metaphysics or categories of mere

---

affert secum calorem, sed eciam splendorem; ut bona arboris radix et medulla non tantum conservat internam arboris bonitatem, sed eciam producit extrinsecus bonos fructus nec cohiberi potest ceteris paribus, quin eos proferat, si modo bona arbor fuerit, ita fides non solum affert secum iusticiam coram Deo, sed eciam operatur iusticiam coram hominibus, quae est exercitium bonorum operum." See also Brenz, *ad Romanos*, 117, 11–21.

[153] Brenz, *ad Romanos*, 101, 30–35: "Ac sequuntur quidem fidem bona opera; sed iusticia non contingit propter opera, quae praecedunt fidem, nec propter opera, quae sequuntur fidem, sed tantum propter Christum, qui per fidem comprehenditur. Quare hoc nobis praecipue omnium agendum est, ut ex evangelio Christum discamus et ipsum per veram fidem apprehendamus." Christian righteousness is passive righteousness (*iusticia passiva*), which does not consist of human activity (*iusticia activa*). See Brenz, *ad Romanos*, 32, 15–21.

[154] On Osiander, see section 4.1. On Andreae, see section 6.1.

[155] Martin Stupperich, "Lehrentscheidung und theologische Schematisierung. Die Sonderrolle Württembergs im Osianderischen Streit und ihre Konsequenzen für die Formulierung des dritten Artikels der Solida Declaratio," in *Widerspruch, Dialog und Einigung*, hrsgb von Wenzel Lohff et al. (Stuttgart: Calwer Verlag 1977), pp. 174–175.

effect. The forensic and effective aspects of justification are not to be understood in a cause and effect relationship. Justification consists of both the renewal of individual's relationship with God and a renewal nature of the human being (*renovatio*$_1$). The basis of salvation is located outside of the person, but it becomes actualized in the person through faith. Consistent with Luther, Bugenhagen and Brenz both understood justification as an effective act (*renovatio*$_1$): new life is participation in the life of Christ. It is also important to stress that justification must be distinguished from good works. Faith and apprehending Christ are not synonymous with good works and love. In this sense justification is different than sanctification and renewal (*renovatio*$_2$).

CHAPTER THREE

PHILIP MELANCHTHON: JUSTIFICATION AS THE RENEWAL OF THE INTELLECT AND THE WILL

Melanchthon has had the dubious honor of being the *lupus fabulae* of the history of Lutheranism. The reason for this hostility must be understood in context of controversies which followed Luther's death and resulted in party-forming. The followers of Luther were split into a number of rival parties, two of which the most prominent were the Philippists, who were supporters of Melanchthon's theology and style, and the Gnesiolutherans, who tried to identify themselves as the genuine followers of Luther.[1]

Melanchthon tried to formulate Lutheran theology in such a way as to maintain a connection with Calvinist theologians. During Luther's lifetime, he had already sought an alliance with the Roman Catholic Church. Melanchthon's ecumenical interests became apparent in Regensburg (1541) and in the Leipzig interim (1548). The formulations of the interim in particular was interpreted as a deviation from Luther's teachings. These accusations came from Joachim Mörlin, among others, whose comment embodies the ambivalent status of Melanchthon.

> He is our Preceptor, and Preceptor he shall be called. But when he speaks about the Lord's Supper, free will, justification of man, or actions concerning interims, then you, Philip, shall be praised by the devil, but me nevermore.[2]

Melanchthon's notion of justification evolved over the years so that the role of renewal in justification varied. His greatest difference from Luther was his way of depicting renewal as the causal renewal of the

---

[1] A third minor party was the Swabachian group, who were followers of Johannes Brenz. Robert Kolb, *Luther's Heirs define His legacy. Studies on Lutheran Confessionalization*, Collected studies series C539 (Norfolk: Variorum 1996), V, 66.

[2] "Er ist unser Präceptor und müssen ihn einen Präceptor nennen; wenn's aber kommt ad locum de coena Domini, de libero arbitrio, de justificatione hominis, de interimisticis actionibus, da lobe dich der Teufel, Philippe, ich nimmermehr." Quoted in Erich Roth, "Ein Braunschweiger Theologe des 16. Jahrhunderts: Mörlin und seine Rechtfertigungslehre", *Jahrbuch der Gesellschaft für niedersächsische Kirchengeschichte* 50 (1952), pp. 68–69.

powers of the soul by the Spirit, whereas Luther understood renewal as participation in Christ.

3.1. *Justification as Reordering of Affects in the* Loci Communes *(1521)*

In 1521, Melanchthon published the first edition of his introduction to theology, *Loci Communes*.[3] Luther declared the book "worth canonization",[4] praise which indicates something of the relationship between these two men. Luther and Melanchthon were colleagues and close friends, and never criticized each other in public.[5]

Melanchthon's description of justification in *Loci* 1521 demonstrates his humanist-pedagogical interests. Practical piety and conversion form the context for justification: the Law condemns and the Gospel revives the person.

> We are justified when we are mortified through the Law and the word of grace promised in Christ revives us. In other words: the Gospel forgives us, and we hold on to that word in faith, and do not doubt that Christ's

---

[3] The best-known revised editions were published in 1535 (*CR* 21) and 1559 (*MW* II/1–2). As the study material of the universities, Lombard's Sentences were replaced by the doctrinal treatments based on Melanchthon's and his students' *loci* method. Thomas Kaufmann, "Martin Chemnitz (1522–1586). Zur Wirkungsgeschichte der theologischen Loci" in *Melanchthon in seinen Schülern*, Hrsgb. Heinz Scheible, (Wiesbaden: Harrassowitz Verlag 1997), p. 113.

[4] *WA* 18, 601, 3–11. On Luther's comments on Melanchthon's works, see also *WA TR* 4, 610, 17–20; *WA TR* 5, 661, 28–29. *Loci* 1521 does not provide a clear picture of Melanchthon's theology. The work includes ideas derived from medieval theology and Luther, which are sometimes in conflict with each other. At the end of the work, there is evidence of the effects of correspondence with Luther. Once the work has already discussed the doctrines of Sin, Law, and Grace, the treatment starts anew, these additions including Luther's suggestions and appendixes. See Lohse, *Dogma und Bekenntnis in der Reformation: Von Luther bis zum Konkordienbuch.—Handbuch der Dogmen- und Theologiegeschichte*, hrsgb. Carl Andresen, Band 2, Die Lehrentwicklung im Rahmen der Konfessionalität (Göttingen: Vandenhoeck & Ruprecht 1980), pp. 75–76.

[5] On the relationship between Luther and Melanchthon in general, see Timothy Wengert, "Melanchthon and Luther/Luther and Melanchthon" in *Lutherjahrbuch* (Göttingen: Vandenhoeck & Ruprecht 1999); Lohse, "Philipp Melanchthon in seinen Beziehungen zur Luther," in *Martin Luther: Ein Einführung ein sein Leben und sein Werk* (München: Beck 1983), p. 860.

> righteousness is our righteousness, that Christ's reconciliation is our expiation and that Christ's resurrection is our resurrection.[6]

Here Melanchthon comes close to Luther's idea of salutary exchange, a notion which appears in Luther's text written at the same time.[7] However, the connection between christology and justification is not well developed in *Loci* 1521. For the young Melanchthon, Christ's incarnation has a preconditional and informative role, not a salvific one.[8] According to Melanchthon, "to know Christ is to know His benefits (*beneficia*) and not, as scholastics teach, pondering over his natures or the ways of his incarnation."[9]

The way Melanchthon refers to patristic theology indicates his christological views. Church fathers such as Athanasios, Gregory of

---

[6] *MW* II/1, 106 (*Loci* 1521): "Iustificamur igitur, cum mortificari per legem resuscitamur verbo gratiae, quae in Christo promissa est, seu evangelio condonante peccata et illi fide adhaeremus, nihil dubitantes, quin Christi iustitia sit nostra iustitia, quin Christi satisfactio sit expiatio nostri, quin Christi resurrectio nostra sit."

[7] Luther explains the happy exchange in his *Operationes in Psalmos* (1519–1521) as follows. *WA* 5, 608, 7–8: "...quod admirabili commercio peccata nostra iam non nostra, sed Christi sunt, et iustitia Christi non Christi, sed nostra est."

[8] Melanchthon's tract *De studio doctrinae Paul.* 1520 (*CR* 11, 37) explains the incarnation of the Word as follows: "Carnem aeternus Dei sermo induit, ut et nos significaret divini sermonis commercio ἀποθεοῦσθαι." It is worth noting that the tract speaks about the divinization of God's work, not divinization of the flesh. On christology in early Melanchthon, see Wilhelm Maurer, *Der Junge Melanchthon zwischen Humanismus und Reformation*, Bd. 2, *Der Theologe* (Göttingen: Vandenhoeck & Ruprecht 1969), pp. 341–349, 565; Ernst Bizer, "Reformationsgeschichte 1532 bis 1555," in *Reformationsgeschichte Deutschlands bis* 1555, hrsgb. Franz Lau und Ernst Bizer, Die Kirche in ihrer Geschichte, Ein Handbuch (Göttingen: Vandenhoeck & Ruprecht 1964b), p. 67; Rolf Schäfer, *Christologie und Sittlichkeit in Melanchthons frühen loci* (Tübingen: J. C. B. Mohr 1961), pp. 37–38. In *Loci* 1521, Melanchthon criticizes speculative theology heavily, which neglects the true Christian knowledge of repentance and Gospel for the sake of hairsplitting. *MW* II/1, 19 (*Loci* 1521). Does this imply a negative attitude towards christological approaches to theology? Clearly this is not the case. Melanchthon's christology, however, has been interpreted as psychological. Theodor Mahlmann sees this as reductionism. See Mahlmann, *Das Neue Dogma der lutherischen Christologie. Problem und Geschichte seiner Begründung*, (Gütersloh: Gütersloher Verlagshaus Mohn 1969), p. 71. According to Melanchthon, the speculation of the act of incarnation functions only as a preparation for conversion. This speculation, however, can turn against Christian faith. See E. P. Meijering, *Melanchthon and Patristic Thought. The Doctrines of Christ and Grace, the Trinity and the Creation* (Leiden: Brill 1983), pp. 4–18.

[9] *MW* II/1, 20 (*Loci* 1521). The notion "*beneficia*" refers to Christ's beneficial work, which is actualized in forgiveness of sins and the following renewals, which produce consolation in conscience, joy, and peace. Therefore, *beneficia* means both the historical act of redemption and its application. See Meijering, *Melanchthon*, p. 111; Schäfer, *Christologie*, pp. 59–60; Ralph Quere, *Melanchthon's Christum cognoscere. Christ's efficacious Presence in the Eucharistic Theology of Melanchthon* (Nieuwkoop: B. de Graaf 1977), p. 109.

Nazianzus, and Cyprian appear in Melanchthon as genuine witnesses, but only because the quotations concentrate on the full humanity and divinity of Christ, which form the prerequisite for satisfaction, incarnation functions as the informer of God's salvific will. The individual can find certainty of salvation in this information.[10]

In *Loci* 1521, the concept of justification remains undefined. For example, 'faith', the central soteriological concept in the book, is defined in more detail than 'justification', which is used in the practical context of piety and devotion.[11] The concept is ambivalent in that while justification is only right information concerning Christ and having faith in Him, which means understanding (*cognitio*) His mercifulness,[12] Melanchthon depicts justification as a sanative act as well.[13]

The sanative and effective aspect of justification is illustrated through anthropological changes which evoke faith. Melanchthon uses the notion 'affect' (*affectus*)[14] to depict these changes, following the standard contemporaneous way of illustrating how the two capacities of the soul—knowledge (*intellectus*) and will (*voluntas*)—function. The affects illustrate the actions of the will. The human will is not free but a slave to the affects. In the fallen state one is unable to resist the affects, which

---

[10] Schäfer, *Christologie*, pp. 36–38.

[11] See Albrecht Peters, *Rechtfertigung. Handbuch Systematischer Theologie*, hrsgb. von Carl Heinz Ratschow, Bd. 12 (Gütersloher: Verlaugshaus Gerd Mohn 1984), p. 64: "Der Terminus Rechtfertigung (*iustificatio*) spielt innerhalb des übergreifenden Gnadentraktates neben dem schon präziser durchreflektierten Glaubensbegriff in den Loci Communes von 1521 lediglich eine untergeordnete Rolle; er ist noch nicht denkerisch durchdrungen und begrifflich fixiert." See also Maurer, *Der Junge Melanchthon*, pp. 336–338. The locus *De iustificatione et fide* focuses primarily on the notion of true faith. This is also apparent in Luther's contemporary texts. For example, faith is a more central concept in his response to Latomus (1521) than justification, which does not appear in the book at all.

[12] *MW* II/1, 126 (*Loci* 1521): "Respondeo, cum sola misericordia dei iustificemur fidesque plane sit misericordiae cognitio..."

[13] *MW* II/1, 127 (*Loci* 1521): "Coepta enim iustificatio est, non consummata." See also Otto Ritschl, *Dogmengeschichte des Protestantismus*, IV *Band*, *Orthodoxie und Synkretismus in der altprotestantischen Theologie*, *Das orthodoxe Luthertum im Gegensatz zu der reformierten Theologie und in der Auseinandersetzung mit dem Synkretismus* (Göttingen: Vandenhoeck & Ruprecht 1912), p. 240; Bizer, *Theologie der Verheissung. Studien zur Theologie des jüngen Melanchthon* 1519–1524 (Neukirchen-Vluyn: Neukirchener Verlag des Erziehungsvereins Gmbh 1964), pp. 82–83.

[14] *Affectus* is the central concept in Melanchthon's *Loci* 1521. The affects cause the bondage of the will, for example. Since the human being is dictated by his affects so that the stronger affects dominate the weaker, people are the slaves of the passions. Justification is thus also understood as effective regeneration.

can be overcome only by another affect.[15] The renewal of the affects by the Holy Spirit is prerequisite for faith.[16]

Since justification is a consequence of faith, which the Holy Spirit evokes through renewal (*renovatio*) and illumination (*illuminatio*) of the faculties of the soul,[17] faith is also a new affect.[18] This leads Melanchthon to the notion that faith is a *created* affect, which receives a new object, i.e. Christ, by the power of the Spirit.[19] The renewal of the apprehensive faculty of the soul, i.e., the will, is therefore needed for justification. We can thus conclude that in *Loci* 1521 justification is effective in that the new reality and change in the individual is a part of justification.[20] In *Loci* 1521 Melanchthon uses justification and renewal synonymously. Justification is described as participation in Christ's righteousness while it is actualized in the new affects that are evoked by the Spirit and renewed according to the Law of God. The relation between justification and christology seems ambiguous and incomplete.

While Melanchthon can write that faith in God's mercy is righteousness,[21] faith does not justify because it apprehends Christ, who is the essential righteousness; rather, faith justifies because faith as an affect is directed to Christ and trusts in him. Here Melanchthon follows Luther's

---

[15] *MW* II/1, 27 (*Loci* 1521): "Contra interni affectus non sunt in potestate nostra. Experimentia enim usuque comperimus non posse voluntatem sua sponte ponere amorem, odium aut similes affectus, sed affectus affectu vincitur, ut, quia laesus es ab eo, quem amabas, amare desinis. Nam te ardentius quam quemvis alium amas."

[16] *MW* II/1, 85–87 (*Loci* 1521). According to zur Karl-Heinz zur Mühlen ("Melanchthons Auffassung vom Affekt in den Loci Communes von 1521," in *Humanismus und Wittenberger Reformation*, hrsgb. Michael Beyer et al. (Leipzip: Evangelische Verlagsanstalt 1996), p. 334): "Von diesem sündigen Affekt vermag nur die Gnade zu heilen, die als Gunst Gottes alle Sünden vergibt und rechtfertigt und als Gabe der Gnade das Herz erneuert und zu Glaube, Liebe und Hoffnung wie zu den übrigen Tugenden instandsetz." See also Hägglund, *Rechtfertigung*, p. 182; Hans-Georg Geyer, *Von der Geburt des Wahren Menschen. Probleme aus den Anfängen der Theologie Melanchthons* (Neukirchen-Vluyn: Neukirchener Verlag des Erziehungvereins Gmbh 1965), p. 283; Wolfgang Matz, *Der befreite Mensch. Die Willenslehre in der Theologie Philipp Melanchthons* (Göttingen: Vandenhoeck & Ruprecht 2001), pp. 42–50.

[17] *MW* II/1, 109 (*Loci* 1521): "Quid igitur fides? constanter assentiri omni verbo dei, id quod non sit nisi renovante et illuminante corda nostra spiritu dei."

[18] *MW* II/1, 108 (*Loci* 1521): "Nam de cordis affectu loquor, nec timebat iram dei nec fidebat benignitate."

[19] See also Seils, *Glaube*, pp. 93–94, 100–101.

[20] Hypothetically, justification could belong only to intellect but even this would require some sort of renewal. Generally, Lutheran theologians identify the change of mere intellect with *fides historica*, i.e., *notitia*, which does not justify without trust in the will (*fiducia*).

[21] *MW* II/1, 106 (*Loci* 1521): "...sed sola fides de misericordia et gratia dei in Iesu Christo iustitia est."

thinking. The early Luther ascribes the renewal of the intellect to Christ and the renewal of affects to the Holy Spirit in his sermons of 1520. While this distinction never becomes structural for Luther, Melanchthon strengthens it and develops it further. Christ is for Melanchthon primarily an object of the intellect and knowledge, to which the Holy Spirit redirects human affects.[22] The connection with Christ is not ontological participation in God's nature but correct information (*notitia*) and the correct relation to it, i.e., trust (*fiducia*). God justifies the believer for the sake of this faith and trust.

The chapter on grace (*De gratia*) gives the fullest account of the ontology of salvation. Melanchthon's brief explanation is that God, who is merciful, wishes for the sake of Christ to show His mercy towards mankind. This favor is termed grace (*gratia*).[23] Because of this favor God gives gifts to those whom he loves. God's gift (*donum*) is the Holy Spirit, which He infuses (*effundit*) into the hearts of believers.[24] The Holy Spirit evokes faith, regenerates (*regeneratio*) and sanctifies (*sanctificatio*) their hearts. *Loci* 1521 does not introduce a temporal or logical consequence between grace and gift. Both are donated in the promises of the Gospel and are obtained through faith.[25] Melanchthon understood grace as a state of God's mind which causes God to act savingly towards a person. Grace, however, has no effect before the donation of the gift, which enables justifying faith. The donation is illustrated by such words as *renovatio, illuminatio, sanctificatio*, and *regeneratio*. For Melanchthon, the

[22] See, e.g., *WA* 9, 463, 14–15 (*Predigt 27. Mai* 1520): "Audiendum est verbum divinum, audito adherendum est certa fiducia. Quum audio, Christum pro me mortuum, et credo, tum delabitur in me spiritus sanctus. Nam ea fides excitat in me amorem, qui amor est spiritus sanctus." See also Kärkkäinen, *Luthers trinitarische theologie*, pp. 65–78, 85–89. According to Lohse ("Dogma und Bekenntnis," p. 74) these sermons greatly influenced the young Melanchthon.

[23] *MW* II/1, 104 (*Loci* 1521): "Non significat ergo gratiae vocabulum qualitatem aliquam in nobis, sed potius ipsam dei voluntatem seu benevolentiam dei erga nos." Here Melanchthon opposes the thomistic notion that grace was interpreted as a property of the soul. See, e.g., Aquinas, *Summa*, I q. 27, a. 6. See also Matz, *Der befreite Mensch*, pp. 63–68.

[24] Pihkala (*Gnadenmittel*, p. 42) has claimed that for Melanchthon *donum* is pneumatological while for Luther *donum* is Christ himself.

[25] *MW* II/1, 105 (*Loci* 1521): "Donum ipse spiritus sanctus, quem in eorum corda effundit, quorum est misertus. Fructus spiritus sancti fides, spes, caritas et reliquae virtutes. Et haec quidem de nomine gratiae. In summa, non aliud est gratia nisi condonatio seu remissio peccati. Donum est spiritus sanctus regerans et sanctificans corda... Tam gratiam quam donum promittit evangelium."

internal aspect of justification is faith, a psychological affect evoked by the Spirit, which is realized as trust (*fiducia*) in God's grace.[26]

The justifying content of justification is faith in Christ, which requires the redirection of the affects in regeneration. *Renovatio*$_1$ thus forms part of justification and means a change from a state of unbelief to one of faith. This type of change is distinguished from consequent love and good works (*renovatio*$_2$).[27]

3.2. *The Augsburg Confession and the Apology of the Augsburg Confession*

In the *Augsburg Confession* (CA, 1530), which was written by Melanchthon and deemed the most important confessional writing of Lutheranism, justification is described along the lines of *Loci* 1521.

> Likewise, they teach that human beings cannot be justified before God by their own powers, merits or works. But they are justified as a gift (*gratis*) on account of Christ through faith, when they believe that they are received into grace and their sins are forgiven on account of Christ, who by his death made satisfaction for our sins. God reckons (*imputat*) this faith as righteousness.[28]

CA depicts justification as an extrinsic act, which means that justification is entirely outside human endeavors. Mercy is unconditional and without prerequisites from the human side. "Their own powers, merits, or works" do not acquire the righteousness that avails *coram Deo*; instead God reckons (*imputat*) the righteousness of Christ to sinners. Simultaneously CA claims that righteousness is something intrinsic, i.e., located in the person who is the object of imputation. God reckons *faith*, which is a new reality in this person, as righteousness.[29] This means that there is

---

[26] *MW* II/1, 110 (*Loci* 1521): "Est itaque fides non aliud nisi fiducia misericordiae divinae promissae in Christo adeoque quocunque signo."

[27] *MW* II/1, 130–133 (*Loci* 1521).

[28] *BSELK CA* IV: "Item docent, quod homines non possint iustificari coram Deo propriis viribus, meritis aut operibus, sed gratis iustificentur propter Christum per fidem, cum credunt se in gratiam recipi et peccata remitti propter Christum, qui sua morte pro nostris peccatis satisfecit. Hanc fidem imputat Deus pro iustitia coram ipso."

[29] Traditionally, it has been difficult to combine these two aspects. For example, Leif Grane interprets the concept of faith instrumentally so that faith in itself is the mere reception of Christ's righteousness. See Grane, *The Augsburg Confession. A Commentary* (Minneapolis: Augsburg Publishing House 1987), p. 61. On the other hand, Grane (*op. cit.*, p. 62) claims that this act of imputation is not fictitive; "rather, it means that imputed righteousness is a renewal of the whole person." The interpretation has been

something present in man which forms the basis for imputation. Even so, justification does not take place *propter fidem*, but *propter Christum*.

It is important to note that faith should not be understood here as a virtue. Faith as righteousness is the converse of meritorious deeds. Since faith justifies because it apprehends Christ and applies His righteousness for the believing person, so justification does not happen *simpliciter propter fidem*. In other words, faith justifies as a present new reality because it is directed outside of itself through its essence. This ontological emphasis is especially apparent in theological documents that precede CA, such as the Swabach[30] and Marburg[31] articles dating from 1529. These documents give the necessary hermeneutic framework for the concise text of CA. Faith is described as "the gift and work of God", "a powerful, new and living entity" and "participation in the Son's righteousness, life and all the goods."

---

difficult because the text of CA is so concise. On the interpretations of *CA*, see also Greschat, *Melanchthon*, p. 111; Wenz, *Theologie der Bekenntnischriften*, p. 126; Harding Meyer et al., *Confessio Augustana. Bekenntnis des einen Glaubens. Gemeinsame untersuchung Lutherischer und Katholischer Theologen* (Frankfurt am Main: Verlag Otto Lembeck 1980), pp. 122–126; Maurer, *Historischer Kommentar zur Confessio Augustana*, Bd. 2., *Theologische Probleme* (Gütersloh: Gütersloher Verlagshaus Mohn 1978), p. 85; Regin Prenter, *Das Bekenntnis von Augsburg. Eine Auslegung* (Erlangen: Martin Luther-Verlag 1980), pp. 83–85; Schlink, *Theologie der Lutherischen Bekenntnischriften*, p. 141; Vinzenz Pfnür, *Einig in der Rechtfertigungslehre? Die Rechtfertigungslehre der Confessio Augustana* (1530) *und die Stellungnahme der katholischen Kontroverstheologie zwischen* 1530 *und* 1535 (Wiesbaden: Abteilung Abendländische Religiongeschichte 1970), pp. 140–143; Nestor Beck, *The Doctrine of Faith. A Study of the Augsburg Confession and Contemporary Ecumenical Documents* (St. Louis: Concordia Publishing House 1959), pp. 80–85.

[30] *BSELK*, 57: "Das ist aber Weg zur gerechtigkeit und zur Erlosung von Sunden und Tod, so man ohn alle verdienst oder Werk gläubt an den Sohn Gottes, fur uns gelitten etc., wie gesagt. Solcher Glaub ist unser gerechtigkeit, denn Gott will fur gerecht, frumm und heilig rechnen und halten, alle Sunde vergeben und ewigs Leben geschenkt haben allen, die solchen Glauben an seinen Sohn haben, dass sie um seines Sohns willen sollen zue Gnaden genommen und Kinder sein in seinem Reich etc..." It is important to note that faith is here depicted as "essence" (*Wesen*); this underlines the efficacy of faith. *BSELK*, 59: "Das solcher Glaube sei nicht ein menschliche Werk noch aus unsern Kräften muglich, sondern es ist ein Gotteswerk und Gabe, die der heilige Geist durch Christum gegeben in uns wirket, und solcher Glaub, wo er nit ein loser Wahn oder Dunkel des herzens ist, wie die Salschgläubigen haben, sondern ein kräftiges, neues, lebendiges Wesen, bringet er viel Frucht, tut immer Guts gegen Gott mit Loben, Danken, Beten, Predigen und Lehren, gegen dem Nächsten mit Lieb, Dienen, Helfen, Raten, Geben und Leiden allerlei Ubels bis in den Tod."

[31] Luther wrote the Marburg articles by himself. *BSELK*, 57: "Zum siebenden, dass solcher Glaube sei unser Gerechtigkeit fur Gott, als umb wilchs willen uns Gott gerecht, fromme und heilig rechnet und hält, ohn alle Werk und Verdienst und dadurch von Sonden, Tod, Helle hilft, zu Gnaden nimpt und selig macht umb seines Sohns willen, in wilchen wir also gläuben und dadurch seines Sohns Gerechtigkeit, Lebens und aller Güter geniessen und teilhaftig werden..."

The Marburg articles, in particular, which were written by Luther, help to understand how Luther may have read CA's article on justification. Faith can be understood not only as the instrumental cause but also as the *formal cause* of justification. This is possible because faith's relational essence makes the divine actions and attributes of God (e.g., the Son's life) present, although CA itself does not explicitly mention the presence of divinity itself in faith. Faith can thus be reckoned as righteousness; this is the only way to avoid the idea of faith as a meritorious virtue.

The Roman Catholic Church never approved of CA. By way of response, the emperor composed two rejoinders. The first was *Catholica Responsio*, very sharp-tongued and critical,[32] which claimed that it is erroneous to teach that faith alone saves since love also is essential for Christian faith.

> When the other party claims that we become righteousness through faith alone, this is the biggest mistake and particular incitement. When they reckon for faith what belongs to love and God's grace, they incite people. And Luther undertakes a treacherous venture when he adds to Romans 3 this saying 'alone', which does not exist in either the Greek or Latin examples. Paul states clearly in 1. Cor. 13 that faith alone does not justify: "and though I have complete faith, so that I could remove mountains, and have not charity, I am nothing." This apostle, the teacher of the nations, undoes all sayings of adversaries, who claim that faith alone justifies.[33]

However, this was not Rome's official rejoinder to CA. Soon after *Catholica Responsio* Rome produced a more applicable rejoinder, *Confutatio Confessionis Augustanae* (also known as the *Papal Confutation*). The *Confutatio* emphasizes the primacy of grace but reaffirms the meritoriousness

[32] For the edition of the text, see J. Ficker, *Die Konfutation des Augsburgischen Bekenntnisses. Ihre Gestalt und ihre Geschichte* (Leipzig 1891). Both the emperor and the gentlefolk considered the tone of the paper too extreme, even insulting; thus, it did not serve the emperor's attempts to establish unity. Herbert Immenkötter, *Die Konfutatio der Confessio Augustana vom* 3. *August* 1530, bearbeitet von H. Immenkötter, Corpus Catholicorum 33 (München 1979), p. 38.

[33] Ficker, *Die Konfutation*, p. 19: "Altera parte cum inquiunt fide nos iustificari, is est magnus error et precipuus concionatorum. Nam soli fidei tribuunt quod est charitati proprium et gratie dei, veluti populo inculcarunt. Et Luther ausus est falsare et addere ad Ro. 3. hanc dictionem solam, que nec in grecis nec in latinis exemplaribus invenitur. Quod enim fides sola non iustificet expresse testatur Paulus 1. Cor. 13: Si omnem fidem habuero ita ut montes transferam, charitatem autem non habuero, nihil sum. Hic apostolus, doctor gentium, contundit omnia dicta adversariorum, quia fides sola non iustificat."

of human deeds. Meritoriousness, however, is based on the effect of God's grace. As such human deeds are worthless, but God makes them worthy by His grace.[34] Faith and works are intertwined as hope and charity are infused simultaneously (*simul infunduntur*) in baptism with faith.[35] For this reason, it is false to claim that faith alone justifies since faith must be active through love. *Confutatio* presents justification simply according to the *fides charitate formata* model.[36] In spite of the more courteous tone, the emperor's wishes were not fulfilled and the attempts to reconcile the parties failed. *Confutatio*, however, was an important document in the sense that it enabled further discussions in Regensburg. Melanchthon answered the *Confutatio* with his Apology of the Augsburg Confession (*Apologia Confessionis Augustanea*, AC, 1531). Forensic and effective aspects of justification are also maintained in the Apology, as Melanchthon states:

> And because 'to be justified' means that out of unrighteous people righteous people are made (*effici*) or regenerated, it also means that they are pronounced (*pronuntiari*) or regarded as righteous. For Scripture speaks both ways.[37]

Justification is not strictly a forensic act because it also involves an effective and regenerative change by which the unrighteous person becomes righteous.[38] Melanchthon emphasizes the regenerative character of faith at several points and relates the gift of the Holy Spirit and inner renewal to justification.[39] He strongly denies that "the bestowing of the

---

[34] Immenkötter, *Die Konfutatio*, p. 87: "Attamen omnes catholici fatentur opera nostra ex se nullius esse meriti, sed gratia dei facit illa digna esse vitae aeternae."

[35] Immenkötter, *Die Konfutatio*, p. 87/89.

[36] Immenkötter, *Die Konfutatio*, p. 85/87. See also Martens, *Die Rechtfertigung*, pp. 50–52; Athina Lexutt, *Rechtfertigung im Gespräch: das Rechtfertigungsverständnis in den Religionsgesprächen von Hagenau, Worms und Regensburg* 1540/41 (Göttingen: Vandenhoech & Ruprecht 1996), pp. 56–59.

[37] *BSELK AC* IV, 72: "Et quia iustificari significat ex iniustis iustos effici seu regenerari, significat et iustos pronuntiari seu reputari. Utroque enim modo loquitur scriptura."

[38] Meyer, *Confessio Augustana*, p. 126: "Gerechtmahnung, Heiligung und Gerechterklärung bilden also verschiedene, wenn auch eng zusammengehörige Momente des Rechtfertigungsgeschehens, bei dem laut Confessio Augustana und Apologie der Aktive teil stets auf der Seite des trinitarischen Gottes liegt." See also Nüssel, *Allein aus Glauben*, pp. 36–39; Schlink, *Theologie der Lutherischen Bekenntnischriften*, pp. 138–144; Flogaus, "Luther versus Melanchthon?", pp. 16–20; Peters, *Rechtfertigung*, pp. 78–79. The interpretations of the doctrine of justification in AC have been various, the central issue being the role of efficacy in the act of justification. Wenz (*Theologie der Bekenntnischriften*, pp. 126–142) summarizes this discussion.

[39] *BSELK AC* IV, 117: "...et quod sola fide iustificemur, hoc est, ex iniustis iusti efficiamur seu regenemur." Justification is understood as an inner renewal in the follow-

Holy Spirit is without any effect".[40] Faith causes hearts to "have spiritual and holy impulses", which in turn cause good works.[41]

Although the notion of affect is not as apparent in AC as in *Loci* 1521, it clearly governs his argument. Hence the intrinsic aspect of justification is outlined through the changes in the emotions and other movements in the mind. Justifying faith is knowing (*notitia*) Christ and his benefits.[42] However, faith is not located in the perceptive part of the soul, i.e., the intellect. Faith means positive reception of God's promises; it is the active response of the will, which trusts in God's promises.[43] Faith understands (*sentit*) Christ as the Savior,[44] In addition, several affectual concepts (consolation, joy, peace, tranquility) are used to describe vivification, which means freeing the conscience from the feeling of guilt. This vivification is effected by the Holy Spirit.[45]

In spite of this efficacy, Melanchthon strenuously denied that vivification means becoming righteous because of these changes and impulses. In that case human deeds and merits would become decisive in attaining the certainty of salvation. An individual would put faith in the process of change, which is effected by inherent love or other virtues, not in Christ. In order to prevent this interpretation, Melanchthon stresses

---

ing passages: *BSELK AC* IV, 99, 115–117, 304–305, 366 VII, 13–16, 28, 31. On faith as internally renewing, see, e.g., *BSELK AC* IV, 99, 115–117, 304–305, 366 VII, 13–16, 28, 31. In 1531 slightly before AC, Melanchthon wrote a disputation on justification with a similar tone. Faith apprehends Christ, and sets him against God's wrath. (*apprehendimus Christum mediatorem, et opponimus eum irae dei.*) Melanchthon emphasizes the importance of the person of Christ, while the notion of "merit" appears in the christological sense only once. Faith regenerates and makes the unrighteous acceptable before God (*ex iniustis acceptos efficiat et regeneret*). Faith is depicted as an efficient ontological reality that receives the Holy Spirit and starts to fulfill the Law through virtues such as love for God. Love, however, does not regenerate (*non igitur regenerat dilectio*), faith does (*principio igitur iustificat fides, quae regenerat*). See Melanchthon, *Disputatio*, 252–253. For more on the disputation, see Johannes Haussleiter, "Melanchthons Loci praecipui und Thesen über die Rechtfertigung aus dem Jahre 1531," in *Abhandlungen Alexander von Oettingen zum siebenzigsten Geburstag* (München: C. H. Beck'sche Verlagsbuchhandlung 1898).

[40] *BSELK AC*, 63.

[41] *BSELK AC*, 125.

[42] *BSELK AC* IV, 101: "Quid est autem notitia Christi, nisi nosse beneficia Christi, promissiones, quas per evangelium sparsit in mundum? Et haec beneficia nosse, proprie et vere est credere in Christum, credere, quod, quae promisit Deus propter Christum, certo praestet."

[43] *BSELK AC* IV, 304: "...ita fides est non tantum notitia in intellectu, sed etiam fiducia in voluntate, hoc est, et velle et accipere hoc, quod in promissione offertur, videlicet reconciliationem et remissionem peccatorum."

[44] *BSELK AC* IV, 86: "...seu quia sentit (fides), quod Christus sit nobis factus a Deo sapientia, iustitia, sanctificatio et redemptio."

[45] *BSELK AC* IV, 113–116.

the extrinsic and relational character of justification, as is apparent in the sections using forensic-declaratory language.[46]

To summarize, justifying faith means 'assent', 'desire' and 'reception' of God's mercy in the promises of the Gospel in AC. These affects are effects of the Holy Spirit, which free a sinner from the captivity of death and make him alive. While Melanchthon indicated that he wants to exclude love and works from justification, his main soteriological theme,[47] it is obvious that justification is also an effective act of God. The solution in AC is thus the same as it was in CA. AC does not mention the presence of Christ in faith, although faith clearly means divine activity in man. Both of Melanchthon's texts in BC depict justification as both forensic and effective. Justification means some sort of renovation, not merely imputation. One who has been justified and who has received the promise of forgiveness of sins is also made capable of good works and love (*renovatio*$_1$). The active love (*renovatio*$_2$), however, does not justify, only faith does.[48]

3.3. *Justification as Imputation in the* Commentary on Romans

Johannes Brenz's view on the effective presence of Christ caused Melanchthon to reconsider his theology soon after AC. The idea of change in the context of justification seemed particularly suspect.[49] Melanchthon saw a danger of backsliding to the scholastic teaching that a person is justified to the extent that grace renews him or her.[50] Melanchthon

---

[46] *BSELK AC* IV, 252, 305. See also Seils, *Glaube*, pp. 116–119; Wenz, *Theologie der Bekenntnischriften*, pp. 141–147; *BSELK AC* IV, 74–77, 147–148.

[47] *BSELK AC* IV, 74.

[48] *BSELK AC* IV, 292–294; XII, 36–38.

[49] Greschat, *Melanchthon*, p. 118; Ritschl, *Dogmengeschichte des Protestantismus* II, p. 247. The German edition of *CA* (1530) emphasizes imputation more. *CR* 26, 552–553. So also *CA Variata* 1533. (*CR* 26, 726–728.) On Melanchthon's changes in the articles of justification in *CA* and *AC*, see Christian Peters, *Apologia Confessionis Augustanae. Untersuchungen zur Textgeschichte einer lutherischen Bekenntnisschrift* (1530–1584) (Stuttgart: Calwer Verlag 1997); Flogaus, "Luther versus Melanchthon?", pp. 24–27.

[50] Brenz explained his ideas in a letter which has since vanished. Melanchthon, however, answered him in 1532 in a letter that provides some information on Brenz's views. However, it must be noted that Melanchthon does not necessarily criticize Brenz's true position. For example, Brecht (*Die Frühe Theologie*, p. 241) states that there is no reason for accusations on the grounds of Brenz's other writings. Generally, the doctrine condemned was not necessarily taught explicitly. There were enough reasons

interpreted Brenz to mean that faith is an effective reality which is the fountain and root (*radix*) of good works. In addition, an individual is justified on the grounds of fulfilling the Law, which is caused by the Spirit.[51] Melanchthon does not deny that all of this is God's work in the person. However, if justification and obedience to the Law are linked too closely with each other, it could be possible that the progress of renewal stands out as the pledge of salvation. A more correct way to put it would be: "faith justifies, not because it is the new work of the Holy Spirit in us, but because it apprehends Christ, for the sake of whom we are pleasing, not because of the gifts of the Holy Spirit."[52]

Interestingly, Luther also added an appendix to Melanchthon's letter, where he advised Brenz as follows:

> And I, dear Brenz, in order to get a better grip on this issue, frequently imagine it this way: as if in my heart there is no quality that is called faith or charity, but instead of them I put Christ himself and say: this is my righteousness; He is the quality and my formal righteousness (*iustitia formalis*), as they call it. In this way I free myself from the perception of the law and works, and even from the perception of this object, Christ, who is understood as a teacher or a giver; but I want Him to be my gift and teaching in Himself, so that I may have all things in Him. So he says: I am the way, the truth and the life. He does not say: I give you the way, the truth and the life, as if He worked in me while being placed outside of me. He must be such things in me, remain in me, live in me, speak not through me but into me, 2 Cor. 5; so that we may be righteousness in Him, not in love or in gifts that follow.[53]

---

for condemnation if one could doubt the consequences of particular teachings, as happened in the Osiandrian and Flacian controversies. On Melanchthon's and Brenz's correspondence, see Brecht, *Die Frühe Theologie*, pp. 241–247. See also Green, *How Melanchthon helped Luther*, pp. 223–225; Wenz, *Theologie der Bekenntnischriften*, pp. 37–42.

[51] *CR* 2, 501: "Deinde imaginatur, nos iustos reputari propter hanc impletionem legis, quam efficit in nobis spiritus sanctus. Sic tu imaginaris, fide iustificari homines, quia fide accipiamus Spiritum Sanctum, ut postea iusti esse possimus impletione legis, quam efficit spiritus sanctus.... Ideo sola fide sumus iusti, non quia sit radix, ut tu scribis, sed quia apprehendit Christum, propter quem sumus accepti, qualis sit illa novitas, etsi necessario sequi debet, sed non pacificat conscientiam." Compare *MW* V, 40–41 (*Römerbrief*).

[52] *CR* 2, 502: "Fides enim iustificat, non quia est novum opus Spiritus S. in nobis, sed quia apprehendit Christum, propter quem sumus accepti, non propter dona Spiritus sancti in nobis."

[53] *CR* 2, 502: "Et ego soleo mi Brenti, ut hanc rem melius capiam, sic imaginari, quasi nulla sit in corde meo qualitas, quae fides vel charitas vocetur, sed in loco ipsorum pono ipsum Christum et dico: haec est iustitia mea: ipse qualitas et formalis, ut vocant, iustitia mea, ut sic me liberem ab intuitu legis et operum; imo et ab intuitu

Both Luther's and Melanchthon's answers are broadly similar. Both stress apprehending Christ and his righteousness in faith. In addition, both deny that consequent gifts, such as good works or love, belong to the righteousness that avails *coram Deo*. It is, however, interesting that the letter has been quoted both in favor and against the unity of the Reformers.[54] It is evident that their answers are not contradictory. Melanchthon, however, speaks in general about apprehending Christ (*apprehendere Christum*) as the content of the faith, whereas Luther goes further and claims that Christ is *iustitia formalis*. While Melanchthon says only *what* is included in the evangelical doctrine of justification, Luther speaks about *how* righteousness is actualized in the believer. Luther answers that it is not through spatial extrinsicness but through Christ present in faith.[55]

The essential difference between the Reformers is *how* the apprehension of Christ is considered righteousness. Melanchthon does not address this question in the Brenz letter, but his answer can be read from other contemporary sources. His *Commentary on Romans* (1532) is

objecti istius, Christi, qui vel doctor vel donator intelligitur; sed volo ipsum mihi esse donum et doctrinam per se, ut omnia in ipso habeam. Sic dicit: ego sum via, veritas et vita. Non dicit: ego do tibi viam, veritatem et vitam, quasi extra me positus operetur in me. Talia in me debet esse, manere, et vivere, loqui non per me an *eis* me. 2. Cor. 5: ut essemus iustitia in illo, non: in dilectione aut donis sequentibus."

[54] According to Timothy Wengert, this demonstrates that Luther and Melanchthon differed in the matter of language, not content. See Wengert, "Melanchthon and Luther", p. 69: "Whatever the consequences of these differences may have been for later theology, it was clear that both represented acceptable approaches to the issue and united the reformers against those who would turn Christians either inward in a search for qualities worked by the Holy Spirit or outward to the law or Christ's extrinsic work." Wenz (*Theologie der Bekenntnischriften*, pp. 48–50) sees the letter as a testimony of their "beautiful unity in the doctrine of justification". See also Flogaus, "Luther versus Melanchthon?", pp. 23–24; Wilhelm Pauck, "Luther und Melachthon" in *Luther und Melachthon. Referate und Berichte des Zweiten Internationalen Kongresses für Lutherforschung Münster*, 8.–13. August 1960, hrsgb. Vilmos Vajta (Göttingen: Vandenhoeck & Ruprecht 1961), pp. 21–22.

[55] Luther's response underlines the importance of *renovatio*$_f$. Christ exerts influence from the inside, not from the outside. Moreover, this presence is not an object of observation, and it does not function as the basis for certainty of salvation since Luther declares he will keep himself from thinking of the qualities of faith and love. Instead, he bases his trust on the promise that Christ Himself gives, not only new qualities.

especially interesting in this respect.[56] Melanchthon defines justification in his commentary as an extrinsic act of imputation.[57]

> 'To justify' means primarily reckoning righteous, i.e., an acceptation through imputation. It is understood as a matter of relation (*relative*), as justification was used in Hebrew public forums, which means pronouncing righteous, as if someone should say: "The people of Rome justified Scipio, who was accused by the tribunal, i.e., they pronounced him just, absolved him, approved him." Although it is necessary that the new movements will occur in those who are reconciled, justification does not, however, mean having new virtues. It is understood as a matter of relation (*relative*), which refers to God's will of those who are approved and accepted by God.[58]

More clearly than any of his previous works, Melanchthon's *Commentary* defines justification as fixing the relation between the individual and God. The imputation of God's righteousness means acceptance by God. This acceptance is opposed to human qualities, virtues, and infused habits.[59] 'Believing' (*credere*) and 'doing' (*facere*) are mutually exclusive

---

[56] Brenz's view is clearly closer to Luther than Melanchthon. In his appendix, Luther "gives in" to Brenz and affirms his views on the presence of Christ, although he gives additional advice to Brenz not to observe the presence. See also Brecht, *Die Frühe Theologie*, p. 243. Since the original letter by Brenz is missing, scholars should not draw overly dramatic conclusions premised on Melanchthon and Luther's letter alone. The other reformers had already discussed the letter. In *Tabletalks* (*WA TR* 3, 180–181), there is an interesting note by Conrad Cordatus (1476–1546), who thinks that the appendix was also written by Melanchthon, and who frowns on the emphasis on renewal. Cordatus, hence, is more Lutheran than Luther himself.

[57] Maurer (*Der Junge Melanchthon*, p. 338) claims that Melanchthon intruduces forensic terminology, such as *reputari* and *imputatio*, in his early *Commentary on Romans* (1520–1521). See also Hägglund, *Rechtfertigung*, p. 319. However, the case may be that Melanchthon merely repeats the language of the Vulgate. Green (*How Melanchthon helped Luther*, p. 205) has found similar terminology in the earliest drafts of *Loci* in 1519. These may be borrowed from Erasmus's *Novum Instrumentum omne* (1516), in which he suggests that *imputatum est* may be a proper translation for Greek λογίζεσθαι. However, the mere use of *imputare* does not indicate forensic ontology. For example, Aquinas (*Summa*, I–II 113 a 2) uses imputation to refer to the infusion of habit.

[58] *MW* V, 39 (*Römerbrief*): "'Iustificari' proprie significat iustum reputari, h.e. acceptum reputari. Sic intelligitur relative, sicut in foro usurpatur Hebraica consuetudine iustificari pro eo, quod est iustum pronuntiari, ut si quis dicat: Populus Romanus iustificavit Scipionem accusatum a tribuno plebis, h.e. iustum pronuntiavit, absolvit, approbabit. Quamquam autem novos motus exsistere in his, qui reconciliantur, necesse est, tamen iustificari non significat proprie habere novas virtutes. Sed relative intelligatur de voluntate Dei pro eo, quod est approbari seu acceptari a Deo."

[59] *MW* V, 135 (*Römerbrief*): "Iustificatio est remissio peccatorum, est non-imputatio peccati, est reconciliatio seu acceptatio, qua Deo per misericordiam, non propter nostras virtutes, accepti sumus." *MW* V, 132: (*Römerbrief*) "Deinde Paulus enarrat et agitat verbum 'imputandi' et dialectice definit iustificationem, quod videlicet 'iustificatio'

ways to depict receiving the gift of salvation. 'Doing' means an accidental quality as well as an actual good work for Melanchthon, which could function as a basis for justification. 'Believing' means receiving the grace promised in Christ.[60]

What has changed since *Loci* 1521? Justification is now described clearly as a single unit, or phase, of salvation, which does not include intrinsic renewal of the faculties of the mind. Melanchthon's *Commentary* is thus representative of a purely forensic doctrine of justification.

Despite this demarcation, the depiction of God's salvific act remains similar to *Loci* 1521 and his confessional documents (CA, AC). On the one hand, faith is primarily trust in God's mercy, and is depicted instrumentally,[61] which secures consolation for consciences and prevents the danger of self-righteousness. This leads Melanchthon to emphasize the relational aspect of justification. On the other hand, relational renewal is related to affectual renewal, apparent in his interpretation of Romans 5:5—Paul's notion of 'God's love infused in our hearts'. According to Melanchthon this love is not our love of God, i.e., a human faculty, but God's love for us. This love is comprehended and experienced (*agnoscitur et sentitur*) as the feeling of consolation (*consolatio*).[62]

From *Commentary on Romans* onwards Melanchthon explicitly adds vivification (*vivificatio*), which finds its expressions in felt joy and peace along with justification, as one of the effects of faith. Faith effects imputation but imputation coheres with intrinsic Spirit-evoked affects: peace (*pax*), joy (*gaudium*), and life (*vita*).[63] The infusion of God's love means the renewal of the affects and the birth of the affect of faith,

---

significat non qualitatem aut virtutem in nobis aut infusionem habitus, sed relative acceptationem, qua gratis per misericordiam a Deo reputamur iusti."

[60] *MW* V, 270–271 (*Römerbrief*): "Antithesis est harum partium 'facere' et 'credere'. 'Facere' significat non solum opus nostrum, sed etiam qualitatem in nobis. Econtra 'credere' seu apprehendere verbum est accipere miseriacordiam, quae offertur propter Christum, h. e. est sentire, quod accepti simus non propter aliquam nostram qualitatem aut opus, sed per misericordiam propter Christum."

[61] *MW* V, 40–41 (*Römerbrief*).

[62] *MW* V, 166 (*Römerbrief*): "Nam 'dilectio Dei' significat dilectionem, qua Deus nos diligit. Haec effunditur in corda nostra, h.e. in consolatione agnoscitur et sentitur."

[63] *MW* V, 66 (*Römerbrief*): "...duo enim tribuit fidei, videlicet iustificationem et vivificationem. Fide iusti pronuntiamur et fide vivificamur, quia fides, dum consolatur corda et erigit conscientias, dum erigit credit peccata remitti et Deum esse placatum propter Christum, affert pacem, gaudium et vitam animis, sicut infra dicitur: 'iustificati ex fide pacem habemus'."

which actually enables the other affects. Knowing God's grace results in joy and peace.[64]

Without the Holy Spirit both intellect and will are incapacitated in knowing God.[65] The prerequisite for the affect of justifying faith is therefore the donation of the Spirit.[66] Justification and donation are, however, consequential.[67] Even though both the favor (*gratia*) and the gift (*donum* i.e. the Spirit) are given and received simultaneously (*simul*) through the Gospel,[68] Melanchthon still explicitly denies that *donum* belongs to justification. While *donum* signifies qualitative renewal by the

---

[64] *MW* V, 166 (*Römerbrief*): "Ac plane desperandum est, si nostra dilectio esset causa spei, cum diligere non possimus, nisi prius fide apprehendimus misericordiam." *MW* V, 167 (*Römerbrief*): "'Dilectio Dei effusa est est in cordibus nostris', sc. in ipso actu spei aut fidei. Et discimus ex his locis, quos motus pariat spiritus sanctus in piis, sc. fidem et spem; et in his ipsis motibus concipitur gaudium et pax conscientiae, cum agnoscitur bonitas et misericordia."

[65] *MW* V, 232 (*Römerbrief*): "'Secundum carnem esse' est non habere spiritum sanctum, sed tantum uti naturalibus viribus, non solum sensu, sed etiam ratione. 'Sapere secumdum carnem' significat non solum appetitum sensitivum seu beluinum, sed etiam superiora, videlicet cogitationem rationis et appetitum rationalem. Complectitur enim Paulus λόγον και ὁρμήν, notitiam et appetitum.... Nec intelligunt spiritualia nec appetunt spirituali, i.e. non vere norunt Deum, h.e. non statuunt, quod Deus nos rescipiat, quod irascatur peccatis, quod misearetur." See also *MW* V, 233 (*Römerbrief*).

[66] *MW* V, 226 (*Römerbrief*): "Gubernatio spiritus, quae vivificat apprehenso Christo, i.e. fides in Christum, liberat me a lege peccati et mortis..." *MW* V, 233 (*Römerbrief*): "Sensus spiritus est vita est pax", i.e. fides, quam in corde afficit spiritus sanctus, vivificat et consolatur cor in iudicio Dei, sicut et Christus docet: "Qui credit in me, non morietur", item: "Haec est vita aeterna, ut et cognoscant Deum verum et, quem misisti, Iesum Christum." *MW* V, 290 (*Römerbrief*): "...opera spiritualia cordis et affectus spiritus sancti in corde, videlicet omnia opera decalogi: timor Dei, credere Deo, invocatio, gratiarum actio, confessio..."

[67] *MW* V, 334–335 (*Römerbrief*): "Faciam igitur docendi causa quattuor gradus libertatis christianae. Primus gradus est, quod a peccato et a morte aeterna liberamur ita, quod non propter legem aut virtutes nostras, sed gratis per misericordiam propter Christum donantur nobis remissio peccatorum, imputatio iustitiae et vita aeterna, modo ut credamus haec nobis contingere propter Christum. De hoc gradu contionatur in evangelio Christus: 'Si vos filius liberaverit, vere liberi eritis.' Secundus gradus est, quod donatur nobis spiritus sanctus, qui nos adiuvet, ut legi oboedire possimus, qui gubernet et defendat nos adversus insidias diaboli. Hic gradus ita cum superiore coniunctas est ut non possit ab eo divelli." This passage may indicate logical consequence, but here Melanchthon explains four different aspects of Christian freedom (freedom from sin and eternal death, God's guidance and help, freedom from the Old Testament cult Law, and freedom from outward actions that appear as conditions for salvation). Additionally, Melanchthon emphasizes the inseparability of the first two aspects.

[68] *MW* V, 185 (*Römerbrief*): "Et complectitur gratia haec duo: remissionem peccatorum et imputationem iustitiae. 'Donum per gratiam' significat donationem spiritus sancti et vitae aeternae. Nam evangelium simul offert in remissione peccatorum spiritum sanctum, qui quidem fide accipitur, et, dum erigit et consolatur conscientiam, parit novos motus et novam vitam."

Spirit, the renewal is not perfect, and is unable to offer a foundation for certainty of salvation as *gratia* does.[69]

What of christology in this respect? For Melanchthon, justification does not take place through participation in Christ even as Christ is the object of the affect of faith. Melanchthon can certainly speak about 'having Christ' (*habere*) but this simply indicates belief in Christ, not participation.[70] The connection with Christ occurs as participation in the Holy Spirit.[71] Christ is present only as the object of the intellect, as is apparent, for example, in Melanchthon's interpretation of Romans 13:14.

> Therefore we interpret it this way "Clothe yourselves with Jesus Christ," i.e., the knowledge of Christ, faith and hope. 'Clothing' metaphorically means apprehending (*apprehendere*), and apprehending means knowing (*agnoscere*) Christ.[72]

While apprehending Christ is an act of intellect, apprehension alone is unable to justify. The individual must trust in the Gospel, which is a matter of will. Here lies the basic problem of Melanchthon's *Commentary*: his theory of the will forces him to emphasize affectual renewal and simultaneously deny the role of renewal within justification in order to prevent amalgamation of the righteousness of faith with good works.

---

[69] *MW* V, 186 (*Römerbrief*): "Ideoque Paulus diserte separat 'gratiam', h.e. acceptationem a 'dono'; testatur nos habere propter Christum non modo donum, sed etiam gratiam, et quidem non propter nostram perfectionem, sed propter Christum."

[70] *MW* V, 266–267 (*Römerbrief*): "...qui habet Christum seu qui credit in Christo, est iustus et hoc, quod lex postulat, habet imputative, h.e. reputatur iustus, etsi re ipsa non satisfecit legi. Quidam exponunt effective: Christus est consummatio legis, i.e. dat spiritum sanctum ad faciendam legem.—Haec interpretatio, etsi vera est, tamen hic est intempestiva, quia non reputamur iusti propterea, quod non legem faciamus, sed propter Christum fide." On Melanchthon's difficulty in speaking about change in the context of justification, see also *MW* V, 266–267 n. 32 (*Römerbrief*).

[71] *MW* V, 235 (*Römerbrief*): "'Si Christus in nobis est, corpus mortuum est', i.e., si Christus per spiritum sanctum in nobis est, corpus mortuum est, i.e. mortificatur." Luther, typically, describes *unio cum Deo* as union with Christ, which takes place in Christ. In addition, the Holy Spirit renews the sinner for good works. See Kärkkäinen, *Luthers trinitarische Theologie*, pp. 107–112; Peura, *Mehr als ein Mensch?*, pp. 204–211. Melanchthon never mentions union with Christ in any other than cognitive sense. Union with God is markedly pneumatological albeit the text under examination suggests christological communion. See *MW* V, 200–204, 236–237 (*Römerbrief*).

[72] *MW* V, 330 (*Römerbrief*): "Quare sic interpretabimur: 'Induere Christum', h.e. notitiam Christi, fidem et spem. Nam 'induere' metaphorice significat apprehendere, apprehendere autem est agnoscere Christum." Johannes Gerhard uses the term *induitio* but gives it effective and unifying meaning. See Martti Vaahtoranta, *Restauratio imaginis divinae. Die Vereinigung von Gott und Mensch ihre Voraussetzungen und Implikationen bei Johann Gerhard* (Helsinki: Schriften der Luther-Agricola-Gesellschaft 41, 1998), pp. 249–267.

In the *Commentary* the two main soteriological concepts are the Gospel (*evangelium*) and faith (*fides*). While these justify the believer, on whom the righteousness of Christ is imputed, they also produce new life in the believer. Although Melanchthon tries to dissociate justification conceptually from all types of renewal, he still depicts justification as an event parallel to affectual renewal. The act of the individual's salvation flows from the affect of faith, which has imputation as *one* of its effects. Melanchthon depicts justification as a relational act of declaration that still takes place in the effective context. Justification is the consequence of affectual renewal. The demarcation between this renewal (*renovatio*$_I$) and justification is the most significant difference from his earlier works. Interestingly, *renovatio*$_I$ is not depicted as the consequence but as the parallel, or contextual, event of justification.

The *Commentary on Romans* formulates the concept of 'justification' more strictly, but the event of salvation as a whole is described in ways similar to Melanchthon's earlier works.[73] Even if the change is only conceptual, this still opens up a new possibility of interpreting the relation between the individual and God, without the unitive aspect.

3.4. *Justification as Imputation and Donation of the Spirit in the Later Works*

Melanchthon was not satisfied with his definition of justification in the *Commentary on Romans*. His writings during and after the Osiandrian controversy (1550–1553) consider the intrinsic aspect of justification more extensively.[74] The basic ideas, which had already appeared in *Loci* 1521, find their culmination in these texts. Andreas Osiander brought the *unio cum Christo* theme back in to the discussion by claiming that

---

[73] Thus also Hägglund (*Rechtfertigung*, p. 319): "Es ist die Terminologie—vor allem der Begriff justificatio—die umgeprägt wird; das Geschehen selbst—das initium des Christenlebens, die Erneurung des Glaubens—wird aber in anderen Zusammenhängen bei dem späteren Melanchthon in ähnlicher Weise beschrieben wie bei dem früheren. Aus besonderen Gründen hat er den Begriff *justificatio* anders gedeutet, aber damit meint er nur, eine logische Distinktion zu machen, und zwar eine Distinktion, die auch theologisch notwendig sei. Die Sache, das, was geschieht, wenn ein Mensch gerechtfertigt wird, hat er nicht anders aufgefast als vorher."

[74] Osiander cannot be considered as the reason for change in Melanchthon's thought. The "merely forensic" period, starting from the *Commentary on Romans*, does not last long. The *Loci secundae aetas* of 1535 speaks about donation of the Spirit within justification. See, e.g., *CR* 21, 421–425.

Melanchthon had removed concept of 'indwelling' from justification. Osiander stressed against Melanchthon that God's essential righteousness, or more precisely Christ's divine nature, is the substance of righteousness of faith.[75]

In his response to Osiander, (*Antwort auff das Buch Herrn Andreae Osiandri*, 1552), Melanchthon stated that there is no disagreement regarding God's presence in the believer.[76] When a person is forgiven through faith in Christ, God simultaneously makes the heart of the believer His dwelling place. This indwelling is felt as consolation (*trost*), which frees one from the fear of God's judgment (*angst*).[77] The Gospel simultaneously offers both the favor (*gratia*), meaning forgiveness of sin, and the gift (*donum*), meaning divine presence. No temporal and logical difference is indicated.[78] Melanchthon, however, considers it erroneous to say that one is justified *only* through God's essential righteousness. He does not deny the role of *donum* in justification, as in his *Commentary on Romans*,

---

[75] On Osiander, see section 4.1.

[76] *MW* VI, 456 (*Antwort*): "Von diser gegenwertigkeit saget Osiander, davon zwischen uns kein streit ist, und beschweret unsere Kirchen gleich, als reden sie nichts von der gegenwertigkeit Gottes in uns, daran er uns offentlich unrecht thut." See also Erikson, *Inhabitatio*, 88–95. Flogaus, "Luther versus Melanchton?", 40–41.

[77] *MW* VI, 458 (*Antwort*): "Welches alles muss also verstanden werden, das wir vergebung der sünden haben, und angenem sind vor Gott durch den verdienst Christi, so wir mit warhafftigem glauben den Herrn Christum annemen und gleuben, das uns gnädig sein wölle, und ist zugleich war, das als denn Gott in uns wohnet, so wir durch diesen trost aus rechter angst erret werden."

[78] *MW* VI, 454 (*Antwort*): "S. Paulus spricht Rom. 5. Die gnade Gottes und die Gabe durch die liebe gegen einem Menschen Jhesu Christo ist gegen vielen mechtiger gewesen denn die Sünd. Hie fasset S. Paulus zwey ding. Die gnade, das ist die gnedige vergebung der sünden und annemung unser person bei Gott. Und zugleich wird mit gegeben die Gabe, das ist die göttliche gegenwertigkeit in uns, dadurch wir verneuet werden und fülen trost und anfang des Ewigen lebens. Uns diese beide haben wir durch das verdienst Jhesu Christi, wie dieser Text offentlich saget, das wir solchs haben von wegen der liebe, die der ewige Vater zu disem Son hatt, welchen S. Paulus hie nennet den Menschen Jhesum Christum, und wird solches nicht durch unsere werck verdienet, sondern allein durch glauben an den Herrn Jhesum Christum erlanget, welcher glaube in uns in rechter bekerung angezundet wird, so wir das Evangelium hören, damit der herr Christus selbs wircket. Denn Gott wird durch sein ewiges Wort und den Heiligen Geist geoffenbaret." *MW* VI, 455 (*Antwort*): "Und dieser glaube mus für und für beides annemen und behalten, Gratiam et donum umb des mittlers Christi willen, auch wenn gleich die wiedergeburt angefangen ist." Grace can be interpreted as the enabler of the event of salvation, although grace as forgiveness is actualized in the gift, which renews the individual. While Melanchthon stresses the forgiveness of sins, grace without the gift clearly is only unactualized potentiality.

but teaches their internal connectivity. However, the most essential thing is the apprehension of forgiveness of sins, which Osiander omitted.[79]

> Now Osiander says: "I call that righteousness, which makes us do good." In these words, there is no word of forgiveness. Instead, we put it like this: "We call righteousness the Lord Christ, through whom we have forgiveness and merciful God, and even the divine presence in us, as Paul says in his speech Rom. 3 "we are justified freely by Christ's grace, whom God had set forth to be the propitiation through faith in his blood," and Isaiah 53: "by his knowledge shall my righteous servant justify many." Here, without a doubt, both favor and gift are mentioned, as it was said before.[80]

Although Melanchthon previously tried to define justification only as imputation, he still understood justification in effective terms since faith is the product of the renewal of the Holy Spirit, an idea advanced in his *Response to Osiander*. Both the favor and the gift belong to justification, and justification includes not only a relational aspect but also God's real presence in the believer. In contrast to his *Commentary on Romans*, justification is here depicted as a more effective event.

However, Melanchthon's interpretation of efficacy does differ from Luther's despite the apparent semantic identity. Melanchthon wrote several late texts in which he defines justification in christological language

---

[79] *MW* VI, 457 (*Antwort*): "Und kan im Wort 'wir werden gerecht' nicht allein dieser verstand sein, wir werden gerecht durch die wesentliche gerechtigkeit des Vaters, Sons und heiligen Geists, sondern wir müssen vergebung der Sünd und gnad mit fassen und den verdienst des Sons, der da ist zum Erlöser gestalt, unterscheiden vom Vater und heiligen Geist." Melanchthon had stated in a letter to Staphylus (1.3.1551) that regarding Osiander "man kann folgende Formel zugestehen: Wir werden gerecht durch das Verdienst und die wesentliche Gerechtigkeit des Sohnes, die in uns die Gerechtigkeit bewirken." Melanchthon only occasionally speaks about the essential righteousness of the Son as the righteousness of faith. This quote may thus seem surprising, since it claims that the essential righteousness is not actualized in faith since this righteousness *effects* righteousness in the individual. This is apparent in: "Osiander bemüht sich nicht um das Stückchen 'extra nos'. Es ist zwar zuzugestehen, dass der Sohn Gottes in den Heiligen wohnt, gemäss vieler Sprüche, aber Luther sagt; extra nos, d.h. unsere Gerechtigkeit ist nicht unsere Qualität, sondern wird ausserhalb unser bewirkt." For the letter in its entirety, see Stupperich, *Osiander in Preussen*, p. 184. See also *AO* 9, 674, 7–14 (*Melanchthon an Osiander*).

[80] *MW* VI, 458 (*Antwort*): "Nu spricht Osiander offt also: Ich heisse gerechtigkeit dieses, das uns macht recht thun. In diesen worten ist nichts geredt von vergebung der sünden. Dagegen sagen wir also: Wir nennen gerechtigkeit den Herrn Christum, dadurch wir haben vergebung der sünden und einen gnedigen Gott, und dazu in uns Göttliche gegenwertigkeit, welches alles S. Paulus fasset in seinem heubtspruch Rom. 3. 'Justificamur gratis per gratiam Christi, quem proposuit propitiatorem fide per sanguinem'. etc. Und Esa. 53. 'Und mein knecht, der gerechte, wird durch seine erkentnus viel gerecht machen', hie fasset et on zweifel beides, gratiam et donum, wir droben gesaget ist."

similar to Luther's. For example, *Confessio Saxonica* (1551) describes how faith receives Christ, who is the righteousness of the Christian.

> Justification means the unrighteous becoming righteous, which this explanation tries to describe correctly. The unrighteous, i.e., guilty and disobedient and without Christ, become righteous, i.e., free from guilt for the sake of the Son of God, apprehending in faith Christ himself, who is our righteousness as Jeremiah and Paul say, because He is our righteousness for whose sake we are reckoned righteous, and because He makes us alive and regenerates us by the Holy Spirit. As it is said in John 5: "This is the life in his Son. Who has the Son, has the life. Who does not have the Son, does not have the life", and Romans 3: "that he might be just, and would justify the sinner."
>
> Even if renewal starts simultaneously, we do not, however, call a person righteous in this life for the sake of new qualities, but for the sake of the Mediator, who has suffered and risen; who rules, prays for us, and makes us alive.[81]

Melanchthon later describes justification from the Trinitarian point of view, defining particular functions for each divine Person. God's real presence has now a more central place in these texts. *Explicatio symboli niceni* (1561), for example, defines justification as follows.

> Two gifts are also mentioned. The favor and the gift through the favor, and the mode of their reception is formulated. The beginning relates to hearing the Gospel, while the voice of the Gospel makes us alive in conversion. These things take place simultaneously. The Father loves us,

[81] *MW* VI, 99–100 (*Saxonica*): "In declaratione vocabuli Iustificari usitate dicitur: iustificari significat ex iniusto iustum fieri, quod recte intellectum hic quoque quadrat. Ex iniusto, id est reo et inobediente et non habente Christum, fieri iustum, id est absolutum a reatu propter Filium Dei, et apprehendentem fide ipsum Christum, qui est iusticia nostra, ut dicunt Ieremias et Paulus, quia est iusticia nobis imputatur et propter eum iusti reputamur, et quia dato Spiritu suo sancto nos vivificat et regenerat, sicut et Ioh. 5. Dicitur, 'Haec est vita in Filio eius. Qui habet Filium, habet vitam. Qui non habet Filium, vitam non habet.' Et Ro 3: 'Ut sit ipse iustus et iustificans impium.' Quanquam autem simul inchoatur novitas, tamen non dicimus personam iustam esse in hac vita propter novas qualitates, sed propter ipsum mediatorem passum, resuscitatum, regnantem, deprecantem pro nobis, nos obumbrantem et vivificantem. Et quanquam sunt inchoatae virtutes, tamen adhuc sunt imperfectae et haerent in nobis reliquiae peccati. Ideo tenenda est haec consolatio, placere personam propter Filium Dei, imputata nobis ipsius iustitia, sicut Rom. 4. Dicitur, 'Credidit Abraham Deo, et imputatum est ei ad iustitiam.' Item 'Beati quorum remissae sunt iniquitates et quorum tecta sut peccata.' Itaque et correlative intelligenda est haec oratio: 'Fide iustificamur', hoc est fiducia Filii Dei iustificamur, non propter nostram qualitatem, sed quia ipse est propiciator, in quo cor acquiescit fiducia promissae misericordiae propter eum, quam fiduciam ipse Spiritu suo sancto exuscitat, sicut inquit Paulus, 'Accepistis Spiritum adoptionis filiorum, quo clamamus, Abba Pater.'"

i.e., receives us mercifully for the sake of the Son. The Son consoles our hearts and shows us the mercifulness of the Father and revives the repentant sinners, drawing them out of the sufferings of Hell. The Father infuses the Holy Spirit in the heart through the Son, so that we could have similar movements of the mind as He has; we would rest in God, love and call for him, submit under his command, confess our weakness and ruination, and we would know that we have aid against our weakness and the raging devil by the mercy of God. Against him we ask the help of the present God, as it is said: "I do not rescue you in heavenly arches but in our Lord God, i.e., in the Son, who really is Immanuel, truly present in believers, because he makes us alive and gives us the Holy Spirit through the voice of the Gospel." As it is said in 1. John 4, "Hereby we know that we dwell in him, and he in us, because he has given us of his Spirit."[82]

While Melanchthon speaks about Christ's presence, for him the apprehension of Christ is first and foremost a cognitive event in which the divine Logos illuminates (*illuminat*) the mind through the Gospel. The Word, i.e., the Son, has an informative role; the Word is heard and the mind (*mens*) understands (*cogitabat*) God's love. The Spirit, infused through the Word, takes over control of the will and evokes new movements of the mind. These can be felt (*sentiebant*) as new states of mind.[83]

The presence of the Son occurs in a 'word-event' when the Son as the Word is in the mind (*in mente*) of one who hears the Gospel.[84] The Son is not present through salutary exchange but correlatively, in

[82] *CR* 23, 454 (*Explicatio*): "Hic quoque duo illa beneficia recitantur, Gratia et donum per gratiam, et modus exprimitur, quo accipiuntur. Initium est ab auditu Evangelii, cum in conversione voce evangelii nos sustentamus, simul haec fiunt, Pater diligit nos, id est, percipit consolationem in corde, ostendit misericordiam Patris, et vivificat credentes retractor ex doloribus inferorum, et Pater per eum effundit Spiritum sanctum in corda, ut tales motus habeamus qualis ipse est, laetemur in Deo diligamus et invocemus eum, et nos ei subiiciamus, agnoscamus infirmitatem et pericula nostra, et sciamus nobis immensa misericordia Dei propositum esse auxilium divinum, contra infirmitatem nostram, et contra Diabolorum rabiens. Adversus ista petamus Dei praesentiam, sicut dicitur: Salvabo vos non in arcu, sed in Domino vestro, id est, in Filio, qui vere est Emanuel, vere adest in credentibus, cum voce Evangelii sustentantur, et simul dat Spiritum sanctum: Sic. 1. Joh. 4. dicitur: in hoc sciamus, quod in ipso maneamus, et ipso in nobis, quia de Spiritu suo dat nobis."

[83] *CR* 7, 1068 (*Aurifabro*): "Recte igitur hic ordo cogitatur: cum verbo vocali simul persona, logos, mentem illuminat et effundit spiritum sanctum, qui addidit motus et laetitiam. Ut cum loqueretur in Paradiso filius, foris audiebatur verbum vocale, intus autem mens movebatur τῷ Λόγω, et cogitabat, Deum patrem dicere hanc concolationem et illum loquentem, et deinde sentiebant laetitiam et motus novos."

[84] *CR* 7, 1068 (*Aurifabro*): "In mente mulieris conversae Logos dicit: Deus pater remittit tibi peccata. Hic Logos deinde effundit Spiritum Sanctum, qui laetitiam et novos motus efficit."

a cognitive relation with the understood promise of grace.[85] Christ, as the righteousness of the sinner, is a new state of the intellect.[86] God's real presence occurs through the person of the Holy Spirit.[87] The Spirit is not only information, but an actually present entity in the believer which renews the sinner and produces new affects.[88] Justification as

[85] *CR* 23, 178 (*Catechesis*): "Fide iusti sumus, haec oratio correlative intelligi debet, hoc modo, per misericordiam propter Christum iusti, id est, accepti sumus, non propter nostras virtutes, sed tamen hanc misericordiam oportet fide accipi et apprehendi."

[86] This may result from Melanchthon's understanding of *communicatio idiomatum*, which he takes to mean a rule of grammar that secures correct speech about Christ. The communion of the natures is not as literate as for Luther; for Melanchthon the divine nature is the sustainer of human nature, and human nature is an instrument of God. He sees God's presence in the person of Christ as a special case of God's presence, which basically occurs in the same way as all the other modes of presence with the only expectation that in Christ the mode of presence is forever. The union of the two natures is dialectical without actual ontological communion. See Brandy, *Die späte Christologie*, pp. 30–37. Melanchthon was afraid that the two natutes would be confused. Zwingli and Calvin made a similar accusation against Luther that the humanity of Christ does not remain human. See Albrecht Peters, *Realpräsenz. Luthers Zeugnis von Christi Gegenwart im Abendmal*, Arbeiten zur Geschichte und Theologie des Luthertums, Band V. (Berlin und Hamburg: Lutherisches Verlagshaus 1966), p. 79. Melanchthon's christology did not satisfy Lutherans. For example, pastor J. Bötker attacked his christology, claiming that Melanchthon's Christ is not Bread but only a "breadbasket" (*brottkorb*). See Jörg Baur, "Christologie und Subjektivität. Geschichtlicher Ort und dogmatischer Rang der Christologie der Konkordienformel," in *Einsicht und Glaube. Aufsätze* (Göttingen: Vandenhoeck & Ruprecht 1978c), pp. 193–194; Mahlmann, *Das Neue Dogma*, pp. 75, 119; Reinhold Seeberg, *Lehrbuch der Dogmengeschichte*, IV/2 (Basel: Benno Schwabe & Co.R. 1954), pp. 520–522. The eucharistic christology of the late Melanchthon is illustrated in following passage. *MW* VI, 484 (*Iudicium*): "Non dicit [Paulus], mutari naturam panis, ut Papistae dicunt. Non dicit, ut Bremenses, panem esse substantiale corpus Christi. Non dicit, ut Hesshusius, panem esse verum corpus Christi, sed esse κοινωνίαν, id est hoc, quo sit consociatio cum corpore Christi: quae sit in usu, et quidem non sine cogitatione, ut cum mures panem rodunt."

[87] This is illustrated in *Examen* (1559), where Melanchthon defines the differences between the Trinitarian concepts *nascere* and *genere*. *CR* 23, 3–4: "NASCI est a potentia cognoscente. Quia genitum est imago gignentis. Ut autem in hominibus potentia cognoscens format imagines, et loquitur: Sic Filius est aeterni Patris imago, cogitatione gnota, et est Logos ostendens eum in revelatione Evangelii. Procedere autem est a voluntate, quia Spiritus Sanctus est motor, seu agitator." The birth of the Son from the Father is cognitive action, whereas that of the Spirit belongs to the will. The cognitive nature of the work of the Son is apparent in the passage where Melanchthon explains that the name "Logos" results from the cognitive origins of the Son, and the nature of His salvific work: the son speaks words (λόγον), since He is the Word (Λόγος). The Son consoles (*consolatio*) and infuses the Spirit, who works as *agitator*. The movement of the will follows knowledge (*cogitatio*).

[88] *CR* 23, 369 (*Explicatio*): "Tertius modus est praesentia, qua in hoc mortali vita Deus habitat in Sanctis, qua non solum conservat substantias eorum, sed etiam sanctificat eos non visibiliter, Sed est efficax in eis, quia voce Evangelii Filius accendit in eis novam lucem, et vivificat eos, et effundit in eos Spiritum Sanctum, ut novos motus ipsi congruentes, et laetitiam in eis exuscitet, hanc praesentiam separabilem esse Scriptura

forgiveness of sins and donation of the Spirit is a formulation typical of Melanchthon's late works.[89]

Interestingly, Melanchthon never calls Christ the form of faith as Luther does. Luther used the Aristotelian philosophy of mind—in which the form of an object constitutes the form of the act of knowing—to describe Christ's presence. Melanchthon follows a different theory, in which the form of the object is not transferred to the subject of knowing. Melanchthon's view is close to Luther's adaptation of Aristotle's ideas but is not identical.[90] According to Melanchthon intellect does not receive the form of the object as such but its representation, which is equivalent to its source similar to the way the act of the intellect is identical with its object. The picture of the object in the mind is not the object itself, but represents it.[91] In keeping with this, the object of the faith never truly becomes the form of the faith. The picture—theologically the merit—of Christ is in the mind of the Christian, but not Christ in His person. Since this apprehension always changes its subject, this kind of event is always effective but still unable to justify. For this reason Melanchthon needs the Spirit to take the major role in supplying this deficit. Only the Spirit can renew the affects of the sinner according to the divine life.

affirmat, et tristissimi lapsus Sanctorum ostendunt, et nequaquam est unio hypostatica Filii aut Spiritus sancti cum homine converso seu renato, sed nominatur tantum habitatio Dei in homine converso."

[89] *CR* 23, 449 (*Explicatio*): "IUSTIFICATIO est acceptio remissionis peccatorum, et reconciliationis personae coram Deo, et imputationis iustitiae, et haereditatis vitae aeternae, propter obedientiam Mediatoris, quae acceptio fit fide, consolante et erigente cor in veris doloribus, in qua fit vivificatio per Filium Dei, dicentem consolationem in corde voce Evangelii, et effundentem Spiritum sanctum, quo inchoatur nova obedientia in corde, sicut scriptum est: Dabo Legem meam in corda eorum." *CR* 23, 178, 179 (*Catechesis*). "Et IUSTIFICATIO est remissio peccatorum, et acceptatio coram Deo, cum qua coniuncta est donatio Spiritus sancti.... Tertio necesse est et hoc teneri, quod cum iustificamur, donamur Spiritu sancto, quem ita concipiunt corda, cum audiunt Evangelium, et ei adsentiuntur, ac fide se sustentant in pavoribus. Sic docet Paulus at Galatas: Ut promissionem Spiritus sancti vocatur regeneratio seu renovatio, et est inchoatio vitae aeternae in nobis, sicut Christus inquit: Haec est vita aeterna, ut cognoscant te Deum verum, et quem misisti Iesum Christum." See also *CR* 23, 337, 339 (*Enarratio*); *CR* 23, 17–18 (*Examen*); *MW* VI, 98–99 (*Confessio*); *CR* 23, 651 (*Poenitentia*).

[90] According to Spruit (*Species intelligibilis* II, p. 130), Melanchthon's theory of perception, which cannot be identified with any previous one, constitutes an independent theory of its own.

[91] Melanchthon, *De anima*, 145: "Noticia est mentis actio, qua rem adspicit, quasi formam imaginem rei, quam cogitat. Nec aliud sunt imagines illae seu ideae, nisi actus intelligendi."

One of Melanchthon's most important late works, *Liber de anima* (1553), gives a clear account of the relationship between justification and the renewal of the affects.[92] This work, which concentrates on the doctrine of the soul from a theological point of view, defines the individual as the creation of God. The individual's highest goal is knowledge of God, and the doctrine of the soul serves the purpose of attaining this goal.[93] According to Melanchthon, the functions of the soul are based on entities known as the vital spirits (*spiritus vitales*), which, in effect, mean affects.[94] In the original state, *imago Dei* was constituted by the right ordering of the faculties of the mind.[95] The right disposition of

---

[92] Melanchthon's *Liber de anima* is an augmented edition of his *Commentarius de Anima*, which was a commentary on Aristotle's *De anima. Liber de Anima* contains psychological, medical, and theological material, which Melanchthon tries to synthesize.

[93] Günter Frank, "Melanchthons 'Liber de anima' und die Etablierung der frühneuzeitlichen Anthropologie," in *Humanismus und Wittenberger Reformation*, hrsgb. Michael Beyer et al. (Leipzip: Evangelische Verlagsanstalt 1996), p. 324. Melanchthon's theological anthropology does not actually distinguish between body and soul. A human being is an holistic entity of desires; the lower desires govern the bodily needs, and higher desires, such as intellect and will, minister to the spiritual plane. See also Hägglund, Rechtfertigung, 191; Dino Bellucci, *Science de la Nature et Réformation. La physique au service de la Réforme dans l'enseignement de Philippe Mélanchthon* (Roma: Edizioni Vivere 1998), pp. 606–612.

[94] The doctrine of the vital spirits was the standard medical explanation of the functions of the body and soul. The concept originates from Galen, but he does not articulate it as a doctrine. Arabian philosophers later furthered the notion, and it found its way into the medieval theology. The balance of the spirits guarantees the health of the human being. On this, see Ruth Harvey, *The inward wits. Psychological theory in the middle ages and the renaissance*, Warburg Institute Surveys VI (London: The Warburg Institute 1975), pp. 4–30. Melanchthon applies the same system to theology. *CR* 13, 8. (*De anima*): "Praetera spiritus vitales in homine, nascuntur in corde, et vere sunt flammae, quae in omnium adfectuum incendiis, in laeticia, dolore, amore, odio, ira, et aliis, sparguntur. Et cum motibus voluntatis non simulatis hae flammae in corde congruunt. Ex hac umbra utcunque cogitamus de nomine Spiritus sancti, et discimus ei hanc appellationem in divinis literis tribui, quia sit agitator, et quasi flamma, a voluntate Patris et Filii procedens, qua divinitas immensa bonitate nos sibi copulat et nos leticia complet, sicut effundit mater vitales spiritus osculans infantem filium aut filiam. Haec vocabulorom interpretatio sobrie et pie considerata de multis magnis rebus studiosus admonet." *CR* 13, 88 (*De anima*): "Spiritus vitalis est flammula ex purissimo sanguine in corde nata, calorem vitalem devehens ad coetera membra, et impertiens eis vim exercendi actiones, quas calore vitali efficiunt. Ad hunc usum supra dictum est arterias esse conditas, ut hunc spiritum in omnia membra transvehant."

[95] *CR* 13, 71 (*De anima*): "Nomino igitur imaginem Dei potentias animae, sed lucente in eis Deo." According to Frank ("Melanchthons 'Liber de anima'", pp. 323–5), Melanchthon considers the soul as a picture of God, *exemplum Dei*, and this likeness enables participation in divine things. Melanchthon, however, considered the distinction between the Law and the Gospel, and philosophy and theology of great importance. Does the doctrine of the vital spirit belong to philosophy or theology? Are the spirits used to explain the birth of good works or the birth of faith? On the importance of

the spirits was sustained by God, who ruled the individual by evoking movements of the mind that are according to His nature.[96] Thus God dwelled in *imago Dei*, and sustained the state of bliss.[97] The presence of the Spirit was not only real, but also physical:

> ...and [the vital spirits] exceed the sun with their light, and the light of all the stars, and even more miraculously, in the case of the pious the divine Spirit is mixed (*miscetur*) with these spirits, which makes them shine even more brightly with the divine light, so that their knowledge of God would be even clearer, their ascent to Him stronger and their feelings for Him more ardent. Similarly, if devils occupy the heart, they will disorient the spirits in heart and the brain with their blow; they hinder judgment and produce perceptible insanity, and drive the heart and other members to cruel acts, as when Medea killed her children or when Judas killed himself. So, let us observe our nature and rule it with dignity, praying God's Son to drive devils from us and to pour the divine Spirit into our spirits.[98]

---

the differences, see Melanchthon, *Philosophiae moralis epitomes* in *MW* III, 157; Saarinen, "Melanchthons Ethik zwischen Tugend und Begabung," in *Melanchthon*, hrsgb. Walter Sparn, Erlanger Forschungen, Reihe A, Band 85 (Erlangen 1998), pp. 75–76. *Liber De Anima*, however, functions on many levels, which Melanchthon uses to illustrate good actions, but he never restricts the use of the spirits simply to moral theology. He also uses them explicitly in a Soteriological context.

[96] *CR* 13, 170 (*De anima*): "Et haec bona ita nobis attribuit, ut ipse simul voluerit in nobis habitare, augere sapientiam, et suis motibus nos regere." This teaching appears in the doctrinal treatises as well. See, e.g., *CR* 23, 339 (*Enarratio*): "Deinde magnitudo amoris in aeterno Patre, Filio et Spiritu sancto, erga genus humanum in hoc decreto conspicitur, quod Filius factus est deprecator, et poenam in se derivat, quod pater Filio suo non pepercit, sed voluit eum subiici poenae, ut nos redimeret, quod Spiritus sanctus ipse vult in cordibus reconciliatorum habitare, et Patris, et Filii, et suos motus in nobis accendere."

[97] *CR* 13, 169 (*De anima*): "Fuit autem ante peccatum talis imago, ut potentiae omnes congruerent cum Deo. In intellectu fulsit firma Dei noticia, voluntas et cor congruebant cum Deo, id est, habebant rectitudinem et iusticiam congruentem cum Deo, et libertas voluntatis non erat impedita. Et in hac imagine Deus habitabat, daturus vitam sine morte, et laeticiam perpetuam, si homo non excuisset Deum rectorem." On the natural likeness of human beings to God (*notitia naturalis*), see Frank, *Theologische philosophie Philip Melanchthons* (1497–1560) (Leipzig: Benno 1995), p. 31.

[98] *CR* 13, 88–89 (*De anima*): "Et quod mirabilius est, his ipsis spiritibus in hominibus piis miscetur ipse divinus spiritus, et efficit magis fulgentes divina luce, ut agnitio Dei sit illustrior, et adsensio firmior, et motus sint ardentiores erga Deum. Econtra ubi diaboli occupant corda, suo adflatu turbant spiritus in corde et in cerebro, impediunt iudicia, et manifestos furores efficiunt, et impellunt corda et alia membra ad crudelissimos motus, ut, Medea interficit natos, Iudas sibi ipsi consciscit mortem. Aspiciamus igitur naturam nostram, et diligenter eam regamus, et sciamus, oportere spiritus nostros esse domicilium Spiritus sancti, et oremus filium Dei, ut ipse depellat a nobis diabolos, et spiritum divinum in nostros spiritus transfundat." See also Sachiko Kusukawa, *The Transformation of Natural Philosophy. The Case of Philip Melanchthon* (Cambridge: Cambridge University Press 1995), p. 120.

Since either the Holy Spirit or Satan can have power over the vital spirits, the true knowledge of God is dependent on the disposition of the spirits.[99] This makes the close relation between justification and renewal understandable. In the Gospel, Logos informs the intellect with the Father's love, and the Spirit joins the individual's will to the will of the Father. A person can have a true relation with the Father only if the Spirit is united with his or her spirits.[100] In keeping with this, Melanchthon's later doctrine of justification concerns not only the extrinsic effect of God, but also the real and actual presence of God in the individual.[101]

---

[99] *CR* 13, 171 (*De anima*): "Hic igitur filius aeterni patris, Dominus noster Iesus Christus nobis donatus est, ut fieret victima pro nobis, et placaret iram aeterni patris, et sit sacerdos perpetuus, colligens ecclesiam voce evangelii, in qua decretum de reconciliatione patefecit, quod et ipse... in mentibus nostris effatur, et ostendit nobis patrem placatum, ac Spiritum sanctum effundit in corda nostra, ut vero amore et laetitia cum aeterno patre et ipso copulemur. Ita restituitur in nobis vita et iustitia aeterna, et renovatur imago Dei verbo lucente in mente, ut agnitio Dei sit clarior et firmior, et Spiritu sancto accendente motus congruentes cum Deo in voluntate et corde." As a humanist and natural philosopher, Melanchthon tried to create a comprehensive and regular system; probably for this reason he is seemingly fond of the Law (*lex*). See also Kusukawa, *The Transformation*, p. 74. In order to bring everything under one theory, salvation is also depicted as being in conformity with the Law, and consequently with the cosmos. On Melanchthon's view of the Law, see Maurer, "Lex spiritualis bei Melanchthon bis 1521," in *Gedenkschrift für Werner Elert*, hrsgb. Friedrich Hübner et al, (Berlin: Lutherisches Verlagshaus 1955), pp. 176–177. Melanchthon never abandons the Augustinian *ordo caritatis* whereas Luther does. This gives a rationalistic tone to his theology.

[100] *CR* 13, 158 (*De anima*).

[101] Melanchthon can speak about righteousness as communion with God. See *CR* 23, 17 (*Examen*): "Definitio apud Clementem loquitur de novitate, et simul complectitur universalem et particularem iustitiam: Dikaiosúnee esti koinoonia theoum metà isóteetos, id est, Iustitia est communicatio, qua Deus se nobis communicat, et est conservatio ordinatae aequalitatis. Prior pars loquitur de prima tabula, et de actionibus divinis in renatis. Secunda de aequalitate, loquitur de actionibus ordinatis erga proximum. Haec congruunt ad Legem, sed dextre intelligenda sunt. Osiander ipsum Deum moventem nos ad iusta facienda, nominat iustitiam. Hoc loquendi modo etiamsi quis volet uti, tamen prius dicendum est de Iustitia imputata propter Filium Dei, qua Deo propter Mediatorem credentes placent. Distinguenda est etiam causa, scilicet, Deus ipse, ab effectibus in nobis, et in infinitum anteferenda est obedientia Filii Dei novis actionibus, quae fiunt in nobis." The idea of actuality of presence is also illustrated in Melanchthon's *Dialectics*, in which he explains different modes of predication. Figurative predication is divided between metaphor and synecdoche. Metaphor, for example, is used when someone says that a tyrant is a wolf, i.e., like (*similis*) a wolf. Synecdoche is used about Pentecost, when the Holy Spirit was actually present with the flames. *CR* 13, 524–525 (*dialectica*): "Alia sunt Synecdochae, ut flammae in ore Apostolorum erant Spiritus sanctus, id est, cum illa re visibili vere aderat Spiritus sanctus."

The terminology of 'vital spirits' is indicative of psychological concepts (such as knowledge, assent, trust, joy, consolation) Melanchthon used in describing faith and its effects.[102] Because the spirits primarily manage the movements of the mind, which for their part constitute individual's state *coram Deo*, it is natural that renewal is described in such terms.[103] Theology and psychology are not unconnected disciplines for Melanchthon; the life of faith finds its expressions through cognitive and psychological language.

The basic problem of Melanchthon's soteriology is found in his concepts of the relationship of sanctification and renewal to justification. Being empirical facts, sanctification and renewal are both affirmed and denied in the event of justification.[104]

3.5. *Conclusion*

Over the course of his thought Melanchthon's doctrine of justification undergoes the following changes.

(1) Justification is a process that evolves through qualitative change, which evokes justifying trust in Christ and striving for good works. This trust is reckoned as righteousness. (*Loci* 1521)
(2) Justification refers only to imputation, which, however, is simultaneous with effective change. This, however, is not part of justification. (*Commentary on Romans* 1531)
(3) Justification is both imputation and donation of the Spirit. The qualititative change caused by the Spirit, however, is not righteousness *coram Deo*. (The late works)

---

[102] According to Seils (*Glaube*, pp. 108–111), *Liber de Anima* stresses the aspects of knowledge and trust in faith. Faith is presented as a natural faculty of the soul, which the Spirit empowers to work in a new way. The message about Christ enlightens the cognitive faculties and enables the sending of the Spirit, which activates the appetitive part of the soul.

[103] The background for this may be in Melanchthon's practical style. He attempts to define how righteousness comes to the believer in terms of his understanding of christology and pneumatology.

[104] This difficulty appears in the *Commentary on Romans* but in the later texts as well. See *MW* II/2, 395–7 (*Loci* 1559).

In other words, *renovatio*$_1$ has always been part of the event of salvation, although after the *Commentary on Romans* Melanchthon has difficulty in joining it with justification. The act of salvation involves an intrinsic change, which results from communion with God. This communion, however, has a different ontological structure than Luther's perception; Melanchthon understood the Holy Spirit as the medium whereas Luther understood communion in christological terms. Because *donum* is the Spirit for Melanchthon, he is unable to explain its meritorious nature. Generally, the justifying merit was attributed to Christ, not to the Spirit. If one considers *renovatio*$_1$ as the work of the Spirit, this does not offer a defense against the notion of habitual grace. This is not a problem for Luther, who explains *renovatio*$_1$ as participation in Christ's divine life. Luther's solution did not convince Melanchthon, who may have thought it sounded passive or even fatalistic.[105] Melanchthon's pneumatological anthropology tried to examine the human aspect of justification more deeply: in what sense do the deeds belong to the individual and in what sense are they God's effects? The problem, however, is the transformation of justification's intrinsic aspect into an empirical category. For Luther, *renovatio*$_1$ is a reality beyond the senses, it is "in the cloud". In contrast, Melanchthon makes it a felt reality—*renovatio*$_1$ and *donum* identify with qualitative renewal. For Luther, however, the feelings are consequences of justification and renewal (*renovatio*$_2$). Melanchthon's meticulous system is finally unable to explain the relation between intrinsic and extrinsic aspects of justification. This is apparent in the way Melanchthon's students abandon the *favor-donum* distinction, which is consequently insignificant in the second generation of Lutheran reformers. (Their reason for abandoning the distinction may be the problem the system caused.) It is hard to speak about *donum* or renewal, which enables justification (*renovatio*$_1$) if it is understood as a qualitative change that comes close to Roman Catholic teaching on habitual or infused grace.

[105] Luther clearly understood the difficulties of his own view. See *WA* 40 I, 288, 17–21. Heikki Kirjavainen ("'Minä' ja mystiikka" in *Elevatis oculis*, Studia mystica in honorem Seppo A. Teinonen, ed. Pauli Annala (Helsinki: Missiologian ja ekumeniikan seuran julkaisuja 42, 1984), pp. 111–115) has referred to the problems of mystical language: how can subject x claim that another subject y "lives in him"? Kirjavainen proposes that y can be joined x as an attribute as long as x is a logical subject. If y is joined with x as a logical subject, x will lose its status as logical subject, or x is identical with y.

The doctrine of *Commentary on Romans* in particular was fiercely opposed by Osiander, who saw it as a deviation from Luther's genuine teachings. Melanchthon, however, reconsidered his own thinking and formulated it in a more consistent way by emphasizing God's indwelling in faith. This reconsideration did not bring resolution to this confused situation. Lutheranism was destined to wrestle with the relation between intrinsic and extrinsic aspects of justification for many years to come, as is illustrated in theologies of Osiander and Flacius.

CHAPTER FOUR

ANDREAS OSIANDER AND MATTHIAS FLACIUS ILLYRICUS: THE CONTROVERSY OVER THE GENUINE INTERPRETATION OF LUTHER

Luther had stated laconically before his death: "After me, many sects will be born, and Osiander will found one of them."[1] The Osiandrian controversy broke out only four years after Luther's death, and was in many ways traumatic and internally damaging for Lutherans. Self-confident as he was, Osiander wanted to play the role of the genuine interpreter of Luther and save reformation from the hands of Melanchthon, whom he perceived as corrupting Lutherans with his teaching on justification. However, Osiander's own teaching on justification was so different from Luther's that he never managed to obtain general support from other reformers.

One of the most important antagonists of Osiander was Matthias Flacius Illyricus, who tried to rescue Luther from the hands of Osiander. Osiander's and Flacius's interpretations of Luther were as opposite as night and day. Osiander emphasized essential communion with Christ in faith so strongly that he almost embraced subjectivism. Flacius, however, did not allow anything intrinsic and human to enter the doctrine of justification which would threaten the reality of salvation.

4.1. *Osiander's Attack on Melanchthon's Teaching on Justification*

4.1.1. *Justification as Participation in Christ's Divine Nature*

In 1550 Andreas Osiander[2] challenged Melanchthon's doctrine of justification by holding a disputation on justification in Königsberg

[1] *WA TR* 4, 478, 6–20.

[2] Osiander was a close colleague of Luther and Melanchthon. In 1523, when the eucharist was served in both forms in Nürenberg for the first time, Osiander was there. Two years later, when the city of Nürenberg officially joined the reform movement, Osiander had a great influence on its development. Osiander sided with Luther in the discussion on the eucharist against Zwingli, and at the Diet of Augsburg he looked

(*Disputatio de justificatione*). His official opponents were Melchior Isinder and Martin Chemnitz.[3] Through his disputation and other examinations on the subject,[4] Osiander wanted to demonstrate his loyalty to Luther's teaching and his ability to correct Melanchthon's aberrations.[5] He constantly referred to Luther to prove his point.[6]

In his disputation, Osiander claimed that justification involved becoming alive and righteous (*vivificatio*) through Christ's living presence in the individual through faith.[7] Osiander did not deny the role of imputation, claiming that "Christ's righteousness will be imputed to us (*imputetur*

---

after Melanchthon, preventing him from conceding too much to the Catholics. In 1532, Osiander and Brenz established the church orders for Nürenberg-Brandenburg. He was present at Schmalcalden in 1537 where Luther published his articles and fiercely opposed the interims, having been exiled from Nürenberg for his views. Until the controversy, he had been a reputed reformer and a Gnesiolutheran. See Rainer Hauke, *Gott-Haben—um Gottes Willen. Andreas Osianders Theosisgedanke und die Diskussion um die Grundlagen der evangelisch verstandenen Rechtfertigung* (Frankfurt am Main: Peter Lang 1999), pp. 82–110, 280; Martin Stupperich, *Osiander in Preussen* 1549–1552 (Berlin: Walter de Gruyter 1973); Carl Lawrenz, "On Justification, Osiander's Doctrine of the Indwelling Christ (FC, III)" in *No other Gospel. Essays in Commemoration of the* 400th *Anniversary of the Formula of Concord* 1580–1980, ed. Arnold J. Koelpin (Milwaukee: Northwestern Publishing House. 1980, 150–153; F. Bente, *Historical Introductions to the Book of Concord* (St. Louis: Concordia Publishing House 1965), pp. 152–153.

[3] *AO* 9, 426–447 (Disputatio). On the contents of *Disputatio*, see Gunter Zimmermann, "Die Thesen Osianders zur Disputation 'de iustificatione'," *KuD* 33 (1987).

[4] These include a lengthy examination on justification, *Von dem einigen Mittler Jhesu Cristo und rechtfertigung des glaubens bekanntnus* 1551 (AO 10, 49–300), where Osiander furthers the analysis he had begun in *Disputatio*, and the reply to Melanchthon's criticisms, *Widerlegung Der ungegrundten undienstlichen Antwort Philippi Melanchtonis* 1552 (*AO* 10, 561–670). See also *AO* 9–10, which contain Osiander's correspondence and other writings from 1549–1552.

[5] E.g. *AO* 10, 80, 5–15; 10, 86, 5–15 (Mittler). Erikson, *Inhabitatio*, p. 48; Peura, "Gott und Mensch in der Unio. Die Unterschiede im Rechfertigungsverständnis bei Osiander und Luther" in *Unio. Gott und Mensch in der nachreformatorischen Theologie*, hrsgb. Matti Repo und Rainer Vinke (Helsinki: Scriften der uther-Agricola-Gesellshaft 1996), p. 34.

[6] *Von dem einigen Mittler* especially contains numerous quotes from Luther's writings. See, e.g., *AO* 10, 174 (Mittler). On the comparison between Luther and Osiander, see Zimmermann, "Die Thesen", pp. 233–244; Peura, "Gott und Mensch"; Hauke, *Gott-Haben*, pp. 280–285. Also an interesting piece of work is *Excerpta quaedam doctorum de iustificatione fidei in commentario super epistolam Pauli ad Galatas domini Martini Lutheri* (1551), in which Osiander repeats Luther's core passages of the *Commentary on Galatians*. See *AO* 9, 577–581.

[7] *AO* 9, 428, 1–2 (*Disputatio*, thesis 2): "Nihil enim iustificat, quid non et vivificet. Nihilque vicissim vivificat, quod non simul etiam iustificet." (thesis 4) "Iustificare enim propria et primaria institutione significat ex impio iustum facere, hoc est mortuum ad vitam revocare." (thesis 9) "Anima enim ut peccato dominante mortua est, ita Christo per fidem inhabitante vivit." See also theses 31, 32, 36–41.

nobis), but not without it being present in us."[8] The same emphasis occurs in the other examinations. Justification is to be understood more in the sense of making righteous (*gerechtmachen*) than declaring righteous (*gerechtsprechen*). This "making righteous" does not take place through human merits but belongs exclusively to God.[9]

In spite of this, imputation is still a part of justification. Faith is imputed for righteousness.[10] Osiander did not understand faith as a human virtue, habitus, or a state of mind; rather, faith was a christological entity.[11] Christ comes to the person in the preached Word and is apprehended by faith, whereby He makes the heart his dwelling place and becomes the righteousness of the sinner.[12] Faith is synedochic; imputing faith as righteousness means imputing the present Christ as righteousness.[13]

These traits in Osiander's teaching did not deviate from mainstream Lutheran theology. Osiander was astonished when the controversy broke out, claiming that he had taught in the same way for thirty years.[14] It is no wonder that Jacob Andreae and Johannes Brenz among others claimed that there was no problem in Osiander's teaching as such; it

---

[8] *AO* 9, 444, 13–15 (*Disputatio*, thesis 75): "Iusticia enim Christi nobis quidem imputatur, sed non nisi, quum in nobis est." The central criticism of Chemnitz and Isinder focused on the concept of "imputatio". No exact annotation of the dispute is available. Stupperich, *Osiander in Preussen*, pp. 110–114.

[9] *AO* 10, 144, 29–160, 10 (*Mittler*). On the early doctrine of justification Osiander, see Peura ("Gott und Mensch", pp. 46–52) See also *AO* 1, 299–307 (*Ratschlag*). In his inaugural lecture (*De lege et evangelio*) in Königsberg, he underlined the apprehension of Christ in faith. His opponent, Matthias Lauterwald, criticized Osiander's superficial teaching on conversion. Melanchthon considered the issue frivolous and ordered the parties to quit arguing. Stupperich, *Osiander in Preussen*, pp. 37–38.

[10] *AO* 10, 166, 16–20 (*Mittler*).

[11] *AO* 9, 430, 3–5 (*Disputatio*, thesis 12): "Facile autem sobrie philosophantibus concedimus hanc fidem esse qualitatem, modo ipsi nobis vicissim concedant non esse physicam aut Aristotelicam, sed supernaturalem divinitus in nobis excitatam." Osiander denies that faith justifies since it is *relatio*. Instead, faith justifies "...neque qua relatio...tantum qua objectum suum Christum apprehendit et nobis unit." *AO* 9, 430, 22–25. (*Disputatio*, thesis 19). Moreover, Osiander castigates Melanchthon's view of justification as relational acceptation. See also Zimmermann, "Die Thesen", 228.

[12] On Osiander's theology of the Word, see *AO* 9, 428 (*Disputatio*, theses 10, 14).

[13] *AO* 9, 430 (*Disputatio*, theses 15, 17). *AO*, 10 168, 9–170, 29 (*Mittler*). According to Hauke (*Gott-Haben*, p. 210), for Osiander "Gott, Gottes Wort, Christus als Gottes Gerechtigkeit und der Glaube sind eine differenzierte Einheit".

[14] In 1552, Osiander published *Beweisung, dass ich dreissig Jahre immer einerlei Lehre von der Gerechtigkeit des Glaubens gelehrt habe*. *AO* 10, 421–449. See also Erikson, *Inhabitatio*, p. 49. According to Peura ("Gott und Mensch"), the basic elements of Osiander's teaching were already apparent in the texts of the 1520s.

should simply be re-focused. The present controversy was only a battle over words, *bellum grammaticale*.[15]

While it may be admitted that Osiander remained close to Luther on some points, he still could not represent Luther's views in the correct form. One of Osiander's last writings, *Wider den Nachtraben* (1552), summarizes his teaching:

> What is true righteousness? I answer like this. 1. From pure grace and mercy, God gave His only Son for us. 2. The Son became man under the Law, and redeemed us from the Law and its curse. 3. He took all the world's sins upon Himself, and for them suffered, died, shed His blood, descended into hell, and rose again; and in so doing conquered sin, death, and hell and gained for us forgiveness of sins, reconciliation with God, the grace and gift of justification and eternal life. 4. This is to be proclaimed in all the world. 5. He who believes and is baptized is justified and is saved through such faith. 6. Faith seizes Christ, so that he dwells in our hearts (Eph. 3:17). 7. Christ, dwelling in us through faith, is our wisdom, righteousness, sanctification, and redemption (1 Cor. 1:30; Jer. 23:6; 33:16). 8. Christ, true God and man, dwelling in us through faith, is our righteousness according to His divine nature, as Dr. Luther says: "I am founded on the righteousness which is God Himself; this He cannot reject. That is the simple and true understanding, and don't let yourself be led away from it."[16]

The most significant difference between Luther and Osiander was their respective perceptions of how Christ is the righteousness of the sinner. Osiander understood justification in terms of the indwelling of Christ's *divine* nature. Because righteousness is wholly a property of God, only

---

[15] Bente, *The historical introduction*, p. 154. David Chytraeus had also said of Osiander that "manche sagen, er habe nicht aliud, sondern nur aliter gelehrt." See Stupperich, *Osiander in Preussen*, pp. 171–175; Hauke, *Gott-Haben*, pp. 276–277.

[16] *AO* 10, 412, 9–24 (*Nachtraben*): "Welches ist noch die rechte und ware gerechtigkeit? Ich verstehe es also: 1. Aus lauter gnad und barmherzigkeit Gottes ist es hergeflossen das er seinen einigen son für uns har dargegeben. 2. Der son ist mensch worden und unter das gesetz gethan und hat uns vom gesetz und von dem fluch des gesetz erlöset. 3. Er hat aller welt sünd auff sich genommen, fur dieselbigen gelitten, gestorben, sein blut vergossen, gen helle gefahren, wider erstanden und also sünd, todt und hell uberwunden, uns vergebung der sünd, versonung mit Gott, die gnad und gabe der rechtfertigung und ewigs leben erworben. 4. Das sol man in alle welt predigen. 5. Wer das glaubt und getauft wirdt, der wird durch solchen glauben gerechtfertigt und selig. 6. Der glaub ergreifft Christum, das er durch den glauben, in unsern hertzen wonet, Ephe. 3. [17]. 7. Christus durch den glauben in uns wonendt, ist unser gerechtigkeit nach seiner götlichen natur, wie doctor Luther sagt: "Ich bin gegrundet auff die gerechtigket, die Gott selbs ist, die kan er nicht verwerfen, er must sonst sich selbs verwerfen. Das ist, spricht D. Luther 'der einfeltig, richtig verstand, darvon lass dich nicht füren.'" The excerpt from Luther is found in *WA* 17 II, 450, 29–32.

God himself can be the righteousness of the sinner.[17] If, however, the Christian's righteousness is something other than God, then it must be something created, which is theologically unacceptable. In that case, righteousness would be a created righteousness (*creatürliches gerechtigkeit*), i.e., habitus.[18]

Osiander stressed God's essence so strongly that even forgiveness of sins was considered negligible compared to it. Christ himself—not his works—is the righteousness of the sinner. According to Osiander, Christ is not righteous because He has fulfilled the law, which He has also done, but because He is the Son of God.[19] What Christ does is therefore separated from who Christ is.[20]

Osiander's accusation against Melanchthon turned on his teaching of Christ's work as righteousness. According to Osiander, this kind of teaching is colder than ice compared to the idea of Christ's indwelling

---

[17] *AO* 10, 226, 21–33 (*Mittler*): "Dieweil uns Christus worden ist zur gerechtigkeit und Christus ist ein ein name der gantzen, unzertrenten person, in der beide, göttliche und menschliche natur vereinigt sein, so ist nu die frag, nach welcher natur er unser gerechtigkeit sey, gleichwie man fragt, nach welcher natur er schepfer himmels und der erden sey oder nach welchen natur er gestorben sey. Hie ist nun mein lautere, richtige und klare antwort, das er nach seiner göttlichen natur unser gerechtigkeit sey und nicht nach der menslichen natur, wiewol wir solche göttliche gerechtigkeit ausserhalb seiner menscheit nicht können finden, erlnagen oder ergreiffen. Sonder wan er durch den glauben in uns wonet, so bringt er seine gerechtigkeit, die seine göttliche natur ist, mit sich in uns, die wirt uns dann auch zugerechnet, als wer sie unser eigen, ja sie wirt uns auch geschenkt und fleust dan aus seiner menscheit als aus dem heubt auch in uns als seine glider und bewegt uns, das wir unser glider begeben zu waffen der gerechtigkeit Gott den herren, wie Paulus zun Römern am 6. [13] sagt."

[18] *AO* 9, 661, 7 (*Osiander an Mörlin* 27.4.1551): "Quicquid non est Deus, est creatura." *AO* 10, 228, 19–26 (Mittler): "Ist uns nun Christus worden zur gerechtigkeit, auff das wir uns Gottes oder des göttlichen wesens rhumen sollen, so muss er ja nach seiner göttlichen natur und wesen unser gerechtigkeit sein, wir rühmeten uns sonst nicht des göttlichen wesens, sonder nur einer creatürlichen gerechtigkeit, die erschaffen ist, wir einer aus meinen widersachern geschriben hat, die gerechtigkeit Christi sey nur ein werck Gottes in Christo, darmit er lauter zu verstehen gibt, das er Christum weder nach der göttlichen oder nach der menschlichen natur fur unser gerechtigkeit halte. Das heisst Christum auf einmal gar zunichte gemacht." See also *AO* 10, 153–156, 411 (*Mittler*). Erikson 1986, 75; Stupperich, *Osiander in Preussen*, p. 160.

[19] *AO* 9, 432, 16–17 (*Disputatio*, thesis 27).

[20] *AO* 10, 648, 3–4 (*Widerlegung*): "Daraus volget unwidersprechlich das kein Werck diser person unser Gerechtigkeit sein kan." Andreas Musculus criticizes Osiander for splitting the person of Christ. *Musculus* Responsio, thesis XIIII: "...tamen re ipsa & in effectu separare cum naturas Christi in redemptione & iustificatione..." On Christ's indwelling, Musculus states (thesis XVII): "quòd Verbum, per quod omnia facta, caro factum est, & habitavit in nobis, factum est, quòd sumus nos, ut Irenaeus loquitur, ut nos perficeret esse, quòd ipse est."

in the believer through faith.[21] Melanchthon thought that Osiander's accusation was without proper foundation. He answered Osiander by claiming that righteousness is always accompanied by forgiveness and did not consist merely of Christ's divine righteousness.[22]

Osiander could not understand this. He related the sufferings and the death of Christ to Christ's human nature, simply a precondition that had happened 1500 years prior for the actual provision of justifying righteousness to sinners. In other words, the satisfaction that took away God's anger only opened up the possibility of the real event of salvation. The actual salvation takes place through the union of believer with Christ's divine nature. While the death on the Cross was only a precondition, the most crucial part of justification was the indwelling of divinity. Christ is of no use to sinners without this.[23]

4.1.2. *Why was Osiander condemned?*

In spite of his good intentions, Osiander soon gained disrepute among the reformers. Melanchthon's response culminated in the claim that Osiander's teaching on the indwelling of the divine nature destroys the certainty of salvation.[24] This claim was off the point and gave the wrong impression of Osiander's thinking.[25] For Osiander, trust in God's mercy and righteousness, not in human deeds and good works, was

---

[21] *AO* 9, 444, 7–9 (*Disputatio*, thesis 73): "Glacie quoque frigidiora docent, quicunque docent nos tantum propter remissionem peccatorum reputari iustos et non etiam propter iustitiam Christi per fidem in nobis inhabitantis." *Frigidus* also means powerless, weak, and uninterested. Here Osiander probably refers to thesis 80, which claims that merely imputative teaching does not motivate good works, unlike Osiander's own teaching. Osiander also castigates Melanchthon's frigid eucharistic theology: it is impossible to hold on to the real presence in the eucharist if this is omitted from justification. See also Zimmermann, "Die Thesen", p. 230.

[22] *MW* VI, 457 (*Antwort*).

[23] *AO* 10, 110, 1–10 (*Mittler*): "Es ist aber offenbar, das alles dasjenig, das Christus als der getreue mitler von unserwegen durch erfullung des gesetzes und durch sein leiden und sterben mit Gott, seinem himlischen vater, gehandelt hat, das ist fur funfzehenhundert jaren und lenger geschehen, da wir noch nocht geporen gewest sein. Darumb kan es, eigentlich zu reden, nicht unser erlösung und genugthuung fur uns und unser sünde. Dann wer gerechtfertigt sol werden, der mus glauben; sol er aber glauben, so mus er schin geporen sein und leben. Darumb hat Christus uns, die wir itzo leben, und andere vor uns durch erfullung des gesetzes und sein leiden und sterben icht gerechtfertigt; aber erlöset sein wir dardurch von Gotts zorn, todt und helle." See also Stupperich, "Lehrentscheidung", pp. 179–180.

[24] *MW* VI, 458–460 (*Antwort*).

[25] Stupperich, "Lehrentscheidung", p. 182.

inevitably central. Osiander was unable to recognize his teaching in Melanchthon's critique.[26]

Osiander reacted to this critique by affirming that Melanchthon was right in admitting that the indwelling of God's essential righteousness is part of justification.[27] In spite of this, differences remained between them. Even if Melanchthon did teach the indwelling of the Trinity in faith and its efficacious presence in the believer, the indwelling entity was not God himself, but something he called 'creaturely life' (*creatürliches leben*).[28] Osiander's analysis of Melanchthon was quite accurate.

But are there any suggestions in Osiander's writings that support the claim that the works of the justified person could be understood as meritorious? Thesis 80 in *Disputatio* may be one of the most difficult to interpret in this respect. It became customary to refer to this thesis in order to point out the flaws in Osiander's thought.[29] Thesis 80 claims that "no other doctrine can motivate good works better than this heavenly doctrine of our justification."[30] Although this was not Osiander's

---

[26] *AO* 10, 644, 15 (*Widerlegung*): "Das er aber sagt, es sey nahe sovil geredt, als sprech ich, unser neuigkeit ist unser gerechtigkeit, das ist mir frembd zu hören." On these, see especially *AO* 9, 428 (*Disputatio*, theses 5, 21–26, 77, 79), where the meritoriousness of human works is denied. At the beginning of *Von dem einigen Mittler* (*AO* 10, 100, 1–15) Osiander also writes: "Nun konnen wir aber der beider [lebendig und gerecht macht werden] keins durch unser eigne kreffte, werck und vleis erlangen. Darumb har Got 'seins einigen sons nicht verschonet, sonder in fur uns alle dargeben', 'welchen er auch hat furgestellet zu einem gnadenstuhl durch den glauben in seinem blut, darmit er seine gerechtigkeit darbiete', 'auff das er allein gerecht sey und gerecht mache den, der da ist des glaubens an Jhesu Christo', denn der ist der mitler zwischen Gott und dem menschen, der durch seinen gehorsam den Vater uns versohnet hat und seiner gerechtigkeit durch den glauben uns gerecht machen."

[27] *AO* 10, 594, 19–37 (*Widerlegung*).

[28] *AO* 10, 598–599 (*Widerlegung*): "Nun spricht aber Philippus alhie erstlich, das Vater, Sohn und heyliger Gaist würcken in uns trost und leben, und bald darnach spricht er zum andern mal, Gottis Sohn hab durchs evangelion in Adams und Eva hertzen gewürckt trost und leben, und gibt darmit lauter, klar und unwidersprechlichen zu verstehen, das er nicht redet vom leben, das Gottis sohn selbs ist, sonder von eim andern vil geringern, creatürlichen leben, das der sohn Gottis in uns wirckt." See also Hauke, *Gott-Haben*, p. 247.

[29] E.g., Chemnitz, *Loci* I, 118a (146): "Osiander, obedientiam nostram esse essentialem iustitiam Dei dixit: ita ut praeter & extra Christum renovatio nostra opponatur iudicio Dei." See also Andreae, *Concilium* 78; Selnecker, *Institutionis* I, Iii; *BSELK FC SD* III, 2. McGrath (*Iustitia Dei*, p. 213) writes on the relation between Osiander and Chemnitz: "[For Osiander] Justification must therefore be understood to consist of the infusion of the essential righteousness of Christ. Although some of his critics, such as Martin Chemnitz, argued that this made justification dependent upon sanctification, it is clear that this is not the case." McGrath's analysis is correct.

[30] *AO* 9, 446, 10–12 (*Disputatio*, thesis 80): "Nulla doctrina magis impellit homines ad bene operandum quam haec coelestis de iustificatione nostri doctrina."

intention, the thesis was interpreted to mean that good works belong to justification.

A similar reading was made of Osiander's claim that "...God is not unrighteous and not a kind of lover of unrighteousness, who considers righteousness something which does not have whole and real righteousness as is written [Ps. 5:5]: For thou art not a God that hath pleasure in wickedness."[31] As already noted, Osiander's view of imputation was based on the righteousness present in the justified person. Faith makes the believer the part-taker of divine nature and the believer becomes a new creature (*eine neue creatur*).[32] However, Osiander makes a distinction between this new human righteousness and its cause, present divine righteousness. He stresses that only divine righteousness can save a person, although this new righteousness in the person is real.[33] New life and good works are necessary effects of Christ's presence in the individual. Christ and His effects in the justified individual should be considered distinctly. In keeping with this, the real righteousness is Christ alone.[34] When Osiander speaks about God acting wrongly if he reckons as righteous some one who is not righteous *in re*, he does not refer to human properties but to God, who is the justifying righteousness through faith.[35]

The passage in which Osiander defines the word 'righteousness' is also problematic. He understood righteousness to imply that "the justified person does good works."[36] He then hastens to state that there are two kinds of righteousness: human righteousness, which is based on obedience to the Law, and divine righteousness, i.e., God himself.[37] The righteousness that avails *coram Deo* is the latter.[38]

---

[31] *AO* 9, 444, 13–15 (*Disputatio*, thesis 74): "Non enim tam iniquus est Deus aut iniquitatis amans, ut eum pro iusto habeat, in quo verae iusticiae prorsus nihil sit iuxta illud: Quoniam non Deus volens iniquitatem tu es."

[32] *AO* 10, 216, 2–9 (*Mittler*).

[33] *AO* 9, 432, 4–5 (*Disputatio*, thesis 21): "Cum enim duplex iustitia sit, Dei scilicet et hominem, fide non hanc humanam, sed illam Dei iustitiam apprehendimus."

[34] See, e.g., *AO* 10, 166, 216, 248 (*Mittler*).

[35] *AO* 9, 444 (*Disputatio*, thesis 70, 74).

[36] *AO* 10, 160 (*Mittler*): "So antwort ich: Gerechtigkeit ist eben das das den gerechten recht zuthun bewegt und das er weder gerecht sein noch recht thun kan."

[37] *AO* 10, 158 (*Mittler*).

[38] *AO* 10, 164 (*Mittler*): "...das die gerechtigkeit, die fur Gott gilt, nemlich die gerechtigkeit des glaubens, sey warlich Gottes gerechtigkeit, die Gott selbs ist..." *AO* 10, 622 (Widerlegung): "Dann du must dich in disem leben nicht auff dein gehorsam, noch auff dein rainigkeit verlassen, sonder auff den gehorsam und rainigkeit meins Sohns, der das gesetz vollkommenlich fur dich erfüllet hat, dann sein gerechtigkeit wirdt dir

Melanchthon, however, either was not aware or did not speak out about the background of Osiander's teaching. The problem was not the indwelling of God in faith. All Lutherans openly taught this doctrine. The main problem in Osiander was in the realm of christology, as it was for Melanchthon. Basically, the collision of Osiander's and Melanchthon's opinions arose from different theological structures.[39] Neither of them could genuinely represent Luther's idea of Christ's human-divine person as the righteousness of the sinner.

It can be argued on the basis of the letters Melanchthon sent to his colleagues that he had at least a hunch that Osiander's aberration was due to his doctrine of God.[40] Melanchthon was clearly right in this observation. A fundamental aspect of Osiander's theology was the idea of the absolute oneness of God's essence. This prevented him from examining Christ's work as a part of righteousness given to believers in faith, since it would have implied attributing human properties (such as suffering, death, and change) to the divine essence, which was impossible for Osiander, who considered God immutable.[41]

In addition, Osiander's definition of Christ's natures maintained their separate distinctiveness in which no real communion was shared.[42] Osiander did not use *communicatio idiomatum*, which means definition of the unity of Christ's person, in a traditional sense. On the contrary, he used it to separate the natures and to describe their characteristic properties. *Communicatio idiomatum* is only a grammatical rule and does

von mir nicht zugerechnet, darumb das sie dise oder jhene grosse oder geringe werck in dir würckt, sonder allein darumb, das sie durch den glauben in dir ist." See also *AO* 10, 644–645 (*Widerlegung*).

[39] Osiander's character may also have caused problems. According to Carl Lawrenz ("On Justification", pp. 150–157), Osiander used to speculate a lot. Michael Noting, a teacher from Nürenberg, had stated that Osiander typically knows things otherwise, and better, than the others. Osiander's status as a close colleague of Luther and Melanchthon gave him confidence to declare his views and expect them to be approved. This attitude was familiar to Luther as well, who had been irritated by Osiander's comments on his own theology. See *WA TR* 4, 498.

[40] Melanchthon's letter to Justus Jonas 26.1.1552. (*CR* VII, 927). Melanchthon to Chytreaus and Aurifaber 10.9.1552. (*CR* VII, 1067). See also Stupperich, "Lehrentscheidung", p. 181.

[41] Stupperich, *Osiander in Preussen*, pp. 200–203; *Hauke, Gott-Haben*, p. 200.

[42] *AO* 10, 200 (*Mittler*). On the grammatical rules of christology and the relationship between the two natures, see *AO* 10, 200, 7–208, 2 (Mittler). Stupperich "Lehrentscheidung", p. 184; Peura, "Gott und Mensch", pp. 37–39, 49. Nüssel (*Allein aus Glauben*, p. 25) correctly claims, leaning to Mahlman (*Das Neue Dogma*, p. 93), that Osiander took advantage of Melanchthon's christology and developed it to the extreme.

not refer to actual exchange of properties between natures.[43] What one nature does is always something that the other nature does not do. For example, divine nature has created the world, which human nature certainly did not do.[44] In keeping with this, Christ's satisfaction cannot be a part of righteousness given to sinners—it is not even a part of Christ's person. This separation of work and person also involves undervaluing Christ's satisfaction on the Cross.[45] This Osiander depicts with the following parable. The son of a doctor disobediently drinks from one of his father's bottle, which, unknown to him, contains poison. A plea for forgiveness, or the father's forgiving act, is not enough to save the boy from death. The poison must be taken away from the body.[46]

Osiander's attempt to associate renewal with justification and the understatement of satisfaction seemed suspect to reformers who feared that the objectivity of justification was jeopardized. Even if Christ's fulfillment of the Law and His death were objective and independent of human effects, Osiander could not tie this objectivity to Christ's person and presence. Thus he could do no other than speak about God's essential righteousness, which is also objective reality in a way. There is no trace in Osiander's writings of an attempt to cling to the idea of certainty of salvation in a historical event, Christ's satisfaction.[47] As creaturely thing it cannot be a part of righteousness that avails *coram*

[43] *AO* 10, 200 (Mittler). See also Mahlmann, *Das Neue Dogma*, pp. 97–99.

[44] *AO* 10, 200 (Mittler). Hauke (*Gott-Haben*, pp. 221–222) has claimed that Osiander's interpretation of *communicatio idiomatum* is fully Lutheran, even "strongly Chalcedonian"; Osiander's intention is just to prevent the mixing of the natures. Against Hauke, it must be noted that Osiander's inability to speak about Christ's work as part of Christ's person reveals some deeper differences between him and other Lutherans. See also Peura, "Gott und Mensch", pp. 37–39.

[45] Of 81 theses only 3 (theses 29, 58 ja 66) examine Christ's vicarious death and forgiveness of sins. Stupperich 1973, 112; Peura 1996, 49–58. Nevertheless, Christ's suffering is necessary for justification. See *AO* 10, 106, 15–19. Osiander cannot be accused of the denial of historical satisfaction despite focusing more on participation in the divine nature.

[46] *AO* 10, 476 (*Gutachten*). See also Hauke, *Gott-Haben*, pp. 261–262.

[47] Henry Hamann, "Righteousness of Faith before God" in *Contemporary look at the Formula of Concord*, ed. Robert Preus (St. Louis: Concordia Publishing House 1978), pp. 147–149. According to Hauke (*Gott-Haben*, p. 251) there is at least one such quotation. *AO* 6, 198, 25–27. "…so kan man dannoch in einem rechten verstand sprechen, die gerechtigkeit sey nicht in uns, sondern in Christo, dan sie ist in Christo eingewurtzelt und ewigklich befestiget." This passage, however, does not address Christ's satisfaction since Osiander refers here to righteousness as the attribute of the Creator, not of created beings.

Deo.[48] On the contrary, certainty is to be found in the consciousness that Christ's divine nature dwells in the heart of the believer and swallows his or her sins.

In constrast, Luther attached the certainty of salvation to Christ's satisfaction, which is actualized in the union with Christ's person in faith. The indwelling of Christ is not an empirical quantity that can be measured through knowledge or emotion. It is understood only through the promise of the Word. The believer does not observe the indwelling of Christ but of Christ crucified.

If satisfaction is only a prerequisite, it can no longer function as a source of the objective certainty of salvation. Correspondingly, the role of renewal starts to cause problems concerning justification. Osiander is unable to use objective imputation and Christ's satisfaction as objects of faith, in which case renewal (*renovatio*$_I$) would be only the context of justification. Subjectivism causes the main difficulty in Osiander's system. Even if Osiander himself tries to ensure objectivity, the christological flaws in his theology mean that he is unable to achieve his goal.

Later Lutheranism was forced to stress Christ's obedience (*oboedientia*) as the most crucial part of justification in order to meet Osiander's challenge. While the term already appears in the earlier documents it became the trademark of genuine understanding of justification especially after Osiander.[49] Thus Christ's obedience developed into a term that underlines the objectivity of justification against subjectivism.

The *possibility* of falling back on Roman doctrines of infused righteousness and meritoriousness of good works caused opposition to Osiander's theology.[50] As noted already, Osiander tried to resist all kinds of teaching about created grace as the basis for justification; his whole

---

48 *AO* 9, 644, 9–11 (*Osiander an Mörlin*): "...certissimum sit iusticiam, quam tu asseris, esse rem creatam, quam interdum oboedientiam, interdum meritum Christi vocas."

49 Luther uses the concept *obo(e)dientia* to illustrate the nature of satisfaction. See, e.g., *WA* 4, 652, 17–30; *WA* 39 I, 52, 26–28; 53, 1–3 (*Promotionsdisputation von Medler und Weller*). For Brenz (*Ad romanos*, 174, 19–175,9), obedience means Christ's assent to the will of the Father in heaven, and His submission to the salvific work as whole. The incarnated Christ fulfills the Law perfectly (*oboedientia activa*) and suffers for the sins of the world (*oboedientia passiva*). Chemnitz has the same understanding. See section 5.2.2. For Mörlin (*AO* 9, 621, 4 [*Mörlin an Osiander* 18.4.1551]) obedience belongs to the form of the slave (*forma servi*), which Christ has assumed in *kenosis*. These theologians do not understand *oboedientia* simply as forensic but incarnatory as well. Both senses are used to oppose Osiander.

50 Hamann, "Righteousness of Faith", pp. 148–149: "Osiander compels the inward look by his teaching. His teaching may not be subjectivism in its essential structure, but it inevitably leads to subjectivism in its practical application." On the other hand,

theology was targeted against such ideas.[51] It is ironic that Osiander was convicted of what he resisted. FC's declarations aimed at Osiander do not meet the real problem of Osiander's theology.[52]

Melanchthon never entered into a detailed discussion with Osiander. Perhaps he was afraid that the controversy would escalate beyond control and damage Lutheran unity even more. The proper solution of the Osiandrian controversy would have required a detailed account of the unity of Christ's person and work and the modes of the presence of Christ. This, however, could have brought to the surface the dissimilarities between other Lutherans on the issue, such as Brenz and Melanchthon himself—the matter had already been on the table in the form of the Holy Supper controversy. Melanchthon probably knew that the Württembergers could have appealed to Luther to their advantage. It was safer to convict Osiander without immersing oneself in the problem too deeply.[53]

When Osiander died in October 1552, the controversy started to recede gradually.[54] Despite this, the adherents of Osiander were in charge of church life in Prussia until 1567. Ten years later, Osiander's

Osiander has been castigated for teaching justification based on infused grace. See, e.g., Bente, *The historical introduction*, p. 152. This accusation is flawed.

[51] Osiander explicitly distances himself from the *gratia infusa* doctrine. See, e.g., *AO* 9, 634, 32–34. (Osiander an Herzog Albrecht) See also Hauke, *Gott-Haben*, p. 290.

[52] *BSELK FC Epit.* 3, 15–16.

[53] Stupperich, "Lehrentscheidung", pp. 181, 186–187: "Es ist deutlich, dass Melanchthon unter seinen Zeitgenossen in der Ergründung der Lehre Osianders am weitesten vorstiess. Zwar felht in seiner Analyse noch nie Hervorhegung der skolastischen Wurzel, die zu der spezifisch osianderischen Gotteslehre führte, doch ist Melanchthon der einzige, der überhaupt auf die abweichende Gotteslehre Osianders aufmerksam würde. Entsheidend für den weiteren Verlauf der Auseinandersetzung mit Osiander ist jedoch, dass Melanchthon aus taktischen Rücksichten—er wollte eine Ausweitung des Streits auf weitere Themenbereiche auf jeden Fall verhindern—seine erkenntnisse weitgehend geheim hielt. In der öffentlichen Auseinandersetzungen haben sie daher nie eine Rolle gespielt." See also Nüssel, *Allein aus Glauben*, p. 30.

[54] Osiander's death, however, was followed by some absurd events. Someone had spread rumours that when Osiander had died the devil himself had tormented Osiander on his deathbed and gouged out his eyeballs. On his own behalf, Duke Albrecht of Königsberg, dug up the body of Osiander and set it up for everybody to see that such accusations were only rumours. Wigand published a summary of Osiandrian teachings *De Osiandrismo* in 1586, which he spiced up with accounts of the unnatural deaths of Osiander's followers. See Roth, "Ein Braunschweiger Theologe", p. 65.

teaching was once again condemned in FC, even though this teaching was no longer practiced.[55]

4.1.3. *Francesco Stancarus's Response to Osiander*

As a curiosity, it may be worth noting Italian philologist Francesco Stancarus (1501–1574). Stancarus was driven out of Catholic Italy because he openly expressed his support for the reformers. In 1551, Duke Albert, who had hoped that as a specialist in ancient languages Stancarus could bring something new to the dialogue between Melanchthon and Osiander, called him to the university of Königsberg. Sadly, his hope was in vain. Stancarus stated bluntly that both Osiander and Melanchthon were fools and antichrists. The presence of Stancarus intensified the atmosphere to an extent that weapons were carried into the disputation hall. Within the same year the people of Königsberg had lost patience with him and he was exiled to Frankfurt an der Oder, from where Andreas Musculus soon drove him away.

Stancarus was driven away over ten times altogether during his career. The reason for such mobility lay both in his person and his theology. As a person, Stancarus was very annoying; wherever he went, he was always embroiled in controversy. One of his friends (!) compared him to "a snail, which leaves a trace of slime behind it."[56] Stancarus was unable to accommodate himself to any camp within the reformation. While he supported the movement by and large, he had a general distaste for both German and Swiss reformers. He did admire Peter Lombard.[57]

Stancarus joined the Osiandrian controversy by claiming that Christ is the righteousness of the sinner on behalf of his human nature, which he

---

[55] Robert Kolb, *Andreae and The Formula of Concord. Six sermons on the way to Lutheran Unity* (St. Louis: Concordia Publishing House 1977), p. 128; Robert Preus, "Historical Backround of the Formula of Concord" in *Contemporary look at the Formula of Concord*, ed. Robert D. Preus (St. Louis: Concordia Publishing House 1978), p. 40.

[56] George Williams, *The Radical Reformation* (Philadelphia: Westminster Press 1962), pp. 572–573, 654; Waclaw Urban, "Francesco Stancaro d. Ä," in *TRE* 32 (2001), pp. 110–111.

[57] The following claim of Stancarus demonstrates his attitude towards other Reformers: "Peter Lombard alone is worth more than a one hundred Luthers, two hundred Melanchthons, three hundred Bullingers, four hundred Peter Martyrs, and five hundred Calvins, and all of them ground in a mortar with a pestle would not amount to an ounce of the true theology." Cited in Williams, *The Radical Reformation*, p. 660.

considered to be the view of Lombard.[58] In order to maintain the idea of God's immutability he was ready to separate Christ's divine nature from satisfaction.[59] Stancarus accused Osiander and Melanchthon of Arianism due to their claim that Christ's divine nature took part in satisfaction. Stancarus argued that the person of the Son did something that the Father and the Spirit did not do. In keeping with this, the Son should have a nature distinct from the other persons of the Trinity. God sent only the human nature of the human-divine person to save humanity. Stancarus adopted Anselm's idea of satisfaction, which was interpreted in terms of vicarious atonement. The human nature, not the divine nature, sheds blood for the sins of the world. In addition to this, God is one immutable whole without any change, which explains why satisfaction can be the property of human nature only.[60]

In 1553, Melanchthon answered Stancarus's teachings in his *Responsio Philippi Melanchthonis de controversiis Stancari*. Melanchthon declared that satisfaction involves not only suffering and fulfillment of the Law but also victory over death and crushing the head of the serpent, something that mere human nature cannot do. Rather, both human and divine natures are at work in salvation.[61] In 1585, Johannes Wigand published an examination, *De Stancarismo*, confuting Stancarus's teachings. Generally, the effect of Stancarus was quite slight within the Osiandrian controversy, since he never managed to recruit theologians of good repute as followers. He caused bewilderment in Eastern Europe after the confrontation with Osiander and Melanchthon. Stancarus's doctrine was eventually condemned, along with Osiander, in FC.[62]

---

[58] Lombardus, *Sententiae*, III d 19 Cap 7 (61): "Mediator dicitur secundum humanitatem, non secundum divinitatem." Lombard's text does not have anything to do with Osiander and his teaching since the passage concerns the office of Christ. Reinhold Seeberg, *Lehrbuch der Dogmengeschichte*, p. 507.

[59] Williams, *The Radical Reformation*, p. 655.

[60] Bente, *The Historical Introductions*, 159; Reinhold Seeberg, *Lehrbuch der Dogmengeschichte*, pp. 507–508.

[61] *MW* VI, 272 (*Responsio*): "Mediator, Rex, Salvator, non tantum intelliguntur de natura patiente et moriente, sed de persona victrice. Sicut personam victricem comprehendit promissio: "Semen mulieris conteret caput serpentis." Conterit haec persona non tantum merito in passione,sed etiam quia vincit mortem in suo corpore et in nobis, et restituit vitam et iustitiam aeternam."

[62] *BSELK FC* Epit. 3, 14.

4.2. *Flacius's Attempt to guarantee the Objectivity of Justification*

4.2.1. *Justification as Real Imputation*

A more prominent opponent of Osiander than Stancarus was Matthias Flacius Illyricus (1520–1575).[63] Flacius, as the leader of the gnesiolutheran party, was one of the most visible figures of early Lutheranism; gnesiolutherans were even occasionally called 'Flacians'.[64] Eventually Flacius was condemned for heresy because of his radical understanding of the nature of original sin. Despite this, his knowledge and terminology in other matters was widely accepted among Lutheran theologians. Flacius opposed Osiander and Roman Catholic theology by developing and further radicalizing Melanchthon's ideas in his examinations *De voce et re fidei* (1549), *De iustificatione liber* (1563), and *Clavis Scripturae sacrae* (1567).[65] Flacius's view remains much the same in all the works mentioned. His understanding of justification was largely formed in 1549 before the Osiandrian controversy broke out. Later developments consisted mostly of specifying concepts.[66]

---

[63] Flacius (Matija Vlacic, Croat.) studied liberal arts in Venice, where he changed his name into Matthias Flacius. In order to emphasize his origins he added his place of birth (Illyria) to his name. Flacius moved to Germany in 1539, where he studied languages under Melanchthon's supervision and was graduated in 1543. Deep spiritual crisis and the fear of Hell shadowed his studies, from which he was freed by Luther's teachings in 1542. Flacius soon became a strict Gnesiolutheran, who fiercely opposed interims and participated in controversies on adiaphora, synergism, and original sin. For his straightforward style, Jörg Baur has called Flacius a "radical theologian". See Baur, "Flacius—Radikale Theologe," in *Einsicht und Glaube. Aufsätze* (Göttingen: Vandenhoeck & Ruprecht 1978), pp. 179, 181. Flacius participated in the Osiandrian controversy fairly late in 1552, but still managed to produce 16 writings opposing him. Wilhelm Preger, *Matthias Flacius Illyricus und seine Zeit* I–II, (Erlangen: Verlag von Theodor Bläsing 1859), pp. 15–22, 219; Peter Barton, "Matthias Flacius Illyricus," in *Gestalten der Kirchengeschichte*, bd. 6, hrsgb. Martin Greschat (Stuttgart: Verlag W. Kohlhammer 1981), pp. 277–280; Stupperich, *Osiander in Preussen*, pp. 292–293; Baur, "Flacius", pp. 175–176, 178.

[64] Barton, "Matthias Flacius", pp. 287–288.

[65] Flacius states that both Osiander and the Catholics come close to each other since both of them confuse inchoate obedience with justification. Flacius, *Verlegung*, Niij: "Denn das wort iustificare rechtfertigen bedeutet beiden dem Osiandro und Papisten mit der that gerecht machen / Sie sagen beyde das wir gantz und gar und mit der that gerecht werden / und verkleinen die Erbsünde / die noch ubrig bleibet... Er vermengt auch den Newen gehorsam mit der Gnedigen annemung."

[66] E.g., on the concept *regeneratio*, see Lauri Haikola, *Gesetz und Evangelium bei Matthias Flacius Illyricus. Eine Untersuchung zur lutherischen Theologie vor der Kondordienformel*, Studia Theologica Lundensia (Lund: CWK Cleerup 1952), pp. 315–317.

Flacius was the main reason that Lutheran theologians started to emphasize imputation over Christ's indwelling. The Philippist and Gnesiolutheran parties opposed Osiander using this emphasis—a way of thinking which eventually spread throughout the entire reformation.[67] The most significant development involved the detailed definition of different modes of imputation. At the Council of Trent, justification was specified through Aristotelian concepts of cause (material, formal, efficient, and final causes).[68] Flacius adapted this language, taking advantage of Aristotelian distinctions to seek as detailed an account of justification as possible.[69] Like Melanchthon, he defined justification in more detail as 'reckoning', i.e., imputation that takes place in God's mind:

> The justification of the sinner is the act of God in which He transfers or transcribes, all the time, like a Judge on his seat, the righteousness of His Son to believers, i.e., those who come to the throne of grace...in a rational although imputative application (*rationali quidem aut imputativa applicatione*), which however is powerful, real and effective.[70]
>
> Generally, imputation seems to mean a transfer of something (*translatio*), not however essential, but only rational transfer.[71]

On the other hand, Flacius saw that the Bible and Lutheran theologians spoke not only about imputation of Christ's righteousness but also about imputation of *faith* as righteousness.[72] Faith as righteousness is here a personal, present property within the individual. This was something

[67] Nüssel, *Allein aus Glauben*, p. 71.

[68] Heinrich Denzinger, *Kompendium der Glaubensbekenntnisse und kirchlichen Lehrentscheidungen*, 37. auflage (Freiburg im Bresgau: Herder 1991), p. 506 (*Tridentinum*).

[69] Flacius (*Clavis* II, 36) claims that the controversy between Osiandrians and Catholics centered on the instrumental and material causes of justification. "At contra maxima contentio est cum Papistis, primum de causa instrumentali; an sola fide apprehendamus justitiam? Secundo, cum Osiandro & Papistis, de causa materiali; quid id sit, quod nobis applicatum & quasi appositum, nos ut proxima causa, efficiat iustos?" The worst mistake was: "At Osiandristae & Papistae dicunt, illam adhibitionem justitiae fieri, non rationali quadam imputatione, sed reali infusione." Against Osiander, Flacius states that God's essential righteousness is a consuming flame for sinners; thus, the essential righteousness is incommunicable to humans as such. Flacius, *De iustificatione*, 117.

[70] Flacius, *De iustificatione*, 135: "Iustificatio peccatoris est, actio Dei, qua ille quotidie, tanquam iudex pro tribunali sedens, Filii iusticiam ad credentes, seu fide thronum gratiae accedentes & misericordiam per & propter Christum quarentes & implorantes, ob eius intercessionem transfert aut transscribit, rationali quidem aut imputativa tantum applicatione, sed tamen potenti, vera ac efficaci."

[71] Flacius, *De iustificatione*, 126: "Imputatio igitur in genere videtur significare quandam translationem alicuius rei, sed non essentialem, verum tantum rationalem."

[72] So CA IV and Rom. 4:3. Flacius, *Clavis* I, 422; *De iustificatione*, 126, 132.

that Flacius could not affirm. For this reason he saw a need to define the imputation of faith as righteousness such that faith as a present entity could not be regarded as a part of the formal righteousness (*iustitia formalis*) that avails *coram Deo*. Otherwise imputation would cease to be a rational act located in God's mind and would consequently be founded on something within the believer. The danger of this idea was its close resemblance to Catholic teaching on habitual grace, or Osiandrism.[73]

In order to define imputation of faith as righteousness as a forensic act, Flacius distinguished between two main classes of imputation (see appendix 1).[74] First, personal imputation (*imputatio personalis*), in which a person's real merit or guilt is reckoned to another person. This kind of imputation takes place when the righteousness of Christ is imputed to the sinner. This means that God transfers Christ's merit in his mind to the person involved in the act of justification, and, accordingly, the sins of the person are related to Christ. This kind of imputation does not imply considering a thing to be something other than it actually is. Imputation signifies exchange of a real entity between persons in a rational, not habitual sense. Christ's merit and human guilt change places in God's mind (*cogitatione*), although the people remain intact and without change.[75]

Second, real imputation (*imputatio realis*) occurs, which is comprised of two subcategories. First, a real virtue or personal property can be synedochically imputed to relate to the person as a whole. Second, a thing can be imputed to be real without its being so.[76] For example,

[73] Flacius, *Clavis* I, 424: "Verbum imputare... nusquam significare aliquam realem transfusionem, effectionem, exhibitionem, aut communicationem illius rei, de qua agitur: ut vel justitiae, vel iniustitiae: sed rationalem tantum, mentalem, aut consensus cogitationis, aut voluntatis tractationem."

[74] Flacius, *De iustificatione*, 127: "Duplex est imputatio: altera est realis, seu in re ipsa manens: altera personalis, seu in rei translatione ab alia persona ad aliam sita." On the modes of imputation, see also Haikola 1952, 318–323; Nüssel, *Allein aus Glauben*, pp. 74–76.

[75] Flacius, *De iustificatione*, 126–7: "Cum igitur iusticia aut meritum obedientia aut passio Christi nobis imputari dicitur, idem plane est, ac imputatione, ratione, seu firma ac solida cogitatione & decreto (ut est Dei) a Christo in nos transferri: ut alterius solutio aut debitum in alterum transferri, seu in alterum transscribi, eique acceptum aut datum ferri solet. Hic igitur in imputatione obedientiae Christi (ut dixi) imputare est, aliquid ab aliquo in alium transcribere, aut solo decreto transferre. Transfertur enim eius iusticia in nos, sicut antea fuit nostra iniustitia in eum transripta." Flacius hence uses the notion of salutary exchange but without participation in the person of Christ.

[76] Flacius, *De iustificatione*, 127: "In re aut realis imputatio est, cum res non vera, pro ipsa vera re, quae adesse debebat, suo quodam modo ab aliquibus habetur aut accipitur."

the banking system can impute the value of, say, 50 euros, to a nearly worthless piece of paper. Imputation of faith as righteousness is this kind of operation. In this view God accepts faith that receives Christ's merit as *the substitute* for original righteousness lost in the Fall.[77] Faith itself does not have any real form that could work as righteousness *coram Deo*. Trent states that this kind of imputation is only an illusion.[78] Flacius responded that it may be so if a human being performs the imputation; but if God does it, it is real.[79]

4.2.3. *The Order of Salvation as the Guarantee of the Reality of Justification*

The accusations of illusoriness made Flacius consider more deeply how justification and salvation actually affect the individual. As a result, the following order of salvation (*ordo salutis*)[80] emerged which depicts depicts the phases a person goes through in conversion. According to *De justificatione liber* the first phase is contrition (*contritio*), followed by faith (*fides*) generated by the promise of the Gospel. The third phase is justification (*iustificatio*), followed by donation of the Holy Spirit or renewal (*renovatio*).[81] In Flacius's order of salvation contrition and faith

[77] Flacius, *De iustificatione*, 76: "Alias contra, res nullius momenti pro vera re, eximioque bono, ob misericordiam aliquam, dispensationem, aut etiam stulticiam imputatoris imputatur; ut Romanis rubor ac verecundia Demetrii fuit pro innocentia regis Philippi patris: supplex deprecatio saepe fonti est, imputaturve pro innocentia: scita adulatio aulici saepe est regi loco eximiae virtutis, ut eum perinde complectatur ac sit industrius, fidus & utilis minister. Sic divitiae pro virtute sunt, habentur aut imputantur multis: sic adulatio in communi vita pro fida amiticia multis est. Hac ratione fides dicitur imputari ad iustitiam, quod externa quadam specie, aut saltem quod ad modum moremque loquendi, quoniam precario apprehendit veram iusticiam, locum eius utruncue suppleat, ut mox plenius dicitur." Flacius, *Clavis* I, 429: "Fidem alicui imputari ad justitiam, Rom. 4. v. 5. proprie significat, esse illi loco justitiae: non, quia re ipsa sit justitia, aut ullo modo vicem justitiae subeat: sed tum, quia is illa, veluti mendica manu, acquirit alienam justitiam..."

[78] Denzinger, *Kompendium*, p. 518 (*Tridentinum*). See canons 11 and 12 especially.

[79] Flacius, *De iustificatione*, 139: "Denique sicut illa imputatio nostrae Christo imputatae iniusticiae non quiddam leve, ioculare aut umbratile, aut denique fictum fuit, sed tam grande et grave onus, ut eum usque ad inferos deprimeret: ita vicissim eius quoque iusticia a Deo efficacissime nobis imputatur, adeoque nobis fructuosa ac salutaris sit, ut nos ab imis inferis usque ad coelum attollat & inter filios Dei ac haeredes aeterneae vitae sistat & considere faciat."

[80] Although Flacius tried to form a coherent system of the order of salvation, the exact notion of *ordo salutis* was not introduced until the beginning of the 18th century. Flacius (*De iustificatione*, 136) speaks about the order of justification (*ordo justificationis*).

[81] Flacius, *De iustificatione*, 136–137.

are prerequisites of justification, followed by justification and renewal. The ordering implies a process that develops through time and cannot be reduced merely to logical or terminological distinctions.[82]

This is implied in *De voce et re fidei*, which describes the movements of faith (*motus*) in the believer. The movement begins with knowledge of the Law. This causes terror and fear of damnation, i.e., contrition. Third, cognition of the Gospel (*cognitio evangelii*). The fourth phase is prayer (*oratio*), in which the individual asks to receive the things promised in the Gospel. The fifth phase is trust that the prayer has been heard. Sixth, trust in the mercy of God.[83] Regeneration takes place in phase four as a part of the prayer, because prayer is an empirical sign of the regenerate mind.[84] Contrition is a life-long process of fear and trust. It is an actual event effected by God, which repeats itself again and again. In this way, Flacius can define the process of faith without change in the person.[85]

In order to emphasize the free nature of justification, Flacius defined it according to Aristotelian theories of causes. The *causa efficiens remotior* is God's mercy and *causa efficiens propinquior* is Christ's obedience, death and intercession. The *causa materialis ex qua* is Christ's fulfillment of the Law through obedience and suffering. The *causa materialis in qua* is the person as an object of imputation. The *causa formalis* is the imputation of Christ's righteousness. Faith on the part of the believer is the *causa instrumentalis*. For God, the instrumental cause is the Word and the Sacraments (see appendix 2). Flacius uses this definition to represent faith as an entity that is not a new meritorious quality in the individual but signifies simply apprehension of Christ's merit. The form

[82] Flacius, *De iustificatione*, 149: "Licet autem necessario sequatur hanc imputativam iusticiam, etiam quaedam realis, seu (ut Scholastici loquntur) infusa, aut (ut nostri) inchoata, qua Deus nos per Spiritum suum renatos iam, reipsa quoque ex iniustis facere incipit iustos, tum intus renovando tum vero etiam foris bona opera per nos efficiendo: non tamen haec est nostra illa vera Evangelica aut fidei iustiticia, vel etiam pars aliqua eius, qua coram Dei iusti & vitae eternae haeredes constituimur: sed diversum planè eiusdem servatoris nostri beneficium, & effectus, aut etiam consequens iustificationis." Haikola, *Gesetz und Evangelium*, p. 313; Nüssel, *Allein aus Glauben*, p. 83.

[83] Flacius, *De voce*, 25–31.

[84] Flacius, *De voce*, 31: "Atque ita fide iustificati, pacem habemus & gaudium Spiritus sancti, ubi simul & regeneratio fit, quae tamen iam antea in quarto motu, id est in expetitione agniti boni fieri incoeperat: ac omnes actiones regenerati hominis, omniaque bona opera consequuntur."

[85] Haikola 1952, 314–315; Nüssel, *Allein aus Glauben*, pp. 90–91.

of justification is the apprehension of forgiveness.[86] Faith justifies only because it grasps Christ's merit.

> ...Faith justifies only to the extent that it gazes on Christ's work, merit, fulfilling of the Law, and redemption, and apprehends it, not to the extent that it clings to Christ's essential righteousness infused into us.[87]

God, not the believer, is the cause of all this.[88] In order to secure this, Flacius formulated his grim doctrine that makes original sin the substance of man. Man is thus no longer the image of God, but the image of the devil (*imago diabolii*). However, Flacius's view was not as extreme as it appears ostensibly, and as it was commonly interpreted. Flacius made a distinction between material substance (*substantia materialis*) and formal substance (*substantia formalis*). In the human being, original sin is a formal substance, not a material one. The material substance is the body and the soul. Continuity in material substance remains after the Fall; radical change occurs in the formal, theological substance. Before faith the human being is in the power of sin according to his or her formal substance and all meritorious action is a sheer impossibility.[89] Ultimately Flacius's view was too radical and never gained general acceptance: FC condemned it as a Manichean heresy.[90]

---

[86] Flacius, *De iustificatione*, 153: "Secundo, si consideretur ut nobis applicatur, causa formalis est, nobis porrò eam obedientiam sic imputatam esse, seu ipsa ratio applicationis eius, quae idem est cum remissione peccatorum, aut iustificatione quae aliquo modo effectus, sed valde vicinus prioris dici posset."

[87] Flacius, *Verlegung*, Kij 2f: "Hieraus erscheinet klerlich / Das D. Luthers meinung gewest ist / das uns der glaube Gerecht mache/ so fern er die Werck / verdinst / Gnugthuung / und Erlösung Christi ansihet und ergreyfft / Nicht / so fern er von Gott erlangt / das uns die wesentliche Gerechtigkeit Christi eingegossen werde."

[88] Günter Moldaenke, *Matthias Flacius Illyricus. Schriftverständnis und Schriftauslegung im Zeitalter der Reformation*, teil I. (Stuttgart: Verlag von W. Kohlhammer 1936), pp. 454–456, 470.

[89] Flacius, *Clavis* II, 663. See also *Haikola, Gesetz und Evangelium*, pp. 118–128; Nüssel, *Allein aus Glauben*, p. 94. Flacius opposed Strigel, who had claimed that original sin is only an accidental quality. After all, Flacius's view is quite close to Luther, for whom Christ is the form of the justified person. Before this can occur, the Law must annihilate the previous form perverted by sin. Of the Gnesiolutherans, at least Musaeus, Wigand, and Heshuss sided initially with Flacius but later also turned against him.

[90] *BSELK Epit.* I, 19–24 (774–775). *FC* did not address Flacius's distinction between material and formal substances. However, it condems the use of concepts such as substance and accidence as problematic since lay people do not understand them. The learned can use them if needed. On Flacius's anthropology, see Walter Sparn, "*Substanz oder Subjekt? Die Kontroverse um die anthropologischen Allgemeinbegriffe im Artikle von der Erbsünde*," in *Widerspruch, Dialog und Einigung*, hrsgb. Wenzel Lohff & Lewis Spitz (Stuttgart: Calwer Verlag 1977).

Although Flacius repeated the forensic and extrinsic aspect of Melanchthon's doctrine of justification, it was the intrinsic that caused him problems.[91] Flacius admitted that Luther used the word 'righteousness' in the sense of 'essential' (*wesentlich*). Flacius interpreted this as contrary to 'actual'. In other words, God's righteousness is permanent and not evanescent.[92] Surely, Christ is essentially righteous but the imputed righteousness is based on Christ's obedience, not on His essence.[93] Flacius claimed—contrary to Osiander—that what Christ does justifies the sinner, not who Christ is.[94] Justification does not consist of participation in the divine since it actually takes place in the life to come.[95] Here Flacius departs from Luther. Flacius seems to be the first Lutheran

---

[91] Melanchthon's doctrine of justification was clearly not forensic enough since Flacius omits the donation of the Spirit and focuses merely on the correlative aspect.

[92] Flacius, *Verlegung*, Iiij 3: "Es redet aber D. Luther am selben ort in keinen weg von der wesentlichen Gerechtigkeit Gottes / sonder zeigt an mit klaren worten / warumb er die Gerechtigkeit des glaubens Essentialem / wesentlich nenne / nemlich weil (wie gesagt) sie allezeit bleibt / und nicht auffhöret / wie die actualis..." Flacius, *Verlegung*, Kiij 3f: "Also leret Doct: Luther alhie klerlich und unterschiedlich / das es ein ander ding sey / durch den Mitler Christum mit Gotte versünet oder Gerechtigkeit / und Gottes freund werden / und ein anders / nach dem du nu Gerechtfertigt bist / und Gotte zum freunde und Vater hast / das du seiner Göttlichen Natur / und aller seiner Güter / teilhafftig wirst." Erikson (*Inhabitatio*, p. 108) claims that "man kan märka en tydlig tendens hos Flacius att mer eller mindre 'bortförklara' de ställen där Luther talar om hur Kristus genom tron bor i människans hjärta." See also Erikson, *Inhabitatio*, pp. 102–103; Flacius, *Verlegung*, Ciij 2–D.

[93] Flacius, *Verlegung*, Giij 2ff: "Durch diese Argument acht ich / sey klerlich gnug beweiset / das Christus warhafftiger Gott nicht allein die ewige wesentliche gerechtigkeit habe / sonder auch die / durch welcher er das Gesetz erfüllet / und der gerechtigkeit Gottes / welche straff und gehorsam von dem menschen erfordert / auffs aller reiclichste und uberflüssigste / für uns gnug thun hat...das unsere Gerechtigkeit darinne stehe / das unsere Sünde auff Christum gelegt / und Christi gehorsam oder Gerechtigkeit und gnugthuung uns zugerechnet wird / dadurch wir vergebung der Sünden / Gerechtigkeit / und endlich die Kindschafft erlangen." See also Preger, *Matthias Flacius*, pp. 232–238.

[94] Flacius, *Verlegung*, Hij: "Denn diese wort / Gerechtigkeit, Weisheit & c. bedeuten alhie nicht eine qualitaté, was Christus fur eine art an sich habe, Sonder eine Actionem oder Effectum / was er Thut / Ausrichtet / und in uns wircket / Ja die zwey wörter Sanctificatio & Redemptio / heiligung und Erlösung / sunt nomina verbalia seu actionem / bedeuten That und nicht substantiam oder qualitatem / Das also wenn sie gleich der Gottheit zugelegt würden / so könten sie gleichwol nicht wesentlich davon verstanden werden, Denn Gott ist ja nicht eine Action oder Wirckung."

[95] Flacius, *Verlegung*, Miij 2: "Aber die erbschafft / teilhafftijkeit / und genissung der Göttheit uns aller ihrer güter / welche uns endlich in ienem leben volkömlich widderfaren wird / ist nicht proprie die Rechtfertigung / sonder viel mehr gleichsam eine belonung der Rechtfertigung / und das ewige leben oder seligkeit...Hie hören wir klerlich / das unsere (so zu reden) Gottheit oder teilhafftigkeit der Gottheit / von welcher wir itzt nur geringe erstlinge haben / eigentlich zu der künfftigen seligkeit und geniessung Gottes gehöret." See also Haikola, *Gesetz und Evangelium*, pp. 316–317.

theologian who makes so sharp a distinction between justification and indwelling.[96] Justification is not a participatory event; it is depicted with relational concepts. Renewal (in the sense of both *renovatio*$_1$ and *renovatio*$_2$) is distinguished from justification. Although Flacius describes the effective changes in the believer in great detail, his basic solution is similar to Melanchthon, who stated in in his *Commentary on Romans* that renewal is understood in the sense of becoming affected by the Spirit, which does not belong to justification.

Flacian terminology effectively safeguarded faith against ideas of faith as an infused virtue. On the other hand, one may ask whether faith is not actually a human virtue if it does not have divine form. Faith is something non-divine, which God considers as divine, even though it is not actually so.[97] Here Flacius comes very close to the *meritum de congruo* doctrine.

Flacius is unable to offer a holistic picture of the essence of faith: while faith occurs in the person, anything internal is excluded from justification. The following gift of the Spirit is a divine entity, of course, but it is explicitly excluded from justification. Additionally, Flacius's way of meticulously defining the empirical movements in the mind is juxtaposed with his emphasis on extrinsicness. The crucial question remains: how can the Spirit effect faith or change towards faith without being present?[98] How can salvation occur *sola fide*, if the prerequisite of faith, the change in the theological substance of the person, is a matter of sanctification, rather than justification?

Later Lutheranism never used the exact Flacian modes of imputation, perhaps because of Flacius's radical views on original sin. In spite of this, justification was conceptually defined as imputation from Flacius onwards, a notion supported by Luther's late disputations.

---

[96] Flacius, *De iustificatione*, pp. 172–175, 182. According to Haikola (*Gesetz und Evangelium*, pp. 254–258), Flacius manages to keep the person of Christ together better than Osiander. For Flacius, redemption is not just a prerequisite for but also the substance of justification. The merit applied in justification is based on Christ's works as true God and true man.

[97] Flacius's theology has substantial differences in relation to Luther. For Flacius, faith as present reality is not righteousness. Compared to Luther, he has less understanding of the ontological status of faith. Luther thinks that faith justifies because of the present *iustitia formalis*, whereas Flacius tried to explain such notions away. Because Christ is the essence of faith, it is consequently *the actualization of the original relationship with God* that was lost in the Fall. For Luther, faith is not just a substitute for original righteousness. See Nüssel, *Allein aus Glauben*, pp. 108–111.

[98] Flacius, *De iustificatione*, p. 173: "Primum ergo est fides, postea Spiritum sanctum inhabitans, ex quo renovatio."

4.3. *Conclusion*

The examination of Osiander's and Flacius's thought shows the theological disunity and instability of early Lutheranism. Both Osiander and Flacius wanted to be genuine followers of Luther despite their great mutual differences. Osiander understood justification as participation in Christ's divine nature. On the contrary, Flacius denied the role of participation as a part of justification. They taught different notions on the effective character of justification. Osiander spoke about it even more forcefully than Luther, which caused the danger of mixing *renovatio*$_1$ and *renovatio*$_2$. Flacius wanted to play the whole issue of participation down, as Melanchthon did in his *Commentary on Romans*.

The controversy reveals how the nature of justifying faith plays the main role. Is it to be understood through Christ's presence and participation or should faith be described only by relational concepts? Must faith have the divine form in itself or is it enough that God reckons the movements in the mind aroused by the Spirit as a substitute for original righteousness?

Despite the apparent weaknesses in Osiander's thought, particularly on the issue of the nature of faith, his position was more congruent with Luther than that of Flacius. The merit of Flacius is the safeguarding of presuppositionless nature of salvation and the emphasis on the certainty of salvation. Later Lutheranism had to survive the pressure of both Flacius and Osiander: how was the christological and intrinsic nature of faith to be maintained and the dangers of subjectivism prevented at the same time? This problem was taken up, among others, by Joachim Mörlin and Martin Chemnitz.

CHAPTER FIVE

JOACHIM MÖRLIN AND MARTIN CHEMNITZ: TOWARDS A SYNTHESIS OF EXTREMES

Martin Chemnitz, Melanchthon's student and a specialist in patristic theology, was one of the leading figures in early Lutheranism. His formulation of the doctrine of justification can be positioned in a category between Osiander and Flacius. Like Flacius, Chemnitz wanted to maintain justification as an objective event yet simultaneously relate it to communion with Christ. The same idea can be found in the texts of Joachim Mörlin, a close friend and a colleague of Chemnitz.

5.1. *Joachim Mörlin: Incarnated Christ as the Righteousness of the Sinner*

While there are only a few studies available on Joachim Mörlin (1514–1571),[1] his theology had a great impact on early Lutheran theology in two ways.[2] First, he was one of the leading figures of the anti-osiandrian front. His letters and examinations on the development of the controversy formed the impressions of other Lutherans for a long time, even after the conflict.[3] Second, he worked closely with Chemnitz, who took

---

[1] Mörlin studied in Wittenberg under Luther and Melanchthon. Luther especially considered Mörlin a promising theologian, and states about him that "if anyone will follow my teaching after I have passed away, it'll be this man" After his promotion (1540), Mörlin served as superintendent in Arnstadt and Göttingen. In 1550 he fled to Königsberg for the sake of the Interim, where he made friends with Osiander. In 1554 Mörlin was selected as superintendent of Braunschweig. During his office he participated actively in theological discussion, even vainly trying to heal the rift between Melanchthon and Flacius. Mörlin was not polemical like many other Gnesiolutherans. He appreciated Melanchthon, despite disagreeing with him on many points. Stupperich, *Osiander in Preussen*, pp. 193–194; Roth, "Ein Braunschweiger Theologe", p. 60.

[2] One of the reasons for the small number of studies is the lack of source material. This study uses Mörlin's *Historia* and *Repetitio*, which, however, are relatively short. The most important source is Mörlin's correspondence with Osiander (*OA* 9).

[3] Roth, "Ein Braunschweiger Theologe", p. 59; Hauke, *Gott-Haben*, p. 285. Mörlin's influence can be seen in *Wigand's* exposition of Osiander's teachings (*De Osiandrismo*).

advantage of some of his theological formulations.[4] Especially interesting is Mörlin's response to Osiander's doctrine of justification.

When Mörlin arrived in Köningsberg in 1550, where the conflict surrounding Osiander was just gaining momentum, he considered Osiander to be in agreement with Luther.[5] For a while Osiander and Mörlin were close friends. Osiander rejoiced in this, since now he had a friend with whom he could defend the genuine (γνήσια) teaching of Luther.[6] However, the friendship ended as the controversy deepened. Although Mörlin had first defended Osiander, he became his fierce opponent.[7] While Mörlin criticized Osiander extensively he never denied Osiander's thesis on the relation between Christ's indwelling and justification. In his own texts Mörlin also emphasized the indwelling of Christ in faith. In spite of this, he saw dangerous aberrations in Osiander's teachings. Mörlin depicted the development of the crisis and the teachings of the various parties in his most prominent work *Historia Welcher gestalt sich die Osiandrische schwermerey im lande zu Preussen erhaben* (1554). *Historia* lists fifteen theses that united the anti-osiandrian front.[8]

> I. Christ is not our salvation 'by half' so that we would have no more than forgiveness of sins through Him, as the Interimists imagine. II. But He is wholly our righteousness so that we receive through Him both forgiveness of sins and imputation of righteousness; i.e., in justification there is nothing that belongs to the sinner but everything belongs to Christ or is Christ himself. III. This righteousness is received only through the word. IIII. And this word of justification does not bring with itself any other than Christ, Son of God and Son of Mary. V. The only way to apprehend and grasp this word is through faith. VI. I.e., through faith everyone actually receives Christ the Mediator as their own. VII. In whom we also are righteousness before God. VIII. This is not through infused virtues dwelling in our person, or virtues flowing from us. IX. And not because of the great glory and value of the faith. X. But in the person of Christ XI. However, not outside of us. XII. But for the sake of Him

[4] J. A. O. Preus, *The Second Martin*, 98.

[5] Scholars have considered Luther's and Mörlin's doctrines almost identical. According to Stupperich (*Osiander in Preussen*, p. 195): "Rechtfertigung und Heiligung wollte (Mörlin) nicht in zwei akte auseinandergenommen sehen, sondern er betonte im Sinne von Luthers "fröhlichen wechsel" die Einheit von Rechtfertigung und Heiligung, die sich in einem Zuge vollzügen..." See also Roth, "Ein Braunschweiger Theologe".

[6] *AO* 9, 448, 7–10 (*Osiander an Mörlin* 24.8.1550).

[7] *Stupperich* (*Osiander in Preussen*, pp. 114–165) offers a detailed account of the relations between Osiander and Mörlin. See also Roth, "Ein Braunschweiger Theologe", pp. 61–66, 69.

[8] Mörlin, *Historia*, Eii^{v}–Fii^{v}. See also Stupperich, *Osiander in Preussen*, p. 115.

> who is given and offered to us and whom we apprehend and to whom we are joined. XIII. Also, we are not righteous for the sake of our own or other human piety, against all papacy, and the gates of Hell. XIIII. But only through God's righteousness. XV. For Christ is God, who has died for our sins and risen for our justification.[9]

Although these theses are not examined any further in *Historia*,[10] together they form a coherent system of thought which is examined in what follows. Mörlin's concept of divine righteousness donated to the believer in faith was different than Osiander's. As already noted, Osiander had claimed that Christ's work cannot be the righteousness that avails *coram Deo*. This was derived from his understanding of *communication idiomatum*, according to which there is no real communication of the attributes between Christ's human and divine natures.

In principle, it is in accord with Luther's teaching to claim that justifying righteousness is God's essential righteousness.[11] However, Osiander's emphasis suggested rereading Luther to discern a better understanding of what Luther actually meant. Mörlin denied that justifying righteousness is God's essential righteousness. The reason for this distinction was his interpretation of Osiander. For Mörlin, Osiander's concept

---

[9] Mörlin, *Historia*, Fi^{v}–Fii: "Diese lauten zu deutsch also des seind wir einig. I. Das Christus nicht allein zum halben teil uns erlösung sey / als hetten wir nicht mehr an im / denn vergebung der Sünden / wie die Interimisten davon trewmen. II. Sondern das er alle unsere Gerechtigkeit sey / dermassen / das wir an im haben beide vergebung der Sünden / und zurechnung der gerechtigkeit / Also / das in der rechtfertigung nichts sey des Sünders / Sondern alles allein Christi / oder Christus selbst. III. Das alle diese Gerechtigkeit niemands anders wird angetragen / denn allein durchswort. IIII. Und das das wort / in dem handel der Rechtfertigung / nichts bringe / denn allein Christum Gottes und Marien Son. V. Welchs wort / keinerley weg mag ergriffen / oder jemands zugeeignet werden / denn allein durch den Glauben. VI. Also das der Glaube / diesen Mitteler Christum / wahrhafftiglich einem jedern zu eigen möchte. VII. In welchem wir auch wahrhafftiglich vor Gott gerecht seind durch die zugerechnung. VIII. Das ist / nicht umb einiger eingegossener oder von uns selbs erlangeter tugend willen / in unser person. IX. Darumb auch nicht von wegen der grossen wirdigkeit oder ansehens des Glaubens selbs. X. Sondern in person Christi. XI. Doch nicht ausser uns. XII. Sondern umb seinet willen / wie er uns geschenkt / angetragen / zugeeignet / und durch den vereinigt ist. XIII. Und seind wir also gerecht / nicht von wegen einiger unserer oder auch anderer Menschlicher frömigkeit willen / wider das gantze Bapstumb und alle pforten der hellen. XIIII. Sondern allein durch Gottes gerechtigkeit. XV. Denn Christus ist Gott / welcher umb unserer Sünde willen gestorben / und umb unserer rechtfertigung willen widerumb ist aufferstanden."

[10] The *Historia* is a kind of companion, which contains correspondence, short texts, and a section with a comparison of quotes from Luther's and Osiander's texts.

[11] According to Peura (*Mehr als ein Mensch?*, pp. 49–50, 244–245), Luther did not separate God from His attributes. Consequently, participation in the grace of God is equivalent to participation in God Himself.

of essential righteousness means *righteousness that has been separated from Christ's salvific acts.*[12] Mörlin deemed it suspect that Osiander spoke out about Christ's indwelling but was silent about Christ's actions and their meaning for the individual's salvation.[13]

Mörlin was thus obliged to describe in more detail how it is possible to speak about God's essential righteousness as the righteousness given to sinners. The distinction between the two concepts of God's righteousness comes to the fore in the correspondence between Mörlin and Osiander, which eventually ended their friendship. In his letter to Osiander on 18.4.1551, Mörlin accuses him of three things. First, Christ's merit is not given its due.[14] Second, Osiander denies the notion of two different righteousnesses. According to Mörlin, the righteousness of Christ is based on His relation to the Father *before the incarnation* and also *based on the incarnation.*[15] Third, Mörlin claims that it is wrong to teach that justifying righteousness is the former, as Osiander does, since the righteousness given to sinners is based on the incarnation.[16] Osiander denied this, and in the next letter Mörlin wrote again to Osiander: "if my friendship is not good enough for you, it suits me fine, for I am a friend of the truth."[17]

---

[12] Hauke, *Gott-Haben*, p. 288.

[13] Mörlin, *Wieder*, Di: "Osiander hat gestritten / das nicht der gehorsam Christi / sondern die inwonende wesentliche Gerechtigkeit / unsere Gerechtigkeit des Glaubens sey." See also *Stupperich* 1973, 156–157. Mörlin concluded that this caused uncertainty about the forgiveness of sins since the believer starts to observe the effects of the renewal; the present righteousness was identified wrongly with internal change. Mörlin, *Antwort*, Biii. "Dieselbige gerechtigkeit sey nichts vergebung der Sünden / Sondern die verneuerung." See also *Antwort*, Biv.

[14] *AO* 9, 620, 13–15 (*Mörlin an Osiander*).

[15] *AO* 9, 620, 19–621, 4 (*Mörlin an Osiander*).

[16] *AO* 9, 621 (*Mörlin an Osiander*): "Tertio ne igitur de mea sententia haesites, si forte me antea non satis intellexisti, statuo fortiter, fortius, fortissime et sum super omnia certus iusticiam hominis peccatoris non esse illam iusticiam, qua Pater, Filius et Spiritus sanctus absolute extra incarnationem positive sunt iusti, quia hoc est simpliciter facere beneficium et meritum Christi in incarnatione merum nihil; deinde non esse novitatem aut ullas qualitates divinitus infusas vel acquisitas, sed esse iusticiam Filii incarnati, qui Deus et homo, natus ex Maria virgine, mortuus est propter peccata et resurrexit propter iustificationem nostram, nobis credentibus in sua persona hoc meritum cum omnibus virtutibus tribuens per imputationem. Extra hanc mediatricem quae ab incarnatione incipit, non tempore, sed forma, nullam aliam audiemus, quia ad hanc unam et solam remittit nos scriptura, cum de iustificatione hominis peccatoris loquitur." See also Stupperich, *Osiander in Preussen*, p. 139; Hauke, *Gott-Haben*, pp. 285–288.

[17] *AO* 9, 626, 7–9 (*Mörlin an Osiander*). Osiander had underlined the words of Mörlin: "Hanc obedientiam Filii esse iusticiam", and the word "negamus" appears in the margin. *AO* 9, 621, 3–4.

Mörlin's anti-osiandrian strategy culminated in the realistic nature of the *communicatio idiomatum*.[18] Emphasizing the reality of the communication of attributes within Christ's natures, Mörlin managed to keep Christ's actions as part of His person. God as such, in His essential righteousness and before the incarnation, is terrifying for sinners. Through the incarnation Christ has reconciled the world with God the Father. For Mörlin, *communicatio idiomatum* guarantees the unity of the essence and actions of Christ because He has not fulfilled his reconciling work simply in one nature but as a person. It is therefore no longer something that exists only in the created realm, as Osiander thought.[19]

This argument is further explained in his *Disputatio de Communicatio idiomatum* (1571), which points out that it is correct to say that God suffers *in Christ.*, or that this human being is omnipotent. In Christ the natures do nothing apart from each other. Everything Christ does, He does as one person. Accordingly, Christ's suffering, death, and resurrection all belong to the person who is both God and man. It is the realistic notion of the communication of the attributes that makes coherent christology and soteriology possible: the righteousness of the sinner is Christ who is both God and man. Therefore, Christ's acts can be a part of His person.[20]

In his later writings, Mörlin often emphasized the blood of Christ (*Blut Christi*) as the matter of righteousness. This notion works as a metaconcept for the afore-mentioned christological and soteriological constructs, especially for righteousness based on the incarnation. During

[18] Stupperich, *Osiander in Preussen*, p. 195.

[19] Mörlin, *Historia*, Xii: "Darumb wenn ich sage / das leiden / das sterben / der tod / die aufferstehung / ist meine Gerechtigkeit / so ist gar viel ein anders / denn wenn ich sage / das werck / die Creatur ist meine Gerechtigkeit / jenes ist von der person formaliter nicht gescheiden / die Gott ist / und in dem der Gott unser Gerechtigkeit ist / sondern bringet mir allezeit die mit / ja das thun die andern Creaturn nicht." *AO* 9, 648, 29–31. (*Mörlin an Osiander* 25.4.1551): "iusticiam non esse creaturam, quia Christum non est creatura, nec esse ullius hominis obedientiam vel meritum, imo nec humanitatis Christi." *AO* 9, 649, 4–6 (*Mörlin an Osiander* 25.4.1551). "Haec omnia sunt idiomata divinae naturae, sed non in divinitate absoluta contra omne tuum figmentum—sed incarnata. Itaque Deus est iusticia nostra in forma servi, ut divus Paulus vocat."

[20] Mörlin, *Communicatione*, theses 19, 22, 40 and 41: "19. Recte dicitur, Deus est passus... 20. Et recte dicitur, hic homo potens est rerum omnium.... 40. Non ergo quidquam nunc facit vel patitur natura vel divina vel humana. 41. Sed omnia patitur et facit persona, quae Deus est et homo."

the course of the debate, Mörlin got the nickname '*Bluttheologe*' from Osiander.[21]

Mörlin claimed, as Osiander did, that God himself is the *iustitia formalis* of sinners, but only because He has become sin in Christ.[22] This is underlined by the concept of 'obedience' (*Gehorsam*).[23] The essence of righteousness can be described in terms of various concepts, such as the blood of Christ, the forgiveness of sins, and Christ himself, as long as the unity of the person is maintained since Christ is both God and man.[24]

Osiander had stated that if Christ does not become one with the sinner, the merit of Christ is of no use, and Mörlin agreed on this point. The concept of application (*applicatio*) comes to the fore in the writings of Mörlin. The merit of Christ must be owned personally by the individual in order to have effect. Christ is not the savior of the sinner outside (*ausser*) of himself or herself, otherwise the whole world would

---

[21] E.g. Mörlin, *Apologia*, G iii: "...das unsere Gerechtigkeit des Glaubens / sey das Blut Christi." See Hauke, *Gott-Haben*, 285.

[22] *AO* 9, 649, 10–12. (*Mörlin an Osiander* 25.4.1551): "Deus est formalis iusticia nostra, non quando est iustus in sese ab aeterno, quia hoc semper est, sed quando fit peccatum pro nobis." Mörlin's doctrine of kenosis is similar to Luther: Christ has truly become sin. E.g., Mörlin calls Christ "the dumping ground of Braunschweig." Kolb, *Luther's Heirs*, VIII, 145.

[23] Hauke, *Gott-Haben*, p. 292.

[24] Mörlin, *Repetitio*, Ii: "Nemlich / die gantze Erlösung im Todt und Blut christi / mit der Vergebung der Sünden in der Person dieses einigen Mitlers zu unser Rechtfertigung gehören / Darumb redet es die Schrifft ohn unterscheid / Wir seind gerecht durch die Erlösung. Roman. 3. In seinem Blut / Roman. 5. Vergebung der Sünden ist unsere gerechtigkeit. Joha. 16. Oder Christus ist unsere gerechtigkeit /1. Cor. 1. Denn da wird Christus nicht verstanden / allein nach der menschlichen Natur / wie Stanckar Schwermet / auch nicht allein nach der Göttlichen / wie Osiander treuget. Sondern es wird der Gott verstanden / der aus dem Stam Davids geborn / ein recht Naturlich Mensch / und seines Volcks König und Erlöser ist / Jerem. 23. und 33." *Mörlin Historia*, Xii. "Es saget ja Christus elbst / das sey die gerechtigkeit / das er zum Vater gehet...So wenig aber wir die person ausschliessen / wenn wir sagen / das leiden und sterben ist unser Erlösung...also wenig schliessen wir auch die person damit aus / wenn wir sagen / Der Gang Christi ist unsere Gerechtigkeit...Jene geschehen von Gott / ja ausser seiner person / hie gechiet alles...inder person / die der ware Gott selbst ist." Roth, "Ein Braunschweiger Theologe", 73 offers a relatively positive judgment on Mörlin's formulation: "Schöner kann man die Einheit von Werk und Person Christi ja noch mehr: die Einhet von Gott und Golgatha, kaum ausdrücken." See also Hauke, *Gott-Haben*, 221. According to Hauke (*Gott-Haben*, pp. 293–294), the basic difference between Osiander and Mörlin is that: "Für Mörlin ist das Konsequenszmacherei, die die Grenzen der vom Glauben bezeugten Einheit des Werkes Christi überschreitet. Er will mit seiner Position sichern, dass Jesu Werk keiner Ergänzung bedarf, dass er wirklich 'genug getan' hat, Osiander hingegen will auf die Verankerung des Erlösungwerkes in Gottes Wesen aufmerksam machen." However, Mörlin seeks to bind justification to God's essence as well.

be saved. Of course, Christ has completed his salvific work completely outside of the sinner so that it is free from human merits,[25] but the righteousness of Christ must still become *formaliter* the righteousness of the believer. This takes place in application, where the righteousness of Christ, namely Christ himself, is communicated to the believer.[26]

The union (*vereinigung*) with Christ takes place in faith, which enables the believer to apprehend Christ's righteousness.[27] Justification means communion between Christ and the sinner, a communion that involves salutary exchange: what the sinner is, is given to Christ and accordingly what Christ is, is given to the sinner. The fact that Christ gives himself does not make the believer perfect, and he or she still needs imputation to cover the sin that clings in his or her flesh. Because sanctification never reaches completion in this life, contrition and belief that sins are forgiven never cease. In justification, *communicatio* precedes *imputatio*, which means that union with Christ is prerequisite for justification.[28] Even so, renewal (*renovatio*$_2$) is not reckoned as justifying righteousness, for such is apprehended in Christ alone through faith.[29]

---

[25] Mörlin, *Historia*, Ci^v–Cii: "Christus ist nicht ein versüner ausser uns / denn also weren alle menschen durch ihn versünet / Er hat ja das werck der versünung auser uns für alle volnbracht / wo das nu sine applicatione gnug were / so were alle welt selig / und zu gleich ganz und gar niemands verdampt / darumb mus uns das werkc adplicirt werden / das werck aber lesst sich von der person Christi nicht scheiden / denn sonst ohne diese person were es auch keine versünung / noch Got gefellig oder angenem / Aber darumb ist so köstlich / wichtig und gros / das es von dem lieben Sohn geschehen / der warer Gott und mensch ist." See also Mörlin, *Repetitio*, Jiiii^v–Ki.

[26] *AO* 9, 651, 29–652, 3 (*Mörlin an Osiander* 25.4.1551): "Non est respective iusticia Christi in forma servi crucifixi et resuscitati, sed formaliter, ita ut non modo attulerit nobis tanquam internuncius, non meruerit tantum, vel per applicationem nobis communicaverit iusticiam, ipse—quem praedicamus crucifixum, 1. Cor. 1 [23]—factus est nobis iusticia etc."

[27] Mörlin, *Historia*, Fi^v–Fii: "X. Sondern in person Christi. XI. Doch nicht ausser uns. XII. Sondern umb seinet willen / wie er uns geschenkt / angetragen / zugeeignet / und durch den vereinigt ist."

[28] Mörlin, *Historia*, Cii–Cii^v: "Doch macht illa communicatio das unser /sein / id est, peccatum & infirmitatem nostram transfert in eum, quia nos in eum transfert / Unnd widerumb machet sie das seine unser / id est, iusticiam & vitam aeternam, Quia donavit illum nobis, & transtulit eum in nos / Und absorbit er das unser in im / Aber macht das seine nicht volkomen in uns / nisi per imputationem, donec corruptibile incorruptionem induat / darumb mus auch poenitentia, fides, & peccatorum remissio / nimermehr in disem leben auff hören."

[29] Mörlin, *Historia*, Zi–Zi^v: "Objectio. Der Glaube wird wol unser Gerechtigkeit genennet / er ists aber darumb nicht / denn Paulus spricht / der Glaube werde zugerechnet / was nun fur ein ding gerechtnet / das ist das ding nicht. Responsio. Contra, Eben darumb / das Gott uns den Glauben zur Gerechtigkeit rechnet / darfur auffniemet / So ist er unsere Gerechtigkeit vor Gott / darinnen wir nun allein sollen und müssen Gerecht werden. Er ist ja die Gerechtigkeit nicht / die Gott im Gesetz

In a late text by Mörlin, *Repetitio Corporis Doctrinae ecclesiasticae* (1567), a new distinction is introduced with respect to a description of justification. Justification takes place through mercy alone, not because of new powers or the succeeding indwelling of the divine nature.[30] This distinction is not explained further. In fact, it may seem contradictory to his earlier writings, and even with respect to *Repetitio* itself, in which Mörlin repeated the earlier claim that justification involves an intrinsic change in the believer and is not an extrinsic event. In justification the Holy Spirit cleanses hearts through faith and creates a new being (*Newen wesen*).[31] The justified person is a good tree (*ein guter Baum*)[32] since justification involves apprehending both the favor and the gift.[33] Mörlin considered justification an effective reality (*renovatio$_1$*) as well, although he still stated that it is a papal heresy that good works and renewal (*verneuerung*) could avail *coram Deo*.[34] However, the christological basis of faith and renewal falters if they are disconnected from participation in divine reality.[35]

---

erfordert / das ist zwar / Dieweil aber Gott den Glauben darfur anniemet / so ist das auch allein / uns sonst keine andere / so vor Gott gilt / und darinnen wir allein Gerecht und selig werden. War ists / nun fraget sichs weiter / wie und worumb Gott den Glauben fur unsere Gerechtigkeit auffneme / do antwortet sichs / darumb / das er Christum ergreiffet / mit ganzen vertraeun auff in sezet / als der den gehorsam des Gesetzes (welcher die Gerechtigkeit ist) von unsertwegen zweierley weise ausgerichtet." Mörlin, *Historia*, Cii: "Solcher Glaube aber ist zu gleich ein erhaschen oder ergreiffen und annemen / damit man Christum zusich nimmet / als ein eigen gut / und lieben werten schatz." Although faith does not fulfill the Law as a good work and is not in this sense a substitute for original righteousness, it does fulfill the Law so that faith apprehends Christ, who has fulfilled the Law. Mörlin, *Repetitio*, Hiiii: "Also ist nu die Gerechtigkeit vom Gesetz erfordert in uns erfüllet / Roman. 8. Weil alles von Christo gehalten ist in aller unschuld / was das Gesetz erfordert / was aber wir nicht gehalten / mit gebürlicher Straff nach dem Sententz und urtheil des Gesetzes bezalet auch von Christo..." Mörlin, *Historia*, Zi^v.

30 Mörlin, *Repetitio*, Hiiii: "Sondern ohn alle Werck pur lauter allein aus Gnaden / nicht durch eingeben newer Krefften / oder folgenden einwohnung Göttlicher Natur."

31 Mörlin, *Repetitio*, Iiii^v: "Solchs aber wirckt und gibet der Heilige Geist / der das Hertz durch den Glauben reiniget und zu einem Newen wesen zurichtet."

32 Mörlin, *Repetitio*, Iiii^v.

33 Mörlin, *Repetitio*, Hiiii^v: "Doch kompt die Gerechtigkeit auff uns nicht von art in der Natur / wie die Sünde / Sondern wir müssen solche gnade und gabe empfahen / und uns appliciren. Romanor 5."

34 Mörlin, *Repetitio*, Iiiii.

35 The lack of texts prevents more detailed analysis. However, Mörlin's passage seems strange when compared to his other works. The limitation can be interpreted in two ways. First, Mörlin may have changed his view later in his life. Second, the passage refers only to the use of essential righteousness according to which the good produced from renewal belongs to justification. The latter seems more plausible.

Mörlin, at least in his earlier writings, repeated Luther's central themes more loyally than Melanchthon, Osiander or Flacius. Faith connects the believer to Christ. Both the forgiveness of sins through Christ's personal presence and the birth of new being take place in this faith. In Mörlin's theology, justification is based on the constitution of Christ's person, which accounts full meaning to the person of Christ in the act of salvation.

5.2. *Martin Chemnitz*

5.2.1. *Christ as True God and Man*

Martin Chemnitz (1522–1586),[36] Joachim Mörlin's assistant, followed him as the superintendent of Braunschweig. Chemnitz was soon to become the leading theologian of Lutheranism.[37] His historical influence on Lutheranism has been outlined in the adage: "if Martin

[36] Chemnitz studied Greek, mathematics, and astrology under the supervision of Melanchthon in Wittenberg. Since he was not a theology major, he did not attend Luther's lectures, which he regretted deeply. In 1546 Chemnitz moved to Königsberg to work as a librarian, which enabled him to familiarize himself with the history of theology. During his three-year term he read the church fathers especially, which was a great benefit for his career as a theologian. Chemnitz then returned to Wittenberg, where he immediately won Melanchthon's favor, and was later selected to lecture on Melanchthon's *Loci Communes*. Although Chemnitz was one of the students closest to Melanchthon, he in fact was mostly self-educated, and Melanchthon was never an unquestionable authority for him. See Paul Strawn, "Kyrill von Alexandrien als eine Quelle der Christologie bei Martin Chemnitz. Ein überblick als Werkstattbericht," *Lutherische Theologie und Kirche* 19 (1995), pp. 75–82. Moreover, Chemnitz never approved any of Melanchthon's later works—not even *Loci*, which he had lectured on—as a part of the local *corpora doctrinae* preceding BC. See J. A. O. Preus, *The Second Martin*, p. 164. In 1554, Chemnitz accepted Mörlin's invitation to assist him in his office in Braunschweig and Johannes Bugenhagen ordained him. Chemnitz followed Mörlin as superintendent of Braunschweig in 1567. During his period in office he wrote his most important works, and influenced the formulation of FC greatly. Fred Kramer, "Biografical sketch of Martin Chemnitz," in Martin Chemnitz: *Examination of Council of Trent*, Part I, transl. Fred Kramer (St. Louis: Concordia Publishing House 1971), p. 23; Kramer, "Martin Chemnitz," in *Shapers of religious traditions in Germany, Switzerland and Poland* 1560–1600, ed. Jill Raitt (New Haven: Yale University Press 1981), pp. 39–41; Mahlmann, "Martin Chemnitz," in TRE, Bd. 7 (Walter de Gruyter: Berlin 1981), pp. 714–715; J. A. O. Preus, *The Second Martin*, pp. 93–99; *Kaufmann*, "Martin Chemnitz (1522–1586). Zur Wirkungsgeschichte der theologische Loci," in *Melanchthon in seinen Schülern*, hrsgb. Heinz Scheible (Wiesbaden: Harrassowitz Verlag 1997), pp. 192–214.

[37] J. A. O. Preus, *The Second Martin*, pp. 335–338; Jobst Ebel, "Jacob Andreae (1528–1590) als Verfasser der Konkordienformel," in *Zeitschrift für Kirchengeschichte* 89

[Chemnitz] had not come along, Martin [Luther] would hardly have survived."[38] Chemnitz made his major contribution during an era of great importance for the survival of Lutheranism: between Luther's death and the signing of FC. He has been honored as the repository of Luther's heritage; he has even received the nickname 'the Second Martin' (*Martinus Alter*).[39] Since Chemnitz has been regarded as the greatest single factor behind the declarations of FC,[40] the criticisms levelled at FC's doctrine of justification have also implicitly been

(1978), p. 115; Ebel, "Die Herkunft des Konzeptes der Konkordienformel", *Zeitschrift für Kirchengeschichte* 91 (1980), p. 253.

[38] Lat. "Si Martinus [Chemnitius] non fuisset, Martinus [Lutherus] vix stetisset." The origins of the adage are unknown but it has been used since the beginning of the 17th century. E.g., Eduardo Preuss, "Vita Martini Chemnicii," in Martin Chemnitz: *Examen concilii Tridentinii*, hrsgb. E. Preuss (Darmstadt: Wissenschaftliche Buchgesellschaft 1972), p. 956. A note from the year 1719, relates its origins to Catholic theologians. "Ipsimet Pontificii ad hunc virum (sc. Chemnitz) digitum intendentes dicere solent: Vos protestantes duos habuistis Martinos, si posterior non fuisset, prior non stetisset." Cited in Kaufmann, "Martin Chemnitz", p. 193. See also Inge Mager, "Das Testament des Braunschweiger Stadtssuperindenten Martin Chemnitz (1522–1586)," in *Braunschweigisches Jb.* 68 (1987b), p. 121.

[39] The name *Martinus Alter* probably originates from the texts of *Livy* (Liv. 21,10,8), which were generally known in the middle ages. In this passage, Hanno of Carthage calls Hamilcar, the father of Hannibal, The Other Mars (*Mars Alter*), comparing him to the Roman god of War.

[40] Ebel, "Die Herkunft," p. 252. See also Martens, *Die Rechtfertigung*, pp. 87–112. Chemnitz formulated *FC* together with Jacob Andreae, Nicolaus Selnecker and David Chytraeus. Jacob Andreae composed a document known as *Schwäbische Konkordie* in 1573. On the edition of the text, see H. Hachfeld, "Die Schwäbische Confession," *Zeitschrift für historische Theologie* 36 (1866). Before this Andreae had already written drafts, which are analyzed in the section focusing on Andreae (6.1.). Chemnitz edited *Schwäbische Konkordie*, which was augmented into *Schwäbisch-Sächsische Konkordie* in 1575. On the edition of the text, see Christopher Pfaffius, *Acta et scripta publica Ecclesiae Wirtembergicae* (Tubingae 1720). The theologians of Württemberg responded to this with *Maulbronner Formel.* On the edition of the text, see Theodor Pressel, "Zwei Actenstücke zur Genesis der Concordienformel, aus den Originalie des Dresdener K. Archivs mitgetheilt von Dr. Th. Pressel," in *Jahrbüch für Deutsche Theologie* (1866). In 1576, Jacob Andreae chaired a meeting in Torgau that formulated *Torgisches Buch*, containing the basic structure of *FC.* The final proper meeting evaluated the feedback of *Torgisches Buch* in Bergen in 1577. Andreae, Chemnitz, and Selnecker composed a text that was commented on by a broader group of theologians. As a result, they published *Bergisches Buch*, which is almost exactly the same as *FC*, only minor alterations being made to the text during the publishing process. On the edition of the text, see Heinrich Heppe, *Der Text der Bergischen Concordienformel verglichen mit dem Text der schwäbischen Concordie, der schwäbisch-sächsischen Concordie und des Torgauer Buches*, zweite Ausgabe (Marburg: Koch & Sipmann 1860), who has compared *Bergisches Buch* to the earlier editions.

against Chemnitz.[41] He has been studied here in more detail than his contemporaries because of his great theological influence.

In many respects Chemnitz's influence culminates in his writings on christology.[42] Chemnitz clarified the Lutheran understanding of christology against the Calvinists through his examinations on the doctrine of the Holy Supper, *Repetitio sanae doctrinae* (1561), and its extension *Fundamenta sanae doctrinae* (1570).[43] These examinations formed the basis for his christology and the doctrinal treatment of theHoly Supper. His wide-ranging introduction to christology, *De Duabus naturis in Christo* (1570), which discuss the same subjects as the works already mentioned, soon became the basic Lutheran handbook on christology. Chemnitz can be accredited with achieving intra-Lutheran doctrinal unity concerning christology[44] and the Holy Supper.[45]

---

[41] Gottfried Hoffman, "Die Rechtfertigung des Sünders vor Gott nach dem Examen Concilii Tridentinii von Martin Chemnitz," in *Der zweite Martin der Lutherischen Kirche*, Festschrift zum 400. Todestag von Martin Chemnitz, hrsgb. W. A. Jünke (Braunschweig: Ev.-luth. Stadtkirchenband und Propstei Braunschweig 1986), pp. 85; Nüssel, *Allein aus Glauben*, p. 174.

[42] Other prominent works include *Examen concilii tridentinii* (1566–1575), which is a detailed analysis of the theology of the Council of Trent. In his *Handtbüchlein* (1569, lat. *Enchiridion*) Chemnitz advises pastors in their office. Chemnitz's lectures on Melanchthon's *Loci Communes* were published posthumously as *Loci Theologici* (1591). This work passed Melanchthon's theological method to the later generations and to some extent his theology as well. Some contemporaries called Chemnitz "the second Philip" (*secundus Philippus*) for this reason. See Kaufmann, "Martin Chemnitz," p. 263.

[43] Melanchthon accused Mörlin (*CR* 9, 962) of teaching transubstantiation. Chemnitz's *Repetitio* was originally the defense of Mörlin. Ebel, "Herkunft," p. 240.

[44] Mahlmann, *Das Neue Dogma*, pp. 205–249. The Calvinist christology, which denied Christ's real presence in the eucharist, made Chemnitz focus on christology. The basis for this was the Hardenberg Controversy, in which Albert Hardenberg and Johann Timann disputed on the right interpretation of Luther's understanding of the eucharist. Hardenberg sided with Melanchthon, and Timann was allied with Andreae, Brenz, Chemnitz, and Mörlin. Chemnitz, *De Duabus*, Epistola Dedicatoria (20–22). Mahlmann, *Das Neue Dogma*, p. 205. On this controversy, see Wilhelm Neuser, "Haardenberg und Melanchthon. Der Haardenbergische Streit (1554–1560)," *Jahrbuch der Gesellschaft für niedersächsische Kirchengeschichte* (1967), pp. 142–186.

[45] On Chemnitz's doctrine of the eucharist, see Bjarne Teigen, *The Lord's Supper in the Theology of Martin Chemnitz*, (Brewster: Trinity Lutheran Press 1986); Frank-Georg Gozdek, "Der Beitrag des Martin Chemnitz zur lutherischen Abendmalslehre—dargestellt anhand seiner Schrift 'Repetitio sanae doctrinae de vera praesentia corporis et sanguinis Donini in coena'," in *Der zweite Martin der Lutherischen Kirche. Festschrift zum* 400. *Todestag von Martin Chemnitz*, hrsgb. W. A. Jünke (Braunschweig: Ev.-luth. Stadtkirchenband und Propstei Braunschweig 1986); Tom G. A. Hardt, *Venerabilis & adorabilis Eucharistia. En studie i den lutherska nattvardsläran under* 1500-talet, Studia doctrinae christianae Upsaliensia 9 (Stockholm 1971); Bernt Torvild Oftestad, "Traditio und Norma. Hauptzüge der Schriftauffassung bei Martin Chemnitz," in *Der zweite Martin der Lutherischen Kirche*; Helmut Gollwitzer, *Coena Domini. Die altlutherische Abendmahlslehre in*

In keeping with Chemnitz's central interests it is appropriate to consider his thought from its christological fundamentals. Even though his theology was formed during controversies it is clear that his doctrine of Christ forms the basis of all his theology, and not simply to matters related to the eucharist. This was the standard understanding of both Luther and the later Lutheranism. Comprehending christology is thus of vital importance in understanding the doctrine of justification.[46]

Chemnitz structures his christology, and implicitly his whole theology, on the concept of hypostatic union (*unio hypostatica*) and on the essence of Christ's two natures; Christ must be both true God and true man in order to reconcile the world.[47] Chemnitz's christological and soteriological *sedes doctrinae* is based on Colossians (2:9): "For in him the whole fullness of God lives in bodily form. And you have been brought to fullness in him, who is the head of every ruler and authority." To establish a connection between the sinner and the fullness of God, Christ as the object of faith must be true God.[48] Equally important is Christ's true humanity. First, the assumed nature of Christ is true (*solidum*), not merely an apparition (*fantasma*) that resembles the human body only in outward form.[49] If Christ's body had been only an apparition, then the life He gives would be only a shadow of life (*spectrum*).[50]

---

ihrer Auseinandersetsung mit dem Calvinismus dargestellt an der lutherischen Frühortodoxie (München: Chr. Kaiser Verlag 1937), p. 8; O. Ritschl, *Dogmengeschichte*, p. 72.

[46] David P. Scaer, *Christology. Confessional Lutheran Dogmatics*, Vol. VI. (Fort Wayne: The International Foundation for Lutheran Confessional Research 1989), pp. 1–2; Kimme, *Rechtfertigung und Heiligung*, pp. 9–14; Brandy, *Die späte Christologie*, pp. 267–270.

[47] Chemnitz, *De Duabus*, 52a–b (147–148); 82a–b (219–220), the numbers in parentheses refer to English translations. Chemnitz offers 14 reasons why Christ had to be both God and man, which primarily concentrate on the qualitative difference between God and humanity. This means that *by their natures* human beings are sinners, while God is holy. From this comes the guilt and juridical difference, to which Chemnitz makes only two references.

[48] Chemnitz, *De Duabus*, 6b (41); 123b (313); *Examen* 240b–241a (II, 56); *Loci*, 71a–b (113).

[49] E.g., the appearances of God in OT (e.g., Gen. 32:24–30; Dan. 3:25; 7:13).

[50] Chemnitz, *De Duabus*, 10b (51): "Si incarnatio Christi, & tota redemptionis οἰκονομία, phantasma fuit, cùm Christus incarnatus in officio Mediatoris sit redemptio, justitia, salus et vitae nostra: putative igitur & non in veritate, redempti sumus, nec verè, sed μετὰ τὸ δοκεῖν justificabimur, h.e. sine liberatione, sub ira Dei in aeterna damnatione manebimus, & pro vita aeterna, quam speramus, spectrum vitae nobis objicietur."

Second, since Christ's human nature was perfect, it had to include a soul.[51] Because sin dwells in the soul and its faculties (not only in the body) Christ assumed all desires, actions, and functions typical of human nature.[52] Chemnitz appeals to an adage of St. Gregory of Nazianzus: "For that which he has not assumed, He has not healed" (τὸ ἀπρόσλεπτον ἀθεράπευτον).[53]

Third, everything Christ feels, he feels genuinely. Since his human nature is united with the Godhead, one could erroneously conclude that the sufferings of Christ are not real, like a spear goes through water or fire, leaving a certain mark behind but no wound,[54] or that Christ dies only putatively.[55] According to Chemnitz, the denial of the reality of Christ's sufferings is equivalent to denying the reality of salvation. Just as human sufferings (and hell) are real, Christ carries them in reality. A true thing must be given a true counterpart.[56] The sufferings of Christ are even greater than the sufferings of any individual person.

---

[51] Chemnitz derives this from Apollinaris of Laodicea, who identified the mind (*nous*) and the self (*ho autos*). If Christ assumed both of these, Christ would have two selves, His own and the assumed one. Chemnitz offers the following solution. The divine nature of Christ has existed from eternity while his human nature did not exist before conception in which case there would have been an individual with a body and a soul, i.e., a person *ens in se*, which Christ had assumed. At the assumption, Christ did not assume the body and soul of somebody else; he assumed human nature but not a human person. Chemnitz, *De Duabus*, 22b (76). On the assumption of the soul in patristic theology, see Steven A. McKinion, *Words, Imagery and the Mystery of Christ. A Reconstruction of Cyril of Alexandria's Christology*, Supplements to Vigiliae Christianae LV (Leiden: Brill 2000), pp. 149–159.

[52] Chemnitz, *De Duabus*, 15a (60): "Non autem pars tantum aliqua natura nostrae, sed tota peccato infecta et vitiata est. Nec partem tantum aliquam, sed totam & integram servandam suscepit. Totam ergo & integram, hoc est, corpus & animam assumpsit. Anima enim praestat corpore, & contagione peccati magis infecta est, quam corpus. Quomodo ergo illa, quae praecipue erat curanda, non esset assumpta?"

[53] Chemnitz, *De Duabus*, 15b (60). Chemnitz quotes Gregory's letter to Cledonius. *MPG* 37, 181 (*Epistola* 101). This dictum has been usually associated with Gregory of Nazianzus. Origen and Tertullianus however used it before him. See M. F. Wiles, *Soteriological Arguments in the Fathers*, Studia Patristica, (Berlin: Academie Verlag 1966), p. 322.

[54] So, e.g., Hilarius, *MPL* 10, 361–362 (*De Trinitate*); Chemnitz, *De Duabus*, 15b (61).

[55] Against the actuality of Christ's sufferings, the Manicheans claimed that Christ did not die truly but only seemingly. See, e.g., Damascenus, *MPG* 94, 717 (*De haeresis*).

[56] This axiom was common in patristic theology. See Edward Hardy, *Christology of the Later Fathers* (Philadelphia: Westminster Press 1954), p. 219.

A human suffers only for his or her own sins; Christ suffers for the whole world.[57]

Fourth, Chemnitz emphasizes that Christ's human nature is of the same essence (ὁμοούσιος) as humans. In theory, Christ could have brought a heavenly body with Him or even created it anew from the dust of the earth.[58] According to Chemnitz, the reality of salvation is dependent on the essence of assumed nature. This is why Christ did not "take on him the nature of angels; but he took on him the seed of Abraham" (Heb. 2:16).[59] Death is destroyed within the same nature which once brought death upon creation.[60] The assumed nature is exactly what humans have after the Fall. Mary was under the influence of sin, like everyone else.[61] However, at the moment of conception the Holy Spirit sanctified the assumed sinful flesh born from Mary so that it became clean and holy.[62] As a consequence, Christ in his human-divine person was perfectly sinless.

Nevertheless, Christ participates in sin and its consequences through kenosis and imputation. As a result of incarnation, there is no sin in the person of Christ but He still experiences the consequences of sin:

---

[57] Chemnitz, *De Duabus*, 15a–16b (61–62).

[58] Chemnitz, *De Duabus*, 12b (54).

[59] Chemnitz emphasizes this in his dissertation *Genelogia Christi*, which attempts to demonstrate how Christ is the heir of Adam who heals the sin of Adam. E.g., Chemnitz, *Genelogia*, B: "Adam enim principio ad imaginem Dei creatus conivis fuit regni DEI & habuit communionem cum Deo: sed per lapsum & se & totam suam posteritatem ad illacum Deo conjuctione avulsit, quae in Christo demùm restituta est. Hujus enim redintegrationis vinculum seu nexus est Christus Deus & homo: in quo divina natura τῷ λόγῳ personaliter sibi univit humanam naturam, assumptam quidem ex massa, quae in Adamo corrupta fuerat [ex iis enim, quos post lapsum Adam genuit, Genelogia Christi deduetur:] ut ad nostram corruptam naturam redemtionem pertinere sciamus: sed spiritu superveniente sanctificatam."

[60] Chemnitz, *De Duabus*, 12b (55): "Nostrum corpus est corpus mortis. Sed in illo ipso nostro corpore, quod Filius a nobis assumpsit, mors rursus destructa est." Chemnitz, *Duabus*, 12b. (55–56): "Caro invexit mortem in hunc mundum. Et rursus, caro Filij hominis data est pro mundi vita, ut qui manducat carnem Christi, habeat vitam aeternam." The eucharist unites the receiver of the substances to the assumed nature of Christ in which death is destroyed. Without the consubstantiality of the natures, the eucharist would have no effect.

[61] Chemnitz, *Examen*, 120b (377).

[62] Chemnitz, *De Duabus*, 13b (57): "Et illam massam, quam de Maria carne & sanguine, in illa conceptione, Filius Dei assumpsit, Spiritus Sanctus ita sanctificavit, & mundavit ab omni labe peccati, ut sanctum sit, quod nascitur ex Maria." See also Chemnitz, *De Duabus*, 13a–13b; 78a–b (210). So also Cyril of Alexandria. See Koen, *The Saving Passion*, p. 78. Cyril (380–444) in particular was a great authority for Chemnitz in terms of christology. See Strawn, "Kyrill von Alexandrien," pp. 65–66. *De Duabus Naturis* contains 1280 quotations of patristic texts, 279 of which refer to Cyril.

weakness, sickness, and the ability to die.[63] These are not individual or personal defects (such as blindness or particular diseases) but general defects that influence the whole of humanity in the same manner. Christ has willingly assumed these frailties along with human nature in order to make reconciliation through death possible.[64] In addition to general failings, he has also submitted himself to the influence of the devil and other destructive powers, and he restrains himself from using his divine powers against them.[65] Submission under the threatening powers is to be considered more characteristic of *kenosis* than incarnation.[66]

For Luther, it was crucial that Christ had become sin. The same point is found in Chemnitz in a more detailed manner. While Luther did not define the way Christ becomes sin, Chemnitz taught that Christ is made sin imputatively (*imputative*).[67] The sin that causes Christ's death on the cross is not sin made by him—it is not of his person—but it is in him through imputation.[68]

The assumed nature remains part of Christ's person forever. Humanity is not absorbed into divinity. At the resurrection Christ keeps the same nature in him, although in glorified state, and did not receive a new substance. The human nature heightened on the right hand of the Father is the "tie and bond" upon which soteriology is based.[69]

> It is a great comfort that the surest pledge of our salvation and glorification is the human nature of Christ seated at the right hand of the Father

---

[63] Chemnitz, *De Duabus*, 9b (49).
[64] Chemnitz, *De Duabus*, 11a–12b (53–55).
[65] Chemnitz, *De Duabus*, 9b (49); 174b (427).
[66] Chemnitz, *De Duabus*, 203b–204a (490).
[67] Chemnitz, *Examen*, 161a (502): "Illum qui non noverat peccatum, pro nobis peccatum fecit, ut efficeremur justitia Dei in ipso. Quomodo vero Christus factus est peccatum? Certe imputative. Et ita nos in ipso efficimur justitia Dei."
[68] Chemnitz follows Luther in his understanding of incarnation and kenosis; both claim that the assumed nature was sinful, not neutral. They claim however that after the conception the person of Christ is pure but still shares the death and consequences of sin. Luther uses paradoxes to illustrate this: "Christ does not represent his own person; he is no Son of God, born of a virgin, but a sinner." *WA* 40 I, 433, 28–30. Luther does not explain the meaning of 'representation'. Chemnitz, however, tries to describe this imputation, which probably originates from the Latin words of Isaiah 53:12 according to which "(Christ) was reputed an evildoer" (*et cum sceleratis reputatus est*). Christ does not cease to be God but he is reckoned a sinner. For both Luther and Chemnitz, despite the terminology, becoming a sinner is equally actual: sin kills Christ and condemns Him. Becoming a sinner may happen in *kenosis* as Luther seems to think (see *WA* 40 I, 437.), or on Calvary, where Christ is ultimately rejected and suffers the punishment of sin. Chemnitz, however, does not deliberate on this in the sources.
[69] Chemnitz, *De Duabus*, 16b–17a (63–64).

> where He appears before the face of God on our behalf (Heb. 7:25), leading us and joining us to the Father (John 17:24), in order that then we may be made to conform (*conformes*) to His glorious body (Phil. 3:21). In the very nature by which we are flesh of His flesh and bone of His bones we will come to judgment, in order that we may the more eagerly love His appearing (1. Tim. 4:8). By this tie and bond (*nexus et copula*) we shall be joined forever to God in eternal life.[70]

In Christ the natures are united inseparably (ἀδιαιρέτως) and undividedly (ἀχωρίστως) for all eternity.[71] Because of the hypostatic union it is impossible to observe the person without the human nature. As such, Christ is also the object of faith because the majesty of God is inaccessible. The sinner can approach God as much as straw can approach flame.[72] Christ is now ὁμοούσιος in his person with both God and man. In Christ's person God is now accessible.[73]

In this context, the word 'nature' (*natura*) requires definition. From the viewpoint of the Trinity, the One who assumes human nature is one person (God the Son), whose nature is identical with the other persons of the Trinity. Likewise the assumed nature consists of only one human nature (*natura*) which is common to all humans. The assumed nature is an individual unit (*massa*), not the whole (platonic) universal humanity or the idea of humanity.[74] The whole of divinity does not assume

---

[70] Chemnitz, *De Duabus*, 17a–b (64): "Et dulcis est consolatio, quod certissimum pignus salutis & glorificationi nostrae est humana natura in Christo, ad dexteram Patris collocata, in qua vultui Dei apparet pro nobis, Heb. 7. Adducens & conjungens nos Patri, Joh. 17. Ut conformes aliquando reddamur corpori ipsius glorioso, Philip. 3. In illa ipsa natura, qua sumus caro de carne ejus, & os de ossibus ejus, veniet ad judicium, ut eo alacriores diligamus adventum ipsius. 2. Timoth. 4. Hoc nexu & hac copula perpetuo adhaerebimus Deo in vita aeterna."

[71] Chemnitz, *De Duabus*, 23a (77).

[72] Chemnitz, *De Duabus*, 24a–b (79): "Imò cùm ad nudam divinam maiestatem nobis miseris peccatoribus non pateret aditus, tanquam stipulae ad ignem consumentem..."

[73] Chemnitz, *De Duabus*, 24a–b (79); *Epistola Dedicatoria* (17).

[74] According to J. A. O. Preus, "the term massa is difficult to translate. It refers to the individual unit of human nature, which was assumed by the Logos in contradistinction to all other men or units of human nature. It might be translated as lump or mass, but the term "individual unit" seems most appropriate." See Chemnitz, *Two Natures in Christ*, transl. J. A. O. Preus (St. Louis: Concordia Publishing House 1971), p. 36. At some point in the history of theology the human nature of Christ meant universal human nature, which contained all individual natures. However, Chemnitz's authority Cyril understands the assumption of humanity (ἀνθρωπότης) not as the platonic universal nature, but as the fact that Christ is truly human with regard to all his faculties of body and soul. The assumed nature is an individual unit. See McKinion, *Words*, pp. 166–171. In this sense, the concept of "natura" used by Lutherans refers analogically to the human nature of a human person's and Christ's natures. See Häg-

the whole of humanity; in this case humanity would be absorbed into divinity, which would cause some kind of apokatastatic state. This was not, of course, the intention of the reformers. Instead, the salvation of the individual takes place through participation in the person of Christ in faith.

5.2.2. Communicatio idiomatum *as the Guarantee of the Reality of Salvation*

The two natures of Christ form a new hypostasis (*unio hypostatica*).[75] This union is analogical to the union of body and soul, which do not inhere in the person side-by-side but permeate each other. The natures of Christ relate to each other perichoretically (περιχώρησις): the divine nature permeating the human nature.[76] The natures nevertheless remain distinct and intact; they do not mix with each other or go through substantial transformation.[77] Even so, the union of the natures (*communio naturarum*) is real, not verbal.[78]

Chemnitz builds his doctrine on communication of attributes (*communicatio idiomatum*)[79] on the basis of the union of the natures. To put it more clearly, the former provides the substance and explanation of

glund, "Majestas homini Christi". Wie hat Martin Chemnitz die Christologie Luthers gedeutet?," in *Lutherjahrbuch* (Göttingen: Vandenhoeck & Ruprecht 1980), pp. 74–76. Ockham (III sent. D 1 q 1 ad tertium; Quodlibeta 5 q 10) emphasizes this as well. On the disputations in the middle ages, see Heiko Oberman, *Harvest of Medieval Theology. Gabriel Biel and Late Medieval Nominalism* (Cambridge: Harvard University Press 1963), pp. 249–261.

[75] Chemnitz confesses that no explanation or formulation explains fully the nature of the hypostatic union. *Duabus* contains a whole chapter with patristic quotations stressing the ineffability of incarnation. Chemnitz, *De Duabus*, 51a (143): "Caput X. Sententiae quaedam scripturae et vetustatis, monstrantes, totam plenitudinem mysterii hypostaticae unionis in hac vita imperscrutabilem & ineffabilem esse, ut meminerimus, mediocri explicatione & cognitione nos debere contentos esse."

[76] Chemnitz, *De Duabus*, 114a (292); 116a–b (297).

[77] Chemnitz, *De Duabus*, 59a–b (162–163). Chemnitz lists 14 different kinds of union, which do not meet these requirements since the parties to the union either change or merge together. Chemnitz, *De Duabus*, 35b–36a (105–107).

[78] Chemnitz, *Examen*, 58a (160): "Quia vero Unio non est verbalis, sed vera, non enim nuncupativè tantum vel verbaliter, conjunctae sunt duae naturae in Christo, sed verè, reipsa, revera, quod usitatè vocamus, Realiter. Et ab eo, si res enunciater vel est, vel non est, oratio dicitur vera vel falsa, Ideò communicatio vocatur non Verbalis, sed Realis, Ut hoc vocabulo distinguatur à fictitia, commentitia, imaginaria, seu putativa communicatione."

[79] Chemnitz, *Theses*, 55. *Communicatio idiomatum* was rarely used in the middle ages; only Gabriel Biel and Nicholas Oresme consider it of some importance. At the time the essence of the doctrine, according to Oberman (*Harvest*, pp. 262–264), was that the

the latter. The meticulous distinction of different genera of *communicatio idiomatum* underlines the reality of the communion of Christ's natures. One reason for this is the Reformed doctrine of ἀλλοίωσις, according to which natures have their own functions in relation to the person as a whole.[80]

For Chemnitz, *communicatio idiomatum* is first and foremost a soteriological concept.[81] In *De Duabus Naturis* salvation is structured according to the genera of *communicatio idiomatum.* The first genus (*genus idiomaticum*) creates the foundation for a right relation between humanity and divinity. In other words, it answers the question of the character of Christ the Saviour's essential being. The second genus (*genus apotelesmaticum*) describes how Christ's natures work together for salvation, and what Christ does in order to save the individual. The third genus (*genus majestaticum*) helps to understand what takes place in the person of Christ in order that His person be salvific. Since speaking correctly on *communicatio idiomatum* leads to a correct understanding of justification, christological rules do effect soteriology as whole, and not merely the doctrine of the eucharist.[82] The genera are good examples of Chemnitz's use of the

---

hypostatic union was the basis for communion of the attributes, and the communication of the abstract attributes was denied so that one could not mix humanity with deity.

[80] Werner Elert, *Der Christliche Glaube. Grundlinien der Lutherischen Dogmatik*, Sechste Auflage (Erlangen: Martin Luther-Verlag 1988), pp. 330: "Ohne die Lehre von *communicatio idiomatum* ist die *communio naturarum* nur ein Begriff, unter dem sich niemand etwas vorstellen kann." See also Richard A. Müller, *Dictionary of Latin and Greek Theological Terms. Drawn Principally from Protestant Scholastic Theology* (Grand Rapids: Baker Book House 1985), p. 30.

[81] Hägglund, "Majestas homini Christi," p. 72: "Die sorgfältig entwickelte Terminologie und die streng logisch aufgebaute Darstellungweise sollen nicht verbergen, dass diese Arbeit mit bewusster Rücksichtnahme auf die forma doctrinae und auf die Sprache des lebendigen Glaubens einen praktischen Zweck erfolgt." On the importance of *communicatio idiomatum* for Luther, Kvell Ove Nilsson remarks that "Die Lehre von der communicatio idiomatum ist überhaupt keine blosse Konsequenz der Einheit in Christus, sondern ein Ausdruck dieser Einheit selbst und des ganzen Fundaments, worauf für Luther Leben und Seligkeit ruhen." See Nilsson, *Simul. Das Miteinander von Göttlichem und Mensclichem in Luthers Theologie* (Göttingen: Vandenhoeck & Ruprecht 1966), p. 228.

[82] *Communicatio idiomatum* thus makes it impossible to separate Christ's person and work without endangering the actuality of salvation. According to Chemnitz, the denial of the hypostatic union equates to denial of the incarnation and annulling salvation. Chemnitz, *De Duabus*, 183a (443). On the connection between *communicatio idiomatum* and soteriology, see also J. A. O. Preus, *The Second Martin*, p. 276. On the same theme in Cyril and Gregory of Nazianzus, see Koen, *The Saving Passion*, pp. 80–82; Ezra *Gebremedhin, Life-Giving Blessing. An Inquiry into the Eucharistic Doctrine of Cyril of Alexandria* (Uppsala: Acta Universitas Upsaliensis 1977), pp. 39–40.

nomilistic theory of language.[83] While *communicatio idiomatum* is *modus loquendi* safeguarding the biblical mode of speech, it is not merely a grammatical rule; it depicts how Christ's natures are related to each other in reality, not merely verbally.[84]

The first genus of *communicatio idiomatum* is *genus idiomaticum*, which illustrates how the natures communicate their attributes to the person while retaining their own natural attributes. As already noted, *genus idiomaticum* protects the real divinity and humanity of Christ because only the true God-man can save humanity. While the first genus primarily protects the unchangeability of the natures, the second genus (*genus apotelesmaticum*) underlines the unity of the person: how Christ as one person is the Mediator. In accordance with its name (Gr. ἀποτέλεσμα = work, effect) this genus describes how Christ accomplishes salvation through His suffering and resurrection.[85] *Genus apotelesmaticum* illustrates that one nature is not passive when the other performs some deed, but works in co-operation with it.[86] For example, when Christ dies

---

[83] Chemnitz follows the nominalistic tradition according to which language comes before metaphysics and ontology. In practice, this means examining how words work, and where they refer in the sentence. Chemnitz was not interested in the ontology of the world in general, rather in how one must speak to speak in terms of biblical revelation. Correct biblical speech does not need examination of the principles of the reality as its basis. On nominalistic use of language, see Graham White, *Luther as nominalist. A study of the logical methods used in Martin Luther's disputations in the light of their medieval background* (Helsinki: Schriften der Luther-Agricola-Gesellshaft 1992), pp. 41–42, 47–48. Chemnitz's notion of reality is dependent on the *modus loquendi*, which tries to avoid utterances that conflict with biblical revelation. Hägglund, "Majestas homini Christi," p. 72; Martens, *Die Rechtfertigung*, 87. Although semantic analysis leads to a view of reality's ontological structure, ontological analysis is a consequence of semantic analysis. The structure of being is derived from the correct mode of speech. Chemnitz, *De Duabus*, 77a (207): "Ita prosessio rectae fidei conspicua extat in ipsis modis loquendi, & hac diligentia conservari potest."

[84] Chemnitz, *Wiederholte*, Fi^{V}: "...non verbaliter, sed realiter, quia unio non est verbalis." Chemnitz uses Paul's statement on the identification of his sufferings with Christ's sufferings as an argument for the actuality of the communion. Chemnitz, *Theses*, 352: "Non enim est tantum relatio idiomatum. (sicut Paulus suas passiones uocat passiones Christi, Coloss. 1.) sed communicatio. Nec est confusio sed κοινωνία idiomatum." See also Chemnitz (*Theses*, 70–73), where Chemnitz refers to the old metaphor of fire and steel; fire is a genuine property of heated steel.

[85] Chemnitz, *De Duabus*, 79b (212): "Sed plenior explicatio, quomodo divina natura λόγου, per passionem & mortem assumptae naturae, operata sit redemptio & salutem nostram, pertinet ad secundum genus."

[86] Chemnitz, *Repetitio*, 374: "Ad officium enim redemptionis pertinent duo, PRIMO, pati, mori, & c. Lu. 24. & hae actiones siunt in humana natura proprie. SECUNDO, per passionem vincere mortem. Heb. 2. Restituere vitam aeternam. Joan. 10. & hae actiones, sunt divinae naturae, propriae. Non sunt autem separatim illae actiones, ut humanitas separatim agat in passione, & divinitas separatim in destructione mortis,

according to His human nature, this occurs in accordance and with the permission of the divine nature, even though the divine nature as such is incapable of dying. Still, the divine nature sustains the human nature in the midst of sufferings so that it may endure the burden of the sins and the wrath of God.[87]

What elements do Christ's work of redemption actually contain? Chemnitz referred to different theories of atonement to demonstrate the meaning of Christ's death. He used the *Christus victor* theory and the anselmian theory of *satisfactio vicaria* in a complementary way.[88] *Loci* and *Examen* in particular use the satisfaction theory. This particular emphasis may be due to the nature of the works, both of which contain heavy criticism of scholastic theology. An emphasis on the forensic nature of justification is the most effective way to resist the notion of habitual grace.

The central concept of the theory of vicarious satisfaction is the divine Law.[89] Because God has revealed His will in the Law, He cannot overrule his own revelation and save in a way that neglects the Law. Someone has to suffer adequate punishment, and the Law must be fulfilled with perfect obedience.[90] Because this is impossible for human beings Christ becomes man, fulfills the Law, and suffers the punishment for humanity. Christ thus becomes the righteousness of the sinner.[91]

---

sed unitae sunt sicut ipsae naturae in una persona, & ita coniunctim peragunt opus redemptionis." Chemnitz, *Repetitio*, 375. "Persona agit secundum utramque naturam. Persona habet actiones in utraque natura simul et una natura agit cum communicatione alterius." The Reformed view is that the natures function separately for the same goal. Reinhold Seeberg, *Lehrbuch der Dogmengeschichte*, p. 144; Gottfried Locher, *Die Theologie Huldrich Zwinglis im Lichte seiner Christologie* (Zürich: Zwingli-Verlag 1952), pp. 128–132; Müller, *Dictionary*, p. 74.

[87] Chemnitz, *De Duabus*, 80b (216).

[88] Both theories appear side by side, e.g., in Chemnitz, *De Duabus*, 83a (221–2).

[89] Kolb (*Luther's Heirs*, p. 148) regards Chemnitz's theory of satisfaction as speculative: "Luther's concepts of alien and proper righteousness are present, but alien righteousness is treated in terms of satisfaction of the divine law in a manner not found in Luther, who shied away from venturing so deeply into an explanation of the atonement."

[90] Chemnitz, *Loci* II, 275a (530): "Ergò iuxta illam reuelatam voluntatem Deus non vult aliquem iustificare sine iustitia, hoc est, nisi iuxta Legem satisfactum sit pro peccato, & lex perfectâ obedientiâ fuerit impleta."

[91] Chemnitz, *Examen*, 159b–160b (500–501); *De Duabus*, 9b (49); 11a–b (53); 52b (147); 83a (221); *Examen*, 168b (524): "Quod Christus satisfactione plenissima et obedientia perfectissima, legem pro nobis impleverit: et ita factus sit iustitia nostra." Chemnitz does not use the words *activa et passiva obodientia*, but replaces them with *meritum / satisfactio et obodientia*.

However, obedience (*obedientia*) does not mean simply the acquisition of forensic merit and fulfillment of the Law. Chemnitz understands obedience as obedience of the Son to the will of the Father, who desires to save the world. In obedience to the will of the Father, Christ assumed the human condition and did not use His divine power to avoid suffering.[92] In keeping with this, obedience refers to all salvific events from the the moment of incarnation to the ascension.[93] Obedience can signify both the fulfilment of the Law and salvation's *oeconomia* in the aggregate.[94] The latter was more commonly used in early Lutheranism.

For Chemnitz, redemption involves incarnation as well, not simply forensic merit. When Christ assumed human nature in Mary's womb, the incarnation as such joined humanity and divinity together; the Holy Spirit purified the sinful nature that Christ received from Mary in the act of conception.[95] Incarnation thus implies the future union of the sinner and God, which also brings consolation to terrified minds.[96]

---

[92] Chemnitz, *Examen*, 168b (524); *De Duabus*, 84a–b (223); 205b (491).

[93] Chemnitz, *De Duabus*, 204a–b. (490–491): "Cum Filius à Patre missus esset in carne, ut in ea talem subjectionem & obedientiam pro nobis praestaret, noluit praeter vocationem & ante tempus, rapere usurpationem & ostentionem Divine poteniae & operationis in assumta, & per assumtam humanam naturam, sed exinanivit se, factus obediens Patri usq; ad mortem, & propterea Deus dedit illi nomen super omne nomen, & c." Chemnitz, *De Duabus*, 84a (223): "Proponit igitur considerandam, admirandum illam obedientiam Filii Dei quiescentis, hoc est, quod divina ipsius natura, non usa est sua potentia, non exercuit suas vires, ad prohibendas à carne sua injurias, passiones & mortem, Sed cessit irae aeterni Patris, adversus peccatum generis humani, volens humanam suam naturam pro salute generis humani pati, ac permittens, ut caro illa crucifigi & mori posset."

[94] See Chemnitz, *Theses*, 88, according to which incarnation is God's *oeconomia*. Thus, the obedience can be joined with the *Christus Victor* theory of atonement. This also is a typical patristic interpretation of the concept. For Cyril's use of the term, see Koen, *The Saving Passion*, p. 90.

[95] Chemnitz, *De Duabus*, 13a (56): "Sed voluit concipi, in utero gestari, ex utero nascendo progredi, sicut habet nostra naturalis conceptio & nativitatis excepto per superventum Spiritus sancti peccato, ut eo minus dubitaremus, esse carnem nobis consubstantialem, & certi redderemur, nostrae conceptioni, nativitati & toti naturae nostrae reparandae & salvandae incarnationem Filii Dei impendi."

[96] Chemnitz, *Theses*, 20: "Summa & suavissima est consolatio, cum misera nostra natura per peccatum á Deo qui ipsa vita est esset auulsa & abalienata, Esai. 59. Ephes. 4. Quod massa eius in persona Christi, rursus arctissima copulatione, hypostatica scilicet, unita est divinae naturae, ut ea ratione & nos vicissim participes efficemur divinae naturae, sicut Petrus inquit, & communionem acciperemus cum Patre, Filio & Spiritus sancto, sicut Joannes loquitur." A good example of Chemnitz's use of incarnation in practice is his sermon on the wedding of the King's son (Matt. 22), where he identifies both the bride and the guests with Christ's human nature. Chemnitz, *Von dem König*: "Aber weil in dieser Parabel die Braut und die Geste unterschiedlich genennet / und

De Duabus Naturis emphasizes the *Christus victor* theory. While the critique was directed against the Reformed theologians, it is evident that christology now plays the major role. Christ suffers punishment as a result of humanity's transgression of God's will. Through incarnation, sufferings, death, resurrection, and ascension, Christ restores life to humanity in the human nature He has assumed, which brings about victory over sin, death and hell.[97] Chemnitz also referred to the patristic metaphor of Christ's human nature as the worm, and the divine nature as the hook, which catches Satan.[98]

The death of Christ has significance for both theories. The role of resurrection is to witness to the fact that Christ's death is sufficient for redemption and efficacious (*efficacia*). The risen Christ now prays for believers that they should be saved and His merit become effective.[99]

The ascension of Christ also implies the ascension of human nature.[100] In the person of Christ the fallen nature of Adam has now

---

die auserwehlten durch die Geste bedeutet werden / so wird durch die Braut in dieser Parabel recht verstanden / die Menschliche Natur / welche in einigkeit der Personen mit dem Sohn Gottes vereiniget...Das ist ein herzliches pfandt unser erlösung uns seligkeit / das die Menschliche Natur / welche der Sathan durch die Sünde von Gott so weit hatte abgegriffen / nun wiederumb so nahe und genawe mit Gott vereinigt ist / das numehr zu der ganzen Persone des Sohns Gottes / nicht alleine seine Göttliche Natur / sondern auch unser von ihm angenommene Menschliche Natur gehöret / und das er das werck unser Seligmachung / nicht alleine durch seine Göttliche / sondern auch durch die angenommene Menschliche Natur / nach welcher er unser Bruder / und wir fleisch sein von seinem Fleisch/ verrichten will."

[97] Chemnitz, *De Duabus*, 83b (222): "...quod per illam passionem & mortem, placata est ira Patris, contritum caput serpentis, Mors destructa, vita restituta, captiui liberati & c." See also Chemnitz, *De Duabus*, 4b (37); 53a (148); 84b–85a (224–225); 132b–133a (332). Chemnitz, *Repetitio*, 374. In *Duabus* Chemnitz defines his theory of satisfaction in terms of patristic theology, appealing to Irenaeus (*Contra Haeresies*, V), Athanasios (*MPG* 26, 100–104, 276–293 [*Orationes adversus Arianos*]) and Cyril (*MPG* 73, 161; 74, 432 [*In Joannis evangelium*]; *MPG* 76, 17 [*Adversus Nestorium Lib* I.]; 77, 785–787 [*Homilia Paschalis*]) among others.

[98] Chemnitz, *De Duabus*, 83b (222). Among others, Gregory of Nyssa (*MPG* 45, 60–69 [*Oratio Catechetica*]) and Ambrosius (*MPL* 16, 1115, 1245–1246 [*Epistolae in duas classes distributae*]) have used the metaphor.

[99] Chemnitz, *Examen*, 170b (530): "Ideo Paulus in imputatione justitiae conjungit mortem et resurrectionem Christi. Consideretur et haec ratio: quia Christus Salvator noster est, non tantum merito, verum etiam efficacia, ut qui tanquam advocatus noster intercedit, et apparet vultui Dei pro nobis, ut per vitam ejus servemur ab ira."

[100] Chemnitz, *De Duabus*, 175a (428): "...Certum est, Christi corpus per Ascensionem, seu transitionem ex hoc mundo ad Patrem, glorificatum seu gloriosum factum esse, in summo gradu gloriae."

ascended from the power of sin.[101] In his original state the human being experienced God's inhabitation, but now his or her relation to God is much deeper. Humanity was not originally a part of Triune life; it is now since the assumed human nature has ascended to the right hand of the Father.[102]

In fact, everything Christ goes through belongs to salvation because of the assumed human nature. In keeping with this, salvation takes place first in this nature.[103] Christ heals human nature first in himself, as the Head, and then He gives it to the body, i.e., the Christian congregation.[104]

> This is the most comforting and salutary exchange (*salutaris permutatio*), that the Son of God has received from us a human nature and sanctified and blessed and exalted and glorified it in his own person.[105]

The third genus (*genus majestaticum*) refers to the supernatural gifts and attributes Christ's human nature receives in the hypostatic union. Since God's attributes and essence are inseparable, these supernatural gifts and attributes are God's essence.[106] Soteriologically the most important

---

[101] Chemnitz, *De Duabus*, 127a (320): "...humana nostra natura, quae in Adamo in infirmam deiectionem prolapsa, & in potestatem tenebrarum redacta fuerat, in Christo rursus euecta & exaltata sit."

[102] Chemnitz, *De Duabus*, 203b (489–490).

[103] Chemnitz, *De Duabus*, 123b (313): "Paulus igitur Col. 1. cum corpori, carni, sanguini, cruci, morti Christi, tribuisset recõciliationem, pacificationem & c. Ut sciremus solida & efficacia esse illa beneficia, & ad nos fratres etiam, illam restaurationem, quae in assumpta natura primogeneti facta est, pertinere, dicit Paulus complacitum esse, ut ominis plenitudo in ipso inhabiter."

[104] Chemnitz, *De Duabus*, 14b–15a (60): "Quia peccato corrupta & depravata est, ut eam in seipso primum repararet & restitueret, ac deinde ex ipso tanquam ex capite, ad nos, qui membra ejus sumus, sanatio, sanctificatio, seu renovatio derivaretur." See also Chemnitz, *De Duabus*, 90a–b (239); 123b (313).

[105] Chemnitz, *De Duabus*, 12b (55): "Et suavissima est salutaris illa permutatio, quod Filius Dei a nobis humanam naturam accepit, & illam in sua persona sanctificavit, beatificavit, exaltavit, & glorificavit."

[106] Chemnitz, *De Duabus*, 103b (270): "Et quia idiomata Divinitatis sunt ipsa essentia Divina, separari ab ea non possunt." Chemnitz, *De Duabus*, 6b–7a (42). Chemnitz states that in principle one could speak about divinization (*deificatio*) of the flesh but, because of Schwenkfeld, the concept has become useless. Instead, more proper terms include "participation" (*participatio*), "putting together" (*collatio*), and "communication" (*communicatio*). Chemnitz, *De Duabus*, 161b (396–7). "Sed propter Eutychis certamina, & propter Schwenckfeldii deliria, nostro tempore sparsa, de conversione & exaequatione naturarum, vocabulum Deificationis incommodius jam factum est, nec velle ejus usum revocari, semper enim prolixa addensa esset declaratio & praemonitio."

attribute is Life, since Christ is Life personified.[107] The life lost in the Fall is now restored in the person of Christ; consequently now everyone who is in communion with Christ becomes the recipient of Life.

> For the divine nature of the Logos, essentially or in essence, in, according to, and through itself, by nature, in its very being, is life giving, omnipotent, and omniscient, indeed it is life and omnipotence itself. But the assumed human nature in Christ is in no way life giving or omnipotent, essentially, or in essence, in and through itself, by nature, formally, or in its very being but only by possession, that is, because it possesses the divine majesty and power of the Logos personally united to itself; and by virtue of the Logos which is wholly united with it, it makes all things alive, knows all, can do all, just as hot iron by virtue of its union with the fire can glow and give heat.[108]

The restoration of life is closely related to the notion of anointing (*unctio*). In incarnation, humanity was anointed with the Spirit, which implies the special presence of God. This comes close to the capacity of the human in his original state to have the Spirit within. Under sin the Spirit is driven out, but in the person of Christ humanity is anointed again, and the capacity to have the Spirit is restored.[109]

The person of Christ, especially His human nature, is perceived as the place of salvation—the individual is saved in union (*copulatio*) with Him.[110] The humanity of Christ is the *nexus conjunctionis* between the individual and God.[111] According to Colossians 2:10, Christ is the

---

[107] Chemnitz, *Theses*, 86. "...quae ab aeterna fuit ipsa vita vivificans."

[108] Chemnitz, *De Duabus*, 114a–b (293).

[109] Chemnitz, *De Duabus*, 131a (329). An illustrtion of this is Chemnitz's explanation of the creation of the soul by God's breath (1. Moos. 2:7). Chemnitz compares this to the donation of the Holy Spirit, when Christ breathed into the apostles (John. 20:22). Chemnitz, *Loci* I, 115b (165): "Nam & Christus instauraturus imaginem Dei in homine, usus est inspiratione, cum insussiando Apostolis dabat Spiritum Sanctum. Ioan. 21 v. 22. Et voluit sine dubio nos deducere ad cognitionem primae inspirationis."

[110] Chemnitz, *Fundamenta*, 62b (188–189): "Ut autem certi redderemur haec ad nostram etiam miseram naturam in nobis pertinere, & verè nobis communicari, Christus ipsam illam naturam, quam à nobis assumpsit, & in se primo reparavit, rursus nobis in Coena sua praebet, ita, ut haec misera nostra carne eam sumentes, non dubitemus de salute nostra etiam naturae per Christum. Hoc enim modo, sanctissime & vivificae suae massae. Miseram & depravatam nostram naturam quasi inserit, sicut Cyrillus loquitur, ut ejus depravatio & miseria, per acrissimam antidoti hujus copulationem, sanctificetur & reformetur."

[111] Chemnitz, *Fundamenta*, 62b (188): "Atque; ita humanitas Christi est nexus conjunctionis nostrae cum ipso Deo..." This is a typical patristic notion. See Koen, *The Saving Passion*, p. 78.

Head, and everyone who clings to Him and apprehends Him grows together with God (2:19).

> Thus Paul concludes that he who grasps and clings to this Head, that is, to this individual human nature which in Colossians 1 he calls the body, flesh, and blood of Christ, at the same time grasps, holds, and possesses the whole fullness of the Godhead. For this fullness dwells in the assumed nature, which is akin to us, of the same substance with us, and personally united with us, because there and in that way He has willed that He be sought, found, apprehended, and possessed. For in His absolute deity we cannot approach Him, since we have been alienated and barred from Him because of our sin. But now, since this fullness has been made akin to us in the flesh, not indeed through a transformation or conversion of the natures and essences but through the personal union, we are permitted to approach Him. And since we have an approach and access to the assumed nature of Christ on account of our consubstantial relationship through faith, we also through this same means have an approach to the whole fullness of the deity of the Logos, which dwells in the assumed nature; and thus we are finally brought to fellowship not only with the Son but also with the Father and the Holy Spirit because of the consubstantiality of the Trinity.[112]

The Head must be joined to the body if it is to provide life. In order to enable the union, the following conditions must be fulfilled. First, the Head must be of the same essence as the body; this occured through the incarnation. Second, the Head must contain the fullness of God so that it can vivify the body. This occurs for the sake of Christ's divinity (Col. 2:9). Third, this fullness of God must be transferred to the body, which is possible only if the Head and the body are connected. Chemnitz explains this as follows:

> It is required that the Head not be cut off or separated from the body, but be joined with it, and it is also necessary that the members adhere

[112] Chemnitz, *De Duabus*, 124b (315–6): "Atque hinc Paulus concludit, qui hoc caput, in illo scilicet obiecto naturae humanae, quam capite primo nominat corpus, carnem & sanguinem Christi, apprehendit ac tenet illum, simul apprehendere, tenere & habere, omnem plenitudinem Deitatis, illa enim in assumpta natura, nobis cognata & consubstantiali, personaliter unita inhabitat, ut ibi ac ita velit quaeri, inueniri, apprehendi, & teneri, quod in absoluta Deitate assequi non possumus, quoniam per peccatum ab ea nimium abalienati & dissiti simus, Sed iam in carne nobis cognata, non quidem per physicam seu essentialem, vel effusionem, vel confusionem, sed per hypostaticam unionem deposita est. Cumque ad assumtam Christi naturam, propter cognationem imò consubstantialitatem, fide aditum & accessum habeamus, per illam, ad totam plenitudinem Deitatis τοῦ Λόγου in ea habitantem, peruenimus, atque inde propter ὁμοούσια Trinitatis ad communionem non Filij tantum, sed & Patris & Spiritus Sancti deducimur."

> to the head in a firm union. Thus it is also imperative that the complete Christ is present in the members according to both natures, and that He graft the members into Himself.[113]

Salvation is possible for the individual believer only if Christ's human-divine body is omnipresent and capable of apprehension. Communion with God is possible because divine ubiquity has now taken on human nature. The human nature of Christ has been raised to right hand of the Father,[114] making Christ salvifically present in the Word and Sacraments.[115]

5.2.3. *Faith as Apprehension of Christ*

All of what has been said so far leads to the notion that Christ, *as a human-divine person*, is the salvation of the human race. The life of Christ becomes actual and effective for the sinner only when the sinner is made to participate in that life through Christ and in Christ (*per eam & in ea*).

> ...the flesh of Christ vivifies the believers not only meritoriously but also efficaciously by application and communication.... For Christ imparts and lavishes His blessings on us by the communication of Himself and by union with Himself.[116]

---

[113] Chemnitz, *De Duabus*, 135a (336): "Requiritur ut caput non sit praecisum aut separatum à corpore, sed ei coniunctum, & membra etiam oportet capiti adhaerere, per certas iuncturas. Ita oportet Christum totum, secundum utramque naturam, ut caput membris suis praesentem adesse, ac membra sibi inferere."

[114] Chemnitz, *Repetitio*, 385: "Sola enim illa massa, personali unione copulata est divinitati, ita quod verbum in tota illa lucet. Sola illa massa exaltata est, ad dextram virtutis, & maiestatis Dei." According to Chemnitz the Bible never understands God's right hand as a literal place; rather, the concept refers to the power and action of God. Christ is the right hand of God *par excellence* since God works everything through Christ. When the Bible speaks about Christ sitting at the right hand of the Father (as in Math. 26:64), this means ascension of human nature and its participation in the divine ubiquity. Chemnitz, *Duabus*, 127a–b (323). Chemnitz, *Repetitio*, 17. Both Luther and Lutheran orthodoxy have always understood God's right hand like this. See Erwin Metzke, *Coincidentia oppositorum: Gesammelte Studien zur Philosophiegeschichte* (Witten: Forschungen und Berichte der Evangelischen Studiengemeinschaft 19, 1968). Calvin and the Reformed theologians have usually understood the concept spatially, see Calvin, *Institutio* II, XVI, 14.

[115] Chemnitz, *Fundamenta*, 80–83 (235); *De Duabus*, praefatio (27).

[116] Chemnitz, *De Duabus*, 132b (332): "Caro Christi, non merito tantum, verum etiam efficia, applicatione & communicatione, credentes vivificat. Dupliciter enim caro Christi Johann. 6. datur: Primo, quando ut victima in mortem pro mundi vita datur. Secundo, quando audientibus & credentibus datur, ut per eam, & in ea, vitam aeternam habeat. Christus enim sui ipsius communicatione & coniunctione, beneficia sua, & vitam

Apprehension (*apprehensio*), reception (*receptio*), and application (*applicatio*) of Christ take place through faith,[117] the essence of which is depicted in Melanchthon's terminology of movements in the mind.[118] As an anthropological state of mind, Chemnitz divides faith into five steps (*gradus*), the first of which is knowledge (*notitia/scientia*). The facts about Christ must be known and understood.[119] Second, the individual must assent (*assensus*) to knowledge; the believer must be convinced that the promise of grace applies to him or her personally.[120]

Although knowledge and assent belong to the intellect, they effect longing and desire (*desideria*) in the will. The individual now understands his or her state under the wrath of God and begins to yearn for forgiveness.[121] Trust (*fiducia*) in Christ is attributed to the believer as justifying faith.[122] This is not a detached 'epicurean' opinion but a genuine joint movement of the intellect and the will that results in ardent trust in the promise of grace.[123] The last step is courage clarify

---

aeternam nobis impertit & largitur. Non autem solius Divinae suae naturae, verum rumentiam carnis suae ac sanguinis, (haec enim Joh. 6. Expresse aliquoties nominatur) communione ac coniunctione hoc efficit, ac fides apprehendes, tenes & applicans sibi Christum, non tantum Divinam eius naturam, sed inprimis eam naturam, qua nobis cognatus & consubstantialis est, in qua, & per quam opus redemptionis perficit, apprehendit." See also Chemnitz, *Examen*, 241a (II, 57); *Fundamenta*, 94 (267).

[117] Chemnitz, *Loci* II, 241a (490): "Est enim fides unicum medium & organum, per quod iustitiam Christi apprehendimus, recipimus & nobis applicamus."

[118] Martens, *Die Rechtfertigung*, pp. 97–98; Bernt Oftestad, "Lehre, die das Herz bewegt. Das Predigtparadigma bei Martin Chemnitz," *Archiv für Reformationsgeschichte* 80 (1989), pp. 151–152.

[119] Chemnitz, *Loci* II, 252a (502).

[120] Chemnitz, *Loci* II, 252a (502): "Oportet igitur huic notitiae conjunctam esse assensionem, non quidem generalem tantum: sed qua firma persuasione, quam Paulus pleerophoria vocat, quisque statuat, universalem illam promissionem privatim ad se quoque proprie & peculiariter pertinere, se quoque includi & comprehendi in illa universali promissione."

[121] Chemnitz, *Loci* II, 252a (502): "Deinde ex hac notitia & assensione. Quae in mente est, cor seu voluntas & concipit operatione Spiritus sancti gemitum seu desiderium, ut quia serio sensit, se oneratum esse peccatis & ira Dei, velit, expetat, quaerat sibi donari illa beneficia, quae in promissione Evangelij proponuntur."

[122] Chemnitz, *Loci* II, 252a (502): "...Necesse est accedere fiduciam, quae firma persuasione ex verbo Dei statuat, Deum tunc tibi donare, communicare & applicare beneficia promissionis gratiae, & te hoc modo vere apprehendere & accipere ad justitiam, salutem & vitam aeternam ea, quae gratuita Evangelij promissio offert."

[123] Chemnitz, *Loci* II, 244a (493): "Diligenter considerentur pondera illorum testimonium, quae manifeste ostendunt, Fidem in Articulo Justificationis intelligendam esse, non tantum pro notitia & generali assensione, quae in genere statuat veram esse promissionem Euangelii; sed complecti simul motus voluntatis & cordis; hoc est, esse desiderium & fiduciam, quae in lucta cum peccato & ira Dei, singulis credentibus promissionem gratiae ita applicet, ut in generalem promissionem quisque credentuim se

characters (παρρησία) which appears as peace in the conscience and as deep spiritual joy even in the midst of sufferings.[124] This last step does not constitute the essence of faith precisely since it is the outcome of faith. In addition, God can occasionally remove this joy and certainty.[125] The intensity of other steps may also vary individually. One believer may have less knowledge of spiritual matters than another, and another may have stronger trust than the other.[126]

In Chemnitz's definition faith as trust is the antithesis to the Roman Catholic notion of faith, which is only knowledge and assent.[127] Consequently the form (*forma*) of faith is described as apprehending the promise of grace (*promissio gratiae*).[128] However, Chemnitz emphasizes that faith does not save because of its psychological characteristics, but receives its form from Christ apprehended.[129] Generally, Chemnitz uses the notion of form in a broad sense to mean, faith, Christ, God's grace, forgiveness of sins, and so on, which are not mutually exclusive entities.[130]

---

quoque includat, & ita se erigat, ut sine haesitatione statuens promissionem Euangelii sibi quoque firmam esse, inde consolationem & vitam in tentationibus concipiat."

[124] Chemnitz, *Loci* II, 252a (502): "Postremo sequitur ex hac fide παρρησία, qua habet accessum ad Deum, Ephes. 3, v. 12. Pax conscientiae, Rom. 5, v. 1. Gaudium Spiritus, Rom. 14, v. 17. ut cor sentiens novam vitam & laetitiam in Deo, suaviter acquiescae in promissione gratiae, etiam in cruce, persecutione, in ipsa denique morte, & habet indubitatam spem gloriae Dei, Rom. 5, v. 2."

[125] Chemnitz, *Loci* II, 252b (503): "Quia quintus ille gradus sequitur fidem, non est de essentia fidei, & Deus sensum illum pacis credentibus saepe substrahit."

[126] Chemnitz, *Loci* II, 252b (503).

[127] Chemnitz, *Examen*, 181b, 15 (I, 563).

[128] Chemnitz, *Loci* II, 251b (502): "Est igitur apprehensio, acceptio, seu applicatio promissionis gratiae, formale fidei justificans, juxta phrasin Scripturae."

[129] Chemnitz, *Loci* II, 252b (503): "Justificamur enim fide non propterea, quod sit virtus tam firma, robusta & perfecta; sed propter objectum, quod Fides apprehendit Christum, scilicet Mediatorem in gratiae." Chemnitz, *Examen*, 161b, 6 (503): "Non quod fides per se sit talis virtus, sed quia apprehendit, accipit, amplectitur, et possidet Christum, qui est perfectio legis ad justitiam omni credenti. Illa enim est justitia, quam Deus imputat sine nostris operibus, iis qui beati redduntur: per redemptionem enim, quae est in Christo Jesu, justificamur, Rom 3." Chemnitz, *Examen*, 188a, 24 (581).

[130] Chemnitz, *Loci* II, 296a (554): "Haec simplex ratio ideo mihi probatur, quia multae disputationes hinc possunt dijudicari. Quidam causam formale ponunt fidem, quidam Christum: alij misericordiam Dei: alij remissionem peccatorum seu acceptationem. Et hae sententiae saepe ab imperitis committuntur, quasi pugnantes inter se & diversa, saepe ab Adversarijs exagitantur." In *Commentary on Galatians*, Luther also uses Melanchthonian distinctions such as *certa fiducia*, *firmus assensus*, and *cognitio*, but in the same passage faith is described as darkness, which does not see anything, although Christ is present in this faith. See *WA* 40 I, 228, 27—229, 35.

Disregarding the saving power of psychological aspects of faith suggests that there is something more powerful behind the empirical reality that transforms mere trust into saving faith. An emphasis of trust over knowledge is not the most essential antithesis of the scholastic notion of faith; justifying power is somewhere other than in the faculties of the individual, as apparent in the paragraphs where Chemnitz criticizes soteriologies based on the *fides charitate formata* notion.[131]

> However, the life which faith brings to the believers it does not borrow or receive from love but from Christ, whom it embraces, who is our life and salvation.[132]

Love does not make faith perfect. Only Christ who is Life and Salvation can give faith its justifying nature. Although the reception of the promise of grace can be termed the form of justification, this is possible only because Christ is present in the promise.[133] Christ and His merit is thus applied to the sinner (*applicet in promissione Christum cum omnibus suis meritis*).[134] This is illustrated in *Loci* where Chemnitz disproves three erroneous ways of understanding the relation between Christ and faith.

> (1) Faith in itself, as a quality, without Christ, is not our formal righteousness. (2) And Christ, unless He is apprehended by faith, is not your

---

[131] According to Hoffman ("Die Rechtfertigung des Sünders," pp. 63, 68–69, 76–77, 82) the substantial difference between Chemnitz and Trent is the grounds on which the sinner is saved. Both parties describe the act of salvation similarly. Lutherans admit that the justified person is renewed, while Trent admits the pastoral meaning of forgiveness of sins. From this it does not follow however that the saving principle is the same. Chemnitz interprets Trent to mean that renewal and love are the *causa formalis* of justification, while Lutherans consider faith as formal righteousness.

[132] Chemnitz, *Examen*, 188b (I, 582): "Vitam autem quam fides affert credentibus non mutuatur, aut accipit a charitate sed a Christo quem complectitur, qui est vita et salus nostra."

[133] Chemnitz does not explicitly use the *fides Christo formata* formulation, but it occurs implicitly as an antithesis for *fides charitate formata*. E.g. Chemnitz, *Loci* II, 253b (504): "Quòd si quaeritur, quo respectu, seu qua vi & virtute fides justificet, Scholastici respondent, Fidem hanx virtutem & efficaciam justificandi mutuari à charitate, & hanc vocant Fidem formatam. Scriptura verò affirmat, Fidem ideò justiticare, quia Christum, quo nobis est factus à Deo justitia, apprehendit et sibi applicat."

[134] Chemnitz, *Examen*, 185a, 14 (573): "Altera quaestio est, quomodo et qua ratione fides justificans circa illud suum objectum versetur ut justificet, scilicet non frigida cogitatione, non generali et superficiali assensione: sed ita ut agnoscat, intueatur, expetat, quaerat, apprehendat, accipiat, complectatur, et singulis credentibus applicet in promissione Christum cum omnibus suis meritis, et in Christo misericordiam Dei remittens peccata."

> righteousness. (3) But if faith lays hold on Christ, but does not in Him also lay hold on the grace and mercy of God, it does not thereby establish that it will receive forgiveness of sins or acceptance, and it is certainly lacking the form of righteousness before God. For justification is absolution or acceptance.[135]

First, this concise and cryptic paragraph condemns the notions of faith as a human deed, virtue, or any other non-christological event. Apparently Chemnitz thought that one can have all the psychological and empirical aspects of faith without actually having justifying faith. Even if faith has empirical aspects, they do not justify *simpliciter* without the presence of Christ. Second, the apprehension of Christ is of importance. Chemnitz repeats Mörlin's notions of the importance of personal apprehension in order for Christ's merit to become effective. Third, Chemnitz criticizes the Osiandrian notion that separates Christ's person from His work, which downplays the role of Christ's merit. Abstract and mystical speech about apprehension of Christ in itself does not create Christian belief. While Christ's mystical presence in faith is part of Christian belief, it needs to be related to redemption through the Cross.

The apprehension of Christ in faith is the essence of faith, which one cannot produce oneself. Through the Word and Sacraments God infuses (*effundit*) the Holy Spirit into the hearts of believers and thus donates faith.[136] According to Chemnitz, faith embraces Christ and apprehends (*apprehendit, accipit, amplectitur, et possidet Christum*) Him.[137] Faith is the bond (*Band*) which connects the individual with Christ.[138] Chemnitz explicitly denies that Christ's presence is only a matter of relational re-disposition of the will.

---

[135] Chemnitz, *Loci* II, 296a (554): "Fides per se, ut qualitas, sine Christo, non est formalis nostra iustitia. Et Christus nisi fide apprehendatur, non est tua justitia. Quòd si fides Christum apprehendat, non autem in eo gratiam & misericordiam Dei. Nec statuat illa se apprehensione consequi remissionem peccatorum seu acceptationem, certum est deesse formam justitiae coram Deo. Justificatio enim est absolutio seu acceptatio."

[136] Chemnitz, *Enchiridion*, 154: "Deus ipse, quò firmam & certam haec fiduciam reddatur, iusticiam fidei obsignat per sua Sacramenta... & per Spiritum sanctum suum, quem ideo in corde credentium effundit."

[137] Chemnitz, *Examen*, 161b, 6 (503): "...apprehendit, accipit, amplectitur, et possidet Christum..." See also Chemnitz, *Examen*, 186a, 17 (576).

[138] Chemnitz, *Handtbüchlein*, 125: "Und ist das (Glaube) Band / dadurch Christus in uns wohnet / Ephe 3. Und wir in ihme gefunden werden / Philip 3." See also Chemnitz, *Loci* II, 254b (505), where he states that faith is "verbum, quo inferiamur in Christo."

> Thus we must consider that Christ is in us, not only by relationship (Gr. σχέσις) or by conformity to a favorable disposition which is covered by the term 'love', but also by participation in our very nature. Just as if one should mix hot liquid wax with some other similar liquified wax in such a way that that which would produced would seem to be one thing, so by communication of His body and blood Christ is in us and we in Him.[139]

The presence of Christ in the believer is also illustrated in the following way.

> But the real reasons that Paul says Christ dwells in us by faith are: (1) that He may show that faith is the means, the organ, or instrument by which we lay hold on Christ in the Word, receive and retain Him, so that He does not pass by as a pilgrim or only spend the night as a guest in our midst, but remains through the grace of indwelling (*gratia inhabitationis*) and always abides in us, so that we may always be and remain in the household of God; (2) that in this passage faith is put in opposition to actual sight and sense perception, as in 2 Cor. 5:7, "We walk by faith not by sight," or outward appearance. And in John 20:29, "Blessed are they who do not see," or touch, "but believe"; (3) That Christ is said to dwell in us by faith because He dwells in our hearts in a divine and incomprehensible manner which is believed alone by faith in the promise, not by our reason or by some perceptible or visible or local condition of this world which can be grasped by the senses or comprehended by our intellect and reason; so that even though we do not feel or understand that Christ is in us or how He is in us, yet by faith, according to his promise we understand with certainty that He truly dwells in our hearts. I think that Nazianzus is trying to say this when he writes in his first epistle to Cledonius that Christ dwells in our hearts not by appearance [phenomenally] but by rational apprehension [noumenally]; that is, in a manner which is above and beyond the phenomenal.[140]

---

[139] Chemnitz, *De Duabus*, 194a–b (468): "Unde considerandum est, non σχέσις habitudine seu affectionum conformitate solum, quae per caritatem intelligitur, Christum in nobis esse, verumentiam participatione naturali. Quemadmodum, si quis igne liquefactam ceram, alii cerae similiter liquefactae ita miscuerit, ut unum quid ex utrisque factum videatur, sic communicatione corporis & sanguinis Christi, ipse in nobis est, & nos in ipso." Although the passage speaks about salvation with regard to the eucharist, the context shows the wider application of this idea. The passage is from the section that examines the consolation of God's indwelling. See also Chemnitz, *Fundamenta*, 53a (164).

[140] Chemnitz, *De Duabus*, 16b–187a (451): "Verae autem caussae, quod Paulus dicit Christum fide inhabitare in nobis, hae sunt, ut ostendat fidem esse medium, organon seu instrumentum, quo Christum in verbo apprehendimus, accipimus ac retinemus, ut non quasi peregrinus transeat, vel ut hospes pernoctet tantum apud nos, sed ut per inhabitationis gratiam maneat, ac perpetuo in nobis inhabitet, ut semper nos simus ac maneamus domestici Dei.2. Quia fides hoc loco opponitur apertae visionis & sensibus,

According to Chemnitz, the presence of Christ is not obvious to the senses but is understood to be true on the basis of God's promises. This allowed Chemnitz to avoid the dangers of Osiandrianism; the observation of Christ's indwelling does not provide the basis for the certainty salvation. God's indwelling is the source of great joy and consolation even if it can be obtained only by faith, not with emotions.[141] The mystical presence of Christ is related to Chemnitz's notion of incarnation, which forms the foundation for the idea of Christ's person as the location of eternal blessing, salvation having already taken place in Christ's person. For Chemnitz, justifying faith is first and foremost apprehending Christ (*apprehendere Christum per fidem*), which takes place through actual participation in the person of Christ.

In summary, faith is evoked by the Spirit and has empirical qualities. However, these qualities do not justify since it is Christ who gives faith its form. The crucial question is whether justifying faith that is part of justification involves change. This problem will be examined next.

5.2.4. *Justification and Renewal through Participation in Christ*

Chemnitz's interpretation of the doctrine of justification incorporates both extrinsic and intrinsic motives. The motif of extrinsicness is underlined by excluding particles (*particulae exclusivae*) such as 'alone' (*sola*), 'grace' (*gratia*), 'without works' (*sine operibus*), 'faith' (*fides*), and 'freely' (*gratis*).[142]

---

ut 2. Corinth. 5. Per fidem ambulamus, non per speciem seu visionem. Et Johan. 20. Beati qui non vident, aut palpat, sed credunt. 3. Christus dicitur fide inhabitare, quia non ratione aut conditione aliqua huius seculi, sensibili, visibili, aut locali, quae vel sensibus percipi, vel intellectu seu ratione comprehendi possit, sed coelesti divino ac incomprehensibili modo, qui sola fide ex promissione creditur Christus inhabitat in cordibus nostris, ut etiamsi nec sentiamus, nec intelligamus, quod & quomodo Christus sit in nobis, Fide tamen juxta promissionem certò statuamus, ipsum verè habitare in cordibus nostris, ut etiamsi nec sentiamus, nec intelligamus, quod & quomodo Christus sit in nobis, Fide tamen juxta promissionem certò statuamus, ipsum verè habitare in cordibus nostris. Et hoc existimo Nazienzenum velle, quando scribit Epist. 1. Ad Cledonium, Christum habitare in cordibus nostris οὐ κατὰ τὸ φαινόμενον ἀλλὰ κατὰ τὸ νοούμενον."

[141] *De Duabus Naturis in Christo* (194a) contains a section entitled "Quàm dulces consolationes veteres inde sumant, quod vivificatio & instauratio naturae humanae in nobis, ex carne & per carnem Christi, quae nobis cognata est, nobis communicetur & immittatur, quodque Christus non tantum Spiritu, verum etiam corpore suo, se nobis conjungat & uniat."

[142] Chemnitz, *Loci* II, 282b–283a (538–534).

Chemnitz used these concepts to emphasize three things. First, the object of justifying grace is the Gospel alone, which offers mercy for those who receive it. Second, the concepts refer to the cause of redemption. The merit and the cause are demarcated outside of us so that Christ alone is the foundation of salvation. Third, the concepts illustrate the mode of application of salvation, which is faith. All human merits are thus excluded.[143]

In addition to exclusive particles, the free nature of justification is stressed by the interpretation of the word 'to justify' (*iustificare*) as a forensic term (*verbum forense*).[144]

> Paul everywhere describes the article of justification as a judicial process wherein the conscience of the sinner, accused before the tribunal of God by the divine law, convicted, and subject to the sentence of eternal damnation, flees to the throne of grace and is restored, absolved, and freed from the sentence of condemnation and received to eternal life for the sake of the obedience and intercession of the Son of God, our Mediator, which is laid hold of and made one's own through faith.[145]

The person is saved by Christ's righteousness alone; human righteousness—not even where it is perfected with divine righteousness—is enough. The righteousness of Christ means primarily Christ's obedience (*obedientia*), which is reckoned for righteousness.[146] As already noted, apprehending Christ's obedience and apprehending Christ do not exclude each other since they are mutually complementary or synonymous concepts.[147] Thus, Chemnitz did not make an essential

---

[143] Chemnitz, *Loci* II, 287a (544).

[144] Chemnitz, *Loci* II, 230a–b (476–477). Chemnitz, *Examen*, 149a, 3–150a, 5 (449–450). According to Chemnitz, the Greek word δικαιόω means either 1) "pronouncing judgment or declaring righteous", or 2) "to inflict punishment based on court decisions" Torbjörn Johansson has summarized Chemnitz's argument for the forensic use of *iustificare*. See Johansson, *Reformationens huvudfrågor och arvet från Augustinus. En studie i Martin Chemnitz' Augustinusreception* (Göteborg: Församlingförlaget), pp. 207–210.

[145] Chemnitz, *Loci* II, 233b (480): "Paulus igitur articulum Iustificationis ubique describit, tanquam processum judicialem, quod conscientia peccatoris coram tribunali Dei Lege divina accusata, convicta & sententiae aeternae damnationis subjecta, confugiens ad thronum gratiae restituitur, absolvitur, & a sententia damnationis liberata, ad vitam aeternam acceptatur, propter obedientiam & intercessionem Filij Dei Mediatoris, quae fide apprehenditur & applicantur."

[146] Chemnitz, *Loci* II, 237b (485): "In his testimonijs, iustitia Dei significat iustitia, que coram Deo acceptatur ad vita aeterna, & haec est obedientia Mediatoris nostri, quam Deus credentibus imputat ad iustitiam, si fide eam apprehendat."

[147] Esim. Chemnitz, *Examen*, 185a, 14 (573): "Altera quaestio est, quomodo et qua ratione fides justificans circa illud suum objectum versetur ut justificet, scilicet non frigida cogitatione, non generali et superficiali assensione: sed ita ut agnoscat, intueatur,

distinction between Christ's person and Christ's work; God cannot be separated from His attributes.[148] The emphasis on Christ's obedience underlines the significance of salvation history: When the believer apprehends Christ, who exactly is apprehended?

The extrinsic concepts do not imply spatial outwardness. The idea of actual inwardness is stressed when Chemnitz claimed that Christ is not somewhere else when He forgives sin. As a general principle of Christian doctrine, Chemnitz taught that Christ's presence (*praesentia*) is always joined with Christ's deeds (*operationes*).[149] He wrote:

> For the power, grace, efficacy, merits and blessings of Christ are not communicated to believers outside of or without His person, as if He Himself were not present, as the adversaries themselves admit. They also admit that it is necessary above all things that Christ himself be given to us, that He become ours and that He be present in with us and joined to us, so that from Him and in Him and through Him we might be filled with all the fullness of God.[150]

The *gratia-donum* distinction of Luther and Melanchthon did not appear often in the texts of the second-generation Reformers.[151] According to Chemnitz the locus of justification consists of merit (*meritum*) and its application (*applicatio*).[152] This new distinction is substantially identical with the previous one while it is certainly more informative. Merit means Christ's fulfilled work, which exists as potentiality and outside

---

expetat, quaerat, apprehendat, accipiat, complectatur, et singulis credentibus applicet in promissione Christum cum omnibus suis meritis, et in Christo misericordiam Dei remittens peccata." Although the emphasis of the theory of forensic satisfaction may cause rationalism, according to Martens (*Die Rechtfertigung*, pp. 91–92, 95) Chemnitz avoids this by his emphasis on the unity of the person and the work of Christ. See also Elert, *Morphologie des Luthertums, Erster Band: Theologie und Weltanschauung des Luthertums hauptsächlich im* 16. *und* 17. Jahrhundert (München 1952), pp. 102–103.

[148] Chemnitz, *Loci* I, 28b (61): "Sed quia misericordia eius non distinguitur ab essentia eius..."

[149] Chemnitz, *De Duabus*, 186a–b (450): "Et Christus ipse hasce cogitationes praeuenit, utramque enim coniungit, & operationem suam Marci 16. & praesentiam suam Matth. 28."

[150] Chemnitz, *De Duabus*, 196a (472): "Neque enim virtus, gratia, efficacia, merita & beneficia Christi, extra ipsius personam, & sine ea, etiamsi ipse non adsit, credentibus communicantur, imo sicut Aduersarij ipsi fatentur, Christum ipsum ante omnia nobis donari, & nostrum fieri, nobis adesse, ac nobiscum coniunci oportet, ut ita ex ipso, in ipso, & per ipsum, impleamur in omnem plenitudinem Dei, Eph. 3."

[151] This may result from the several interpretations and confusing uses of *donum* in early Lutheran theology.

[152] Chemnitz, *Loci* II, 228b (474); *Fundamenta* 94b (267).

the sinner. Merit is of no use as such. In order to become effective it must be applied,[153] which causes justification and regeneration.[154]

The next question concerns the method of application. Chemnitz depicted the relation between God and the human being in terms of a distinction between foundation (*fundamentum*), relation (*relatio*), and goal (*terminus*).[155] The foundation is Christ's obedience and his salvific work. The relation is God's gracious will, which desires to save every human being. Since this will is revealed in the promises of the Bible, the foundation and executive power are wholly outside of the individual. The goal is the believing person, who owns grace by faith.[156] These three factors together constitute the form of justification. In other words, the form of justification is application of the foundation to its goal.

> Justification is a matter of relationship. The righteousness which is imputed to us, or on account of which we are accepted to eternal life, is not something inhering in us, either in whole or in part, but it is firmly rooted in the obedience of Christ alone. Therefore, in the simplest terms, the formal cause can be stated this way (as we state the formal cause in

---

[153] E.g. in *Handtbüchlein* (123) Chemnitz understands the application of the merit unitively. "Denn das Verdienst Christi mus unser werden. Roma 8. Und einem selben applicieret werden / das ers empfange und anneme / Johan. 3. Und also Christus in uns sey / Johan. 6. Und wir in im gefunden werden Phi. 3."

[154] Chemnitz, *De Duabus*, 133b (333): "Testatur autem Scriptura, Christum non sola sua Divina natura mundare conscientias à peccato, Sed ad illam mundationem adhibere etiam assumtam humanam suam naturam. Primo in merito Matth. 26. Sanguis effunditur in remissionem peccatorum. Ebr. 1. Sacta per semetipsum purgatione peccatorum. Secundò, etiam in applicatione, regeratione, iustificatione & efficacia." Chemnitz, *De Duabus*, 132b (332).

[155] The tripartite distinction appears in Melanchthon's *Erotemata Dialectices*, where he explain the modes of various relations (*CR* 13, 545): "Omne relativum versatur inter duo, quorum alterum vocatur fundamentum, alterum terminus. Fundamentum est res, ad quam ordinata est relatio. Inter haec relatio est, ipsa applicatio seu ordo fundamenti ad terminum, ut, cum de patre dicimus, fundamentum est persona quae genuit, terminus persona genita, ordo a patre ad filium dicitur paternitas." Chemnitz uses this distinction to explain how God can declare the individual just even if he is not actually so. In himself or herself the sinful person receives and shares the righteousness of Christ.

[156] Chemnitz, *Loci* II, 275b (530): "Ita habebimus integram relationem, fundamentum est in obedientia & redemptione, in Christo Jesu Domino nostro. Relatio est gratia & misericordia Dei. Terminus est persona credens, cui propter justitiam Christi peccata non imputantur; sed per Christum reputatur justa coram Deo ad vitam aeternam, imputatâ ipsi justitiâ Christi. Et Fides apprehendens illam iustitiam Christi, & in ea gratiam & misericordiam Dei in promissione dicitur imputari ad justitiam, non quatenus fides est virtus inhaerens in nobis; sed quia hoc medio & organo relatio Dei applicat fundamentum ad terminum."

> relationships): it is the very application of the foundation to the purpose, and the justification of the sinner comes from this application as its result, so to speak.[157]

Thus, the extrinsic (*fundamentum*) and intrinsic aspects (*terminus*) of justification become one. Justification requires actual participation in Christ, which does not mean participation only in the Holy Spirit or the divine nature of Christ.[158] Faith means sharing the consubstantial relation, in which a connection with Christ is established on the grounds of the consubstantiality of the natures; for the sake of hypostatic union Christ has the same nature as the sinner.[159] In faith, the believer first becomes a sharer (κοινωνός) of Christ and, eventually, of Triune God.[160]

This real communion with God effects justification and subsequent renewal. As Christ's human nature possesses the fullness of God, so the person who is united with it shares all the gifts of God and God himself.[161] Christ, who is consubstantial with both God and humankind,

---

[157] Chemnitz, *Loci* II, 296a (554): "1. Quòd iustificatio sit relatio quaedam. 2. Quod justitia illa, quae nobis imputatur, seu propter quam acceptamur ad vitam aeternam, non sit aliquid inhaerens in nobis, sive ex toto, sive ex parte, sed illam in solidum sitam esse in sola Christi obedientia. Simplicissimè igitur causa formalis ita potest constitui (sicut in relationibus formale est) ipsa applicatio fundamenti ad terminum, & quod ex illa applicatione quasi resultat, ut ita dicam."

[158] Chemnitz, *De Duabus*, 196b–197a (473): "Existimant [Scholasticos] enim merita Christi ab ipsius persona ita separata esse, ut per Spiritum Sanctum conferri possint credentibus, etiamsi persona Christi non adsit, vel solius Divinae naturae in Christo praesentia, operatione & efficacia, applicationem meritorum Christi, ac reliqua officij eius beneficia conferri, sine communione alterius naturae."

[159] Chemnitz, *De Duabus*, 124b (316): "...ad assumptam Christi naturam, propter cognationem imo consubstantialitatem, fide aditum & accessum habeamus, per illam, ad totam plenitudinem Deitatis τῷ Λόγω in ea habitantem, pervenimus, atq; inde propter ὁμοούσιαν Trinitatis, ad communionem non Filij tantum, sed & Patris Spiritus sancti deducimur." Chemnitz, *De Duabus*, 124a (314): "Ac inde concludit Paulus nullus aliis elementis mundi nobis opus esse ad salutem, cum totam ejus plenitudinem habeamus in Christo." See also Chemnitz, *Theses*, 128–130. Generally, scholars have not noticed participatory notions in Chemnitz. See, e.g., Johansson, *Reformationens huvudfrågor*, pp. 203–215; J. A. O. Preus, *The Second Martin*, pp. 293–320. Jörg Baur ("Martin Chemnitz," pp. 158–164), however, has interpreted Chemnitz's doctrine of justification as participatory but he does not explain the nature of participation. Is it an existential state of mind or ontological communication?

[160] Chemnitz, *De Duabus*, 122a–b (309); 124b (316). Chemnitz illustrates participation with the Greek concept μετέχειν, "to participate", which Greek Fathers used regularly to depict believers relation to God. Chemnitz, *De Duabus*, 40a (116). The created being, however, never shares such divine attributes as omniscientia or omnipotentia. Chemnitz, *De Duabus*, 121a–b (307).

[161] Chemnitz, *De Duabus*, 6b (41): "...ut ita restitutio & reparatio eius eò esset certior & firmior, ac ea ratione nos vicissim in Christo divinae naturae κοίνωνοι participes

delivers the fullness of God to believers, who become the dwelling place of the Triune God. This starts the renewal and restoration of the image of God.

> ...so there is only one salvation for the human race, if we do not deny it to ourselves and if we lean wholly on the engrafted Christ, that we may be found in Him, having that righteousness which God gives to faith in Christ (Phil. 3:9); that we may be made the righteousness of God in Christ (2. Cor. 5:21); and become branches of the Vine (John 15:5); that we may be able to say, I live, yet not I, but Christ lives in me (Gal. 2:20).[162]

Since the beginning of the 17th century, Lutheran theology had developed a distinction between two types of union.[163] The first type is union with Christ, which precedes justification (*unio fidei formalis / unio Christi*). This 'union of faith' is followed by God's indwelling (*inhabitatio Dei*). While Chemnitz did not employ this distinction his texts contain elements that provide the basis for such a development.[164]

Chemnitz did not introduce his own concept for the union that occurs simultaneously with justification. Instead, he used several concepts such as 'conjunction' (*coniungo*) or 'presence' (*adesse*), but these do not have the status of *theologumenon.*[165] In *Fundamenta*, Chemnitz followed Cyril's terminology, distinguishing three different unions. First, the union of faith reforms (*reformat*) the human being. Second, the union of love effects good works. Third, the sacramental union takes place in the eucharist.[166] Although Chemnitz did not use Cyril's terminology explicitly in

---

efficeremut. 2. Pet. 1. & communicationem acciperemus cum Patre, Filio & Spiritu Sancto. 1. Joh. 1."

[162] Chemnitz, *De Duabus*, 35a (102): "Ita unica salus est generis humani, si nos ipsos abnegamus, & Christo inserti ipsi toti innitimur, ut inveniamur in ipso, habentes eam iustitiam, quam Deus in Christo fidei donat, Phil. 3. Ut efficiamur iusticia Dei Christo, 2. Cor. 5. & simus palmites in vite, Ioh. 15. Ut dicere possimus: Vivo iam non ego, sed vivit in me Christus, Gal. 2." The difference between the person of a Christian and Christ is that in the human Christ's indwelling does not form a hypostatic union.

[163] The two distinct unions appear in Gerhard and Hollaz, among others. David Hollazius, *Examen Theologicum Acroamaticum* (Darmstad: Wissenschaftliche Buchgesellschaft 1971), p. 485. On Gerhard, see Vaahtoranta, *Restauratio*, pp. 243–285.

[164] This may already have begun with Luther's *Commentary on Galatians*. See section 2.1.2.

[165] *Coniungo* appears in Chemnitz, *Fundamenta*, 54a (166); *De Duabus*, 132b–133a (332); 196–b (472), etc. *Adesse* appears in Chemnitz, *De Duabus*, 196b–197a (472–473); *Loci* III, 34a, for instance. The previous passage speaks about union as well.

[166] Chemnitz, *Fundamenta*, 53a (164): "Cyrillus enim in Joannem lib. 11. Cap. 16, distincte tradit tres modos uniones nostrae cum Christo. 1. Unionem unius Sancti Spiritus participatione per fidem, qui sua gratia Spiritum nostrum reformat. 2. Unionem quae fit habitudine, affectu, et pietatis consensu, seu conformitate. Significat autem "σχέσις""

his other works, the way in which the distinction effects his doctrine of justification is easily apparent. Justification requires a *re-forming* union with Christ (*renovatio*$_1$), which enables faith. Still, this must be separated from renewal that causes good works (*renovatio*$_2$).

Chemnitz made an explicit distinction between justification (*iustificatio*) and renewal (*renovatio*). Justification means only forgiveness.[167] On the other hand, in justification the believer is reformed from the state of unbelief to that of belief (*renovatio*$_1$). In *Fundamenta* Chemnitz calls this vivifying (*vivificatio*); Christ cannot be apprehended by faith without this.[168] In this sense Chemnitz can speak about renewal (*renovatio*$_1$) as the prerequisite of faith. The desire for salvation does not arise without the work of the Spirit in the human heart. As mentioned, faith must be the gift of the Spirit, not a human deed. The Holy Spirit awakes the desire for salvation through prevenient grace (*gratia praeveniens*).[169] This is followed by preparing grace (*gratia praeparans*), which effects assent to the call of the Spirit.[170] The effective cause of faith is applied through operating grace (*gratia operans*), which illuminates the intellect (*illuminatio*)

---

affectionem rerum inter se comparatarum, quae indicat, quid una cum altera habeat conuenientiae. Σχέσις igitur, quae per dilectionem, sicut Chrysostomus & Cyrillus loquuntur, sit, complectitur efficiam & communicationem proprietatum. Cyrillus vero adhuc tertium genus unionis ponit, distinctum a prioribus duobus, Christum scilicet non tantum spiritu & divinitate esse in nobis, nec tantum vigore & efficacia carnis suae, verum etiam corporali seu naturali participatione carnis suae..., participationem illam fieri in Coena dominica." Chemnitz, *Fundamenta, 54a* (166): "Ita Cyrillus in Iohannem lib. 10. Cap. 13. Tradit spiritualem coniunctionem nostri cum Christo duobus modis fieri. 1. Fide per Spiritum seu divinam naturam. 2. Caritate, hoc sit, efficacia.... Non tamen negamus, fide & caritate nos Christo spirituale coniungi..."

[167] Chemnitz, *Examen*, 146b (462): "...quod homo iustificetur, hoc est, in gratiam recipiatur et acceptetur ad vitam aeternam, sola imputatione justitiae Christi, vel sola remissione peccatorum, fide apprehendente misericordiam Dei, peccata remittentis propter Christum." See also Chemnitz, *Examen*, 149 (468).

[168] Chemnitz, *Fundamenta*, 84a (240–241): "Sed necesse est Spiritum vivificare hominem & illustrare mentem. Ita enim & non aliter, fides ex verbo concipitur, ut possit Christum apprehendere." This notion has been neglected in the research. Hoffman ("*Die Rechtfertigung des Sünders*," pp. 84–85), for example, claims that no internal change can be a reason for justification since justification is *ex fide*. But how can there be faith without change in the individual?

[169] Chemnitz, *Loci* I, 179b (243): "Ex illis ergo Scripturae sententijs Augustinus rectè & verè statuit contra Pelagianos, Incipere non esse nostrum, nec ortum bonae voluntatis nostro conatu emergere, sed sanctam cogitationem, bonum propositum, cupiditatem seu desiderium boni esse gratiam, donum & operationem Spiritus Sancti. Et hanc gratiam docendi causâ vocat PRAEVENIENTEM, praecedentem, antecedentem." In *Loci*, Chemnitz (I, 178–183 (241–247)) uses the distinctions employed by Augustine (*de gratia praeveniente, subsequente, operante, cooperante*).

[170] Chemnitz, *Loci* I, 182a–b (246).

and renews the will (*renovatio*).[171] This inner renewal is something different than antecedent external persuasion.

> In external matters God can touch (*tangere*) or bow (*inclinare*) the hearts, but in spiritual matters the infirmity cannot be cured by so simple a remedy. God can soften the heart, turn it or open it, but because the heart is too hard, He wounds, circumcises, and even grinds it to powder. When this profits nothing, He finally takes it away, gives it a new life (*vivificat*), and even creates a new heart.[172]

Justification as vivifying is distinguished from an understanding of renewal (*renovatio*$_2$) that involves good works. In the later case, renewal is synonymous with conversion (*conversio*), which signifies processual growth of faith starting from justification and lasting until the end of earthly life.[173] In this sense, renewal refers to sanctification, good works and all the changes the Gospel effects. However, Chemnitz nowhere connects God's indwelling and renewal so that God's indwelling takes place only after justification.

Justification and renewal cannot be separated since they are intimately related.[174] They are separated conceptually in the locus of justification

---

171 Chemnitz, *Loci* I, 182b (246): "Huc pertinet, I. Illuminatio mentis & intellectus. 2. Renovatio voluntatis..."

172 Chemnitz, *Loci* I 178b (241): "In externis Deus potest tangere, inclinare corda: sed in spiritualibus tàm leui remedio non potest curari infirmitas. Sed Deus emollit, conuertit, aperit corda. Quia verò corda nimis sunt dura, vulnerat, circumcidit, immò conterit. Sed quando nihil proficit, tandem planè aufert, vivificat, dat, immò cor novum." Scholastic theology used the concept of *inclinatio* as almost synonymous with *habitus*. See Ockham, *Quodlibeta*, III q 22. The concept is very ambiguous, however, and there is no reason to assume that Chemnitz uses it in any particular scholastic sense. Thus, the translation "inclination" or "act of leaning" is sufficient based on its actual use by Chemnitz. Luther uses similar ideas in his idea of annihilation. See Juntunen, *Der Begriff des Nichts*, pp. 378–383.

173 Chemnitz, *Examen*, 136 (432): "Secundo, Multa Scripturae testimonia non tantum de defectu loquuntur, sed ostendunt in locum amissarum virium successisse vitiosum habitum et tristissimam depravationem in mente, voluntate et corde, quod ad motus seu actiones spirituales attinet: vocatur enim ante conversionem seu renovationem, cor durum Rom. 2." Curing (*sanatio*) means the same as renewal (*renovatio*). Chemnitz. *Examen*, 134a: "Ipsa etiam sanatio et renovatio, non est talis mutatio, quae uno momento statim absolvatur et perficiatur."

174 Chemnitz, *Loci* II, 271 (525): "Quia vero ostendunt, vocabulum usurpari pro causa & pro effectu, hoc est pro misericordia, & pro donis: Ideo addenda sunt testimonia firmiora & magis illustria, & ex ipsis rebus sumpta, quae manifeste probent & certó demonstrent, quando Paulus dicit, nos gratis per gratiam Dei justificari. Item, Gratia Dei salvati est, & c. non esse intelligendum, nos vel sola novitate, vel partim misericordia Dei, partim nostra novitate inhaerente justificari & salvari. Sed in hoc articulo Justificationis solam misericordiam Dei, quae est remissio peccatorum, & gratuita acceptatio ad vitam aeternam, propter Mediatorem. Illam vero acceptationem

but outside of this locus they are one because true faith is effective in love and is the generator (*genitrix*) of good works. The works of Christians please God for the sake of their faith.[175] Additionally, true faith does not exist without the works of love.[176] Faith and love are joined together christologically, not simply logically: both reconciliation and renewal are Christ's benefits (*beneficia*).[177] Since both are located in Christ and are given to those who believe in Him, the believer cannot apprehend Christ with only one of his gifts.

> As therefore these and many similar things, even when they are present at the same time, are rightly and necessarily distinguished, so we do not tear apart reconciliation and renewal, faith and love, in such a manner that we remove and deny one of them, but we give to each its place, its function, and its peculiar nature, with the Scripture, which teaches that this is the peculiar function of faith alone that it apprehends and accepts Christ in the promise of the Gospel for righteousness before God to life eternal. Faith does not divide this righteousness between Christ and our newness, or love, but it ascribes it entirely to the merit of Christ. Therefore true faith lays hold of Christ, but true faith is also not without works (Jas. 2:14–18) but works by love (Gal. 5:6). However, that faith justifies and saves, that strength and power it does not borrow, take, and have from this, that it works by love and brings forth good works, but from the fact that it apprehends Christ, who is the end of the Law for righteousness

---

sequuntur dona, Spiritus renovationis, & adeo non possunt haec duo divelli.... Non igitur rejicimus dona renovationis...Sed distinguimus haec duo, & cuique tribuimus illum locum, quem ei Scriptura assignat, articulo scilicet Justificationis misericordiam Dei, articulo vero renovationis dona novitatis, idque propterea, ut fides remissionis peccatorum & reconciliationis cum Deo nitatur, non nostris qualitatibus; sed sola misericordia Dei..."

[175] Chemnitz, *Examen*, 169b: "Omnino enim talem immediatam facit Paulus antithesin fidei et operum, gratiae et operum, meriti Christi et nostrorum operum, in articulo justificationis, cujus extrema nullo modo possint conjungi aut convenire, sed posito uno, statim excludatur et tollatur alterum. Signanter autem dico, in articulo justificationis: alias enim extra hunc articulum, optime convenit fidei et bonis operibus. Fides enim est per charitem efficax, genitrix est bonorum operum, et opera placent fide."

[176] Chemnitz, *Examen*, 201b, 5 (621). Consciously committed sin (*peccata contra conscientiam*) destroys faith as well. See Gottfried Noth, "Peccata contra conscientiam," in *Gedenkschrift für D. Werner Elert*, hrsgb. F. Hübner et al., (Berlin: Lutherisches Verlagshaus 1955), p. 211.

[177] Chemnitz, *Loci* II, 251 (501): "Restat igitur doctrina Evangelij, quod concionatur de duplici beneficio Christi, scilicet reconciliationis & sanctificationis, sive renovationis, hoc est, continet promissionem remissionis peccatorum, gratuitae reconciliationis, adoptionis & acceptationis ad vitam aeternam, propter Christum Mediatorem. Continet etam promissionem Spiritus renovationis, qui operatur velle & perficere, ut postquam justificati sumus, possimus etiam novam obedientiam inchoare."

to everyone who believes (Rom. 10:4). And there is no salvation in any other (Acts 4:12).[178]

In faith, forgiveness of sin and donation of the Holy Spirit are simultaneous (*simul*). Still, the forgiveness and good works are consequential.

> For Christ by His sufferings merited for us not only the remission of sins but also this, that on account of His merit the Holy Spirit is given to us, that we may be renewed in the spirit of our mind. We say, indeed, that these benefits of the Son of God are connected, so that, when we are reconciled, the Spirit of the renewal is at the same time (*simul*) given. But we do not for this reason confuse but rather distinguish them, so that we may assign to each its place, order, and peculiar nature, as we have learned it from the Scripture, namely, so that reconciliation, or remission of sins, precedes and the beginning of love, or of the new obedience, follows after (*postea sequatur*); chiefly, however, that faith may be certain that it has a reconciled God and remission of sins not because of the renewal, which follows (*sequentem*) and which has been begun (*inchoatam*), but because of the mediator, the Son of God.[179]

While justification and renewal are simultaneous (the *simul* aspect in the quote), renewal follows justification (the *postea sequatur* aspect in the quote). The *postea sequatur* aspect illustrates the free nature of justification. First, for pastoral reasons Chemnitz wants to make sure that renewal does not appear as the cause of justification, which would

---

[178] Chemnitz, *Examen*, 188a (580–581): "Sicut igitur haec et similia sunt multa, etiam quando simul adsunt, recte et necessario distinguuntur. Ita nos reconciliationem et renovationem, fidem et charitatem non ita divellimus, ut alterum tollamus et negemus; sed cuique suum locum, suum officium, et suam proprietatem tribuimus cum Scriptura: quae solius fidei hoc proprium esse docet, apprehendere et accipere in promissione Evangelii, Christum ad justitiam coram Deo ad vitam aeternam. Et illam justitiam fides non partitur inter Christum et nostram novitatem seu charitatem, sed in solidum eam tribuit merito Christi. Vera igitur fides apprehendit Christum: vera etiam fides non est sine operibus, Jac 2. Sed per charitatem est efficax. Gal. 5. Quod autem fides justificat et salvat, illam vim et virtutem non mutuatur, sumit et habet inde, quia per charitatem efficax est, et bona opera parit: sed quia Christum apprehendit, qui est impletio legis ad iustitiam omni credenti, Rom. 10, et non est in alio salus Acto. 4."

[179] Chemnitz, *Examen*, 147b, 1 (465): "Christus enim sua passione meruit nobis non tantum remissionem peccatorum, verum etiam hoc, quod propter ipsius meritum datur nobis spiritus sanctus, ut renovamur spiritu mentis nostrae. Haec beneficia filii Dei, dicimus quidem esse conjuncta, ita ut quando reconciliamur, simul etiam datur Spiritus renovationis. Sed propterea non confundimus, sed distinguimus, ita ut cuique suum locum, ordinem, et suam proprietatem tribuamus, sicut ex Scriptura didicimus, ut scilicet reconciliatio seu remissio peccatorum praecedat et postea sequatur inchoatio dilectionis seu novae obodientiae. Praecipue vero, ut fides statuat se habere placatum Deum, et remissionem peccatorum, non propter sequentem et inchoatam novitatem, sed propter mediatorem filium Dei." See also Chemnitz, *Examen*, 150a, 6 (473).

imply that love actually merits forgiveness. Probably the expression *postea sequatur* is the most natural way to move spiritual observation away from human change. The problem, however, is that pastoral reasons work as a basis for doctrinal formulations, which do not have a correspondence in reality. According to Chemnitz, renewal does not actually antedate justification since they are simultaneous. This causal relation was interpreted more literally later.

The exclusion of good works from justification does not imply the exclusion of sanctification from the orbit of God's grace. Chemnitz emphasizes that while sanctification is necessary for a Christian, the power to perform good works comes from Christ. Justifying faith especially is the source of the good works.[180] When the person is engrafted in Christ, like a branch engrafted in a tree, the power to bear good fruit comes from the trunk, which is Christ, who rules (*regit*) the Christian through the Holy Spirit.[181]

The believer is perfect in the eyes of God for two reasons: first, for the sake of inchoate righteousness, i.e., the obedience the Spirit evokes, and second, while this obedience is not yet perfect in this life, imputation perfects what is still lacking; for the sake of Christ, the privation of good is not reckoned as guilt.[182] Christ's presence in faith enables this imputation.[183]

---

[180] Martens, *Die Rechtfertigung*, p. 106.

[181] Chemnitz, *Loci* III, 35b (602): "Lutherus vero contra docet: sicut inquit, in 15. Cap. Joan. Charitatem, novitatem seu novam obedientiam renatorum, non ab extra per assuefactionem & disciplinam, ut actiones liberi arbitrii, generari aut formari (wird nicht von aussen eingetragen) sed quando per fidem inserimur Christo, qui est vera vitis, participes efficimur pinguedinis & succi illius: hoc est, simul datur Spiritus S. qui cor renovat: & novam creaturam facit, ut ab illa radice ab intus prodeant vere bona opera." Chemnitz, *Loci* III, 31b (597). "...Christum enim per fidem habitans in cordibus, regit voluntatem renatorum per Spiritum Sanctum." This passage is a quotation from Luther. Chemnitz, *Examen*, 215a, 11 (660): "Magna est dignitas, quod renati sicut palmites Christo insiti, fructum faciunt, Joh. 15 et quod ipsorum opera sint fructus spiritus, Eph 5." While justification occurs in relation to Christ, renewal is ascribed to the Holy Spirit. E.g. Chemnitz, *Loci* III, 35a (601): "Spiritus sanctus est causa efficiens renovationis in renatis." See also Chemnitz, *De Duabus*, 181a (439).

[182] Chemnitz, *Loci* II, 9b (341): "Nam quo ad perfectam obedientiam, mandata Dei in hac vita esse impossibilia, antea demonstratum est: sed quod ad imputationem habent credentes perfectissimam impletionem omnium mandatorum Dei. Christus enim, qui perfectissime implevit legem, donatur credentibus cum omnia sua iustitia."

[183] Chemnitz *Loci* III, 34a: "Sed oportet adesse fidem in Christum, ut non imputetur hoc, quod deest impletione legis.... Evangelio verò credentibus adfert & Christum & Spiritum sanctum. Et in Christo credentes habent per imputationem coram Deo perfectionem, quam lex requirit."

> For Paul sharply contends that we are not justified by the Law, but that the righteousness of the Law, that is, the most absolute righteousness which Law demands and requires of us, may be fullfilled not by us but in us, because Christ, who has fullfilled the Law for us, is in us; that is, He dwells in us through faith (Eph. 3:17).[184]

The fact that Chemnitz did not interpret participation in Christ as the consequence of justification helps him to keep justification and sanctification coherently together.

5.3. *Conclusion*

This examination of Mörlin and Chemnitz reveals their distance from the pneumatological anthropology of Melanchthon and his way of explaining the nature of justification and renewal. Likewise, they positioned themselves far from the teachings of Flacius, for whom participation in Christ actually belonged to the life to come. Against Osiander, they emphasized the reality of Christ's salvific work as fully God and fully man; the righteousness of Christ is the obedience Christ has shown to the Father, which was demonstrated in His incarnation and in the work of redemption. A significant point is the emergence of the concept of obedience as the central feature of a genuine doctrine of justification.

Chemnitz used patristic material in his works profusely, which resulted in prioritizing the incarnation as a vital soteriological theme. This may have come through the influence of Mörlin and his controversy with Osiander, where the actuality of the acts of redemption came to the fore.

For both Chemnitz and Mörlin justification was in conjunction with the person of Christ; hence Christ can be termed the formal cause of justification. Christ present in faith gives the *forma* to faith and justification. In faith the believer participates in the person of Christ, who has

---

[184] Chemnitz, *Examen*, 161b, 6 (503): "Paulus enim acriter pugnat, nos per legem non iustificari, sed ut δικαίωμα legis, hoc est justitia absolutissima, quam lex a nobis flagitat et requirit, impleatur, non a nobis, sed in nobis: quia Christus, qui legem pro nobis implevit, in nobis est: hoc est per fidem in nobis habitat, Ephes. 3: Impletio vero legis, quae in nobis inchoatur, non suum, sed alium habet locum, sicut Paulus inquit: Qui Spiritum Christi non habent, in illis Christus non est." Chemnitz, *Loci* III, 29a (595): "Plenitudo enim Legis, sicut Paulus inquit, non est externa operatio, sed charitas; non quae ex natura oritur, sed est donum & operatio Spiritus S. quo fide accipitur."

triumphed over death. From the christological point of view the mode of application of salvation is analogical to the mutual interchange of attributes in Christ's person. As the human nature of Christ shares God's attributes, so the individual believer shares the fullness of God in Christ.

In Chemnitz's works, the union and renewal related to faith and justification (*renovatio*$_1$) is depicted in pneumatological concepts; the Spirit renews the faculties of the soul. Simultaneously the new life of the believer means participation in Christ, who is Life. In a sense, Mörlin and Chemnitz formulate a synthesis of the teachings of Luther and Melanchthon.

CHAPTER SIX

UNIO CUM CHRISTO IN THE THEOLOGIES OF THE OTHER CONTRIBUTORS TO THE FORMULA OF CONCORD

A number of theologians contributed to the development of early Lutheranism along with Chemnitz. Jacob Andreae was responsible for writing the first four drafts of FC. Later versions also involved contributions from David Chytraeus and Nicolaus Selnecker. Only Chemnitz, Andreae and Chytraeus influenced FC directly by writing articles. Selnecker's influence was limited to conversations with other contributors.[1] In addition to the main contributors, three other significant theologians are analyzed. The views of Tileman Hesshus, Johannes Wigand and Jacob Heerbrand illustrate contemporary thinking on justification, although they did not influence FC directly.

6.1. *Jacob Andreae and the First Drafts of the Formula of Concord*

6.1.1. *Consilium*

Jacob Andreae (1528–1590)[2] wrote the first draft of FC in 1568, called *Consilium de praesentibus Religionis Controversijs pie & moderatissime*

[1] From Torgau onwards, Andreas Musculus (1514–1581) and Cristopher Cornerus (1518–1594) attended the discussions as well, but did not actually compose any texts. Ebel, "Herkunft," pp. 271–274.

[2] Jacob Andreae did not have deep theological training. According to Robert Kolb "[Andreae] plunged into complicated theological problems without being a great theologian himself. He was instead first of all a pastor; as a thinker he was something of a simplifier." See Kolb, *Andreae and The Formula of Concord. Six sermons on the way to Lutheran Unity* (St. Louis: Concordia Publishing House 1977), p. 9. However, he decided to bring to together the group that had signed CA. The theologians of Rome commented on the disunity of the Lutherans, especially when the Council of Trent had ended the disunity within the Roman Catholic Church, at least on the face of it. See James Megivern, "The Catholic Rejoinder," in *Discord, Dialogue and Concord. Studies in the Lutheran Reformation's Formula of Concord*, eds. Wenzel Lohff & Lewis Spitz (Philadelphia: Fortress Press 1977), p. 191. Additionally, since the disunity threatened the internal peace of Lutheran congregations, Andreae also had a pastoral motive. See Kolb, *Andreae*, pp. 9–18; Theodor Jungkuntz, *Formulators of the Formula of Concord. Four Architects of Lutheran*

componendis,[3] as a short introduction to the controversial questions of the time. The article on justification describes the connection between imputation and inhabitation in detail. The central problem is the interpretation of the concepts *iustificari*, *iustitia Dei*, and *iustitia fidei*. Andreae offers two possible interpretations. On the one hand, they may refer to God's essential righteousness, which makes a person righteous through God's inhabitation.[4] On the other hand, they may be interpreted as referring to absolution. According to Andreae, justification does not mean the change from sin to righteousness through God's inhabitation, but absolution from unrighteousness and sin.[5]

The effects of the Osiandrian controversy are evident in Andrea's texts, in which God's inhabitation are related to good works. As already noted, the concept 'God's essential righteousness' has different meanings in Luther and in the second Lutheran generation. The subsequent negative connotations of Osiander's aberrations had made the use of the term difficult.[6] In spite of this, Andreae used inhabitation in a soteriological context. The *Consilium* still associates inhabitation with justification.

> Sins are not forgiven because of God's essential righteousness, which is present in faith, but for the sake of the sufferings and death of our Lord Jesus Christ, for believers in whom the Divine Christ dwells. Not because of indwelling but for the sake of obedience that Christ has shown outside of us. But even if these two, the imputation of Christ's obedience and God's essential righteousness, are in believers simultaneously, it must be carefully noted that they should not be mixed or altered. There is no imputation of Christ's obedience for forgiveness of sins before God dwells

Unity (St. Louis: Concordia Publishing House 1977), pp. 14–49; Ebel, "Jacob Andreae (1528–1590) als Verfasser der Konkordienformel," *Zeitschrift für Kirchengeschichte* 89 (1978), p. 79; Mahlmann, "Jacob Andreä im Lichte neuerer Forschung," *LTK* 14 (1990).

[3] On the history and the edition of the document, see Mager, "Jacob Andreäs lateinische Unionsartikel von 1568," *Zeitschrift für Kirchengeschichte* 98 (1987). See also Brandy, "Jacob Andreaes Fünf Artikel von 1568/69," *Zeitschrift für Kirchengeschichte* 98 (1987).

[4] Andreae, *Concilium*, 77: "Alii enim pugnarunt vocabulum iustitiae Dei significare ipsam Dei essentiam, qua Deus sit iustus et iustificet, h.e. reipsa per inhabitationem iustitiae suae essentialis iustum faciat hominem, cui peccata propter passionem Christi remissa sunt."

[5] Andreae, *Concilium*, 77: "Alii vero contra demonstrarunt iustitiam fidei significare non essentialem Dei iustitiam, sed remissionem peccatorum, et iustificari non reipsa per inhabitationem Dei iustum effici, sed ab iniustitia et peccatis absolvi."

[6] See also Andreae, *Concilium*, 78, where Andreae associates inhabitation with good works, borrowing Osiander's thesis of righteousness, which produces good works. *AO* 9, 446 (*Disputatio*, thesis 80).

> in the believer through faith, and there is no indwelling of God in the believer if sins are not forgiven.[7]

At the end of the article Andreae's conviction of the importance of inhabitation is clearly evident. He explicitly anathematized any notion of downgrading or denying it.

> If someone says that a person is justified, i.e., is absolved from sins and forgiven for the sake of God's indwelling righteousness and not simply for the sake of the obedience Christ has performed for the Father for us.
>
> If someone says that a person is justified, i.e., is absolved from sins for the sake of Christ's obedience on the cross but in whom God, who is essential righteousness, does not indwell.
>
> If someone says that the imputation of Christ's obedience for the forgiveness of sins and the indwelling of God the Father, Son and Holy Spirit does not take place simultaneously but that justification takes place without accompanying regeneration.[8]

Consilium does not define imputation as a prerequisite for inhabitation but it does emphasize both temporal concurrence and mutual logical consequence in that both imputation and inhabitation are each others prerequisites.

6.1.2. *Bekändtnitz*

The second draft of FC, Andreae's *Bekändtnitz* (Lat. *Confessio*) of 1568, defines justification briefly as the imputation of Christ's obedience.[9]

---

[7] Andreae, *Concilium*, 77: "...peccata non propter essentialem iustitiam Dei per fidem inhabitantem, sed propter passionem et mortem Domini nostri Jesu Christi remitti vere credentibus, in quibus Christus Deus habitat, idque non propter inhabitationem, sed propter opus obedientiae Christi extra nos factum. Cum autem haec duo tempore sint simul in credentibus, videlicet imputatio obedientiae Christi in remissionem peccatorum et inhabitatio essentialis iustitiae Dei, diligenter attendendum est, ne haec vel commisceantur vel permutentur. Nulla est enim imputatio obedientiae Christi in remissionem peccatorum, priusquam per fidem Christus habitet in credente, et vicissim nulla est inhabitatio Dei in nobis, nisi peccata remittuntur."

[8] Andreae, *Concilium*, 78: "Si quis dixerit Hominem iustificari, h.e. a peccatis absolvi et remissionem peccatorum consequi propter essentialem Dei in nobis habitantem iustitiam et non propter obedientiam Christi solam pro nobis Deo patri praestitam. Si quis dixerit Hominem iustificari, h.e. peccatis absolvi propter obedientiam Christi in cruce praestitam, in quo tamen Deus, qui est essentialis iustitia non habitat. Si quis dixerit Imputationem obedientiae Christi in remissionem peccatorum et inhabitationem Dei patris, filii et Spiritus S. non tempore esse simul in iustificatis, sed iustificationem fieri nulla regeratione comitante."

[9] On the document, see Brandy, "Jacob Andreaes Fünf Artikel". The English translation appears in Kolb, *Andreae*, pp. 58–60.

Imputation and inhabitation are separated in terms of their functions, not temporally or logically. The certainty of salvation is based on Christ's obedience while God's inhabitation evokes good works. *Bekändtnitz* affirms that the Trinity dwells in believers, but this is not the substance of righteousness of faith. Because the effects of the indwelling are not perfect, God's inhabitation cannot be considered as a satisfactory basis for the certainty of salvation. Renewal in all forms is therefore demarcated from justification. The function of inhabitation is to evoke good works and renewal, but its connection with justification is not given a detailed description. The description of inhabitation is accordingly more concise in contrast to the *Consilium*. As a matter of fact, the article on justification is very brief.

> Concerning the article on the justification of the poor sinner before God, we believe, teach, and confess, on the basis of God's word and based on the Augsburg Confession, that the poor individual sinner who is justified before God has his sins forgiven and is pronounced free, for the sake of the innocent, perfect and unique obedience, and the bitter suffering and death of our Lord Jesus Christ, not because of the indwelling essential righteousness of God or because of his own good works that either go before or follow faith. In addition, we deny all teaching which is against this faith and confession. Even if God the Father, Son and Holy Spirit, who is Himself essential righteousness, dwells in believers and incites them to do good and to live according to His divine will, God's indwelling does not make them perfect in this life. Because of this they cannot consider themselves righteous before God for the sake of this indwelling. Instead their consolation should be entirely in unique and innocent obedience, the bitter suffering and death of our Lord Jesus Christ, which is reckoned before God for righteousness for every repentant sinner.[10]

---

[10] Andreae, *Bekändtnitz*, 109: "Vom Artickel der Rechtfertigung des armen Sünders vor Gott / glauben / lehren / und bekennen wir / vermöge Gotter Worts / und Inhalts unser Christlichen Augspurgischen Confession, dass der arme sundhaffige Mensch vor Gott gerechtfertiget / das ist / von seinen Sünden absolvirt und ledig gesprochen werde / und des unschuldigen vollkommenen einigen Gehorsams / bittern leidens uns Sterbens unsers Herrn Ihesu Christi willen / nicht von wegen der Inwohnenden wesentlichen Gerechtigkeit Gottes / oder umb eigener / dem Glauben vergehenden / oder nachfolgenden guten wercken willen / und verwerffen alle Lehr / so diesem Glauben und Bekändtnis zu wider ist. Dann ob wol Gott Vater / Sohn / und Heiliger Geist in den Glaubigen wohnet / der die wesentliche Gerechtigkeit selber ist / und sie treibet recht zu thun / und nach seinem Göttlichen Willen zu leben / so macht sie doch solche Einwohnung Gottes in diesem Leben nicht vollkommen / darumb sie auch unb derselben willen vor Gott nicht für gerecht gehalten werden / sondern all ihr trost stehet allein auff dem einiger / und unschuldigen Gehorsam / bittern Leiden und Sterben unsers Herrn Iesu Christi / welcher Gehorsam allen busfertigen Sündern / zur Gerechtigkeit vot Gott / zugerechnet wird."

Andreae toured Northern Germany in the summer of 1569 in order to get signatories for his articles, but he encountered suspicion and opposition. The greatest opposition came from the members of the Gnesiolutheran party, who argued that the article on the Holy Supper could be interpreted in Zwinglian terms. Andreae's efforts to create connections with the Swiss reformers with respect to the Sacrament also caused suspicion.[11] In spite of Andreae's earnest attempts, *Bekändtnitz* was never approved, not least due to its brevity.

Even so, Andreae's work started to bear fruit. In 1570, Counts Wilhelm and Julius summoned a group of evangelical priests to Zerbst for discussion on the need for a new confession. The delegates of Saxony, who were satisfied with the old confessions, shunned the idea of writing a new confessional document. Andreae, however, insisted on the importance of a new text because opposing parties were quoting the Augsburg confession against each other. After the meeting Andreae tried to summarize the results. The Philippists of Wittenberg disliked Andreae's formulations and criticized him severely, which worsened Andreae's relations with them. He no longer wanted to arbitrate between the opposing views and adopted a clearly Gnesiolutheran stance.[12]

6.1.3. *Sechs Christlichen Predigten*

Nikolaus Selnecker published his introduction to dogmatics called *Institutio Christianae Religionis* in 1573, which he dedicated to Count Ludwig of Württemberg. In the preface he rejoiced in the doctrinal union between Württemberg and Braunschweig. He also explicitly thanked Andreae for the good he had done for Braunschweig through stabilizing local religious conditions.[13] Andreae responded to the compliments by expanding his *Bekändtnitz* into six sermons, called *Sechs Christlichen Predigten*.[14] A substantially more extensive document, the sermons were not directed to theologians but to the lay people. Andreae had taken note of the uncertainty doctrinal disunity caused, which influenced the style of the sermons. The parties to the controversy are briefly introduced in

---

[11] In 1557 Andreae published *Kurzer und einfaeltiger Bericht von des Herren Nachtmal*, in which he tried to define the Lutheran doctrine of the eucharist without offending Swiss Reformers. The book aggravated at least the Gnesiolutheran Nicolaus von Amsdorf, and did not manage to create unity. Kolb, *Andreae*, p. 15.

[12] Kolb, *Andreae*, p. 53.

[13] Selnecker, *Institutio*, praefatio.

[14] Kolb, *Andreae*, pp. 48–49.

each sermon, followed by a detailed answer. The answer is laid out in catechetical question-answer format, in which a layman, after hearing the arguments, poses a question on the truth of their views. Andreae answers the question by recommending one of the views presented as the genuine Christian view.

Sechs Christlichen Predigten marked a turning point in efforts towards intra-lutheran unity. Chytraeus and Chemnitz, among others, read the sermons and agreed on the possibility of attaining unity on this basis. Until now most theologians had been suspicious of the possibility of unity. The sermons initiated the writing process that culminated in the signing of FC in 1580.[15]

According to *Sechs Christlichen Predigten* the doctrine of justification can be interpreted in three different ways. Andreae claimed that the root of the problem, as he had already stated in *Consilium*, was in the interpretation of the concept of *Gerechtigkeit Christi*. One faction used it to refer to Christ's divine nature (Osiander), the other to Christ's human nature (Stancarus) and the third to Christ's obedience (Melanchthon).[16] According to Andreae, the third option was correct. Justification is described almost identically with *Bekändtnitz*: Christian righteousness referred to forgiveness of sins, which is reckoned to the sinner in faith for the sake of Christ's obedience.[17]

Andreae also commented on the clause in the Augsburg confession that states that "faith is reckoned as righteousness" (CA IV). The recognition of faith as righteousness is synonymous with the recognition of Christ's obedience as righteousness. Faith in Christ and the obedience of Christ are metonymous—mutually exchangeable expressions.[18]

---

[15] Kolb, *Andreae*, pp. 48, 53–55, 57; Ebel, *Jacob Andreae*, p. 107.

[16] Andreae, *Sechs Christlicher Predig*, 2–3 (68): "Dann so Christus oder die Gerechtigkeit Christi genennet würdt / finden sich drey underschidne ding / die under dem Namen Christi begriffen seind / Namlich / unnd zum ersten / sein Göttliche Natur und ewige Gottheit. Zum andern / sein menschliche Natur / die er von Maria der hochgelobten Jungfrauen an sich genommen hat. Zum dritten / sein Gehorsam / dener / under dem Gesetz / seinem Himmlischen Vatter / biss in den Todt / geleistet hat…Was under disen dreien Stucken uns durch den Glauben zur Gerechtigkeit zugerechnet werde…"

[17] Andreae, *Sechs Christlicher Predig*, 9–10 (71): "Darumb eigentlich zureden / so ist der Christen Gerechtigkeit auff Erden vor Gott / unnd also die Gerechtigkeit des Glaubens anders nichts dann vergebung der Sünden auss lautter Gnaden Gottes / durch den Glauben / umb des einigen gehorsams Christi des Sons Gottes / unnd Marie / willen / der uns zur Gerechtigkeit zugerechnet wirdt."

[18] Andreae, *Sechs Christlicher Predig*, 7 (70): "Oder / das ichs noch deutlicher sage / Es heisse eigentlich den gehorsam Christi / de uns durch den Glauben zur Gerechtigkeit

Andreae attributed a similar tripartite description of faith to Chemnitz. Justification consists of three parts: God's grace, Christ's obedience and faith.[19] Even if only one is mentioned, all three must be included. When one speaks of faith, Christ and God's grace (towards which faith is disposed) must be included.[20]

Faith is described as an instrument that evokes participation in Christ throughout the sermons. It makes the believer a sharer in Christ's death and resurrection so that His suffering, death, and resurrection are the believer's suffering, death, and resurrection. Since the believer becomes like (*ehnlich*) Christ in faith, God considers the sinner to be righteous, just as Christ is righteous.[21]

---

zugerechnet werde / gleich wie auch der Glaube an Christum / mit gewächselter Rede / uns zur Gerechtigkeit würdt zugerechnet."

[19] Andreae, *Sechs Christlicher Predig*, 13 (73): "Dann in der Gerechtigkeit des Glaubens allwegen drey ding zusamen kommen / unnd beieinander seind / und keins ohne das ander den Menschen vor Gott rechtfertiget. Erstlich / ist es die lauttere Gnad Gottes. Zum andern / der Gehorsam oder Verdienst Christi. Zum dritten / der Glaube. Dan wa die Gnad Gottes des Vatters nicht ist / da ist weder der Verdienst Christi / noch der Glaube. Unnd widerumb / wa man Christum in seinem Gehorsam nicht hat / da ist kein Gnad Gottes zuhoffen. Item: Wa der Glaub nicht ist / da nutzet weder die Gnad Gottes / noch der Gehorsam Christi."

[20] Andreae, *Sechs Christlicher Predig*, 14 (74): "Die würdt allein der Glaub genennet / der zur Gerechtigkeit zugerechnet würdt. Aber es muss dabey verstanden werden / Christus / an den er glaubet / und die Gnad Gottes / auss wölcher Gnaden wir glauben."

[21] Andreae, *Sechs Christlicher Predig*, 11 (72): "Hie erkläret S. Paulus deutlich die Gerechtigkeit des Glaubens / warinn sie bestehe / unnd was Gott an seinem Sone ansehe/ umb desswillen er uns unser Sünden nicht entgelten lesst / sonder für gerecht halte / ob wir gleich unserer verderbten Natur halben noch Sünder seien. Namlich die Krafft seiner Aufferstehung / und die Gemeinschaft seines leiden/ das Christus Leiden und Tod / unser Tod ist / dem wir durch den Glauben ehnlich werden / und der Krafft seiner Aufferstehung geniessen." See also Andreae, *Ein christliche Predig*, Fiv^{v}: "...weil wir mit Christo durch den Glauben seindt warhafftig von den Todten erstanden..." Andreae, *Ein christliche Predig*, Di^{v}–Dii: "Wer nun durch Glauben disess Angesicht der Gerechtigkeit Christi unnsers Herren Jhesu Christi anzeücht/die er uns mit seiner herrlichen Aufferstehung von der Todten erworbe hat / dem ist sein alte / hessliche / feindselige / runzelete / Schiemen zugedeckt /und ist mit der Gerechtigkeit Christi unsers Herren / die er durch sein Aufferstehung mit sich gebracht / dermassen gezieret und angezogen / das er frälich und unerschrocken / für das Angesicht Gottes Himmelischen Vatters tretten darff. Dan als schön und herrlich Christus in seiner Aufferstehung ist / eben so schön sind auch in disem leben durch den Glauben alle arme Sünder / denen dise Gerechtigkeit des Herren Christi zugerechnet würdt / wolche stehet in dem volkommene Gehorsam unnd herrlichen Auffstehung unsers Herren Jesu Christi...Alles was unser Herr Christus ist und hat / das ist unser / demnach auch seine Aufferstehung unser Aufferstehung ist / wie er dann selbst sagt: Ich bin die Aufferstehung uñ das Leben..."

However, the exact nature of this sharing remains obscure. In the sermons it is stated that after (*nachdem*) absolution, God, who is essential righteousness, inhabits in the believer, sanctifies them, and stimulates them to do good. Nevertheless, one should not observe this inhabitation in order to find certainty of salvation.[22] Participation in Christ in justification is something other than God's sanctifying indwelling in the believer. Inhabitation is therefore explicitly consequent on justification. In contrast to the earlier drafts, Andreae now introduces a temporal-logical distinction in the place of a functional distinction.

6.1.4. *Schwäbische Konkordie*

Andreae's sermons won the approval of Chemnitz and Chytraeus. Their sole criticism concerned style of presentation: they felt that his catechetical style should be replaced by something more precise. In 1574, Andreae published *Schwäbische Konkordie*, for which he obtained signatures from the theologians of Tübingen and the consistory of Stuttgart. Count Julius considered the document a good start and ordered Chemnitz to accompany Andreae in the follow-up negotiations.[23]

The article on justification in *Schwäbische Konkordie* is considerably shorter than that in the Sermons but its content begins to take its final shape in this document.[24] The righteousness of faith signified absolution and a pronouncement of freedom from sin.[25] This takes place through faith and for the sake of the sufferings and death of Christ, which is reckoned for the repentant as righteousness.[26] This faith is never without

---

[22] Andreae, *Sechs Christlicher Predig*, 18 (76): "Unnd nachdem er zum Gnaden auffgenommen / unnd seiner Sünden vergebung erlanget hat / so wohnet alsdann nicht allein Christus sonder auch der Vatter unnd Heiliger Geist / in einem solchen armen sünder / unangesehen / dass in desselben Natur noch die Sûnde stecket / aber nocht beherschet / helffen ime darwider streitten / unnd faben an / ihne auch frömmer und heiliger in seiner Natur zumachen / biss die ewige volkomne Gerechtigkeit volget..."

[23] Jungkuntz, *The Formulators*, p. 38.

[24] *Schwäbische Konkordie* is not dependent on the earlier drafts, since it has been written completely anew. However, the doctrine of justification remains the same. Ebel, "Jacob Andreae," p. 107.

[25] Andreae, *Schwäbische*, 250: "Von der Gerechtigkeit des Glaubens vor Gott, glauben, lehren und bekennen wir einhellig, das der Arm Sündig Mensch, vor Gott gerechtfertiget, das ist, Absoluirt und ledig gesprochen werde, vonn allen seinen Sünden."

[26] Andreae, *Schwäbische*, 250: "Allein durch den Glauben ohn Alle vorgehende gegenwertige oder nachvolgende werck, umb dess einigen verdients gantzen gehorsams bittern leydens und Sterbens unsers Herren Christi willen, dess gehorsam allen Buesfertigen unnd Rechtgleubigen Christen zur gerechtigkeitt zugerechnet würdt."

love; justifying faith is always faith active through love.[27] The indwelling of God in the believer also takes place through faith. Nevertheless, this is the consequence of righteousness of faith.[28] This distinction is followed by speculation on how Christ is the righteousness of the sinner. As a rejoinder to Osiander and Stancarus, Andreae emphasized that the full obedience of Christ's whole person is reckoned as righteousness for sinners. Humanity must be present in Christ because it is humanity that has rebelled against God. Accordingly, Christ must be simultaneously God and man in order to fulfill the law, pay the penalty of sin, and reconcile humanity with God.[29]

Andreae's notion of inhabitation starts to lose its soteriological significance soon after *Consilium*. Only *Consilium* gives an explicitly positive sense for God's inhabitation within justification. Later it is increasingly interpreted as the source of good works and the consequence of justification. The direction Osiander's theology offered to Andreae is evident. In his *Drey und dreissig Predigen* (1568) Andreae charged the Anabaptists with a heresy typical of Osiander. In defending his own stance Andreae distinguished two types of christological work. The one is the obedience of Christ and reconciliation, which occurs outside of the individual.[30] The other occurs within the individual through Christ's inhabitation of the believer, at which point He starts to mortify the flesh and stimulates the desire for good.[31] According to Andreae, the work that avails

[27] Andreae, *Schwäbische*, 250: "Diese gerechtigkeit aber dess glaubens ist inn den Ausserweltten Christen nimmer ohne die liebe, denn Alleinder glaub gerecht unnd selig machett, der durch die liebe thättig ist, wie der Apostel zeugett."

[28] Andreae, *Schwäbische*, 251: "Sonder sie volget auff die Vorgehende gerechtigkeit dess glaubens, welche Anders nichts ist, denn die gnedige Annehmung der Armen Sünder, Allein umb Christus gehorsam unnd verdiensts willen."

[29] Andreae, *Schwäbische*, 251–252: "Demnach so glauben leren unnd bekennen wir, dass der ganzen Person Christi gantzer gehorsam, welchen er dem Vatter biss Inn den Allerschmehlichsten tod des Creutzes gelaistet hatt, und zur gerechtigkeit zugerechnet werde. Dann die Mensclich Natur ohn die Göttliche dem ewigen, Allmechtigen Gott weder mit gehorsam noch leiden, für aller weltt Sünde genug thuen, die Gottheit Aber, ohn die menscheit, Zwischen Gott unnd unns nicht mittlen mögen."

[30] Andreae, *Drey und dreyssig Predigen* IV, 12–13.

[31] Andreae, *Drey und dreyssig Predigen* IV, 13: "Zum andern / hat der Herr Christus auch sein Werck in den Glaubigen / in wölcher Hertzen er durch den Glauben wohnet / und anfahet die Sünde in ihnen zutödten unnd ausszufegen / unnd treibt sie / dass sie auch lust und willen zum güten haben / unnd anfangen recht zuthün unnd Gottselig zuleben."

coram Deo is the external justification. The internal inhabitation is not perfect and therefore not suitable for this use.[32]

However, Andreae also taught that even if the sinner's righteousness is not Christ's work in us, it is still faith that is reckoned for righteousness.[33] In addition, a tree must be good in order to bear good fruit. The sinner must be made good before he can perform good works.[34] In other writings dating from the same period Andreae also emphasized the Holy Spirit's effective and regenerative work in sinners.[35] Regeneration is the prerequisite for justifying faith.[36] Saving grace is not an extrinsic act but a new reality, which God effects in the believer.[37]

In his later texts Andreae also referred to renewal (*renovatio₁*) in the context of justification. This renewal is defined as the work of the

---

32 Andreae, *Drey und dreyssig Predigen* IV, 13–14: "…unser Gerechtigkeit / umb wölcher willen wir Gott gefällig und angenem seien / unnd ein gnädigen Gott haben / stehe nicht in den Wercken / die Christus in uns thüt / sonder in dem Werck / das er ausserhalb unser gtheon hat / nämlich in seinem unschuldigen Gehorsam / bitter leiden und sterben." Moreover, in *Ein Christliche Predig von Christlicher einigkeit* (1570) Andreae denies that the sinner is justified through the inhabitation of God. See Andreae, *Von Christlicher einigkeit*, Dii[v].

33 Andreae, *Drey und dreyssig Predigen* IV, 15: "Hie würdt mit klaren worten angezeigt / dass nicht die werck / so Christus in uns wircket / sonder der Glaub an Christum uns zügerechnet werde zur Gerechtigkeit / da ein Christ glaubt / dass Christus für ihne dem Vatter ein volkomnen Gehorsam gelaistet habe."

34 Andreae, *Drey und dreyssig Predigen* IV, 17: "Sonder der Baum müss zuvor güt sein / ehe er güte frucht bringet / also müss der zuvor durch den Glaube umb dess Herren Christi willen fromm / gerecht / unnd Gottsellig sein."

35 Andreae, *Zehen Predig*, rrriii[v]–rrriiii; *Ein unnd fünffzigsten Psalmen*, rrbii–rrbiii.

36 Andreae, *Von Christlicher einigkeit*, Eiii: "In der Wiedergeburt wircket Gott der H. Geist / mit seiner krafft / durch das gepredigte und gehörte wort / und im rechten gebrauch des H. Sacraments der Tauff / dass des Menschen gefangner und verderbter will wiederumb ledig und gut wirdt / zündet an im verstande ein liecht der rechten erkenntnis Gottes / wircket den rechten warhafftigen glauben / darmit das wort Gottes angenommen wirdt / wircket ein recht lebedinh vertrauen auff Gott / ein rechte warhafftige liebe / das des Menschen Herr Gott nicht mehr als ein strengen unbarmherzigen Richter fleucht / Sonder als ein getrewen Vater liebet / unnd sich aller gnaden unnd alles guts und frewden in seinen gebotten wandelt."

37 Andreae, *Ein christliche Predig*, Dii[v]: "…das Reich Gottes ist innerhalb ewer / das ist / in euch / da Gott selbst als in einem Temple wonet /und seine gnaden und himmeliche Gaben reichlich aussgeusset und mitteilt…Weil wir dann mit Christo allbereit seindt aufferstanden / unnd dieselbige sein Aufferstehung durch den Glauben uns zugeeignet / unnd die Gerechtigkeit angezogen die vor Gott gilt / dann sie würdt uns von Gott nicht anderst zugerechnet dann als betten wir selbst gelitten für die Sünd / und weren herrlich widerumb erstanden / nach dem die Sünd / Tod / Teüffel / Hell und Verdamnuss überwunden worden sind." Andreae, *Ein christliche Predig*, D: "Das also alle die so durch ein rechten / waren / lebendigen Glauben (der ein Werck des Heiligen Geists ist / in uns) Christum ergreiffen / volkommene verzeihung unnd vergebung aller irer Sünden haben." See also Andreae, *Ein christliche Predig*, E; Andreae, *Ein unnd fünffzigsten Psalmen*, rrbj–rrbiii.

Holy Spirit, which effects participation with Christ's merit. Previously he could relate justification to God's indwelling, but this solution is now inappropriate because of its Osiandrian connotations.

Andreae's later definitions reflect the same problems evident in Melanchthon's theology. A renewal of some form is needed to evoke justifying faith, a change produced by the Holy Spirit. Nevertheless Christ's work in us cannot be justifying righteousness. In spite of this the justifying entity is faith, which makes a person akin to Christ and effects participation in Christ. This tension is never resolved, which results in incoherence between justification and renewal. Extrinsicness means spatial extrinsicness, which forces Andreae to interpret renewal as a causal effect of the Spirit. Renewal is simultaneously affirmed and denied, similar to Melanchthon.[38] The reason for this may naturally lie in Andreae's simplifying way of discussing controversies. However, his formulations were far-reaching for many of his utterances were affirmed in the final version of FC.

6.2. *David Chytraeus*

6.2.1. *The Doctrine of Justification in the Different Versions of the* Catechism

David Chytraeus (1531–1600), who served as the professor of theology at the university of Rostock and who had been in the inner circle of Melanchthon's students, made substantial contributions to FC's formulations.[39] Formerly a Philippist theologian, he identified increasingly

[38] Not even the disputation *De justificatione* goes any further into this. Andreae, *De Justificatione*, 4a–b: "Fides autem sine Christo & misericordia Dei, non est fides, sed opinio humana, quae sua persuasione frustratur.... Est verò Charitas, sicut & Spes, cum Fide perpetuo coniuncta est... Fides enim non quatenus Charitatem, qua nos Deum diligamus: sed quatenus Christum rescipit, eiusque solius merito confidit, iustificat."

[39] David Chytraeus studied theology in Tübingen, where he met Jacob Andreae and Jacob Heerbrand among others. In 1544 he moved to Melanchthon's house in Wittenberg. There he was able to listen Luther's lectures, which had a deep influence on him. Martin Chemnitz also lived in Wittenberg at the time, and he, Chytraeus, and Tileman Hesshus were members of the inner circle who lectured on Melanchthon's *Loci Communes*. Jungkuntz, *Formulators*, pp. 69–88; Theodor Pressel, "David Chytraeus," in *Leben und ausgewaelte Schriften der Vaeter und Begruender der Lutherischen kirche*, VIII (Elberfeld: R. L. Friderichs 1862); Montgomery, *Chytraeus*, pp. 10–19. On Chytraeus's research in general, see Otfried Czaika, *David Chytraeus und die Universität Rostock in ihren Beziehungen zum schwedischen Reich* (Helsinki: Schriften der Luther-Agricola-Gesellschaft 51, 2002), pp. 379–381. No comprehensive study of Chytraeus's theology has been written to

with the Gnesiolutheran party and finally joined Andreae in writing the preliminary drafts of FC.[40] While Chemnitz was the most influential theologian in the formulations of FC, Chytraeus was the second opinion leader.[41]

Chytraeus's influence also involved a commentary on Melanchthon's catechism, which was published under the name *Catechesis* (1554). His work soon became a widely-read popular introduction to Christian doctrine and had a lasting effect on Nordic Lutheranism. The Swedish and Finnish students who studied in Rostock took advantage of Chytraeus's work when writing their own national catechisms.[42] It is interesting, however, that Chytraeus wrote several editions of the book which differ from each other in substantial matters.[43] His outline of the doctrine of justification is especially interesting.

---

date. Rudolf Keller's study focuses on Chytraeus's *Historia der Augspurgischen Confession*, while Czaika (*op. cit.*) discusses his historical influence. See Keller, *Die Confessio Augustana im theologischen Wirken des Rostocker Professors David Chyträus* (1530–1600) (Göttingen: Vandenhoeck & Ruprecht 1994).

[40] Chytraeus started to identify himself more with the Gnesiolutheran party at the end of the 1550s. Melanchthon's death in 1560 released him to think independently, although their relationship had already deteriorated during Melanchthon's lifetime. In the 1560s Chytraeus castigated Philippist theology openly, which contributed to his career in that he became involved in Andreae's project. Although Chytraeus was not present in Bergen, where the last draft was composed, he was called on to sign the document, which was edited by Chemnitz, Andreae, and Selnecker. These three theologians had made alterations to Chytraeus's texts (on christology), which he resented. Later, Chytraeus identified himself as a signer of FC, but not its editor or author. This raised suspicions on Chytraeus's stance towards FC as whole, but he never disagreed with the document; instead he was angry about the method of condemnation it utilized. Chytraeus's relationship to FC was qualified; he considered the content to be biblical, and Lutherans were to accept it until a better document could be formulated. Detloff Klatt, *Chyträus als Geschichtslehrer und Geschichtsschreiber*, Beiträge zur Geschichte der Stadt Rostock., Bd. V., Heft 1 & 2, (Rostock 1909), p. 17; Jungkuntz, *Formulators*, pp. 83–84; Montgomery, *Chytraeus*, pp. 19–23; Kaufmann, "Die Brüder David und Nathan Chytraeus in Rostock," in *David und Nathan Chytraeus—Humanismus im konfessionellen Zeitalter*, hrsgb. Glaser et al. (Ubstadt-Weiher 1993), p. 112; Keller, "David Chytraeus (1530–1600). Melanchthons Geist im Luthertum," in *Melanchthon in seinen Schülern*, hrsgb. Heinz Scheible (Wiesbaden: Wolfenbütteler Forschungen 73, 1997).

[41] Ebel, "Herkunft," pp. 254–264; Keller, *Die Confessio Augustana*, pp. 166–174.

[42] Otfried Czaika, *David Chytraeus*, pp. 359–378.

[43] The *Catechism* was published in revised editions in 1554, 1561, 1572, 1573, 1576, 1577, 1580, 1585, 1588, 1590, 1593, 1596, 1598, 1599, 1603, 1605, and 1612. See Czaika, *David Chytraeus*, pp. 456–457. The *Catechism* uses the question-answer method, which is utilized in every locus: *De Deo, De Creatione, De Lege Dei, De peccato, De remissio peccatorum seu iusticia in evangelio promissa, De bonus operibus, De sacramentis, De poenitentia, De ecclesia*, and *De Immortalitate hominum, resurrectione corporum, et vita aeterna.* The most original part of the book is the section *De lege Dei*, which takes advantage of Melanchthon's exposition of virtues in his *Regula vitae*, in which every commandment is explained by virtues that are for and vices that are against the commandment.

All editions share the centrality of the distinction between the Law and the Gospel. The Law demands perfection, which is possible only for Christ, who is simultaneously God and man. The Gospel means that the righteousness demanded by the Law is transferred to the believer in faith, who apprehends Christ, who has fulfilled the Law.[44] *Catechesis* always defines justification as apprehending Christ. The sinner is not justified through good works but through faith, which receives the forgiveness of sins.[45] However, his account of the relation between justification and renewal varies from one edition to another. The editions of 1561 and 1573 propose different answers to the question concerning the nature of justifying righteousness.

Quid igitur est Iusticia Evangelii, seu Iusticia Christiana, seu Iustificatio hominis coram Deo? IUSTICIA CHRISTIANA est remissio peccatorum & imputatio iusticiae Christi & acceptatio ad vitam aeternam gratuita, non propter ullas virtutes aut opera, Sed propter solum Christum Mediatorem sola fide apprehensum, cum qua coniuncta est, donatio seu inhabitatio Spiritus sancti, & renovatio naturae, ac inchoatio novarum virtutum, quae in persona iusta, hoc est, fide reconciliata Deo placent propter Christum.[46]	Quid igitur est Iusticia Evangelii, seu Iusticia Christiana, seu Iustificatio hominis coram Deo? IUSTICIA CHRISTIANA est remissio peccatorum & imputatio iusticiae Christi & acceptatio ad vitam aeternam gratuita, non propter ullas virtutes aut opera, Sed propter solum Christum Mediatorem donata & sola fide apprehensa.[47]

[44] Chytraeus, *Catechesis* 1561, F7–F7v: "Ideo Iusticia legis est, vel perfecta omnium virium obedientia erga totam lege Dei, expers omnis peccati, qualis in nullo hominum, solo Christo expecto extitit. Vel est qualicunque obedientia externorum membrorum, praestans externa opera, quae lex Dei flagitat, & nunquam satisfacit legi Dei. Evangelium vero GRATIS promittit remissionem peccatorum, iusticiam & vitam aeternam, non propter nostram obediantiam erga Legem, sed propter solum Filium Dei dominum nostrum Iesum Christum quem sola fide amplectimur."

[45] Chytraeus, *Catechesis* 1561, F6: "Quomodo intelligenda est haec Propositio, Sola Fide sumus iusti? Correlative intelligenda est, videlicet, Quod propter solum Filium Dei dominum nostrum Iesum Christum accipiamus remissionem peccatorum, iusticiam, & vitam aeternam GRATIS, non propter nostra merita. Ideo autem hac forma verborum (Fide iustificamur) utitur scriptura ut utrumque doceat. 1. Quae sit causa seu meritum Iustificationis, seu quae sint beneficia Christi, videlicet, quod per propter solum Christum donetur nobis remissio peccatorum, iusticia & vita aeterna. 2. Deinde quomodo nobis applicari & ad nos transferri debebat, videlicet sola FIDE amplectente promissionem & in Christo acquiescente."

[46] Chytraeus, *Catechesis* 1561, F7v.

[47] Chytraeus, *Catechesis* 1573.

The section in which the donation of the Holy Spirit and renewal is discussed has been omitted from the 1573 edition and all subsequent editions. According to the earlier edition, justifying righteousness include the virtues of God's indwelling and inchoate renewal. Although these virtues are not perfect, they still please God through Christ.[48]

At the same time (probably—at least from 1578 onwards) Chytraeus added two new questions and answers to the *De Deo* section. One, incarnation is now given a fuller treatment. Incarnation means that Christ becomes Immanuel, the Mediator, who is a man of the same essence character clarification (ὁμοούσιος) as God.[49] Two, Christ's name 'Immanuel' (Engl. God with us, Lat. *nobiscum Deus*) is described in more detail. Specifically, the name has four different senses. First, it means the assumption of humanity in the incarnation, as a result of which humanity is now a part of Christ's person so that He is "flesh of our flesh and bone of our bones." (Gen. 2:23.) Second, it means that Christ prays to the Father for us (*pro nobis*). Third, Christ dwells in us (*in nobis*) in faith, controlling us and sanctifying our hearts. Fourth, Christ stays with us (*apud nos*) in all calamities and death through His presence and providence.[50]

---

[48] Chytraeus's *Commentary on Genesis* uses a description on justification similar to *Catechism*. See Chytraeus, *In Genesin* 1557, 292–293. The same definition also appears in the 1561 edition. See Chytraeus, *In Genesin* 1561, 308.

[49] Chytraeus, *Catechesis* 1580, 22: "Incarnatio Filii Dei est unio personalis duarum naturarum, divinae de substantia aeterni Patris ab aeterno genitae, & humanae ex substantia Mariae virginis assumptae, facta mirando, consilio divinitatis, in Christo mediatore, ut sit Emanuel, aeterno Deo & nobis hominibus ὁμοούσιος, reconcilians nobis Deum & sufficienti λύτρω placata iustissima ira Dei adversus peccatum aeternam iusticiam & vitam hominibus restituat." Here Chytraeus probably takes advantage of Chemnitz's theology of the incarnation. The use of ὁμοούσιος was particularly characteristic of Chemnitz. According to Pressel ("David Chytraeus," pp. 37–38), Chytraeus considered Chemnitz's christology as superior once he had read Chemnitz's *De Duabus Naturis in Christo*. Chytraeus was also acquainted with patristic theology, which is used, for example, in *Vom tode*. See Chytraeus, *Vom tode*, L[v]–M. Montgomery (*Chytraeus*, pp. 27, 82–83) has demonstrated the significance of the *Christus victor* theory in Chytraeus's examination of atonement in *De sacrificiis* (1569). The examination is the preface to Chytraeus's commentary on Leviticus.

[50] Chytraeus, *Catechesis* 1580, 23–24: "Emanuel id est, NOBISCUM DEUS vocatur propter quatuor causas. Primum propter assumptionem Nostrae naturae, quia theanthropos seu Deus homo & frater noster, caro de carne nostra, & os ex ossibus nostris, factus est.

At least from 1568 onwards the section on justification explains the differences between justification, regeneration, and renewal. Justification signifies the forgiveness of sins alone, whereas regeneration means the transfer from being under God's wrath to being a child of God, which is effected by baptism.[51] In his Catechisms and *Commentary on Matthew* regeneration is used in an extensive sense to involve both justification and renewal in terms of good works.[52] Renewal means simply new movements of the mind and virtues, which follow justification.[53]

In the *Catechism* justification is notably defined in increasingly strict terms. Renewal is not part of justification, not even when understood as perfected through Christ's merit. In spite of this distinction, the

---

Joh. 1. Verbum caro factum est, & habitavit in Nobis, seu assumpta nostra natura, non tantum effectivè & separabiliter sed σωματικοσ ita ut sit una persona. Deinde, Quia PRONOBIS apud aeternum Patrem intercedit & deprecatur, & precium redemptionis persoluit... Tertio, quia IN NOBIS fide eum agnoscentibus habitat Filius Dei, & corda nostra regit & sanctificat, & sibi conformia reddit. Gal. 2. Vivit in me Christus. Ephes. 3. Habitat Christus per fidem in cordibus nostris. Postremo, APUD NOS in omnibus periculis, doloribus & morte ipsa praesens adest Emanuel noster, Deus & homo protegens & salvans nos..." Chytraeus also discusses the modes of presence in his *Commentary on Psalm* CXVIII. God's indwelling presence in faith has five consolations. First, faith considers God's grace certain. Second, God is present in affliction (*nobis Praesentem adesse in aerumnis*), and he is not "absent in Ethiopia" (*non in Aethiopia abesse*) forgetting the sufferer. Third, God is not a lazy observer (*ociosum spectatorem*), but offers His help. Fourth, God consoles in time of grief. Fifth, God frees the believer from several temporal afflictions and from eternal damnation. See Chytraeus, *Psalmum*, 28–31.

[51] Chytraeus, *Catechesis* 1580, 117–118: "Iustificatio est remissio peccatorum, seu absolutio à peccato & aeterna morte & reconciliatio cum Deo, qua persona Deo iusta seu Deo placens & accepta & vitae aeterna haeres est, propter Christum mediatorem." *Chytraeus* Catechesis 1580, 118: "Regeneratio est actio Spiritus sancti, qua per verbum Dei viventis & baptismum, ex filio irae & mortis, generat Filium Dei & haeredem vitae aeternae."

[52] Chytraeus, *In Matthaeum*, 682: "Regeneramur autem, cum propter Filium Dei remissionem peccatorum, in Evangelio promissa, fide accipimus, & Deo reconciliati in locum filiorum & haeredum Regni Dei adoptamur, & donamar Spiritu sancto, quia reliquias peccati nobiscum nati paulatim expurgat & novam lucem, iusticiam & vitam in cordibus credentium accendit." Accordingly in *Catechesis* 1580, 118: "Regeneratio... complectens duas partes, iustificationem & renovationem naturae per Spiritum sanctum, quae fons est Novae obedientiae & operum bonorum." *Catechesis* 1573 (62–63) does not mention renewal in connection with regeneration.

[53] Chytraeus, *Catechesis* 1580, 118–119: "Renovatio est actio Spiritus Sancti, qua in iustificato habitans, veterem hominem seu peccatum, in mentu caliginem, & dubitationes de Deo, in voluntate vacuitatem timoris Dei & omnes pravas inclinationes: in corde incendia seu furias affectuum vicioforum expurgare & abolere incipit, & novum hominem Seu Dei imaginem, per peccatum amissam, restituit & renovat, accendens in mente lucem verae noticiae Dei, in voluntate & corde novam iusticiam, vitam & laetam obedientiam erga omnium mandata Dei, & relatam ad hunc finem, ut Deus celebretur." Thus, renewal takes place by the Spirit, which is present.

notion of union with Christ remains the same. Since the *Catechism* was a popular and simple presentation it could not achieve the detailed style evident in some of Chytraeus' other, more academic works. One such essential source is his textbook on ethics, *Regula vitae*, in which the nature of faith is described with precision.[54] In *Regula vitae* Chytraeus states that Christ is ἐνδελεχεια of faith. Chytraeus uses the term originating from Aristotle (initially ἐντελέχεια), which practically means the same as *forma*. Aristotle used these concepts to define the connection between the body and soul, the soul being the *entelekheia* of the body.[55] In addition, the concept has a secondary sense of 'object', 'aim' or 'end',[56] which would mean that Christ is the object of the faith, not its form.

Although both Luther and Melanchthon use the concept in the same sense as *forma*, it can be conceded that the secondary meaning is also in accordance with the intentions of the reformers as well as the Bible (e.g., Heb. 12:2). It must be noted, however, that the concept cannot be reduced to signify only the 'object'.[57] In the case of Chytraeus, its most natural use is synonymous with *forma.* Chytraeus defined the term by saying that Christ is the 'soul' and 'life' of the faith. Christ is in faith as the jewel is in the ring.[58] Chytraeus agreed with Luther's notion of Christ as the *form* of faith (*Christus forma fidei*).

---

[54] Although the first edition of *Regulae vitae* dates from 1555, this study uses the 1577 edition.

[55] Aristoteles, *De Anima*, 412a 27. This concept means the form that is actualized. James Urmson, *The Greek philosophical vocabulary* (London: Gerald Duckworth & Co. 1990), p. 55. See also *De Anima* (402a 26), where *entelekheia* and *energeia* are synonymous. However, the distinction is possible when *energeia* means activity or actualisation, while *entelekheia* means the resulting actuality or perfection.

[56] Originating from the Greek word *telos*. See Müller, *Dictionary*, p. 104.

[57] On Melanchthon, see especially *CR* 13, 12–15 (*De anima*), which contains responses to Cicero's criticism of Aristotle. According to Cicero, if *entelekheia* is understood as movement (*motio*), it is an accidental quality and the soul cannot be an accident. *Entelekheia* thus cannot be used to refer to the soul. Melanchthon responds that the concept of *entelekheia* can be used both substantially and accidentally. Substantial *entelekheia* is "ipsa talis rei viventis seu animalis, quae actiones ciet, ut si diceret, animam esse energeian, seu efficaciam." (*CR* 13, 15.) Accidental *entelekheia* can mean movement. Melanchthon's students employ the substantial use; Christ is not the origin of the movement but its substance. Luther uses *entelekheia* in *WA* 39 I, 318, 15–17 (*Die Zirkulärdisputation de veste nuptiali*): "Sed respondeo. Quod non valet, quia fides est ipsa forma et actus primus seu entelekheia charitatis... Charitas autem est opus et fructus fidei."

[58] Chytraeus, *Regula*, C1v–C2: "Formam & Eνδελέχειαν, seu animam & vitam fidei impertit Christus mediator, quem fides, velut anulus gemmam, complectitur."

The *Regula vitae* also contains an analysis of the causes of the justifying faith. First, the Holy Spirit enlightens both the knowledge of and assent to the Gospel in the mind and enables trust in the grace promised through Christ. The second cause is the word of the Gospel, which is heard and understood. The third cause is the renewed (*renovata*) mind and will, which trusts in the promise of grace with the assistance of the Holy Spirit.[59]

Faith, arising from the renewed mind, and subsequent justification functions as a soteriological metaconcept. The same faith is followed by God's indwelling in the believer, joy and peace, true prayer, good works, and eternal life. Therefore, in the thinking of Chytraeus, a distinction also obtains between the renewal involved in justification (*renovatio*$_1$) and subsequent renewal caused by the special indwelling of the Trinity. This indwelling is the cause of good works (*renovatio*$_2$).[60]

6.2.2. *Union with God as the Foundation and the End of Humanity*

In 1581 Chytraeus wrote a short book entitled *Unterricht vom Tode und ewigen Leben*, which depicted the status of the human being in Heaven and Hell. The chapter entitled "Beschreibung des Ewigens lebens / welches ist Gottes anschauung und eine vereinigung mit ihm" contains a detailed description of the nature of union with Christ in the state of glory. According to Chytraeus, eternal life consists of a vision of God (*Anschauung*) and union with Him (*Vereinigung*), which is realized as consolation (*Trost*).[61] This kind of state was the original state of humankind in Eden. The original blessedness meant uniformity and communion

[59] Chytraeus, *Regula* MDLXX, B8^v–C: "Caussae fidei sunt. I. Spiritus sanctus accendens in mentibus noticiam essentiae & voluntatis Dei in evangelio patefactae, & movens mentem ut assentiantur Evangelio: renovans ac addiuvans voluntatem ac cor, ut in misericordia & favore Dei propter Christum nobis reconciliati, firmiter acquiescant... II. Verbum Dei, seu promissio Evangelii audita & cogitata... III. Mens & voluntas humana renovata & adiuta per Spiritum Sanctum, assenties verbo Dei, luctans cum dubitationibus & dissidentia, & in promissione divina acquiescens."

[60] Chytraeus, *Regulae*, C1^v–C2: "Fines & effectus, qui fidei, tanquam causae instrumentali: Christo, tanquam causae impulsivae, seu merito: Deo, tanquam efficienti principali tribuuntur. 1. Iustificatio, hoc est, remissio peccatorum & reconciliatio cum Deo... 2. Donatio Spiritus sancti, & inhabitatio totius divinitatis, aeterni Patris, Filii, & SPIritus sancti. 3. Pax & laeticia conscientiae acquiescentis in Deo...4. Vera invocatio Dei...5. Omnia bona opera...6. Vita aeterna..."

[61] Chytraeus, *Vom Tode*, Rvii: "O welch ein seelig anschauung ist diss (spricht Bernhardus) Christum an sich selbs / in uns / und uns in Christo in sehligher liebligkeit anschauuen." See also Rvi–S.

with God (*gleichförmigkeit oder gemeinschafft mit Gott*), real participation in God and His properties.[62]

> The goal, for which man was originally created and afterwards redeemed, and on which the holy Book and Christian faith is founded, is eternal bliss, which is uniformity or union with God, in which we, like God, are enlightened with divine clarity, wisdom, righteousness, life and peace, in union with God, who dwells in us, and in which we enjoy the way He gives us Himself and all His goods. Therefore we are eternally blessed in Him and through Him. For man was created immortal in order to be the image of God and kin and uniform of his Creator, and the dwelling place and the temple of God, where God, like the sun of righteous virtues, should rest and dwell, and in whom He would infuse His wisdom and the rays of His righteousness, and would make us sharers of His divine nature (as [Gregory] Nazianzus says). And so that God, indwelling in us, would cause similar life and movements in us as there are in Himself, and we would become like him, staying in Him forever.[63]

Chytraeus's *Vom Tode* is a rare text in the post-schwenkfeldian and post-osiandrian era. The book presents the notion of deification (*Vergötterung*) in a positive sense, which means becoming one with God (*Vereinigung*), communion (*Gemeinshafft*), reconciliation (*Vergleichung*), and union (*Unio*). These are realized only partially in this life but are perfected in the life to come.[64]

---

[62] The Latin edition replaces the words *gemeinschafft mit Gott* by *unio cum Deo.* The word *unio* appears in the German edition as well Chytraeus, *Vom Tode*, Oiiv: "...und wird also diese gleichförmigkeit oder union mit Gott / dazu der Mensch anfenglich erschaffen..." Similar definitions appear in Chytraeus, *Explicatio Apocalyptis* 1563, 393–394, 417–418.

[63] Chytraeus, *Vom Tode*, Mvi–Mviv: "Das Ende / zu dem das Menschlicher Geschlecht anfenglich erschaffen / und nachmals erlöst / und darauff die ganze heilige Schrifft und der Christen Glaube beruhet / ist die ewige Seligkeit / welche da ist / eine gleichförmigkeit / oder gemeinschafft mit Gott / also / das wir / wie Gott / mit Göttlicher Klarheit / Weisheit / Gerechtigkeit / Leben und Freude erleuchtet / der gemeinschafft Gottes / der in uns wonet / uns sich selbst / uns alle seine güter uns mitteilet / geniessen / unnd also ewig in im und durch in sehlig sein / denn der Mensch ist also anfenglich erschaffen / das er were ein Ebenbild Gottes / und were dem Schöpffer ehnlich und gleichförmig / unnd ein Wohnung und Tempel Gottes / darinne Gott / als die Sonne der rechtschaffenen Tugenden / ruhet und wohnete / unnd in dem er seiner Weisheit und gerechtigkeit stralen ausgüsse / unnd dem er der Göttlichen Natur Theilhafftig machte / (Wie Nazianzenus davon redet) Unnd das also wir Menschen GOTT der in uns wonet / unnd solch leben unnd bewegung wie er selbst ist / in uns erregt / gleichförmig würden / unnd ihm in alle Ewigkeit einvorleibt blieben."

[64] Chytraeus, *Vom tode*, Miiii–Miiii[v]: "Diese geniessung des höchsten und unendtlichen guts / welche eine uberheuffte fülle und mitteilung alles guten / ohne irgend was arges / in sich helt und begreifft / wird eigendlich die Seligkeit genent / dit da in der ewigen Gemeinschafft mit GOTT / nicht allein was das Objectum bertrifft /

Union was destroyed by sin. In order to heal the damage, God assumed humanity in Christ through the incarnation. In the person of Christ humanity is again grafted (*eingeproffi wird*) on to God. The nature of union is equal to the exposition in Chemnitz's *De duabus Naturis*, in which salvation is based on the incarnation and hypostatic union.[65] According to Chytraeus justification requires real connection with divine properties. However, God's self-giving involves not only his properties; the justifying righteousness is God Himself (*Gott selbst*).[66] The union with God takes place through the Son. Accordingly, the union with the Son is effected by five unifying elements, which are Christ's person, the Holy Spirit, preaching the Gospel, baptism, and Holy Communion.

First, in the union with Christ's human-divine person, the lost relationship with God is restored alongside renewed human nature, which is communicated to the believer.[67] Second, the description of infusion

---

welches das höchste unerschaffene Gut ist / sondern auch was belanget sein Wesen unnd Essents / oder die Versammlung unnd Vereinigung mit Gott dem unendlichen gut / das seine güte den Sehligen mitteilen wird / vollkommen und perfect sein und werden. In diesem leben besitze nur ein jeder so viel von der angefangene Sehligkeit / als viel er von dem höheften gut erreicht / und so viel er / durch wares erkentnis oder durch dem Glauben / und durch brünstige hertzliche liebe / durch weisheit / gerechtigkeit und andere Göttliche tugenden / Gott zu gethan wird. Derwegen nennet Basilius das Christenthumb / eine vergleichung mit Gott / und Dionisius nents eine vergötterung. Die vergötterung ist eine vergleichung und Union mit Gott / welcher also gefasset wird."

[65] Chytraeus, *Vom Tode*, Mviv–Mvi: "Weil aber diese gemeinschafft und vereinigung mit GOtt dem Schöpffer / durch die Sünde zertrennet / unnd der Menschen herzen von GOtt abewendt / unnd Gesetzt abschewelicher sünden und unsauberkeit / uns solche wergzeuge / die GOTT nicht mehr fassen noch halten köndten / ja wonungen unnd leibeinige knecht des Satans / und Gottes abgesagte feinde worden / hat sich Gott aus uberschwenglicher güte / unnd mehr also Vaterliche / uber sein geschöpff das Menscliche geschlecht erbarmet / und hat seinen eingebornen Son zu Mittler verordnet / und Mensch werden lassen / auff das er die Menscliche Natur / mit der Göttlichen in einer einigen Person (wie ein Reisslein dem stam am Baum eingepropfft wird) wider vereinigte / unnd uns / die wir im durch den glauben eingebleibet / und glieder Christi worden sein / durch sich und umb seines willen widerumb einem Haupte anfügte / von dem wir Geist / Leben / Licht / gerechtigkeit / und alles so fur Sehligkeit dientslich / schöpfften / und die Gemeinschafft mit Gott / die wir durch sünde verlohren hatten / wider erlangen / und widerumb mit Gott und in Gott vereiniget werden mögten."

[66] Chytraeus, *Vom tode*, Nii: "Wiewol eben dieses Wort (Himelreich) imselben Capitel bisweilen eine grosse Menge Volcks oder die Kirch / so im unterworfen / bisweilen die samlung und erhaltung der Kirchen durchs Wort / bisweilen alle die Wohlthaten und Güter / die ir König Christus seiner Kirche mitteilt / nemlich Gott selbst / oder das ewige Liecht / die ewige Weisheit / Gerechtigkeit / Freude / bedeutet."

[67] Chytraeus, *Vom Tode*, Mvii–Mvii[v]: "Die Bandt aber dieser wunderbaren vereinigung / oder die mittel und Union / durch welche wir als die Gliedmas / Mit Christo / als warem Gott unsern haubt / gleich am ein leib werden / sind diese: Erstlich die

of the Spirit follows Melanchthon's theology as described in his *Liber de Anima*. The Holy Spirit of the eternal Father and the Son is infused (*ausgegossen*) into the hearts of believers and mingled (*vermenget*) with the individual's spirit. The Spirit evokes the desire to act according to God's will and essence in this way. In addition, the Spirit internally witnesses to childhood in the family of God.[68] Third, the Spirit uses the preaching of the Gospel to invoke faith, which also causes the sharing of Christ's merits.[69] Fourth, baptism engrafts (*eingeplanzt werden*) the baptized believer, who is clothed in Christ.[70] Fifth, the Holy Communion joins the receiver of the sacrament to Christ the Head as a member of His body. The communion with the blessed substances, and consequently with Christ present in them, initiates union with Christ. This is followed by renewal and new life.[71]

These elements function as instruments of salvation on God's part, while faith is the instrument on the individual's part. When faith receives the gifts that are offered to it, union with Christ, the whole of the Trinity,

verwendnis der natur / denn mittel der vereinigung unserer mit Gott dem vater / ist Christus: Uns zwar (wie Cyrillus redet) als ein mensch Gott dem Vater aber als Natürlicher Gott verwandt. Denn es war der Menschlichen / als der sterbligkeit unterworffenen Natur / unmüglich zu der unsterbligkeit zu gelangen / wenn nicht eine unsterbliche / und unverwesliche natur / zu ihr herunter kommen / und durch mitteilung selbst / sein sie von der sterbligkeit erledigt hette. Derwegen so sind wir nun volkommen worden / unnd sind mit Gott dem Vater wider vereinigt durch vermitteilung des Erlösers JEsu Christi."

[68] Chytraeus, *Vom Tode*, Mvii^{v}: "Darnach so ist der heilige Geist von Gott dem Ewigen Vater / unnd dem Sohne / in unsere herzen ausgegossen / das er uns ihnen / widerumb einleibe / und ein solch leben unnd regunge in uns anzünde / wie er selbst ist / und in dem er sich mit unsern Geist vermenget / gibt er uns zeugnis / das wir Kinder und Erben Gottes sind..."

[69] Chytraeus, *Vom Tode*, O: "Das dritte Mittel ist die Predigt des Evangelii / durch die der heilige Geist krefftig ist / und den glauben / dadurch wir Christo eingeplanzet / und der gemeinschafft / und aller wolthaten CHRIsti teilhafftig werden / in unsern herzen anzündet 1. Joh. 1. Das Wort des Lebens haben wir euch Verkündiget / auff das auch ihr mit uns gemeinschfft habt / und unser gemeinschafft sey mit dem Vater und mit seinem Son Jesu Christo. Epher. 3.4."

[70] Chytraeus, *Vom Tode*, O: "Das vierde mittel ist / die Tauffe / darein wir / als die Reislein/ Christo dem Baum des lebens eingeplanzt werden / und Christum anziehen / wie solchs Paulus bezeugt. / Rom. 6. 1. Cor. 12. Gal. 3." Chytraeus, *In Matthaeum* (649–699) contains an extensive account of baptism.

[71] Chytraeus, *Vom Tode*, O: "Das Lezte mittel ist das Abendmal des Herrn / dadurch / so wir des Leibs und Bluts Christi mit gleubigem herzen und Munde geniessen / Christo dem Heubt als ware Gleidmas eingeleibt und eingeplanzt werden / denn der Son Gottes / so dem Vater von natur gleich / wird mit uns / als ein Mensch / durch diss gesegnete Brot / leiblich vereiniget / Geistlich aber verneuert er / als ein Gott / unsern geist / zu einem newen leben / und zu der Gemeinschafft Gottes / wie solches Cyrillus in obgedachten ort / werleufftig ausleget."

and all other goods will result.[72] No qualitative difference exists between union in this life and in life to come. The difference is processual—in Heaven the union is more perfect than in the earthly realm.[73]

Chytraeus constructed his theology quite independently, even if he followed Melanchthon's terminology in some places. An example is the division of justification into forgiveness of sin and the renewal of the Spirit. However, on the eve of FC process he omitted the section on the Spirit. Interestingly, this omission is replaced by the emphasis on incarnation and the presence of Christ's person.

Chytraeus subsumes the *renovatio*$_1$ renewal within his soteriology. This enabler of the justifying faith is depicted as participation with Christ but also as a change effected by the Spirit, which is followed by good works (*renovatio*$_2$). Chytraeus's most important difference from Melanchthon was his desertion of a purely pneumatological soteriology; he preferred to follow Chemnitz closely and gave room for patristic motives of deification.

---

[72] Chytraeus, *Vom Tode*, O: "Durch diese band oder mittel vereiniget uns Christus / aus wunderbaren Rath / in diesem leben / widerumb mit GOTT / und bringet uns zu der Gemeinschafft GOTTes / und allen Geistlichen güter / auff das wir / die nun Wohnungen und Tempel GOTtes worden sind / mit Gott / der in uns wohnet / unsere herzen heiliget / und nun gleichförmig machet / eines werden / wie Christus spricht Johan. Am. 17. Cap. Gleich wie du Vater in mir / und ich in dir / das auch sie in uns eines sein / Ich bin in ihnen / und du in mir / auffdas sie wolkomen sein / in eines. 2. Corinth. 6. Ihr seid der Tempel des lebendigen Gottes / wie den Gott spricht: Ich will im ihnen wohnen / und wil ir Gott sein / Johan. Am. 15. Capitel. Bleibt in mir und ich in euch / wer in mir bleibet / und ich in ihm / der bringet viel Früchte / denn ohne mich könnet ir nochts thun. 1. Corinth. 3. Der Tempel GOTtes ist heilig / der seid ihr. Zum Ephesern am. 3. Capitel. / Christus wohnet durch den glauben in unsern herzen. Das Instrument oder Werkzeug aber dadurch wir diese mittel und bandt unser vereinigung mit Gott in diesem leben / sehliglich ergreiffen / uns zueignen / und mit Gott vereiniget werden / ist einig in uns der Glaube / welcher uns allein mit Gott zu Freunden macht. In dem künfftigen leben aber / werden wir Gott klar anschauen / und werden fromme herzen in anschaung Gottes / mit inbrünstiger liebe gegen Gott / und unausprechlicher Freude enkündet werden / und Gott wird selbs in den Gottsehligen wohnen / und leuchten / und alles in allem sein / unnd wird seine Güte / Weisheit / Glanz / Gerechtigkeit / Leben unnd Freude uber sie ausgiessen / unnd wird sie seinem hertzlichen Glanz gleichförmig machen…"

[73] Chytraeus, *Vom Tode*, Ov^v: "Und ist zwar zwischen der sehligkeit und dem erkenntnis Gottes / in diesem gegenwertigen / und in dem zukünfftigen leben / nicht / was das wesen an im selbst betrifft / sondern allein was die fortsetzung und den Process anlangt."

6.3. *Nicolaus Selnecker*

6.3.1. *Reciprocally Transforming Imputation*

Professor and superintendent Nicolaus Selnecker (1530–1592) was another important contributor to FC process. Although he was present at the meetings where the drafts of FC were formulated, he did not contribute any written articles. He is therefore considered a contributor to FC only in an indirect sense.[74] However, his formulation of the doctrine of justification is interesting because it merges several approaches. Selnecker generally understood justification forensically: to be 'justified' meant absolution from guilt and a pronouncement of freedom, as in a court case.[75] The deeper meaning of justification is expressed through the notion of imputation.

Selnecker defined imputation in two alternative ways. First, the basis (*fundamentum*) of imputation inheres in the object of imputation as a quality (*qualitas*). In this case, the basis and the object (*terminus*) are the same. Second, the basis may be something other than the object of

[74] Selnecker studied in Wittenberg and stayed in Melanchthon's house. In 1557 he moved to Dresden after eight years of study. This time was very productive for Selnecker. Within seven years he published the preface to Aristotle's *Physics*, commentaries on numerous books of the Bible, several books on dogmatics, the Catechism and the guide to catechetics. Selnecker published 175 books altogether during his lifetime. In 1570 he was called to the office of superintendent of Wolfenbüttel, where he became familiar with Andreae's project. Jungkuntz, *Formulators*, pp. 89–109; Erich Beyreuther, *Nikolaus Selneccer* 1530–1592, hrsgb. im Gedenkjahr zum 450. Geburtstag 6.12.1980 (Hersbruck: Karl Pfeiffer's Buchdruckerei und Verlag 1980); Ebel, "Herkunft", pp. 265–271; Werner Klän, "Der 'vierte Mann'. Auf den Spuren von Nikolaus Selneckers (1530–1592) Beitrag zu Entstehung und Verbreitung der Konkordienformel," *Lutherische Theologie und Kirche* 17 (1993).

[75] Selnecker, *Institutionis* II, 32: "Nam iustificari prorsus est forense vocabulum, & significat sisti ad iudicium, absolui à reatu peccati & damnationis, & pronunciari iustum." Albeit he does not explicitly direct his teaching against Osiander, he mentions Osiander's heresy in the beginning of his *Institutio*. Selnecker, *Institutionis* I, Iii: "...ante annos ferè triginta, quidam audebant scribere, essentialem Dei iustitiam in nobis habitantem, & nos moventem ad rectè agendum, esse veram nostram iustitiam..." It is apparent that Osiander's teaching effected Selnecker's formulations. For example, Selnecker seems to avoid the theme of inhabition. Selnecker also interprets Osiander's doctrine of inhabitation to include good works within justification, which implies mixing God with His effects. Selnecker, *Institutionis* I, Iiiv: "Quare Satanicum illud dogma de essentiali iustitia, qua coram Deo in hac vita iustificemur, planè execramur, cum confundat Deum ipsum, cum ipsius effectibus in nobis, & eam iusticiam, qua iusti sumus, fingat esse ipsam essentialem, & aeternam iustitiam, qua Deus essentialiter & immutabiliter iustus est: deinde excludat omnem Christi oboedientiam & impletionem totius iusticia legis..."

imputation.[76] This latter form of imputation takes place in justification when the basis is Christ's work and the object is the believing individual.[77] These two notions of imputation are mutually exclusive. If the basis inheres in the object, the justification is no longer by grace alone. In other words Selnecker identifies the former way of imputation as the Roman Catholic teaching on infused virtues, which function meritoriously.

According to Selnecker, God does not act unrighteously, (i.e., consider sin of no importance) when He reckons the sinner righteous without merits, because the righteousness needed for salvation is virtually in Christ.[78] But how can the righteousness of Christ benefit the sinner in effect? How are Christ's righteousness and sinner's unrighteousness related, and what ontological model does Selnecker use to bring the *fundamentum* and *terminus* together? To answer these questions, Selnecker introduces the new concept of reciprocally transforming imputation (*imputatio commutativa*).

> It is sure that the imputation between us and Christ is reciprocally transforming. Our sins, which He does not have and did not commit, are imputed to Christ. Likewise, Christ's righteousness and His whole obedience, which we do not have in our nature and which we have not carried out, are imputed to us. We receive it in faith, i.e., we believe it is imputed to us from God so that all our stain remains unnoticed and we shine dressed up in most radiant righteousness of the Son of God. That is, God sees us in the human form, which itself is also Jahve, and which lacks all stain and dirt, and He does not look on our own natural form, 1. Kings. 7 & 1. Chronicles 17. He does not look at wrinkles, filth or the dirt of nature, soul, and body, but sees clean cloth, which cover all these. "He clothes me with the garments of salvation and covers me with the robe of righteousness." Isaiah 61:10. This sort of transaction (*mercatoria*), or so to say transformation (*commutatio*), between Christ and us connects

[76] Selnecker, *Institutionis* II, 45: "Interdum enim imputatione vocabulum relativum est ea ratione, ut fundamentum habeat certam qualitatem in illis, quibus sit imputatio, & terminum habeat vel praemium, vel poenam & reatum. Inter haec duo relatio est ipsa imputatio vel ad praemium vel ad reatum.... Interdum verò vocabulum imputationis relativum quidem, sed alia ratione, videlicet, ut fundamentum imputationis non sit in illis inhaerens, quibus sit imputatio, sed sit in alio, & terminus sit persona, cui sit imputatio vel ad bonum vel ad malum, & relatio sit cogitatio & voluntas, sive decretum imputantis."

[77] Selnecker, *Institutionis* II, 137: "Estquè vox iustificationis in praedicamento Relationis, & habet fundamentum ipsum Deum, iustificantem & salvantem nos propter Christum: terminus verò habet personam credentem. Relatio est applicatio misericordia divina, & beneficiorum Christi, ad personam credentem."

[78] Selnecker, *Institutionis* II, 51–52.

> both a wonderful doctrine and consolation. This doctrine implies that imputation is not infusion of things, deeds, qualities or righteousness, as the papists imagine. Instead it is only a rational attribution, application, and ascription in the mind of God, who wishes and wills to justify us in this way. But if imputation means real mixing and inherent quality, this leads to an understanding according to which our sins are imputed to Christ so that he is described as knowing them in part and being guilty in them in his nature, and this is most disgraceful, blasphemous, and false teaching.[79]

In this case Selnecker merges two kind of terminology. While he uses concepts with strong forensic emphasis, such as *ascriptio*, he also uses terminology similar to the notion of salutary exchange such as *mercatoria* and *commutatio*.[80] What is especially interesting is the way Selnecker relates justification to christology: Christ's righteousness is imputed to the sinner and the sins are correspondingly imputed to Christ. In reciprocally transforming imputation, both parties receive something they do not have naturally. Since in this case the imputation of righteousness to the sinner cannot be more real or qualitatively different

---

[79] Selnecker, *Institutionis* II, 47–48: "Secundum est, quòd constet nostram & Christi imputationem esse commutativam. Christo imputantur nostra peccata, quae ipse nec habet nec fecit. Nobis econtrà imputantur iustitia Christi, & tota ipsius obedientia, quam ipsi nec habemus in nostra natura, nec fecimus, sed quam fide accipimus, id est, credimus illam ita nobis à Deo imputari, ut omnes nostrae maculae non conspiciantur, sed ut resplendeamus ornati fulgentissima iustitia Filii Dei. Aspicit enim Deus nos in forma hominis, qui est, & ipse Iehova, omnique labe & macula caret, & non ascipit nos in forma nostra, quales natura sumus, 2. Reg. 7. & 1. Paral 17. Non ascipit rugas, foeditatem & maculas naturae, animae & corporis, sed ascipit vestem pulcherrimam qua teguntur illa omnia. Esa. 61. Induit me vestimentis salutis, & indumento iustitiae circumdedit me. Haec igitur quasi mercatoria quaedam commutatio inter Christum & nos cùm doctrinam, tùm consolationem amplissimam continet. Doctrina haec est, quod imputatio non sit infusio rei aut operis aut qualitatis sive iustitiae, ut Pontificii imaginantur, sed sit tantum rationalis attributio, applicatio vel asscriptio cogitantis Dei, & volentis hoc modo nos iustos fieri. Si enim imputatio realis confusio & inhaerens naturae qualitas esset, tunc etiam Christo peccata nostra imputari ita dicerentur, ut illorum parti conscius & reus sua natura factus fingeretur, quod & contumeliosum, blasphemum, & falsissimum est." See also Selnecker, *Institutio* II, 165–166: "Imputatio est...actio Dei, qua id quod nec sumus, & quod nec habemus, nec fecimus, ex ineffabili erga nos amore & misericordia, nos esse, habere, & fecisse Deus iudicat, cogitat, statuit, & pronunciat, ideò, quòd Filius ipsius, in quem credimus, illud universum pro nobis, nostroque nomine & loco in solidum est, habet & fecit."

[80] Elert (*Morphologie*, pp. 100–101) interprets Selnecker's *imputatio commutativa* as salutary exchange, which occurs in union with Christ. Luther uses *commutatio* in this sense as well. See, e.g., *WA* 17 I, 175a, 10–11 (*Predigten* 1525); *WA* 42, 592, 6–8 (*Vorlesung über* 1. *Mose* 1535–1545).

than Christ's becoming sin,[81] justification cannot indicate transformation into something a thing is not by nature. This kind of transformation is for Selnecker as great an error as the mixing of Christ's natures. In justification the sinner shares Christ's righteousness, just as Christ's human nature shares the properties of the divine nature (*communicatio idiomatum*). In the person of Christ, however, the human nature shares the properties of the divine nature effectively so that, for example, the ubiquity of the divine nature is shared by human nature. How does this emphasis on reality appear with respect to justification?

6.3.2. *The* materia *and* forma *of Faith*

Selnecker used a pneumatological approach in describing the changes in the justified person: the Holy Spirit changes and reforms the individual in order to evoke the faith that justifies.[82] Therefore, faith is completely the work of God, whereas the human mind is *materia*, which is the object of God's work.[83] The human mind is not that which converts but that which is converted.[84]

Faith is a special gift of God that is given through the preached Gospel, accompanied by the infusion of the Holy Spirit into the heart. The Spirit bends the intellect and will to receive the promise of the Gospel.[85] Accordingly, the Spirit evokes a change in the person; the mind

[81] Selnecker, *Institutionis* II, 48: "Consolatio verò haec est: iustitiam nostram, peccatum, meritum, culpam, mortem & poenam Christus in se derivat, ut ipse cum iniustis reputetur, ut in Esaia scriptum est. Nostram obligationem, ingens debitum & chirographum ipse in seipsum transportat, ac sua obedientia cruci affigit, & persoluens dilacerat. Pro nostra vicissim culpa dat nobis suam iustitiam & meritum: pro morte vitam, pro poena praemium."

[82] This may originate from Melanchthon, but it may also refer to Augustine's distinctions of grace. Augustine defines the movements preceding conversion in the individual as acts of the Holy Spirit. See Chemnitz, *Loci* I, 179 (243).

[83] Selnecker, *Institutionis* II, 83–84: "Dei igitur solius est efficacia. Nos tantùm sumus materia..."

[84] Selnecker, *Institutionis* II, 85: "Certum enim est, voluntatem esse rem convertendam, non convertentem."

[85] Selnecker, *Paedagogia*, Fiii: "Das evangelium ist der werkzeug / durch welchs Gott den heiligen Geist in unsere herzen ausgeusset / also / das wir gleuben / unnd darnach auch früchte des glaubens bringen." *Selnecker* Institutionis II, 82: "Vocat fidem opus Dei, non solùm quia à Deo mandatum est, sed quia Spiritus sanctus in mente & corde per verbum promissionem Evangelii auditam & cogitatam accendit & confirmat, & conservat fides.... Et non est tantummodo aliquod generale aut commune donum, quale est saepè in vita communi... sed peculiare, filiorumque Dei proprium donum est, omni rationi humane ignotum, & per Spiritum sanctum nostris mentibus patefactum & datum. Causae igitur fidei sunt, doctrina Evangelii audita, & Spiritus sanctus

is enlightened, changed and moved by the Spirit.[86] The person is not like a log or a donkey that has no will. The will is formed so that it does not resist but consents to receive the promise of the Gospel.[87] Selnecker used the following terminology to describe the material or psychological aspect of conversion in his *Paedagogia Christiana*. The following quotation compares the German and Latin editions of the book.

> In dieser beschreibung / wird erstlich angezeigt / das der Glaube sey ein gabe Gottes / denn er ist ein Iezer, das ist / ein neu gemecht / gescheft oder werck des heiligen Geistes / damit er aus dem altem Menschen / welsches Iezer, oder gescheft / dichten und dencken böse ist zu aller zeit / und von Jugend auff / einen neuen Menschen macht / der an den Son Gottes gleubet / und Gott dem Vater angenehm ist.[88]

> Haec fidei descriptione ostenditur, primum, quod fides sit donum Dei, quia est Iezer, id est, nouum quasi plasma, & figmentum sive poëma Spiritus Sancti, quo ex veteri homine, cuius Iezer malum est omni tempore ab infantia sua, facit nouum hominem, credentem in Filium Dei, & Deo patri acceptum & gratum.[89]

Faith is described as God's gift (*gabe / donum*) which is elucidated by the Hebrew word *iezer* (יצר).[90] The word appears in the Bible in four different senses. First, it describes the work of the potter (Isaiah 29:16); second, carved images (Hab. 2:18); third, the form of the human created from the dust of the earth (Gen. 2:7–8.); and fourth, imagination, impulse,

---

illuminans mentem ad assentiendum, & impellens voluntatem ad acquiescendum in promissione Evangelii."

[86] Selnecker, *Institutionis* II, 83: "Etsi autem voluntas in ipso actu & operatione Spiritus sancti accendentis fidem in homine audiente verbum & promissionem Evangelii, non prorsus sublata, mortua & plane ociosa, sed illuminatur, mutatur & movetur à Spiritu sancto..."

[87] Selnecker, *Institutionis* II, 86: "Haec docendi causa ita exponuntur, & vera sunt, & Deo placent. Rectè etiam dicitur: Spiritus sanctus non convertit saxum aut truncum, aut bovem aut asinum, sed hominem ratione à Deo ornatum, & ad imaginem Dei conditum, qui & audire, cogitare & intelligere potest & debet. Ac etsi homo sua natura post lapsum sit hostis Dei factus, tamen ut hostis ratione praeditus reconciliationem sibi ab adversa parte cuius hostis est, oblatam audit, & Spiritus sancti efficaciam intelligit & recipit, & moveri ac flecti se ad pacem finit, & fit amicus: ita homo audiens promissionem Evangelii, & videns legatum Dei offerentem gratiam & pacem, id est, audiens verbum, sentit motum Spiritus sancti in corde suo, non respuit aut reiicit oblata beneficia, sed laetitia accensus subiicit se divina voci & motui, ut Paulus ait: Dominus, quid vis, ut faciam?"

[88] Selnecker, *Paedagogia* 2 German, Eiiv.

[89] Selnecker, *Paedagogia* 2 Latin, 20.

[90] See also Selnecker, *Institutionis* II, 147.

and goal, where the word can refer to good or bad inclinations in the person. (Gen. 2:5; Gen. 8:21; Isaiah 26:3).[91]

The other words of the quote illustrate the additional senses of *iezer*. In the German edition, explanatory substantives include *gemecht, geschefft*, and *werck*, which all refer to a deed or a creation. The Latin edition is more informative on this point—it uses words such as *plasma, figmentum*, and *poëma*. The meaning of the word *plasma* derives from the verb πλάσσω, which means molding or becoming uniform. *Figmentum* is founded on the verb *fingo*, which means forming, constructing, or building. *Poëma* (ποίημα) is derived from the verb 'to do', and refers to something which is made, such as a statue.[92]

All these words underline the reality of faith in the individual. Faith is not fictitious but involves a real change, as underlined in the use of *iezer*: The naturally evil essence of the person is reformed to please God. The *iezer* of the Holy Spirit replaces the naturally tainted *iezer*. The German translation emphasizes the connotation 'essential' while speaking of deeds and thoughts. Since in faith, God gives a person new form, being and disposition, faith and justification involve renewal and the mortification of sin.[93] However, in his explanation of the nature of imputation Selkecker denies the meritoriousness of new qualities. How does he manage to maintain both the renewal as a prerequisite for justifying faith and his strict denial of the meritoriousness of material renewal? His solution is to consider faith through its *forma*, which is not founded on the renewal of the person.[94] Instead, the form of

---

[91] Francis Brown, *Hebrew and English Lexicon* (Massachusetts: Hendrickson Publishers 1999), p. 428.

[92] Earlier, Origen had understood the words *poieo* and *energei* synonymously in his *Peri Archon*. See Michel Barnes, "The background and use of Eunomius' causal language," in *Arianism after Arius*, eds. Barnes et al. (Edinburgh: T&T Clark 1993), pp. 231–232. This involves the following causal series: *dunamis* (power), *energeia/poiema* (action or actualization), and *erga* (product), which illustrates the origination of the created order from the Creator. In the case of Selnecker, faith is the actualization of God's essence in the believer.

[93] Selnecker, *Paedagogia*, 119v: "Sondern er macht uns selig also / das er unsere Sünde bezahlt / das Gott nicht mehr zürne / das er uns die Sünde vergibt / und nicht zurechnet / und uns seine gerechtigkeit und den heiligen Geist schenkt / der die Sünde tödtet / das sie nicht in uns herrsche / noch uns verdamme. Hieber gehören die Psalmen / so von der Rechtfertigung für Gott lehren / als der ein und funffzigste / da David betet / Entsündige mich mit Isopen / das ich rein werde."

[94] Selnecker, *Institutionis* II, 161: "Forma in nobis, aut nostris viribus nulla est, Nec vivificationem aut regenerationem, nec charitatem in nobis inhaerentem nobisque infusam, sive habitum elicitum per charitatem, ut Pontificii loquuntur, nec vitae novitatem aut dignitatem qualencunque, sive novam obedientiam aut opera & merita nostra, formam

the faith is Christ Himself. Even if faith has a certain material and qualitative aspect, it justifies only because of its content, as a ring has worth because of the attached jewel.[95]

He used the word *entelekheia* to depict the relation between Christ and faith: Christ gives form and being to faith.[96] This is also the case in the parallel passage of *Paedagogia*, in which Christ as the jewel of the ring is described as the life (*leben*) and living power (*die lebendige krafft*) of the faith.[97] Thus, Christ is not only the object of faith and faith is not simply a mental state. Christ gives faith its justifying nature.

In faith it is not the act but its object that counts, just as the ring is precious because of the jewel. Thus, faith has an inherent and material aspect (the ring) which corresponds to faith as a mental capacity. Faith also has a form, which is Christ (the jewel). This presence of Christ as the form of faith is the justifying entity; faith does not justify absolutely,

---

nostrae iustitiae appellare possumus. Et vanum est universam figmentum illud, quod de fide formata affertur. Nam vera iustitia nostra est aliena, extra nos, id est, habet fundamentum positivuum et unicum, non in nobis, aut nostris viribus & qualitatibus, sed in Christo, cuius obedientia nobis in ipsum credentibus imputatur. Quare causa formalis nostrae iustitiae est gratuita remissio peccatorum, sive expiatio, qua peccata nostra nobis non imputantur, imputatio obedientiae, innocentiae, & iustitiae Christi, reconciliatio cum Deo, adoptio in filios & haeredes Dei, cum quo semper coniuncta est pax cum Deo, & fiducia acquiescens in promissione Dei, & merito Filii."

[95] Selnecker, *Paedagogia*, Fiiiv: "Das geschicht aber nicht umb der qualitet oder von wegen unsers gleubens / sondern in ansehen des / darauff der Glaube gerichtet ist / und sihet / nemlich / von wegen des verdiensts Christi des Sons Gottes / welches der Glaube / wie der Ring ein köstlich Berlein / fasset und ergreiffet. Den der Herr Christus ist die form / oder das leben / die lebendige krafft des Glaubens." Selnecker, *Paedagogia*, Eii–Eiiv: "Den vom Glauben und seiner krafft und stercke / sol man nicht urteilen aus des glaubens grösse / oder wie er sey / sondern aus dem obiecto, das ist / aus dem das der Glaube ergreifft und darauff sihet."

[96] Selnecker, *Institutionis* II, 89: "Certum est, cùm fide nos iustificari dicimus, non intelligi opus fidei aut ullam in nobis qualitatem & actionem virium nostrarum, sed more Paulino usurpari nomen fidei relativè, & significari fiduciam Filii Mediatoris, id est: iustos nos esse non propter qualitatis dignitatem, sed propter Filium Dei, quem fides agnoscit, intuetur, apprehendit, & in eo acquiescit, & veluti annulus preciosam gemmam, eum complectitur. Christus enim est endelechia fidei, & fides Christum apprehendit. Rectè igitur dicitur. Non propter nostrum credere, sed propter objectum iustificamur, id est, per misericordiam promissam sumus iusti. Et fides tantùm est instrumentum in nobis, quo apprehendimus oblatam & donatam gratiam."

[97] See note 95. Selnecker borrows Augustine's definition, according to which the soul and God are analogical. Selnecker, *Paedagogia*, Viii^{v}: "Gleich wie die Seele ist das leben des Leibs / also ist Gott der Herr das Leben der Seele."

i.e., for the sake of the combination of matter and form.[98] The priority of the form indicates that justification is not merely a new relation between two distinct entities. The new form now constitutes Christ, the object of justification, who is essentially present in faith.

How does Christ actually constitute the form? Selnecker claimed that the prerequisite for salvation is the presence of God. In fact, God is essentially (*essentialiter*) present in believers through faith when justification or any other event of the *ordo salutis* takes place.[99] The nature of God's presence in conversion, regeneration, justification, and sanctification are all qualitatively similar.[100]

---

[98] Selnecker, *Institutionis* II, 89: "Ex hac communefactione facile responderi potest ad argumenta illa tria. Fide sumus iusti. Fides est opus. Ergo propter opera sumus iusti. Maior correlativè intelligenda est. Fide sumus iusti, non qualitate fidei, sed relatione ad eum, quem fides apprehendit, & eius iustitiam sibi applicat. Nam ratione operis fides nihil valet: ratione verò fundamenti & objecti, quod fides intuetur & apprehendit, fides omnia est..."

Selnecker, *Institutionis* II, 90: "Medium, quo, non est terminus ad quem. Fides est medium quo, sive est instrumentum. Ergo non est terminus ad quem, id est non iustificamur fide. Concedo totum de fidei qualitate & opere. Fides enim absolutè non est nostra iustitia, sed fide iustificamur relativè, & fides est medium sive instrumentum, quò ad terminum & scopum pervenimus, & iustitiam Filii Dei apprehendimus, & nobis applicamus."

[99] Selnecker, *Repetitio*, 196–197: "Tertius modus praesentiae Dei est, quo Deus in ecclesia in hac vita secundum suam promissionem verbo manifesto comprehensam, & ministerio suo praesens adest, & in administratione & usu sacramentorum praesto est secundum verba institutionis uniuscuiusque sacramenti, & vere est & habitat in pijs & renatis per gratiam & efficaciam, non tantum spiritualiter & effective, sed etiam effective & revera, licet de sua essentia & deitate nihil ipsis communicet, efficit in eis per verbum & sacramentorum motus, affectus, cogitationes, sermones, & actiones, sibi placentes, operante in mentibus & cordibus piorum Spiritu sancto, movente, regente, gubernante, flectente, ducente & illuminante mentes & corda, & templa sibi ex illis & in illis constituente...Adest enim Deus in renatis non tantum per dona sua, ut ipse alibi sit, & essentialiter non adsit & inest renatis, & adest suis donis & sua efficaciae, licet adsit invisibiliter, societate, & separabiliter."

[100] Selnecker, *Repetitio*, 198: "Ad hunc tertium gradum pertinent praecipua capita doctrinae Christianae. 1. De predicatione verbi, legis & Evangelij. 2. De ministerio, & praecipuis partibus ministerij. 3. De Ecclesia in haec vita. 4. De conversione hominis per verbum, quod est ministerium & instrumentum Spiritu sancti. 5. De regeratione, & iustificatione hominis, reconciliatione cum Deo, imputatione iusticiae Christi, adoptione in filium, remissione peccatorum, beneficijs, meritis, & oboedientia Christi, sive iusticia fidei. 6. De praedestinatione & electione ad vitam aeternam secundum verbum, promissionem, gratiam, & veritatem Dei in evangelio revelatam. 7. De renovatione, sanctificatione, vivificatione, novitate Spiritus, sive de donatione Spiritus sancti subinde conspicua in fructibus iusticiae & fidei, & de bonis operibus, ac inchoatione. 8. De institutione, & usu sacramentorum, baptismi, & coenae dominicae, secundum verba institutionis uniuscuiusque sacramenti."

Selnecker's notion of incarnation is deeply reliant on Chemnitz. In fact Chemnitz's *De Duabus Naturis* begin's with Selnecker's preface in which he briefly goes through the substance of the book.[101] The same notions are used in Selnecker's own writings. The core of soteriology is the assumption of Christ's human nature and the following salutary exchange. This is illustrated, for example, in a hymn written by Selnecker.

> nichts bin ich / und weis auch kein trost /
> denn das du O Herr Jhesu hast mich / selig gmacht und auch erlost /
> In dem du mein Fleisch an dir hast.[102]

Paedagogia contains a chapter in which Selnecker explains the names of Christ. The exposition of the name *Immanuel* includes a doxological section, where the salutary exchange is joined with incarnation. The assumption of the human nature by the divine nature is the foundation of salutary exchange.[103] The second part of *Paedagogia* is basically an explanation of the second article of faith, in which various soteriological theories are used to shed light on the meaning of Christ as Savior.[104] The theory of satisfaction is of great importance for Selnecker, but by no means the only possible theory. The depictions of the Old Testament, such as Christ as the sacrificial offering, high priest and intercessor, and patristic images of *Christus Victor* are given a detailed account.[105] In addition, the doctrine of justification is discussed in the chapter on resurrection (*Vom Triumph Christi*).[106]

Since the person of Christ is the locus in which human and divine become one, Christ in his person is the material cause of the salvation.[107]

---

[101] Chemnitz, *De Duabus*, 5–6. (15–27). See also Baur, *Luther und seine klassichen Erben. Theologische Aufsätze und Forschungen* (Tübingen: Mohr Siebeck 1993), p. 175.

[102] Selnecker, *Paedagogia*, 120v.

[103] Selnecker, *Paedagogia*, 169v–170: "O admirabile commercium. O culpa nimium beata, qua redempta est natura. Mirabilis natura mirifice induta, assumens quod non erat, manens quod erat, &c. O welch ein wünderlicher handel / verwelchung und vereinigung. O welche ein selige schuld / dadurch die Natur widerumb erlöset ist. Welch ein wünderliche Natur / wie wünderlich ist sie in unser Fleisch und Blut verkleidet / in dem sie das / so sie nicht war / an sich nimpt / und das so sie zuvor war / auch bleibet, O welch ein wünderlich und tewerbarer werd und auffsönung für uns. O welche ein herrligkeit hat unser Menschliche Natur bekommen."

[104] Selnecker, *Paedagogia*, 116–359.

[105] Selnecker, *Paedagogia*, Hiiiv–Hiiii.

[106] Selnecker, *Paedagogia*, 267v–269.

[107] Selnecker, *Institutionis* II, 9–10: "Materia circa quàm objecta sunt Deus & homo peccator reconciliandus Deo per & propter Christum Mediatorem, quam quidem ideo Deum & hominem esse congruit, ut Deum & hominem reconciliaret & coniungeret,

This involves everything Christ does as God and man: descension, suffering, death, bleeding, resurrection, and ascension.[108] In addition, being omnipresent, He is able to hear prayers, forgive sins, be present in His congregation, and breathe his Spirit into believers.[109] Thus, the hypostatic union is not simply a material prerequisite that enables satisfactory merit.

Union with Christ also has pastoral importance. In *Christliche und Sehr Schöne Trostsprüche vor engstige betrübte und verfolgte Christen*, Selnecker emphasizes how Christ has fulfilled the Law and suffered for sinners. This forensic aspect is united with the importance of apprehending Christ. In faith the believer apprehends Christ, who has fulfilled the Law and triumphed over sin and Satan—these can no longer threaten the believer.[110]

---

sicut rectè inquit Cyrillus: Mediator Dei hominum est, quia in eo Deus & homo coniunguntur."

[108] Selnecker, *Paedagogia*, Yiiii^{v}: "Materialis, darinnen solches geschehen / ist der gehorsam / gnugthuung oder verdienst Christi / oder die Erlösung selbst durch ihn geschehen / die erfüllung des Gesetzes / oder wie man pflegt zureden / wenn man etwas oder nur ein stück des allens nennet für alles / nemlich / seine Erniedrigung / Menschenwerdung / Leide / Creuzigung / Tod / Blut / Wunden / Aufferstehung / und hingang des Herrn Christi zum Vater. Formalis, wie es geschicht und zugeht / ist die annehmung zu Kindern und Erben / die zurechnung der Gerechtigkeit / unschulf / des gehorsams und vollkommenheit Christi / die die versönung unnd friede mit Gott / wenn das hertz fühlet / das sichs im vertrauen auff die verheissung Gottes und auff das verdienst seines lieben Sons zu frieden gibt."

[109] Selnecker, *Institutionis* I, 121–123. This is enabled by actual understanding of *communicatio idiomatum*. See Selnecker, *Paedagogia*, 224–254.

[110] Selnecker, *Trostsprüche*, 42–43: "...noch ist Christus mein mit seinem leiden / sterben und leben..." Selnecker, *Trostsprüche*, 81–82: "Ich halt mich an Christum / der sich selbs für meine Sünde dargeben hat / und bin des gewis / das kein verdamnis mehr gelten sol bey denen / die in Christo Jhesu sind. Meine sünde solten und können mich nicht verdammen / es were denn / das sie zuvor Christum meinen lieben Heyland verdammeten / welchs sie wol lasen werden. Darumb / ob gleich die Sünde selbs / oder aber der Sathan / oder das Gesetz mich anklagen / so ergreiff ich doch den Schild des Glaubens / und durch den Glauben den Herrn Christum / der ein Herr uber die Sünde / Teuffel / und Gesetz ist / spreche schlecht: Ich will von euch nichts wissen / machets wie ihr wollet. Sünde / wilt du mich verdammen / so thu es zuvor Christo meinem leiden Heyland / Priester und Fürbitter bey dem Vater. Teuffel / wilt du mich schrecken / Nein / du richtest nichts aus / Denn mein Herr Christus hat dich uberwunden / und deine Werck zustöret. Du bist verdammet / ich aber bin selig. Der Zorn Gottes gehet uber dich. Mit mir aber ist Gottes gnad. Du bist Gottes Feind. Ich bin Gottes Freund / Kind / Sohn / Tochter. Warumb wolt ich mich denn fürchten? Ist Gott für uns / Wer will wider uns sein? Also soll ich auch zum Gesetz sagen: Klage mich an / wie du wilt / so soltu mich dennoch nicht verdammen. Es ist wol war / ich bin ein armer unnd grosser Sünder. Aber ich bin vom Gesetz frey gemacht / dass es mich nicht soll noch kan verdammen. Denn Christus mein Herr unnd heyland hat mir ein andere Gesetz geben welchs selig macht alle /

When the believer embraces (*amplectimur*) Christ in faith, he or she is simultaneously given the Holy Spirit. This occurance indicates the connection (*coniuncta*) of the forgiveness of sins and justification with renewal.[111] According to Selnecker the Holy Spirit can be given in three different ways. First, the Holy Spirit is given in the first act of faith, when the Spirit functions as pledge and seal (*arrhabo et pignus*) of the promise of the Gospel. Justification and infusion of the Spirit thus occurs simultaneously. Second, the Spirit is given to renew and enlighten the intellect and the will, and to evoke spiritual virtues. Third, the Spirit is given to strengthen outward works and carry out the vocation.[112]

The first act of faith already involves the presence of the Spirit when Christ's merit is sealed for the believer.[113] Since Christian righteousness consists of forgiveness of sins and imputation of Christ's righteousness, which is made one's own through faith evoked by the Holy Spirit (*renovatio$_1$*), the efficacious presence of the Holy Spirit cannot be considered

---

die an Christum gleuben / ob sie gleich grosse Sünder sind. Christus ist je gegeben nit für heiligen Gerechtigkeit / noch für der Engel unschuld / sondern für der armen Sünder ungerechtigkeit unnd Sünde. Were ich gerecht / und hett keine Sünde / so dorfft ich des Herrn Christi nicht / der mich Gott versöhnete. Weil ich aber weis / dass ich ein Sünder bin / unnd dass mich mein eigne Sünde / darzu der Teuffel und Gesetz / als ein verdampte Sünder anklagen / aben darumb wil ich desto gestöster gleuben / Ich sey gerecht und heilig / unnd werde gewis selig werden / so war als mein Herr Christus gelidten / und für meine Sünde bezahlet hat."

[111] Selnecker, *Institutionis* II, 78: "Spiritus sanctus datur ex auditu fidei, id est, non propter opera legis, sed propter Christum, quam fide iuxta auditum Evangelium amplectimur & simul Spiritum sanctum accipimus cuis donatio semper est coniuncta cum remissione peccatorum."

[112] Selnecker, *Institutionis* II, 129–130: "Haec questio facilè expediri potest, si consideretur, Spiritum sanctum nobis dari, & in nobis, & in nobis essentialiter & efficaciter habitare, propter has praecipuas causas. 1. Ut obsignet in nobis promissionem gratiae, & fiduciam promissionis Evangelicae. Ipse enim est arrhabo & pignus, quod sponsus filius Dei nobis utpote sponsae suae dat, & nos certificat de veritate promissionum, iustitiae, & vitae aeternae. Deinde datur Spiritus sanctus, ut nos renovet, mentem illuminet vera Dei agnitione, voluntatem regeneret, & flectat ad spontaneam obedientiam, cor moveat, & imbuat piis, placidis & castis affectibus, timore Dei, desiderio vitae & salutis, geminitibus, contritione, dolore propter peccatum, fiducia Christi, consolatione & laetitia, ac spe liberationis, & dilectione etiam proximi, sive operibus charitatis. Postea datur ut in tota vita externa nos regat, ut faciamus opera vocationis, piè & honestè vivamus, nemimem nostra culpa offendamus, non praebeamus scandala infirmioribus, aliis libenter inferviamus & benefaciamus."

[113] Selnecker, *Paedagogia*, 274: "Gott gibt und schenckts uns. Der Herr Christus erlangts und verdiensts uns. Der heilige Geist versigelts in uns. Der Glaub empfehets. Die werk bezeugens."

only as the consequence of the justifying faith.[114] The Holy Spirit, given to the believer in justification, generates and strengthens faith.[115]

The two latter aspects of giving are identified with good works and movements of the mind (*renovatio*$_2$).[116] However, all the aspects join together as implications of the same mode of God's presence and do not show temporal difference. Selnecker can still say that *inhabitatio Dei* is the consequence of faith. In this case, it is identified with the second and third aspects of giving.[117] The consequent inhabitation is only a description of God's special action, as the examples of the giving of the Spirit demonstrate. The giving of the Spirit should not be understood as a literal giving; likewise, the ascension of the Spirit in the form of the dove upon Christ should not be understood to mean that the Spirit was not present in Christ previously. What is in question is a particular function and effect.[118]

---

114 Selnecker, *Paedagogia*, Yii^v–Yiii: "Und diese gerechtigkeit / ideo man nennet / entweder die Göttliche Gerechtigkeit / oder die Gerechtigkeit des Evangelii / oder die Gerechtigkeit des Glaubens / der da gerecht macht / ist nichts anders / denn die vergebung der Sünden / so aus gnaden geschicht / unnd die zurechnung der Gerechtigkeit Christi / so mit dem Glauben ergriffen wird / welcher glaube durch den heiligen Geist angezündet / die angebottene wolthaten / so ohn verdienst der werck des Gesetzes / uns umb sinst geschencket werden / empsehet und annimpt / nur allein nach der verheissung die das Evangelium sonderlich und eigentlich allein hat."

115 Selnecker, *Catechesis*, 238: "Effectus cohaerens, est donatio Spiritus Sancti, accendentis & confirmantis fidem, pax cum Deo, laetitia in corde, tranquillitas conscinentiae, & omnes fructus fidei." *Selnecker* Paedagogia 2, 291: "Donatio spiritus Sancti, qui novam lucem vere agnitionis Dei, fidem, consolationem, iusticiam & vitam in mentibus & cordibus piorum accendit."

116 Selnecker, *Institutionis* II, 176.

117 Selnecker, *Institutionis* II, 163: "Et his subiungimus quoque omnia effecta iustitiae fidei, ut sunt donatio Spiritus sancti, inhabitatio Dei in nobis, renovatio, lux nova sive illuminatio, pax conscientiae, laetitia..."

118 Selnecker, *Institutionis* II, 130: "Praestat autem Spiritus sanctus primum officium secundum promissionem evangelii, quia est nostrae haereditatis, quam promissam habemus in Evangelio, pignus. Secundum officium praestat certo quodam ductu & transitu ex doctrina Evangelii ad regulam & praescriptum legis requirentis internam mentis, voluntatis, cordis, & omnium affectuum hominis puritatem, & integram conformitatem, & simul in hoc ipso ductu nobis monstrat & praefert Filium Dei crucifixum, quem intueri debemus, quoties, quantum desit menti, voluntati, cordi & universae nostrae substantiae, animae, corpori, omnibus viribus videmus.... Tertium officium praestat Spiritus sanctus per tertium usum legis, ut usitatè loquimur. Est enim, ut hoc breviter repetamus, triplex usus legis. Primus regere disciplinam, sine qua nec doceri homines de Deo possunt, nec à Filio Dei vivificantur. Secundus, accusare & condemnare peccatum, & perterrefacere conscientiam. Tertius usus de quo hic loquimur, est docere, qui cultus Deo placeant." In his *Commentary on Acts*, Selnecker distinguishes only two different donations of the Spirit, the first donation being identified with the previous donations one and two. *Selnecker* In acta apostolorum, 38–39: "Primum in genere donatur omnib. Piis, ut sanctificet & purificet corda nostra per fidem, & novos motus cordis

Justification and the subsequent renewal can still be discerned. In faith, the righteousness of Christ is apprehended and is performed through good works in sanctification.[119] Through the Gospel both the favor and the gift are received.[120] The favor is the entity that justifies, and the gift refers to the giving of the Spirit in senses two and three (*renovatio*$_2$).[121]

After all that has been said, it is obvious that Selnecker did not depict the role of Christ in a style similar to Mörlin, Chemnitz, and Chytraeus. The nature of *renovatio*$_1$ remains unclear, which appears as an obscurity on the detailed nature of union with Christ. Selnecker did not define salvation explicitly as union with the divine nature, but used more cautious language. The Holy Spirit creates a new being in faith where Christ is present, giving faith its justifying form.

6.4. *The Relation between Justification and Renewal in Theologies of Other Prominent 16th-century Theologians*

6.4.1. *Tilemann Hesshus*

Tilemann Hesshus's (1527–1588)[122] description of justification follows in some respect the trails of the later Melanchthon. Justification consists

---

per verbum vocale in nobis excitet, ut nova & spiritualis vita in nobis sit, qua Deum glorificemus, invocemus, petamus ab eo bona & c.... Deinde donatur Spiritus sanctus, ut addat nobis robur animi, & nos fortes, ac impauidos faciat in omnibus periculis, ne deficiamus ab evangelio, item, ut donet nobis dona spiritualia, prophetiam, genera & cognitionem linguarum, eruditionem, sapientiam & c. Ad hunc modum nonnullis, non omnibus datur, qui videlicet docere & gubernare debent Ecclesias, ut Apostolis, & piis quibusdam doctoribus."

[119] Selnecker, *Institutionis* II, 129: "Primo enim fides in Christo accipit, habet & possidet per imputationem, integerrimam & perfectissimam impletionem legis, ad iustitiam & salutem. Deinde Spiritus sanctus renovat corda credentium, accensa charitate, ut incipiat sacere legem. Posteà quicquid in inchoata illa obedientia imperfectum & propter carnem immundum est, credentibus propter Christum non imputatur, sed tegitur." See also *Selnecker* Institutionis II, 170.

[120] Selnecker, *Institutionis* II, 142.

[121] Selnecker, *Institutionis* II, 173: "Vivificatio aut renovatio non est causa ulla, vel totalis, vel partialis iustitiae iustificantis, sed est effectus, fructus, finis, seu consequens illius iustitiae, & simul est pars, initium, arrhabo, & primitiae futurae vitae, & est in hac vita semper imperfecta, & non est in omnibus aequalis, sed in alio illustrior & maior, in aliis minus conspicua. Dona enim non sunt aequalia. Gratia autem aequalis, eadem & una est, & continua in omnes et super omnes."

[122] Hesshus studied theology in Wittenberg, Oxford, and Paris. In Wittenberg, he was one of Melanchthon's favorite students. In 1559 he was expelled since he did

of the imputation of Christ's righteousness, forgiveness of sins and the giving of the Holy Spirit.[123] It involves a real change in the believer and is not simply an extrinsic event in God's mind. In conversion the believer is changed and renewed (*mutari & renovari*).[124] This is caused by faith which Hesshus describes as "burning movement in the intellect and will, which is evoked by the Spirit". The presence of God, which causes the transfer of Christ's merit to believers, "gives light to the hearts of the believers, righteousness, life and joy through the Holy Spirit".[125]

According to Hesshus, however, justification also consists of participation with Christ. Faith, evoked by the Spirit, apprehends Christ with all His benefits.[126] This apprehension is similar to the presence of a jewel in a ring; faith as a psychological state is of no value, what counts is the presence of Christ.[127] He makes believers share His perfect and

---

not want to subsribe to CA Variata. He worked as pastor and preacher until he was selected as professor in Jena in 1569, from where the Philippists drove him away because of his christology. After this he worked as professor in Helmstedt. Hesshus was, among others, a good friend of Chytraeus, Wigand, and Flacius. Peter Barton, "Hesshusius, Tilemann," in *TRE* XV (1986), pp. 256–259; Keller, "Der Beitrag von David Chytraeus," p. 118.

[123] Hesshus, *De iustificatione*, 17b: "Propter Filium Mediatorem crucifixum & resuscitatum, aeternus pater condonat nobis omnia peccata: recipit nos in gratiam: imputat nobis iustitiam, donat nobis Spiritum sanctum: constituit nos haeredes vitae aeternae: excudit nostras gemitus: & omnia generis beneficia in nos confert." See also Hesshus, *Examen*, 44[v].

[124] Hesshus, *De iustificatione Libri Sex*, 8: "Etsi autem non negamus hominem in conversione & iustificatione mutari & renovari: & novam iustitiam per Spiritum sanctum in ipso inchoari." See also Hesshus, *Examen*, 95–96. Peter Barton terms Hesshus's doctrine of justification "melanchthonian". See Barton, *Um Luthers Erbe. Studien und Texte zur Spätreformation. Tilemann Hesshusius* (1527–1559) (Witten: Luther-Verlag 1972), pp. 44–45. This may be true in a terminological sense, but Hesshus uses more Lutheran christology than Melanchthon to depict the actuality of justification.

[125] Hesshus, *Ad Colossenses*, 64–65: "Secundus modus est sanctificationis, quo non solum est praesens, sed etiam impertit fidelium cordibus lucem, iusticiam, vitam & laeticiam per Spiritum sanctum: de hoc modo loquitur Paulus 1. Cor. 3. An nescitis quod templum Dei sitis: & Spiritus sanctus habitet in vobis.... Non solum adest pijs ut eos sustentet: verum etiam impertit illis Deus spiritum, sanctificat & vivificat eos: communicat eis sua bona sapientiam, iusticiam, laeticiam, & renovat in eis imaginem suam, & facit illos participes divinae naturae." Here *modus* refers to modes of God's presence. The first mode is general omnipresence and sustentation.

[126] Hesshus, *De iustificatione*, B5, 5: "Fides non est tantum noticia Historiae de Iesu Christo, sed est ardens motus in mente & voluntate, accensus per Spiritus sanctus, promissione Evangelij, quo apprehendimus Christum cum omnibus beneficijs..."

[127] Hesshus, *Zehen Predigt*, Riib: "Pomeranus [Bugenhagen] hat hievon ein solch gleichnuss geben / Gleich wie ein Ring / darin ein Köstlicher Edler stein gefalt / hoch und theuer / etlich hundert Cronen werd mag geschetsst werden / so erdoch am Gold gering ist / Aber von wegen des Edlen steins / das Schmaragds und Rubins:

absolute blessings, first, through imputation and, second, by giving the believer His own righteousness and life.[128] Thus both pneumatological and christological terminology is united with the *renovatio$_1$* theme. New life and righteousness occur in participation with Christ through the Holy Spirit.

Hesshus wrote a fuller account of Christ's indwelling in his *Commentary on Galatians* (1569). The inhabitation of Christ is not only a general presence or sustentation. Through the Spirit Christ effectively sanctifies and vivifies believers; these effects are are known through the promise of the Gospel, and not accessible to the senses.[129] In faith, not only Christ but the Trinity itself, including the human nature of Christ, dwells in the believer—the whole person of Christ functions as a shield (*umbraculum*) against the wrath of God.[130] Regeneration means clothing oneself in Christ (*induitio Christi*). This takes place in two ways. First, the righteousness of Christ is given to the believer through imputation (*per imputationem*). Second, he or she is made effectively (*effective*) a sharer

---

Also wird der Glaube gerhümpt / unnd die gerechtigkeit uns seligkeit im zugerechnet / nicht seiner würdigkeit halben / sondern das er in sich / den Edlen bewerten Edelstein Jesum Christum / mit seinem ganzen reich uñ allen wolthaten fasset. Dann Christus Jesus ist unnd bleibt unsere gerechtigkeit / heiligung / weissheit und erlösung / bis an unsere ende." See also Hesshus, *Ad Galatas*, 153.

[128] Hesshus, *Ad Colossenses*, 75–76: "Perfectam & absolutam felicitatem non solum in se possidet Christus: sed eius nos quoque facit participes: ita ut in Christo omnia possideamus... Primum enim imputatione... Deinde spiritus suo sancto inchoat Christus in nobis suam iustitiam et vitam." Hesshus, *De duabus*, E1^v–E2: "Secundus modus praesentiae est Inhabitationis, & sanctificationis: sanctos enim in quibus habitat Deus, non solum sustentat: neque tantum eis adest sua substantia: verum etiam impertit eis suam gratiam: & coelestia bona per Christum partam: perfundit illos nova luce: accendit in illis vitam aeternam: exornat eos nova iusticia: & facit eos templa spiritus sancti, & participes divinae naturae." Sharing the divine nature does not abolish of humanity, since the believer and Christ maintain their own substances. See Hesshus, *De duabus*, E2^v; *Ad Galatas* 91^v: "Non enim mansit in morte, qui pro me crucifixus est, sed tertia die resurrexit à mortuis virtute patris. Et ego, qui credo in ipsum, cum ipso sum resuscitatus in fide per spiritum vivificantem, & iam habitat in me Christus."

[129] Hesshus, *Ad Galatas*, 94^v: "Etsi autem in hac infirmitate & caligine nostrae mentis, comprehendere non possumus, quomodo in nobis vivat: tamen & promissioni Christi adsentiendum, & uberrima consolatio utraque retinenda est.... Primo sciri oportet, Christum non loqui de universali praesentia Dei, qua caelum & terram implet, sed de speciali, qua sanctificat & vivificat corda per spiritum sanctum."

[130] Hesshus, *Ad Galatas*, 95: "... In Christo habitat Deus σωματικῶς, personaliter: at in sanctis per communicationem spiritus & vitae. Tertio non solum persona Christi sed tota divinitas simul, pater, filius & spiritus sanctus habitat in pectoribus piorum.... non est divellenda humanitas Christi ab ipsius divinitate, quando Christus in nobis habitare dicitur. Totus Christus Deus & homo est umbraculum nostrum, contra iram divinae maiestatis."

of Christ, which results in the indwelling of Christ and the inchoation of new life.[131] These take place simultaneously, with no indication of logical or temporal consequence.

> He that believeth on the Son, says John, hath everlasting life. John. 3. At the same time he is vivified and renewed; that is, faith cannot exist without the Holy Spirit enlightening the mind, bending the will and effecting assent. This truly new light and the assent of the will and belief in God are the life and salvation, effected by the Holy Spirit. Since justification does not take place before renewal (*renovatio*), and renewal does not take place before justification, they take place simultaneously through the Holy Spirit. Paul depicts the whole of Christ's merit with the single word: 'vivification' Eph. 2. However, both justification and renewal are simultaneous. When one receives the promise of the Gospel, the Holy Spirit simultaneously takes over the soul and regenerates the person and changes him into the image of God. However, these gifts must be separated: it is necessary to know on what grounds we are righteous in the sight of God and are received as heirs of eternal life. Without a doubt for the sake of the Mediator, who has shed his blood for us; not for the sake of new qualities, which the indwelling Spirit evokes in us.[132]

---

[131] Hesshus, *Ad Galatas*, 158–158[v]: "Quotquot in Christum baptizati estis, Christum induistis. Christum induere, hic Paulo est sanguine Christi à peccatis absolvi, eiusque merito à Deo recipi in gratiam, regenerari per spiritum sanctum in Dei filium, & arctissime cum Christo copulari; ita ut simus membra corporis eius de carne & ossibus eius: ita ut et ipse in nobis, & nos in ipso simus et vivamus, atq; omnium beneficiorum regni eius participes efficiamur. Totum enim Christii beneficium intelligit Paulus cum dicit: Christum induitis. Hinc vero manifestum est, nos duplici ratione induere Christum. Primum per imputationem, cum nobis aeternus pater Christi passionem, mortem, obedientiam & universum iustitiam imputat per fidem, & propter eam nos pronunciat iustos & vitae aeternae haeredes.... Secundo effective induimus Christum: cum videlicet Christus nos in fide suo spiritu vivificat, facit nos membra corporis sui, habitat & vivit in nobis, impertit nobis lucem, iustiticiam & vitam." This distinction resembles Luther's distinction in antinomian disputations. See section 2.1.3.

[132] Hesshus, *Examen* 1587, 216–217: "Qui credit in Filium, inquit Johannes, habet vitam aeternam. Ioh. 3. Simul etiam vivificatur, & renovatur: fides enim existere non potest, nisi mens illuminetur Spiritu sancto: & voluntas trahatur, & permoveatur ad adsentiendum. Haec vero nova lux, & voluntatis adsensus, & in Deum fides est vita & salus, quam ipse Spiritus sanctus operatur. Non ergo antecedit iustificatio renovationem: neque renovatio iustificationem: sed simul fiunt per Spiritum sanctum. Ideoque Paulus totum Christi beneficium una voce vivificationis complectitur. Ephes. 2.... Etsi autem simul existant & fiant cum iustificatio, tum renovatio. Quando enim homo adsentitur promissioni Evangelij, tum Spiritus sanctus occupat animum & regenerat hominem, atque transformat eum in imaginem Dei: tamen distinguenda sunt haec beneficia: sciri enim necesse est, propter quam rem placeamus Deo Deo, & haeredes constituamur vitae aeternae: nimirum propter Mediatorem qui sanguinem suum pro nobis effundit, non propter novas illas qualitates, quas Spiritus sanctus in nostris habitans pectoribus accendit." Hägglund ("Rechtfertigung," p. 336) correctly claims that here Hesshus manages to bind justification and renewal together coherently.

Hesshus depicts the status of Christ as the form of the believer, and formulates the change of the believer into the likeness of Christ from the perspective of of the Flacian controversy. Flacius had contended that a human being in the state of sin is the image of Satan. In this case, the individual is depraved spiritually, i.e., according to one's formal substance, although the material does not undergo a change. The idea of change in human substance in the Fall and in faith makes Hesshus hesitate, claiming that Christ's role as the form of an individual is not to be understood literally since this would mean the destruction of genuine personhood. Instead, it is possible to say that faith that apprehends Christ is the form of the person—a likeness of Christ—which results in new movements in mind and especially in trust (*fiducia*).[133] The formal cause of righteousness of faith (*causa formalis iustitiae*) is forgiveness of sin and the imputation of Christ's righteousness.[134] This is followed by the effects of the Spirit in the believer (*renovatio*$_2$), which do not belong to justification.[135]

6.4.2. *Johannes Wigand*

Another second-generation reformer of great influence was Johannes Wigand (1523–1587).[136] His significance is based on his rich literary

---

[133] Hesshus, *Ad Galatas*, 190^v: "Lutherus, sanctae memoriae, non dubitavit adserere, hominis christiani formam esse fidem, quo apprehendimus Christum, & novos motus, quia spiritu sancto accenduntur. Cor fiducia praeditum, inquit Lutherus, habet veram formam Christi." *Hesshus* Ad Galatas, 189^v: "Formatur autem in pijs Christus, quando per verbum & spiritum sanctum vera Dei agnitio, sincera fides, dilectio dei, & spirituales motus in ipsis accenduntur.... De hac spirituali regeneratione & formatione, loquitur in multis locis spiritus sanctus Psal. 51. Cor mundum crea in me Deus, & spiritum rectum innova in visceribus meis."

[134] Hesshus, *De iustificatione Libri Sex*, 18b: "Causa formalis nostrae iustitia est ipsa gratuita remissio peccatorum, seu reconciliatio cum Deo, & imputatio iustitiae Mediatoris, qua ipse Deus nos peccatores absoluit, & iustos pronunciat." Hesshus thus opposes the Roman Catholic view that theological virtues such as love and hope are part of the justifying righteousness. Hesshus, *De iustificatione*, 18b: "...sed potius iustitiam inhaerentem & charitatem una cum fide & spe infusam: & ipsam sanctificationem & renovationem interioris hominis esse formalem causam nostrae iustificationis..." See also Hesshus, *Ad Romanos*, 89–90; *Ad Galatas* 70^v. Hesshus (*Ad Galatas*, 15) criticizes Augustine for not distinguishing between the forgiveness of sins and the following renewal.

[135] Hesshus, *De iustificatione*, D2: "Verum donatio & inhabitatio Spiritus sanctus, renovatio, vivificatio & sanctificatio, nec sunt ipsa iustificatio, nec sunt pars eius: sed fructus sequentis eam."

[136] Wigand studied in Wittenberg under Luther, and identified himself with the Gnesiolutheran party. In 1560 he moved to Jena, where his friend Flacius worked as superintendent. Later, Wigand started to castigate Flacius for his views on original sin.

output. *Syntagma* (kr. Σύνταγμα) is his most famous work,, which he wrote with Mattheus Judex. It was the first book that followed Melanchthon's *loci* method.[137]

Wigand also wrote a considerable number of treatises on contemporary theological controversies. These works usually begin with a brief summary of the teaching opposed, described with quotations from the heretic's own books. Argument is analyzed using syllogisms that demonstrate the inconsistencies in the thinking of a given theologian. Wigund treated Osiander in this fashion in his *De Osiandrismo*, a work which illuminates Wigand's own thinking on justification even more than his *Syntagma*.

De Osiandrismo is a good example of how Osiander's teaching actually affected the thinking of other Lutherans. In this text it is evident Wigand had difficulty in speaking about God's essential righteousness in the context of justification. Wigand denies that God's essential righteousness is justifying, a point based on the argument of Mörlin. Also following Mörlin, he emphasized Christ's work and obedience as the essence of righteousness.[138] Christ's ascension (*vadere ad Patrem*, John 16:10) as formal righteousness is a characteristic emphasis.[139] This is to be understood as a polemical answer to Osiander, who claimed that no work of Christ could function as a justifying entity. However, Mörlin taught that God can be said to be the formal cause of justification since through *communicatio idiomatum* God's essential righteousness shares in Christ's work. Wigand denies this. The essential righteousness is surely *causa efficiens*, but in no case *causa formalis*, which Wigand understands to be the application of Christ's fulfilling of the Law for the sinner.[140]

His polemical nature made him manage to break the relations with Hesshus, Chemnitz, Selnecker, and Andreae as well. See Ronald Diener, "Johann Wigand", in *Shapers of Religious Traditions in Germany, Switzerland and Poland* 1560–1600, ed. Jill Rait (New Haven and London: Yale University Press 1981).

[137] Syntagma is an analysis of biblical concepts, employing the *loci* method; every locus is discussed with quotes from the Bible and short conclusing sections. While the book is lengthy, it contain very few thoughts from Wigand himself. On the nature of *Syntagma*, see Robert Preus, *The Theology of Post-Reformation Lutheranism*, Vol. I., A Study of Theological Prolegomena (St. Louis: Concordia Publishing House 1970), pp. 88–90.

[138] Wigand, *De Osiandrismo*, 36–37.

[139] Wigand, *De Osiandrismo*, 43–44, 47, 66.

[140] Wigand, *De Osiandrismo*, 37–38, 64, 87: "Deus est causa efficiens nostrae iusticiae. Sed res ipsa nostrae iusticiae est impletio legis per Christum nostra vice praestita. Forma iusticiae nostrae, est imputatio legis per Christum factae, quam fide accipimus" Wigand's *Commentary on Ephesians* considers salvation or application as the form of justification.

Wigand's terminology raises suspicions about whether he speaks of justification as connected to Christ's work to the exclusion of the person of Christ. In time the content and language started to diverge from Luther.[141] If Christ's essential righteousness is not the formal cause of justification, the interconnectedness of the individual and work is more difficult to maintain, even as Wigand tried to preserve this connection by identifying Christ's work with His human nature. When mentioned, Christ's work refers to His salvific work both as God and human.[142] The apprehension of Christ in faith includes God's essential inhabitation in the believer. Wigand examined this more deeply in his *De Ubiquitate* (1588). God's indwelling (*inhabitatio*) is, Wigand says, God's special action, through which He is essentially (*essentialiter*) present in believers, giving His gifts, vivifying, and saving them (*eos suis donis replens, vivificans & salvans*).[143] The communion with Christ, which means communion with the Triune God,[144] is an inhabitation differentiating believers from unbelievers. The believer is then the *materia in qua* of inhabitation, while God is its *forma*.[145] This union results in sharing God's gifts, which

See Wigand, *Ad Ephesios*, 68. Wigand, *Syntagma*, 831: "Causam formalem iustificationis, docent esse ipsam applicationem gratuitae iusticiae Christi & meriti eius per fidem."

[141] Wigand's soteriology does not build as strongly upon patristic theology as Chemnitz's and Chytraeus's. For example, Wigand's *Commentary on Colossians* (2:10–19) does not employ incarnation (as against Chemnitz). The soteriological meaning of the passage is passed over. See Wigand, *Ad Colossenses*, 115–177. Nüssel (*Allein aus Glauben*, p. 180) has also referred to the tenuous nature of Wigand's christology, although his later works came close to the theology of Tübingen according to which the relation between christology and soteriology was more profound. See also Baur, *Luther und seine klassichen Erben*, pp. 172, 224.

[142] On this, see the section entitled Wigand, *De Osiandrismo*, 48–50: "Paulus personam nominat, nempè Christum, eamque; dicit nobis factam esse iusticiam. Sed persona Christi non est tantum divina, sed etiam huma natura.... Humanam verò, tantum esse instrumentum quasi per quod consequamur iusticiam.... Ideò praedicatum, iusticia nostra, ad utramq; naturam Christi pertinet."

[143] Wigand, *De Ubiquitate*, D1v: "Inhabitatio Dei in renatis, est gratiosa Dei actio, qua Deus essentialiter inhabitat in renatos, seu timente Deum in sua Ecclesia, eos suis donis replens, vivificans, & salvans."

[144] Wigand, *Syntagma*, 219: "Fide autem Christum sibi applicit: id quod sua petitione non obscure significat." Wigand, *Syntagma*, 571: "Iesus Christus vivit in renatis. Gal. 3. Per fidem inhabitat in cordibus nostris." Wigand, *Syntagma*, 817: "Iustitiam autem hác sanquine Christi partam distribuere, communicare, & applicare Patrem, Filium, & Spiritum sanctum, testantur primùm generalibus testimonijs de Deo, qua uoce omnes tres personas complectuntur. 1. Pet. 3." Wigand, Frid & Kircner, *Bekentnis*, B4v: "Sondern der Glaube ist nur des instrument / und unser Bettelhand / damit wir Christi verdienst und wohlthaten ergreiffen und annemen sollen."

[145] Wigand, *De Ubiquitate*, D2.

includes faith.[146] However, this does not indicate that God's essential righteousness justifies, since the justifying entity is only Christ's work.[147] The essential righteousness of God cannot be given to a believer. As such, God's essence is *incommunicabilis* and destructive.[148]

Apprehension of Christ means non-imputation of sins and sharing in Christ's righteousness, which is accompanied by the renewing donation of the Holy Spirit.[149] However, this does not indicate that the Spirit is not already present since the birth of justifying faith is the work of the Spirit.[150] Although the precise nature of participation with Christ remains unclear, the salvation event as such is effective. While the effective renewal is demarcated from justification so that the only justifying entity is Christ's work, the justified person has been transformed into "a good tree, which bears good fruit."[151] Wigand distinguished between justification and good works;[152] good deeds flow from a Triune God,

---

[146] Wigand, *De Ubiquitate*, D3: "Adauctio donorum Dei in renatis, istam tam gratiosam Dei in credentibus inhabitationem, comitatur. Nam Deus non ociosè habitat in eis, sed timorem Dei & fidem auget, & sanctos motus accendit. Sic Paulus ait: Accepistis Spiritum adoptionis filiorum Dei, in quo clamamus Abba Pater. Roma. 8. Docet enim, Spiritum sanctum in nobis habitantem noticiam veri Dei, fidem, invocationem accendere, ac noc certos facere, de benigna Dei erga nos voluntate, & ex audititione."

[147] Wigand, *De Osiandrismo*, 66: "Fides enim complectitur Christum cum suis beneficiis. Qui igitur fide iustus est, habet & Christum ipsum in se habitantem, licet iusticia per fidem imputata, non ipsamet ESSENTIA, seu natura DIVINA Christi, sed opus Christi, hoc est, impletio legis integerrima & absolutissima..." Wigand, *De Osiandrismo*, 43: "Nulla prorsus est connexio. Est´q; noster Deus, & habitat in nobis, licet eius essentia non sit nostra iusticia, qua peccator coram Deo consistit."

[148] Wigand, *De Osiandrismo*, 58.

[149] Wigand, *Syntagma*, 833: "Deinde, quòd sit imputativa iusticia, scilicet cùm non imputantur nobis peccata nostra, sed imputatur nobis aliena iusticia, nempe Domini nostri Iesu Chrisri per fidem, & propter eam absoluimur à iure peccati & mortis, ac donatur Spiritus sanctus & vita aeterna." See also Wigand, *Syntagma*, 729, 809.

[150] Wigand, *Syntagma*, 819: "De Spiritu sancto, quòd is quoque distribuat & communicat nobis iustitiam Christi." Wigand, *Syntagma*, 567: "Operatur [Spiritus Sanctus] veram fidem, & in ea corroborat & confirmat pios. Act. 15. Dans illis Spiritum sanctum, sicut & nobis: nihilique discrevit inter nos & illos, cùm fide purificaverit corda illorum... Iustificat. 1. Corinth. 6. Sed iustificati estis per nomen Domini Iesu, & per Spiritum Dei nostri. Inhabitat in regeneratis."

[151] Wigand, Frid & Kircner, *Bekentnis*, B4^{v}: "Aus solcher zugerechten / geschenkten / des Glaubens an Christum Gerechtigkeit / haben wir friede mit Gott / freude des Gewissens / sind wonungen Gottes / können zu Gott tretten uns sind gewertig ewiges lebens / freude und herrligkeit. Rom. 5. Wo nun wir also für Gott / durch den Glauben an Christum gerecht / und an guter baum worden / da sollen folgen / und folgen auch gute früchte..."

[152] Wigand, Frid & Kircner, *Bekentnis*, E2: "Der mann Gottes D. Luther / wie gar trewlich leret er uns in der Epistel an die Galater / Man sol vleifsig unterscheiden den

who renews the mind and governs the deeds of a person, directing him or her towards good through faith.[153]

The new life is contrived by the Spirit, who takes control of a person's powers of the soul which enables the application of Christ's work. God dwells in believer in this faith, but such indwelling does not justify. Thus, Wigand identified closely with Flacius, who denied participation as the cause of justification, but kept a certain distance from his teaching.

6.4.3. *Jacob Heerbrand*

Jacob Heerbrand (1521–1600) has been termed as one of the founders of Lutheran orthodoxy.[154] His most important work is *Compendium Theologiae, quaestionibus methodi tractatum*, which was first published in 1573. Heerbrand published the revised edition of the book only a year after the completion of FC (1578), in which the loci on justification and faith were interpolated. The revised edition added a paragraph concerning living faith (*fides viva*) to the locus *De Fide*. Faith is made alive by Christ, who Himself is the life.[155] Heerbrand also uses the ring trope: faith is

---

Artickel von der Rechtfertigung und der guten Wercken. Item man sol die guten werck in Artickel der Rechtfertigung nicht ziehen / nicht mengen / sondern abschneiden."

[153] Wigand, *Syntagma*, 904: "Causa bonorum operum, quae à iustificatis fiunt, secundum legem Dei, docent esse Deum patrem, filiù, & Spiritum sanctum, qui per fidem, mentem & voluntatem hominis regeneratam, inspiret, ducat, & regat, ut non secundum carné, seu secundum spiritum, quátum in hac imbecillitate fieri potest, ambulet." See also Wigand, *Syntagma*, 910.

[154] Sigfried Raeder, "Heerbrand, Jacob," in *TRE* XIV (1985), 524. Heerbrand studied in Wittenberg under both Luther and Melanchthon. He then worked as professor in Tübingen. Heerbrand's most important work, *Compendium Theologiae*, which was a product of the discussion between the theologians of Tübingen and the patriarchate of Konstantinopol, was published in 1582 in a two-language edition (Greek-Latin). Robert Preus, *Theology*, pp. 47.

[155] Heerbrand, *Compendium* 1578, 408: "Fides viva est, quae Christum, qui est vita, & in se credentes vivificat, vere apprehendit." *Disputationes Theologiae* (1575) also employs the concept of living faith defining it as apprehension of Christ. See Heerbrand, *Disputationes*, 143, 162. Heerbrand does not distinguish between the apprehension of Christ and Christ's merit. Both are used in Heerbrand, *Compendium* 1578, 435–436. Nüssel (*Allein aus Glauben*, pp. 198–200) does not notice the changes in the revised edition. She claims, however, that the earlier edition reflects the view that faith has the nature of formal righteousness, in spite of Melanchthonian and Flacian terminology. Nüssel, *Allein aus Glauben*, p. 200: "...der Glaube an Christus die Realiserungsgestalt der Rechtfertigung ist und insofern durchhaus als diejenige Veränderung des Menschlichen Seins zu gelten hat, vermittels derer aus einem Ungerechten ein Gerechter wird." Nüssel (*Allein aus Glauben*, pp. 207–209) also mentions that *communicatio idiomatum* has a greater role in the revised edition.

the ring that contains the jewel, Christ, who makes it precious.[156] If, however, faith does not apprehend Christ, it is dead (*mortua*).[157] The form of faith is Christ, not love. Love does not, Heerbrand maintains, give form to faith, while faith gives form to love.

> What is the form of faith? It is not love, for love does not give form to faith, while faith gives form to love. If faith is not present, love is not real but pretense. Love is an effect, not the form of the faith. We know that love works through faith. Reversing this equates to saying that the consequence forms the cause. Or if someone would say that fruits produce a good and fruitful tree. But when He, who before all human children is beautiful [Christ], is apprehended through faith, then faith is sufficiently formed and beautiful, because it apprehends Christ, who is alive and makes alive the one who is in faith Christ's own, and from whom faith is and becomes alive—unless someone dare to call Christ dead and not alive! For this cause the righteous person lives through his faith. But such a faith is dead, which does not have the living Christ and life. For through love faith is active. For Christ the Savior with His righteousness is the form of faith, and Christian Faith does not exist without this.[158]

Faith is followed by justification and new affects, such as peace in conscience, certainty and purity of mind. Other consequences include inhabitation of the Holy Spirit, love of God and neighbor, and witness of faith.[159] Because Christ is Life through faith, He necessarily makes the believer alive. *Renovatio$_I$* is, therefore, participation with Christ's

---

[156] Heerbrand, *Compendium* 1578, 436. Same also Heerbrand, *De Gratia*, 15: "...non iustificamur illa, quatenus est qualitas in nobis...sed quatenus Christum, qui à Deo factus est nobis iustitia, sanctificatio, & redemptio, apprehendit, eiusque merita sibi applicat."

[157] Heerbrand, *Compendium* 1578, 410: "Quid est Fides mortua? Quae Christum, qui vita est, non apprehendit."

[158] Heerbrand, *Compendium* 1578, 414: "Quae est forma Fidei? Non est charitas. Quia charitas non informat fidem: sed contrà, fides informat charitatem. Nisi enim fides adsit, charitas vera non est, sed fucata. Et charitas effectus est, non forma fidei. Scimus, Fidem per charitatem operari, sed informari illam per hanc, dicere, idem est, ac si quis causam per effectum informari dicat. Ut si quis dicat, fructus facere arborem bonam & frugiferam. Sed cúm Fide apprehensus est ille formosus prae filiis hominum, satis formata & formosa est Fides, habens Christum, qui vivus est & vivificans eum, qui ex fide est Iesu Christi, à quo fides est & fit viva. Nisi Christum dicere quis ausit, non vivum, sed mortuum. Hinc iustus fide sua vivit. Mortua autem dicitur fides, quae Christum vivum & vitam non habet. Charitas enim est, per quam fides operatur. Sed Christus salvator, cum sua iustitia, forma est fidei, sine quo Fides Christiana non est."

[159] Heerbrand, *Compendium* 1578, 420: "Qui sunt effectus Fidei? Iustificatio...Pax & tranquillitas conscientiae...Certitudo...Puritas mentis...Inhabitatio Spiritus sanctis in nobis...Charitas erga Deum & proximum...Confessio."

vivifying person. Through this presence Christ brings forth the consequent good works. The believer is now a good tree, which bears good fruits.[160]

Heerbrand defined *causa formalis iustificationis* as forgiveness of sin, which is identified with imputation of Christ's righteousness.[161] Regeneration (*regeneratio*), renewal (*renovatio*), and sanctification (*sanctificatio*), logically distinguishable yet simultaneous events, do not belong to justification even as they are consequences of justification.[162] As a result, favor and gift, and donation of the Holy Spirit are consequent events. In this sense gift and renewal are understood as *renovatio*$_2$.[163] Faith and love are united by an inextricable tie; they cannot be considered equal reason for justification.[164]

[160] Heerbrand, *Compendium* 1578, 408: "Fides viva est, quae Christum, qui est vita, & in se credentes vivificat, vere apprehendit. ... Vera ergò in Christum Fides, numquam est mortua, sed semper viva: non ratione quidem operum, quibus non vivificatur. Hoc enim contra naturarum est. Quia opera non causa, sed effectus sunt Fidei. Et per inde est, dicere: Fidem operibus vivificari, ac si quis affirmaret: fructus arborem facere bonam, cuius contrarium verum est. Quod ipsum quoque Christus docet: Aut, inquit eis, facite arborem bonam, & fructus eius bonos: Aut arborem malam, & fructus eius malos. Sed ratione Christi, qui est vita. Ideoque vera Fides mortua nunquam dici aut esse potest, nisi Christum, quem vera fides cõplectitur, mortuum quis dicere ausit."

[161] Heerbrand, *Compendium* 1573, 212: "Quae est causa formalis Iustificationis? Est remission peccatorum, aut quod idem est, sola imputatio iustitiae Christi, qui factus est nobis à Deo Patre iustitia, sanctificatio & redemptio. Et ut Propheta dociut, vacabunt eum, DOMINUS IUSTITIA NOSTRA."

[162] Heerbrand, *Compendium* 1578, 430: "In qua re consistit Iustificatio, quae est coram Deo? Remissione peccatorum: & imputatione iustitia Christi. Nam regeneratio, vel renovatio, aut sanctificatio, effectus sunt iustificationis, non partes. Etsi enim haec tempore simul fiant, tamen non sunt confundenda, & ordine prior est iustificatio."

[163] Heerbrand, *Compendium* 1578, 398: "Quid est Gratia? Est gratuita acceptatio, qua Deus per & propter Christum recipit agentem poenitentiam, & credentem, gratis: & remissis peccatis imputat ei obedientiam & iustitiam ipsius: ac donat Spiritum sanctum, inchoantem novam obedientiam, ac vitam aeternam. Quomodo differunt Gratia & Donum? Ut causa & effectus. Gratia significat remissionem peccatorum, seu reconciliationem & acceptationem apud Deum gratuitam: Donum autem effectus est gratiae, donationem Spiritus sancti, ac donorum ipsius."

[164] Heerbrand, *Disputationes*, 162: "Etsi enim nexu indissolubili semper coniuncta sint Fides & Charitas, non simul tamen iustificant, nec simul, vel coniuncta utraque nostra sunt iustitia, vel iustificationis causa, sed fallacia est, secundum non causam ut causam."

6.5. *Conclusion*

The theologians examined in this chapter were all Melanchthon's students, the only exception was Andreae, who was affiliated with Brenz. While Melanchthon's influence is apparent in the texts examined, these theologians nevertheless made independent and personal decisions in relation to their common teacher and to one another. The group was not homogenous. What they had in common was the basic structure of justification. This becomes apparent in the use of exclusive particles that denied the meritorious nature of good works. Justification is defined extrinsically but is also related to the intrinsic and renewing gift of the Spirit. Renewal is simultaneous with the forgiveness of sin. Therefore, one who has been justified has also been made 'a good tree'. In addition, all agree with that good works (*renovatio*$_2$) do not justify. *Renovatio*$_2$ renewal is understood generally as the work of the Holy Spirit, which renews the capacities of the soul. However, the *renovatio*$_1$ aspect is interpreted differently. At least for Chytraeus, Selnecker, Hesshus, and Heerbrand renewal occurs in participation with Christ, and renewal is not a new disposition of the powers of the soul, as it was for Melanchthon. Luther's influence is apparent in the widely-accepted (Chytraeus, Selnecker, Hesshus, Heerbrand) *Christus forma fidei* theme. It is thus easy to discern the material and formal aspects of faith. Faith consists of the renewal of the tainted substance of the individual, and the birth of faith in the joint action of intellect and will. This is only the material renewal. The formal renewal, Christ as the form of faith, counts for justification—the new life of faith in the believer is Christ's own life. Since the christological terminology does not, however, enable thorough analysis of renewal in the sense of *renovatio*$_1$, the relation between renewal and justification remains ambiguous. In particular, Andreae's and Wigand's writings on the theme are minimal and obscure.

The similarity with Osiander causes problems with concepts like 'Christ's essential righteousness' or 'God's indwelling'. The reverse order of salvation is impossible since, after Osiander, inhabitation was identified with *renovatio*$_2$. Thus, Lutherans had to invent other ways to speak about the renewing nature of justification. It is plain at any rate that 16th-century Lutheran theology did not employ a purely forensic doctrine of justification, except for Flacius. The majority of the second-generation Lutherans identifed more closely with Luther's thinking, and used such things as the metaphor of the ring and the jewel. This is not just mere repetition, for they employed new concepts such as *entelekheia* to demonstrate Christ's presence in faith. For this reason, christology is not reduced to a mere acquisition of legal merit since Christ's being is the being of the believer, which forms the cause of justification. Still, it must be noted that the second-generation Lutherans did not define one comprehensive system for how God's presence and justification should be understood, and the case remains open.

CHAPTER SEVEN

THE DOCTRINE OF JUSTIFICATION IN THE FORMULA OF CONCORD

The formulators of FC used participatory christological notions in their own writings. What about the document they formulated? In order to examine the nature of justification in FC, we must analyze its christological presuppositions about justification. Chemnitz's tripartite formulation, previously mentioned, is an important hermeneutic tool which characterizes the form of justification.

> The only essential and necessary elements of justification are the *grace of God, the merit of Christ, and the faith that receives this grace and merit in the gospel's promise*, through which Christ's righteousness is reckoned to us.[1]

The tripartite distinction *fundamentum—relatio—terminus* offers a means of analyzing justification in more detail. The analysis of the christology of FC (*fundamentum*) and the notion of faith (*terminus*) demonstrate what kind of relation (*relatio*) takes place in justification. First, we turn to christology.

7.1. *The Interconnectedness of the Person and the Work of Christ*

A central problem in FC is the relation between Christ's person and His work. It may seem that participation in the person of Christ is the consequence of imputation. Hence, the righteousness of faith is not the actual and essential righteousness of God, but the merit of Christ separated from His person. This interpretation is usually offered on the basis of the passages that emphasize the imputation of the righteousness of Christ. Strong forensic language is heavily present in FC, in which justification is depicted in external terms.

> We believe...that poor sinful people are justified before God, that is, absolved—pronounced free of all sins and of the judgment of the

---

[1] *BSELK SD* III, 25.

> damnation that they deserved and accepted as children and heirs of eternal life—without the least bit of our own "merit or worthiness", apart from all preceding, present, or subsequent works. We are justified on the basis of sheer grace, because of the sole merit, the entire obedience, and the bitter suffering, death, and the resurrection of our Lord Christ alone, whose obedience is reckoned to us as righteousness.[2]

In addition, the indwelling of God is defined as the consequence of the righteousness of faith.

> To be sure, God the Father, Son, and Holy Spirit, who is the eternal and essential righteousness, dwells through faith in the elect, who have become righteous through Christ and reconciled with God. For all Christians are temples of God the Father, Son, and the Holy Spirit, who moves them to act properly. However, this indwelling of God is not the righteousness of faith, which Paul treats (Rom. 1:17; 3:5, 22, 25; 2. Cor. 5:21) and calls *iustitia Dei* (that is, the righteousness of God), for the sake of which we are pronounced righteous before God. Rather, this indwelling is a result of the righteousness of faith that precedes it, and this righteousness (of faith) is nothing else than the forgiveness of sins and the acceptance of poor sinners by grace, only because of Christ's obedience and merit.[3]

The essence of the righteousness of faith is the obedience of Christ, which is sharply distinguished from the indwelling of God. In keeping with these passages, the following logical order of salvation is discernible: faith—the imputation of Christ's righteousness—the indwelling of God. FC does not, however, consider Christ's merit as separate from

---

[2] *BSELK SD* III, 9: "...dass ein armer sündiger Mensch für Gott gerechtfertigt, das ist, absolviert, los und ledig gesprochen werde von allen seinen Sünden und von dem Urtel der wohlverdienten Verdamnus, auch angenommen werde zur Kindschaft und Erbschaft des ewigen Lebens ohne einig unser 'Verdienst oder Wirdigkeit', auch ohne alle vorgehende gegenwärtige, oder auch folgende Werk, aus lauter Gnaden, allein umb des einigen Verdiensts, des ganzen Gehorsams, bittern Leidens, Sterbens und Auferstehungs unsers Herrn christi willen, des Gehorsam uns zur Gerechtigkeit zugerechnet wird."

[3] *BSELK SD* III, 54: "Gleichfalls muss auch die Disputation von der Einwohnung der wesentlichen Gerechtigkeit Gottes in uns recht erkläret werden. Dann obwohl durch den Glauben in den Auserwählten, so durch Christum gerecht worden und mit Gott versöhnet sind, Gott Vater, Sohn und Heiliger Geist, der die ewige und wesentliche Gerechtigkeit ist, wohnet (dann alle Christen sind Tempel Gottes des Vaters, Sohns und Heiligen Geistes, welcher sie auch treibet, recht zu tuen): so ist doch solche Einwohnung Gottes nicht die Gerechtigkeit des Glaubens, davon S. Paulus handlet und sie iustitiam Dei, das ist, die Gerechtigkeit Gottes, nennet, umb welcher willen wir für Gott gerecht gesprochen werden, sondern sie folget auf die vorgehende Gerechtigkeit des Glaubens, welche anders nichts ist, dann die Vergebung der Sünden und gnädige Annehmung der armen Sünder allein umb Christus Gehorsam und Vordiensts willen."

His person. It must be noted that this kind of teaching was virtually non-existent in 16th-century Lutheranism, apart from Osiander and Flacius. The separation of the person and the work requires christological formulations, which was abandoned by all the Gnesiolutherans through their actual interpretation of *communicatio idiomatum*. But how does FC describe the relation between soteriology and christology? The person and work of Christ are described as follows.

> ...our righteousness does not rest upon one nature of Christ or the other but rather upon his *entire person*, who, as God and human being, in his full and complete obedience alone, is our righteousness...Accordingly, we believe, teach, and confess that *the entire obedience of the entire person of Christ*, which he rendered to the Father on our behalf unto the most shameful death on the cross, is reckoned to us as righteousness....For this reason, neither the divine nor the human nature of Christ in itself is reckoned to us as righteousness, but only *the obedience of the person*, who is at the same time God and a human being. Therefore, faith looks to the person of Christ, as this person submitted to the law for us, bore our sin, and in going to his Father performed complete and perfect obedience for us poor sinners, from his holy birth to his death. (emphasis mine)[4]

FC condemns the heresies of both Osiander and Stancarus, which regard only one nature of Christ as righteousness. Their heresies articulated the separation of the work and person *par excellence*. Against such teachings FC emphasizes how the work of the whole person is the righteousness of the sinner, and that faith looks to the person of Christ, who redeems the world from sin.

The person of Christ was emphasized for the following reasons. First, according to the theory of *satisfactio vicaria*, the Mediator must be both true God and true man to suffer and die, and thus appease the wrath of the righteous Father and bring reconciliation. Second, according to the

---

[4] *BSELK SD* III, 55–58: "...das unser Gerechtigkeit nicht auf die eine oder die ander Natur, sondern auf die ganze Person Christi gesetzt, wölcher als Gott und Mensch in seinem einigen, ganzen, vollkummnen Gehorsam unser Gerechtigkeit ist....Weil aber (wie oben vermeldet) der Gehorsamb der ganzen Person ist, so ist er eine vollkommene Genugtueung und Versöhnung des menschlichen Geschlechts...Solchergestalt wird uns weder die Göttliche noch die menscliche Natur Christi für sich selbst zur Gerechtigkeit zugerechnet, sondern allein der Gehorsamb der Person, welche zumal Gott und Mensche, und siehet also der Glaube auf die Person Christi, wie dieselbe für uns unter das Gesetze getan, unser Sünde getragen und in seinem Gang zum Vater den ganzen vollnkommen Gehorsam von seiner heiligen Geburt an bis in den Tod seinem himmlischen Vater für uns arme Sünder geleistet..."

FC's *locus* on Christ, everything Christ did for the sinful world, He did as one undivided person (according to *genus apotelesmaticum*). Following the rules of *communicatio idiomatum*, the saving work of Christ cannot be the work of only one nature since redemption is the work of the whole person. Thus, FC sets out to safeguard both the reality of salvation and the doctrine of two natures and the actuality of *communication idiomatum*.[5] FC does not support separation of the work / obedience and the person; it refers to *the obedience of the person*, two aspects of Christ that are closely intertwined.[6] If the work of Christ belongs to His person, the next question will be whether it is possible to apply this work or merit without the presence of the person, as Flacius thought. Flacian influences are apparent in FC, especially in the passages quoted. Is the righteousness that is actualized in faith something other than the essential righteousness of God?

In FC the indwelling of God is connected with good works. This is illustrated by a quotation from Osiander: "who moves them to act properly."[7] "The indwelling of God" refers to its effects, which narrows the meaning and overall use of the concept. In other words, the question of God's indwelling as such is not given its due, since the observation is focused on the Osiandrian heresy; God's indwelling is examined only within the context of *renovatio*$_2$. FC makes it very clear that "*this* indwelling of God, *which moves people to act properly*", is not the righteousness of faith, and there is nothing suspicious about this distinction. Nevertheless, this passage does not respond to the issue of the relation between justification and righteousness as an essential attribute of God.[8]

In addition, FC III contains christological passage that is cryptic and seldom, if ever, quoted or analyzed.

> For if Christ had been conceived without sin by the Holy Spirit and had been born and had fulfilled all righteousness in his human nature alone but had not been true eternal God, this obedience and suffering of the human nature would not be reckoned to us as righteousness. In the same

---

[5] Friedrich Jacob, "Von Christi Tat und unserem Tun. Zur Interpretation von Artikel III und IV der Konkordienformel," in *Bekenntnis zur Wahrheit. Aufsätze über die Konkordienformel*, hrsgb. Jobst Schöne (Erlangen: Martin Luther-Verlag 1978), 54.

[6] See also Martens, *Die Rechtfertigung*, pp. 92, 95–9.

[7] On the Holy Spirit as the source of sanctification, see *BSELK SD* IV, 12; VI, 6.

[8] Since the passage is targeted against Osiander, it must be interpreted as condemnation of the alleged Osiandrian heresies, particularly of undermining atonement and confusing justification with its effects.

> way, if the Son of God had not become a human being, the divine nature in itself could not have been our righteousness.[9]

First, this passage states that the application of Christ's merit is dependent on His *divine* nature. Why? In Chemnitz's christology it is first and foremost *human* nature that enables application. This passage, however, focuses rather on how human nature can become applicable, i.e., omnipresent.[10] Additionally, FC states that mere divine nature cannot function as the righteousness of the sinner. God must assume humanity through the incarnation to establish a consubstantial connection between Christ and a human individual.

It is clear that FC III engages christological themes only from a particular perspective. Generally, FC uses christology principally in its eucharistic theology, and in FC III christology remains in the background.[11] Christological themes provide coherence for the theory of *satisfactio vicaria*.[12] For some reason the formulators of FC add the passage quoted which, despite its conciseness, broadens the use of christology within soteriology. At least, it permits and warrants understanding of justification within a more christologically profound context.

---

[9] *BSELK SD* III, 56: "Dann da Christus gleich vom Heiligen Geist ohne Sünde empfangen und geborn und in menschlicher Natur allein alle Gerechtigkeit erfüllet hätte und aber nicht wahrer ewiger Gott gewesen, möchte uns solche, der menschlichen Natur, Gehorsamb und Leiden auch nicht zur Gerechtigkeit gerechnet werden; wie dann auch, da der Sohne Gottes nicht Mensch worden, die blose göttliche Natur unser Gerechtigkeit nicht sein könnten. Demnach so glauben, lehren und bekennen wir, dass der ganzen Person Christi ganzer Gehorsamb, welchen er für uns dem Vater bis in den allerschmählichsten Tod des Kreuzes geleistet hat, uns zur Gerechtigkeit zugerechnet werde."

[10] A quote in the *Catalogue of Testimonies* addresses the issue of application of the human-divine person. See the words of Cyril in (*BSELK SD*, Catalogis Testimoniorum, 10, 1133).

[11] According to article VIII of *FC*, the consolation, life, and salvation of Christians are dependent on *unio personalis*. *BSELK Epit.* VIII, 18.

[12] On the passive and active forms of obedience, see *BSELK SD* III, 15.The incarnatory themes appear only once in FC, in a quote from Cyril (*MPG* 75, 602 [In Joannis evangelium]). *BSELK SD* Catalogus Testimoniorum IV. The *Catalogue of Testimonies* consists of patristic quotes, which are presented in order to respond to the accusation that FC deviates christologically from the tradition of the church. It would be reductionistic, however, to claim that these quotes function in terms of christology alone.

7.2. *Faith as Actual Change*

The most extensive description of justification in BC is found in FC III, although FC also discusses the essence of faith in articles II (Free will) and IV (Good works). According to article II, the Fall and consequent blindness in spiritual matters taint the human being. Inflicted with spiritual blindness, the individual considers the proclaimed gospel madness. He or she is totally unable to come to God through their own strivings but remains an enemy of God until the Holy Spirit brings about conversion, faith, regeneration, and renewal. This occurs through grace alone, without human co-operation, as an effect of the preached, efficacious Word.[13] In conversion "people are enlightened, converted, reborn, renewed, and drawn back to God by the Holy Spirit."[14] According to FC, human reason and free will are capable only of external fulfilment of the Law, but "the Holy Spirit effects new birth and the inner reception of another heart, mind and disposition."[15] When a sinner believes in Christ through the effect of the Holy Spirit, an inner renewal (*Erneuerung*)[16] and change (*Änderung*)[17] take place. The birth of justifying faith is thus an act which produces real changes.

FC describes the relation between renewal and God's presence in the human being in different ways. For example, FC III states that contrition takes place first. After this the Holy Spirit, who renews and sanctifies them, is also given to the contrite and creates love of God and neighbor

[13] *BSELK SD* II, 5.

[14] *BSELK SD* II, 24: "Aber zuvor und ehe der Mensch durch den Heiligen Geist erleuchtet, bekehret, wiedergeboren, verneuert und gezogen wird..."

[15] *BSELK SD* II, 26: "Die Vernunft und freier Wille vormag 'etlichermassen äuserlich ehrbar zu leben'; aber neu geboren werden, inwendig ander Herz, Sinn und Mut bekommen, das wirket alleine der Heilige Geist." According to Martens (*Die Rechtfertigung*, p. 98) "damit ist gesichert, dass die Rechtfertigung ihren Ort tatsächlich in der Lebensgeschichte des Menschen hat."

[16] *BSELK SD* II, 65: "Daraus dann folget, alsbald der Heilige Geist, wie gesagt, durchs Wort und Heilige Sakrament solch sein Werk der Wiedergeburt und Erneuerung in uns angefangen hat, so ist es gewiss, dass wir durch die Kraft des Heiligen Geists mitwirken können und sollen, wiewohl noch in grotzer schwachheit..."

[17] *BSELK SD* II, 70: "Denn das ist einmal wahr, dass in wahrhaftiger Bekehrung müsse ein Änderung, neue Regung und Bewegung im Verstand, Willen und Herzen geschehen, dass nämlich das Herz die Sünde erkenne, für Gottes Zorn sich fürchte, von der Sünde sich abwende, die Verheissung der Gnaden in Christo erkenne und annehme, gute geistliche Gedanken, christlichen fürsatz und fleiss habe und wider das fleisch streite, etc."

in them.[18] On the other hand, there is a somewhat simpler order in which the Holy Spirit also has a role before the existence of faith.

> For good works do not precede faith, nor does sanctification precede justification. Instead, the Holy Spirit first kindles faith in us in conversion through hearing of the gospel. This faith lays hold of God's grace in Christ, and through it a person is justified. Thereafter, once people are justified, the Holy Spirit also renews and sanctifies them. From this renewal and sanctification the fruits of good works follow.[19]

Thus the Holy Spirit first effects faith, which apprehends Christ's righteousness and justifies the individual. After this, the Holy Spirit renews and sanctifies (*verneuert et heiliget*) him. Renewal and good works follow from this. The person must be good in order to do good, i.e., the tree must be good in order to bear good fruit.[20] Justifying faith is not an idle entity; rather, it brings forth good out of necessity.

> Instead, after a person has been justified by faith, there exist a true, living "faith working through love" (Gal. 5:6) That means that good works always follow justifying faith and are certainly found with it when it is a true and living faith. For faith is never alone but is always accompanied by love and hope.[21]

---

[18] *BSELK SD* III, 23: "Dann wahre Reue muss vorhergehen und die also, wie gesagt, aus lauter Gnaden umb des einigen Mittlers Christi willen, allein durch den Glauben, ohne alle Werk und verdienst für Gott gerecht, das ist, zu Gnaden angenommen werden, denen wird auch der Heilige Geist gegeben, der sie verneuert und heiliget, in ihnen wirket Liebe gegen Gott und gegen den Nächsten."

[19] *BSELK SD* III, 41: "Dann gute Werk gehen nicht für dem Glauben her, auch nicht die Heiligung für der Rechtfertigung, sondern erstlich wird in der Bekehrung durch den Heiligen Geist der Glaub aus dem Gehör des Evangelii in uns angezündet; derselbe ergreift Gottes Gnade in Christo, dardurch die Person gerechtfertigt wird; darnach, wenn die Person gerechtfertigt ist, so wird sie auch durch den Heiligen Geist verneuert und geheiliget, aus welcher Verneuerung und Heiligung alsdann die früchte der guten Werk folgen."

[20] *BSELK SD* III, 27: "...und die Person muss erst gerecht sein, eher sie gute Werke tun kann." SD IV, 8, 10. See also Jacob, "Von Christi Tat," p. 58.

[21] *BSELK Epit.* III, 11: "Sonder nachdem der Mensch durch den Glauben gerechtfertiget worden, als dann ist ein wahrhaftiger, lebendiger 'Glaube durch die Liebe tätig' Gal. 5. Also, dass die gute Werk dem gerechtmachenden Glauben allezeit folgen und bei demselben, do er rechtschaffen und lebendig, gewisslich erfunden werden, wie er dann nimmer allein ist, sondern allezeit Lieb und Hoffnung bei sich hat."

Faith is the mother and source (*Mutter und Ursprung*) of good works.[22] Faith is thus an effective entity, not a fancied one.[23] Article II also refers to Luther's *Commentary on Romans* to shed light on faith's nature.[24]

> Faith is a divine work in us that changes us and allows us to be born anew of God (John 1:12–13). It kills the old 'Adam'. and makes us altogether different people, in heart and spirit and mind and all powers; and it brings with it the Holy Spirit. O, it is a living, busy, active, mighty thing, this faith. It is impossible for it not to be doing good works incessantly.[25]

According to Luther, good works follow from faith, not from the renewal that is apart from faith; faith in itself is a medium of renewal. Even so, faith justifies correlatively, not as a deed or a virtue, but because faith apprehends Christ's righteousness.[26]

It is obvious that in FC *faith* is an act that really changes both the state of the individual *coram Deo* and the internal spiritual capacities. Forensic justification and effective change are not disconnected acts, but parts of the same reality, interconnected through faith in Christ.[27] Even if justification is described as imputation, this cannot take place without effective change, which enables faith. Moreover, justification is not real without its consequences. The Christian positively has both imputed righteousness and inchoate righteousness.[28] However, only imputed righteousness is constitutive regarding salvation.[29]

---

[22] *BSELK SD* IV, 9.

[23] According to Hamann ("Righteousness of faith," p. 157) in FC faith "involves a thoroughgoing reorientation of the sinner's whole being."

[24] The Luther quote is a last phase addition, which cannot be found until *Bergisches buch*. See Heppe, *Torgisches Buch*, pp. 88–89.

[25] *BSELK SD* IV, 10: "So ist der Glaube ein Göttliche Werk in uns, das uns wandelt und neu gebüret aus Gott und tötet den alten Adam, macht uns ganz andere Menschen von Herzen, Mut, Sinn und allen Kräften und bringet den Heiligen Geist mit sich, O es ist ein lebendig, gschäftig, tätig, mächtig Ding umb den Glauben, dass unmuglich, dass er micht ohn Unterlass sollt Guts wirken."

[26] *BSELK SD* III, 12–13.

[27] So also Hamann, "Righteousness of faith", pp. 159–160; Jacob, "Von Christi tat," pp. 54, 56, 61. FC gives two different models on this issue. On the one hand, good works and love are fruits of faith. E.g., SD III, 27. On the other hand, they are connected to God's indwelling in SD III, 54. These expressions are not necessarily contradictory because both faith and renewal are connected through effective faith.

[28] *BSELK SD* III, 32, 54; Jacob, "Von Christi tat," p. 63.

[29] According to Flogaus ("Luther versus Melanchthon?," p. 43): "Die FC vertritt eine rein imputative Rechtfertigungslehre, aber kein rein imputatives Verständnis der Gerechtigkeit des Gerechtfertigten." See also Wenz, *Theologie der Bekenntnischriften*, pp. 594, 600.

It is possible to see in FC the traces of *renovatio*, renewal, since justifying faith involves transformation from the state of unbelief and mutiny to the state of belief and obedience.[30] However, the relation between transformation and justification is problematic. According to FC III, we should "not introduce into the article on justification itself or mix with it what precedes faith or what results from it, as if they were necessary parts of it and belonged to it. For to speak of conversion is not at all the same as to speak of justification."[31] This distinction indicates that the formulators of FC understood salvation as transformative: justifying faith means change, which is never completed. For this reason, this change is not a matter of justification, since it concentrates only on what Christ has done.

Although FC depicts faith as effective reality, its connection to the presence of Christ is absent. Moreover, FC does not examine the form of faith.[32] Compared to Luther and the texts of the formulators of FC, the relation between justification and Christ's presence is described in a perfunctory way.[33] FC denies both antecedent and consequent change as part of the righteousness of faith.[34] The solution in FC involves the same problems as the system of Melanchthon in that the renewal needed for actual faith has no place within justification since renewal is regarded as a causal effect. Not even broadening the christological basis (mentioned in section 7.1.) is sufficient to change the Spirit-powered renewal to participation in Christ's human-divine person. Union with Christ is not the explicitly unitive feature between the different parts of salvation, such as imputation, regeneration, and sanctification.

---

[30] *BSELK SD* II, 60.

[31] *BSELK SD* III, 24–25.

[32] The reason for this may be that *forma* is an Aristotelian concept, which were banned in the other sections of FC.

[33] Bengt Hägglund correctly formulates the difference between Luther and FC. See Hägglund, "Die Rezeption Luthers in der Konkordienformel," in *Luther und die Bekenntnisschriften*, Bd. 2. (Erlangen: Veröffentlichungen der Luther-Akademie Ratzeburg 1981), pp. 116–117: "Nach der Konkordienformel ist die Rechtfertigung der Gehorsam Christi, durch den Glauben als Mittel zugeeignet, wodurch die Sünde nicht mehr als Sünde zugerechnet wird. Nach Luther ist die Rechtfertigung der für uns gestorbene und auferstandene Christus, der im Glauben wirksam ist, so dass der innere Wille verändert wird, vom Unglauben zum Glauben, von Feindschaft gegen Gott zum Vertrauen an ihn. Wir sind trotzdem in uns selbst Sünder, aber die bleibende Sünde wird um Christi willen nicht als Sünde zugerechnet".

[34] *BSELK SD* III, 24.

7.3. *The Formula of Concord and Luther*

Generally, FC discussion of justification does not cover every detail, but only provides concise definitions of the essence of faith, and interpretations of the constitution of the person of Christ. For example, faith is not described in terms of the *Christus forma fidei* notion, and justification is not explicitly related to participation in Christ, since forensic terms are more important. Faith is an instrument of reception without the status of a formal cause. Nevertheless, while the essence of faith is described as effective and transformative, clearly incarnatory themes are virtually absent.[35] Christology is observed only in a particular light, and not as comprehensively as in the formulator's own texts. The question is whether the limitation of God's indwelling as a consequence of justification is at odds with Luther's teaching or, to go even further, whether FC III contradicts its major christological contributor, Martin Chemnitz.

Obviously the formulators, Chemnitz included, did not consider FC and Luther's theology as contradictory. If Luther's views in *Commentary to Galatians* had been regarded as problematic, the contributors could have easily referred to other texts by Luther with different, more forensic emphasis. In this context it must be noted that none of the documents in FC defines justification in participatory terms. This includes CA and Luther's Schmalkaldic articles. Nowhere in BC is the christological foundation of justification analyzed in such detail as they are in the works of the formulators. The doctrine of participation in God appears nowhere in BC, except in the demarcating passage in FC III.[36]

The distinction, however, does not pose a problem if the passage is interpreted according to contemporaneous theology. The passage was written with Osiander in mind, and intended to to exclude good works from salvation. Although the Osiandrian controversy actually arose because of the difference in the relation between union with Christ and

---

[35] This is true with regard to FC III, although the *Catalogue of Testimonies* has a different tone.

[36] FC uses the concept *unio* only in a christological sense (*unio personalis*) and within eucharistic theology (*unio sacramentalis*). The soteriological and conceptually defined use of *unio* had not emerged at the time. Still, according to Rune Söderlund FC does not understand justification as unitive. See Söderlund, "Der Unio-Gedanke in der Konkordienformel," in *Unio. Gott und Mensch in der nachreformatorischen Theologie* (Helsinki: Scriften der Luther-Agricola-Gesellshaft 1996), p. 62.

renewal (*renovatio*$_1$), the controversy was later understood as a debate over sanctification and good works (*renovatio*$_2$). This straw man became the target of FC's condemnations. Indeed, FC does not speak so much about God's essential righteousness as it does about the good works it produces. It also omits completely any notion that resembles *renovatio*$_1$; this is the weakest point of the document.[37]

This problem came to the fore at the beginning of 17th century, when the concept of *unio* was debated again. The formulations of the time tried to simultaneously remain loyal to FC and address the issue, since the issue had not been given its due in FC. The standard model of two unions was as follows. The application of Christ's righteousness means union with Christ (*unio fidei formalis*): Christ is present in faith as its form. As a consequence of this, the Trinity comes to dwell in the believer and causes good works (*inhabitatio Dei / unio mystica*).[38]

Nevertheless, the use of two different concepts to illustrate union with God raises some new questions. For example, from a Trinitarian theological perspective, it is strange if the Father and the Son are only a consequent of faith and absent when faith is created. This distinction serves to fulfill the demands of FC, which seems to consider justification and indwelling as consequent events. Interestingly, the later formulations sought to express it both ways: indwelling remains as a consequence but a new mode of *unio* is represented to fix the apparent deficiencies in FC's formulation.

However, the idea of two unions was already present in patristic writings, as in Cyril's theology (an example which Chemnitz made known). Luther also offers different forms of renewal in his *Commentary on Galatians*. Christ is first apprehended in faith, and then the renewing

---

[37] The text of FC illustrates how difficult it was analyze Osiander's teaching analytically. At the beginning of the Osiandrian controversy, Mörlin, for instance, considered that "God's essential righteousness" meant righteousness fatal for sinners. The presence of God's essential righteousness in faith was confessed openly with the corrective that this meant essential righteousness after the incarnation of Christ. Later the problem of Osiander's teaching was, however, associated with the interpretation according to which God's indwelling righteousness produces good works and, to prevent synergism, the indwelling was moved away from justification. The source of the problem has been changed: is God's essential righteousness problematic since it is fatal for sinners, or because it produces good? Thus, FC's notion of God's essential and indwelling righteousness is ambiguous.

[38] Mahlmann, "Die Stellung der unio cum Christo," p. 178; Nüssel, *Allein aus Glauben*, pp. 279–294.

Holy Spirit is given. Theologians of the 17th century could easily imagine that they were continuing within the orthodox Christian tradition in using these distinctions.

How should FC III be read, then? At the end of the document a reference to Luther indicates that FC is not a comprehensive treatment of justification.[39] FC also states that even the creeds based on the Bible were not equivalent to the Bible but "only witnesses and explanations of the faith, which show how Holy Scripture has at various times been understood and interpreted in the church of God by those who lived at the time in regard to articles of faith in dispute and how teachings contrary to the Scripture were rejected and condemned."[40] The function of the creeds is in a certain sense related to the controversies of the historical context in which they appeared. FC also tries to offer solutions to certain controversies of the 16th century, and actually succeeds in this, at least from the political point of view, in that it secured the internal unity of Lutheranism.[41]

FC is not a complete account of justification, but a response to limited doctrinal questions.[42] In spite of this, the formulators of FC regarded the document as the correct, binding, and lasting interpretation of CA.[43] Indeed, the subtitle of FC is "A thorough, clear, correct, and final repetition and explanation of certain articles of the Augsburg

---

[39] J. A. O. Preus, *Second Martin*, (p. 180) states: "The Formula of Concord was not a complete summary of Lutheran theology. It was an attempt to settle existing controversies on the basis of Scripture, the ancient creeds, the Augsburg Confession, and the other earlier Lutheran Confessions." According to Lewis Spitz the idea of confessional documents is not to explain divine mysteries but convey the substance of Christian belief in the best possible way within the limits of human language. See Spitz, "The Formula of Concord Then and Now," in *Discord, Dialogue and Concord. Studies in the Lutheran Reformation's Formula of Concord*, eds. Wenzel Lohff et al. (Philadelphia: Fortress Press 1977), p. 7.

[40] *BSELK Epit.*, Von dem Summarischen Begriff, 8.

[41] Yet, later Lutheran generations preferred CA to FC if they needed to quote an authoritative text. See Robert Preus, "The Influence of the Formula of Concord on the Later Lutheran Orthodoxy," in *Discord, Dialogue and Concord*, p. 101.

[42] Armin-Ernst Buchrucker claims that FC was intended to cleanse the Lutheran house. For this reason, the articles of FC are often compromising and even contradictory. See Buchrucker, "Einheit im Bekenntis de Wahrheit. Von Sinn, Ziel und Problematik der Konkordienformel," in *Bekenntnis zur Wahrheit. Aufsätze über die Konkordienformel*, hrsgb. Jobst Schöne (Erlangen: Martin Luther-Verlag 1978), p. 18. See Robert Preus, "The Influence of the Formula of Concord on the Later Lutheran Orthodoxy," in *Discord, Dialogue and Concord*, pp. 86–87; Ekkehard Muehlenberg, "Synergia and Justification by Faith," in *op. cit.*

[43] Kurt Marquart, "Contemporary Significance of the Formula of Concord," in *No Other Gospel. Essays in Commemoration of the* 400th *Anniversary of the Formula of Concord*

Confession."[44] In keeping with this the possible augmentation of FC requires adherence to the interpretation of justification contained in FC III. This interpretation does not suffer, however, if we augment the christological notions found in Luther and Chemnitz.[45] Indeed, FC even asks for this. The main purpose of FC is to emphasize that certain elements are *not* essential to justification, i.e., good works. Every possible feature is not examined, including the christological foundations.[46] FC merely refers instead to Luther's texts as the more profound explanation.[47] Hence, FC contains a significant principle of openness.

1580–1980, eds. Arnold J. Koelpin (Milwaukee: Northwestern Publishing House 1980); Buchrucker, "Einheit," p. 22.

[44] *BSELK*, 735: "Gründliche (Allgemeine), lautere, richtige und endliche Wiederholung und Erklärung etlicher Artikel Augsburcgischen Confession..." The words "perfect" and "final" are not to be understood in an absolute sense. These words rather refer to the final resolution of Lutheran disunity in the 16th century. The goal of the document is understood in this way in *BSELK SD* VI, 4.

[45] Hägglund, ("Die Rezeption Luthers," p. 117) suggests following: "Der Hinweis zum Galater—Kommentar Luthers am Ende des dritten Artikels ist besonders wichtig, weil darin nicht nur eine Bestätigung, oindern auch eine wichtige Ergänzung der in der Konkordienformel gegebenen Darstellung der Glaubensgerechtigkeit zu finden ist. Diese Ergänzung ist leider, trotz dieses Hinweis, meistens übersehen und in den Definitionen der lutherischen Orthodoxie weggelassen."

[46] Jacob, "Von Christi tat," p. 59.

[47] Interestingly, the reference to Luther was added at the last moment in Torgau. See Pressel, *Zwei Actenstücke*, p. 86. The content of the doctrine of justification does not go through major changes during the edition. The reason may be that the Osiandrian controversy had ended 30 years before, while christology and the doctrine of the eucharist were more current. FC III is based mostly on Andreae's early utterances. In the final versions, justification has probably attracted interest, and some problems have been noted in the almost finished text. Perhaps discussion on justification was not wanted, and the reference to Luther was added to supply the deficiency.

CHAPTER EIGHT

CONCLUDING REMARKS: WHAT IS THE LUTHERAN DOCTRINE OF JUSTIFICATION?

This study has shown that the central features of the Lutheran doctrine of justification cannot be illustrated by simple distinctions. For example, the well-known thesis that Lutherans understand justification forensically and Catholics effectively is not only reductive but also misleading. Sixteenth-century Lutheranism had a number of ways to define justification. Based on the analysis carried out in the previous chapters, I will present five different models of justification and examine their compatibility.

Model 1: Faith is participation in Christ and His merit

Luther, Bugenhagen, and Brenz combine the imputation of Christ's righteousness with Christ's actual presence in the believer; Christ present in faith is the basis of imputation. The forensic and effective aspects are not distinguished since both are joined in participation in Christ. Thus, the new life and renewal given to the sinner in justification was understood as participation in Christ's righteousness and holiness; new life was not considered a human merit. Justification involves both a change of state before God and a change of essence, albeit the change as such is not the basis for imputation. Renewal in justification (*renovatio*$_1$) and new life is participation in Christ's divine life. The renewal of the Spirit occurs and good works start to emerge (*renovatio*$_2$) as a result. The righteousness of Christ consists of redemption carried out by a human-divine person. The problem of model 1 is its mystical nature: what does it actually mean that "I live; yet not I, but Christ lives in me"? (Gal. 2:20.)

Model 2: Faith is the renewal of the faculties of the soul by the Holy Spirit

Melanchthon did not interpret imputation in connection to Christ's person and His attributes. In spite of this, imputation involved the transfer of Christ's righteousness and His merit, which is given through the inseparable gift of the Spirit. Melanchthon's greatest difference from Luther was his way of depicting communion with God through a Spirit-evoked life. The presence of Christ is replaced by the presence of the Spirit, which causes a new disposition towards God. Because justification and renewal do not occur as participation in God's attributes, the results of the renewal are understood as new qualities. This leads Melanchthon to simultaneously deny that renewal is part of justification and affirm the necessity of renewal as the antecedent of justification. The certainty of salvation is related to Christ's obedience and grace, which are independent and external entities to the believer. Certainty is not dependent on inchoate renewal, which is imperfect.

Model 3: Faith is connection with Christ's divine nature

For Osiander Christ's presence in faith enabled imputation and forgiveness. However, since participation in Christ is exclusively participation in Christ's divine nature, the salvific work of Christ on the Cross is removed from justification. According to Osiander, Christ's righteousness, which is given to sinners, is not based on His sufferings but on His essence as the righteous Son of God. Therefore, the indwelling of Christ is of greatest importance in justification, because in this scheme the external work of reconciliation does not have any role since it only gives God permission to act salvifically. Although Osiander did not claim that observation of Christ's indwelling functioned as the source of the certainty of salvation, his adversaries interpreted him this way.

Model 4: Faith is a causal effect of the Holy Spirit

The fear of Osiandrianism and Roman Catholic theology obliged Flacius to develop Melanchthon's terminology further. The concept of 'imputation' especially was limited to refer only to the external works of God in justification. Flacius was afraid that Lutheran terminology about "faith that is reckoned to righteousness" would lead to the observation of effects of faith in the believer as the basis of the certainty of salvation. The object of faith would be situated in the believer. According to Flacius, justification did not mean participation in God, a position contrary to Luther, Melanchthon, and Osiander. Because the nature of faith is not defined through the presence of Christ or the Holy Spirit, the nature of justifying faith remains ambiguous. Faith as such does not have divine form, which could give faith its justifying nature and simultaneously deny the meritoriousness of renewal. Faith is a movement of the mind, which is reckoned as meritorious. This notion closely resembles the Roman Catholic teaching of *meritum de congruo*, although Flacius denied this.

Model 5: Faith is participation in the person of Christ and His merit, which is effected by the Spirit

The second-generation reformers adapted elements from multiple sources; their formulations were a synthesis of the teachings of Luther and Melanchthon. This group of theologians was by no means uniform. They employed an independent approach and terminology to the issue. For this reason, model 5 has been divided into 3 subcategories.

(5.1) Mörlin, Chemnitz and Chytraeus especially define justification as participation in the person of Christ and the merit He has acquired as true God and man. In this case, Christ is the formal cause of justification, and faith and renewal means participation in new life, which is Christ himself.

(5.2) Selnecker, Hesshus, and Heerbrand do not apply patristic theology to the extent as the theologians in model 5.1. As a result the exact articulation of the presence of Christ is more complex. In any case, Christ is the form of faith. The role of *renovatio*$_I$ is not articulated clearly, although the presence of Christ is considered the basis of justification.

(5.3) Andreae and Wigand deny that Christ is the formal cause of justification, but describe justification as transformation into the likeness of Christ. Additionally, they admit that essential divine righteousness is present in faith, even though it does not have a justifying function.

These five models form the basis of the formulations of FC. One crucial question is whether these models are exclusive or inclusive. A comparison of the models indicates that 3 and 4 are less compatible. Osiander's model 3 was generally considered heresy, and Osiander himself openly confessed the incompatibility of his model with models

2 and 4. On the other, model 3 was not fully compatible with model 1 either. Flacius's model 4 makes sharp distinctions and demarcations, and, possibly due to its exclusive character, never received wide acceptance. The denial of participation in Christ as the basis of justification also makes it fundamentally different from the other models. The centrality of participation links models 1 and 2, although participation is understood through different Trinitarian models. The common theme, however, is that justification requires renewal that is possible only through the presence of God while the distinctive feature is the nature of the renewal. In Melanchthon's model 2, renewal is the Spirit-evoked likeness of God, whereas for Luther renewal is participation in God and His attributes. Christ as the form of faith links models 1 and 5.1/5.2. Union with Christ gives shape to justifying faith, which simultaneously renews the believer through participation in the Life of Christ. The relation between models 5.3 and model 1 is more obscure, since model 5.3 denies the presence of essential righteousness as the form of justification. Model 5.3 is not directed against model 1 but against Osiander's model 3. In spite of this, model 5.3 resembles Flacius's model 4 closely without being identical.

Due to Andreae's major influence on the formulation of the article, FC's article on justificaiton resembles model 5.3 most. However, the similarity may be more due to its concise utterances than the substantial differences in the actual affirmations. FC denies that God's essential righteousness is considered righteousness because it produces good works. The article does not, however, consider the issue of whether God's essential righteousness can have any soteriological significance. In any case, this is the stance adopted by the majority of the formulators of FC.

The most compatible models are evidently 1 and 5.1/5.2, which also have the widest acceptance among the most prominent Lutheran reformers. These models join the doctrine of justification and christology coherently and unite the forensic and effective aspects of justification; since Christ (not renewal) is the form of justification, effectuality does not have justifying status. The righteousness of the sinner is Christ, not inchoate righteousness.

Models 1 and 5.1/5.2 share the features of genuine interpretation of the Lutheran doctrine of justification. Connecting the model 5.3 (and FC) to these models requires additions that are not necessarily against the intentions of the model. The central augmentation would be the formulation of a stronger connection between christology and justification; Christ should not be considered simply as the effective but also as the formal cause.

One cannot understate the significance of FC to the development of Lutheran theology in general and justification in particular. Nevertheless, FC does not claim to represent the doctrine of justification in its entirety. It does not deal with several central questions, including Christ as the form of faith, an issue that does not appear in the text despite its importance in other texts written by the formulators. At the same time, it must be remembered that the same deficiency appears in all the other contemporary confessional documents, including Luther's Schmalcaldic articles.

The confessional documents should not be read and interpreted outside of their theological and historical frame of reference, since this would easily lead to inappropriate questions and anachronisms. The confessional affirmations are in a certain sense limited to their own time. Thus, they do not answer all present questions. For this reason, the affirmations of FC should not be overemphasized to the extent that anything beyond the text is deemed suspicious. In the worst case, an overemphasis would lead to the presentation of FC as the hermeneutic tool that evaluates the texts of Luther and other theologians from its own point of view, and dismisses everything that does not satisfy its own affirmations. According to FC's own advice, the formulations written in the articles, especially on justification, can be broadened in reference to material from Luther's own texts. The texts of the other Reformers also offer rich accounts of justification and christology and can be beneficial.

In conclusion, the Lutheran doctrine of justification strenuously denies the meritorious nature of human deeds and love. This stance can be maintained only if the new life given to the sinner is construed as participation in divine Life in Christ, which He has merited as true God and man through incarnation, suffering, death, resurrection and ascension. All this has occurred in order to reconcile the sinful human race with the Father. The faith that has Christ as its object, and which apprehends Him and His merit, making Him present as the form of faith, is reckoned as righteousness. Only when Christ is the form of faith do human deeds lose their justifying significance. The Lutheran doctrine of justification stands or falls on this christological basis.

Also ist die erkentnis Gottes / und unser Studium Theologiae / in diesem leben sehr gering und kindisch / bis wir in die himlische Universitet unnd hohe Schule / zu Gott dem Brunquell aller Weisheit kommen / aldar wir nicht allein Tittel nach Doctores (wie wir alhie auff erde gemeiniglich sein) sondern von Gott volkômlich unnd zu grund gelerte Theologi sein werden.

Chytraeus, *Vom Tode*, Ovii.

APPENDICES

APPENDIX 1. FLACIUS: THE MODES OF IMPUTATION[1]

Dicitur nobis imputari meritum aut iusticia Christi. Item Fides ad iusticiam. Est autem *imputatio rationalis*, *Non essentialis alicuius rei translatio*. Et est alia

- *realis*, cùm alia res loco alterius habetur, aut precium seu aestimatio ab una in aliam cogitatione transfertur: quod sit, cùm vel
  - *Res perinde bonae*, earumque precium, pro sese invicem ponuntur: ut si debens vestem, det frumentum
  - *Res vicissime*, earum´ue precium, pro optimis, quadam dispensatione accipiuntur: ut si debens pecuniam, precibus aut deprecatione satisfaciat. Sic fides aut precaria condonatio nobis imputatur ad iusticiam
- *Personalis*, cùm res quaepiam bona aut mala, sola cogitatione ab alio in alium tranfertur. Sic transscribitur tum
  - *Iniusticia nostra*, aut debitum in Christum
  - *Iusticia*, aut solutio Christi in nos

[1] Flacius, *Iustificatione*, 130.

APPENDIX 2. FLACIUS: THE CAUSES OF JUSTIFICATION[2]

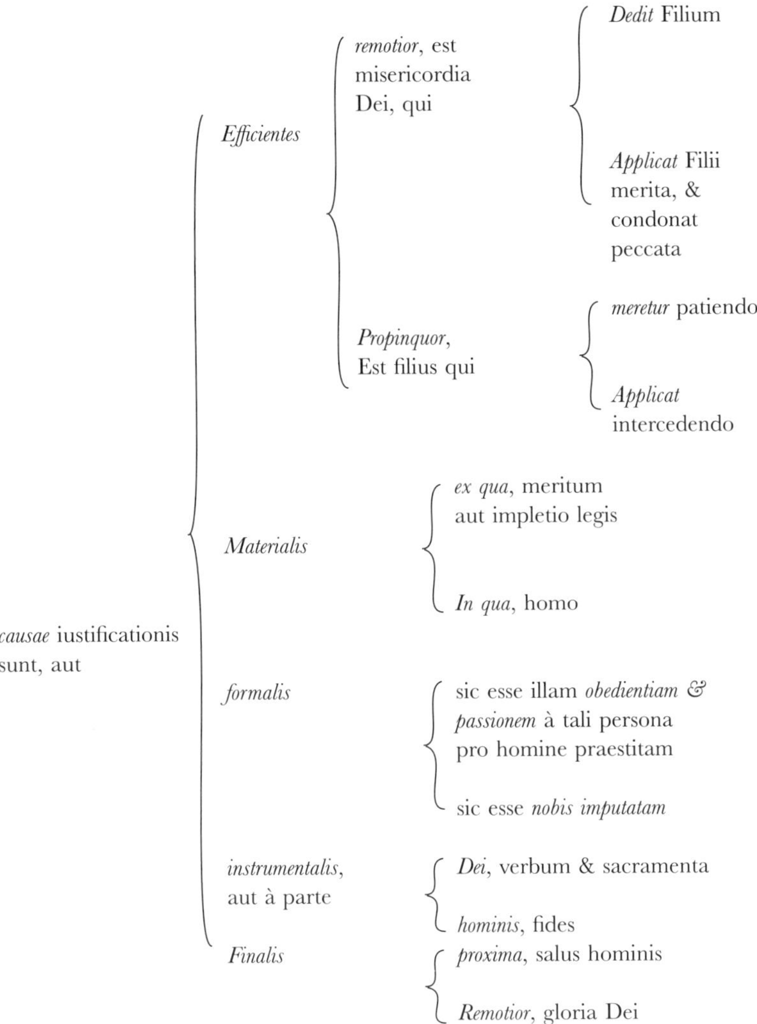

[2] Flacius, *Iustificatione*, 156.

SOURCES AND BIBLIOGRAPHY

Abbreviations

AO	*Andreas Osiander Gesamtausgabe*
AC	*Apologia Confessionis Augustanae*
BC	*The Book of Concord*
BSELK	*Die Bekenntnisschriften der evangelisch-lutherischen Kirche. 11. Auflage*
CA	*The Augsburg Confession* (*Confessio Augustana*)
CR	*Corpus Reformatorum*
FC	*The Formula of Concord* (*Formula Concordiae*)
FC Epit.	*The Epitome of the Formula of Concord* (*Epitome*)
FC SD	*The Solid Declaration of the Formula of Concord* (*Solida declaratio*)
JDDJ	*Joint Declaration on the Doctrine of Justification*
MPG	*Patrologia Graeca*. Migne
MPL	*Patrologia Latina*. Migne
MW	Melanchthon's *Werke. Studienausgabe*
SA	*Schmalcald articles*
StA	Martin Luther*: Studienausgabe*
TRE	*Theologische Realenzyklopädie*
WA	*D. Martin Luthers Werke: Kritische Gesamtausgabe*
WA BR.	*D. Martin Luthers Briefe: Kritische Gesamtausgabe*
WA TR.	*D. Martin Luthers Tischreden: Kritische Gesamtausgabe*

Sources

Andreae, Jacob, *[Sechs Christlicher Predig über den] ein unnd fünffzigsten Psalmen Davids geprediget zu Lawgingen durch Jacobum Andreae der heiligen Schrifft Doctorn*, Tübingen 1561.

——, *Zehen Predig von den sechs Hauptstucken Christlicher Lehr <Catechismus genant> allen Christlichen Haussvattern nutzlich zulesen. gepredigt zu Lawgingen durch Jacobum Andreae der heiligen Schrifft Doctorn*, Tubingae 1561.

——, *Gründtliche Erklärung dreyer Hauptartikel christlicher Lehre*, Tubingae 1563.

——, *Consilium de praesentibus Religionis Controversijs pie & moderatissime componendis, scriptum a D. Iacobo Andreae* printed in Inge Mager: "Jacob Andreaes lateinische Unionsartikel von 1568", *Zeitschrift für Kirchengeschichte* 98 (1987), pp. 70–86.

——, *Drey und dreissig Predigen Von den fürnebsten Spaltungen in der Christlichen Religion so sich zwischen den Baptischen, Lutherischen, Zwinglischen, Zwenckfeldern unnd Wider teuffern halten*, Tubingae 1568.

——, *Ein christliche Predig, wie der Mensch vor Gott gerecht werde*, Tubingae 1569.

——, *[Ein christliche Predigt], von Christlicher Einigkeit der Theologen Augspürgischer Confession*, Wolfenbüttel 1570.

——, *Disputatio De persona Christi: de unione personali in Christo: de earundem Idiomatum communicatione; veraque; praesentia corporis & sanguinis Christi in coena Domini*, Tubingae 1572.

——, *Disputatio de Justificatione*, Tubingae 1572.

——, *Sechs Christlicher Predig von den Spaltungen, so sich zwischen den Theologen Augspurgischer Confession/von anno* 1548, Tübingae 1574.

——, *Bekändtnitz und kurze Erklärung etlicher zwiespaltiger Artickel / nach welcher eine Christliche Einigkeit in den Kirchen / der Christlichen Augspurgischen Confession zugethan / getroffen / und die ärgerliche langwierige Spaltung hingelegt werden möchte*, printed in Hutter: *Concordia concors*, Francofurti & Lipsiae 1690.

——, *Die Schwäbische Confession*, printed in *Zeitschrift für historische Theologie* 36 (1862), pp. 230–301.

Bugenhagen, Johannes, *Von dem Christlichen Glauben und rechten guten wercken*, Wittenberg 1527.

——, *Confessio Fidei Duae altera D. Doctoris Martini Lutheri, altera D. Joannis Bugenhagii Pomerani denuo recognitae, & singulari consilio iam primum latinae editae*, Vitebergae 1539.

——, *Sechs Predigten Johannes Bugenhagens*, Aufgefunden und mitgeteilt von lic. Theol. Dr. Georg Buchwald, Max Niemeyr, Halle 1885.

Calvin, Johannes, *Institutio Christianae Religionis*, Verlag der Buchhandlung des Erziehungsvereins, Neukirchen 1955.

Chemnitz, Martin, *Repetitio sanae doctrinae de vera praesentia corporis et sanguinis Domini in Coena*, Leipzig 1561.

——, *Wiederholte Christliche Gemeine Confession und Erklerung: Wie in den Sechsischen kirchen vermöge der heiligen Schrifft / und Augspurgischen Confession / nach der alten Grundsfest D. Lutheri / wieder die Sacramentierer wirdt*, 1571.

——, *De duabus naturis in Christo. De hypostatica earum unione, de communicatione idiomatum, et de aliis quaestionibus inde dependentibus*, Francofurti & Wittebergae Anno M. DC. LIII.

——, *Theses quaedam de unione duarum naturarum in Christo hypostatica: item de officiis et maiestate Christi mediatoris*, Lipsiae, printed in Nikolaus Selnecker: *Repetitio doctrina de idiomatum communicatione, & humanae in Christo naturae exaltatione, gloria, & maiestate*, Lipsiae 1581.

——, *Enchiridion de praecipuis capiti doctrinae coelestis, latine redditum per Johannem Zangerum*, Lipsiae 1588.

——, *Fundamenta sanae doctrinae de vera et substantiali praesentia, exhibitione & sumptione corporis & sanguinis Domini in Coena*, Francofurti & Wittebergae Anno MDCLIII.

——, *Loci Theologici D.N. Martini Chemnitii, Theologi longe celeberrimi, atque ecclesiae Brunsvicensis quondam superintendentis fidelissimi, quibus et Loci communes d. Philippi Melanthonis perspicue explicantur et quasi integrum christianae doctrinae corpus ecclesiae Dei sincere proponitur*, Editi opera & studio Polycarpi Leiseri D. Francofurti & Wittebergae Anno M. DC. LIII. (Loci I–III)

——, [*Eine Predigt uber das Evangelion Matth.* 22.] *Von dem König der seinem Sohn Hochzeit machet etc.* 1573

——, *Handtbüchlein. Der Fürnemsten heuptstücke der Christlichen Lehre / durch Frag und Antwort aus Gottes Wort einfeltig und grüdlich erkleret*, Magdeburg Anno M. D. LXXIX.

——, *Genelogia Christi*, Magdeburgi 1696.

——, *Examen Concilii Tridentinii*, hrsgb. E. Preuss, Wissenshaftliche buchgesellshaft, Darmstadt 1972.

——, *Two Natures in Christ*, transl. J. A. O. Preus, Concordia Publishing House, St. Louis 1971.

——, *The Examination of the Council of Trent* I–IV, transl. Fred Kramer, Concordia Publishing House, St. Louis 1971–1986.

——, *Lord's Supper*, transl. J. A. O. Preus, Concordia Publishing House, St. Louis 1979.

——, *Loci Theologici* I–II, transl. J. A. O. Preus, Concordia Publishing House, St. Louis 1989.

——, "*Judgment on Certain Controversies concerning Certain Articles of the Augsburg Confession . . . by Martin Chemnitz*", transl. J. A. O. Preus & R. Kolb, printed in *Sources and Contexts of the Book of Concord*, eds. Robert Kolb & James Nestingen, Fortress Press, Minneapolis 2001.

Chytraeus, David, *Davidis Chytraei De Morte Et Vita Aeterna*, Erscheinungsvermerk am Ende von Bd. 1: Rostochii Excudebat Stephanus Myliander Sumptibus Laurentii Albrecht Bibliopolae Lubecensis, Anno M.D. XIC.

——, *In Genesin Enarratio*, Vitebergae 1557.

——, *Catechesis recens recognita a Davide Chytraeo*, 1561.

——, *In Genesin Enarratio*, Vitebergae 1561.
——, *Explicatio Apocalyptis Johannis*, Wittebergae 1563.
——, [*Commentarius*] *in Matthaeum Evangelistam, ex praelectionibus collectus*, Witebergae 1566.
——, *Regulae vitae*, Lipsiae 1570.
——, *Catechesis D. Ch.—i recens. recognita et multis definitionibus aucta*, Excudebat Johannes Lufft, Witebergae 1573.
——, *Catechesis Davidis Chytraei postremo recognita*, Magdeburgae 1578.
——, *Catechesis Davidis Chytraei Postremo nunc ab ipso Autore recognita, & multis in locis aucta*, Johannes Beyer imprimebat, Lipsiae 1580.
——, *Unterricht vom Tode und ewigen Leben*, übers. d. Heinr. Räteln, Berlin 1590.
——, *In Psalmum* CXVIII... *Praelectiones*..., Rostochii 1590.
——, *On sacrifice. A Reformation Treatise in Biblical Theology, David Chytraeus' "De sacrificiis" of* 1569 *Translated for the First Time into a Modern Language and Edited in Translation*, transl. John Warwick Montgomery, Concordia Publishing House, St. Louis 1962.
Flacius, Matthias Illyricus, Clavis Scripturae sacrae, Frankfurt & Leipzig 1719. (Clavis I & II)
——, *Verlegung des Bekentnis Osiandri von der Rechtfertigung der armen sünder durch die wesentliche Gerechtitgkeit der Hohen Maiestet Gottes allein*, Magdeburg 1552.
——, *De voce et re fidei, contra pharisaicum hypocritarum fermentum, cum praefatione Philipp Melanchthonis*, Basel 1563.
——, *De iustificatione liber; multa accuratius alijs quibusdam explicans*, in *De voce et re fidei*, Basel 1563.
Heerbrand, Jacob, *[Disputatio] de Gratia*, Tubingae 1572.
——, *Compendium Theologiae*, Tubingae 1573.
——, *Disputationes Theologicae in inclyta Tubingensi Academia Publice Discutiendae Propositae*, Tubingae 1575.
——, *Compendium Theologiae, nunc passim auctum, & methodi Quaestionibus tractatum*, Tubingae 1578.
Hesshus, Tileman, *Zehen Predigten von der Rechfertigung des Sünders für Gott*, 1568.
——, [*Explicatio Epistolae Pauli*] *ad Romanos, Ienae 1571.*
——, *Examen Theologicum complectens Praecipua capita doctrinae Christianae, Quibus interrogati sunt pastores Ecclesiarum in Franconia & Thuringia in visitatione an* 1569, Ienae 1571.
——, *De iustificatione hominis coram Deo. Propositiones et solutiones objectionum, quibus Pontificij & alii Sectarij sanam doctrinam de Iustificatione impugnare solent*, Ienae 1572.
——, [*Explicatio Epistolae Pauli*] *ad Galatas*, Helmstadij 1579.
——, *Commentarius in Epistolam Pauli ad Colossenses*, Helmstadij 1582.
——, *Examen Theologicum*, 1587.
——, *De iustificatione* [*hominis coram Deo.*] *Libri Sex. Adversus impia decreta Tridentinae Synodi, & blasphemos errores Iesuitarum*, Helmstadij 1587.
——, *De duabus naturis in Christo, Earumque unione hypostatica tractatus, Madgeburgi 1590.*
Hollazius, David, *Examen Theologicum Acroamaticum*, Wissenschaftliche Buchgesellschaft, Darmstad 1971.
Luther, Martin, "Rationis Latomianae", in StA 2, pp. 405–519.
——, "Sermo Lutheri in natali Christi (1515)", in WA 1, pp. 20–29.
——, "Dictata super Psalterium 1513–16", in WA 4.
——, "Operationes in Psalmos 1519–1521", in WA 5.
——, "Schriften und Predigten 1509/21", in WA 9.
——, "Predigten des Jahres 1522", in WA 10 I.
——, "Predigten des Jahres 1522", in WA 10 III.
——, "Predigten des Jahres 1525", in WA 17 I.
——, "Festpostille 1527", in WA 17 II, pp. 251–516.
——, "Fastenpostille 1525", in WA 17 II, pp. 1–247.
——, "Crucigers Sommerpostille 1544", in WA 21.

——, "Vorlesung über Jesaias 1527–1530", in WA 31 II, pp. 1–586.
——, "Predigten des Jahres 1532", in WA 36.
——, "Die Zirkulardisputation de veste nuptiali", in WA 39 I, pp. 264–333.
——, "Die Doktorpromotion von Hieronymus Weller und Nikolaus Medler 1535", in WA 39 I, pp. 40–77.
——, "Thesen de fide (1535)", in WA 39 I, pp. 44–48.
——, "Die Disputation über Daniel 4, 24 (1535)", in WA 39 I, pp. 63–77.
——, "Die Disputation de Justificatione (1536)", in WA 39 I, pp. 78–126.
——, "Die 3. Thesenreihe über Römer 3, 28 (1536)", in WA 39 I, pp. 82–86.
——, "Die Promotionsdisputation von Palladius und Tilemann (1537)", in WA 39 I, pp. 198–257.
——, "Die zweite Disputation gegen die Antinomer (1538)", in WA 39 I, pp. 418–485.
——, "Die dritte Disputation gegen die Antinomer (1538)", in WA 39 I, pp. 486–584.
——, "Die Promotionsdisputation von Joachim Mörlin (1540)", in WA 39 II, pp. 122–144.
——, "Die Promotionsdisputation von Hieronymus Nopp und Friedrich Bachofen (1543)", in WA 39 II, pp. 233–251.
——, "St. Pauli Commentarius ad Galatas", in WA 40 I–II.
——, "Vorlesungen über die Psalmen 2. 51. 45. (1532)", in WA 40 II.
——, "Vorlesungen über Jesaja 9 und 53 (1543/44)", in WA 40 III, pp. 595–747.
——, "Predigten des Jahres 1536", in WA 41.
——, "Vorlesungen über 1. Mose (1535–1545)", in WA 42–44.
——, "Eine schöne predigt von dem Gesetz und Evangelium (1537)", in WA 45, pp. 145–204.
——, "Predigten des Jahres 1538", in WA 46.
——, "Predigten des Jahres 1539", in WA 47.
——, "Von den Conciliis und Kirchen", in WA 50, pp. 488–653.
——, "Eigenhändige Randbemerkungen zu Gabriel Biels Collectorium und Canonis Misse Expositio. Seit 1516/17", in WA 59, pp. 25–53.
Melanchthon, Philip, "Loci Communes 1521", in MW II/1.
——, "Römerbrief-Kommentar (1532)", in MW V.
——, "CA variata (1540)", in MW VI, pp. 12–79.
——, "Philosophiae moralis epitomes libri duo (1546)", in MW III, pp. 149–302.
——, "Erotemata dialectices (1547)", in CR 13, pp. 509–751.
——, "[De] poenitentia (1548)", in CR 23, pp. 643–646.
——, "[IV.] Enarratio Symboli Niceni (1550)", in CR 23.
——, "[Confessio] doctrinae Saxonicarum ecclesiarum (1551)", in MW VI, pp. 80–167.
——, "Aurifabro et Chytraeo (1552)", in CR 7, pp. 927.
——, "Antwort auff das Buch Herrn Andreae Osiandri (1552)", in MW VI, pp. 452–461.
——, "[Liber] de Anima (1553)", in CR 13, pp. 6–178.
——, "Responsio Philippi Melanchthonis de controversiis Stancari (1553)", in MW VI, pp. 462–481.
——, "Catechesis puerilis (1558)", in CR 23, pp. 117–190.
——, "Loci Communes (1559)", in MW II/1 & 2.
——, "Examen eorum (1559)", in CR 23, pp. 1–102.
——, "Iudicium de controversia de coena Domini (1560)", in MW VI, pp. 482–486.
——, "[V.] Explicatio Symboli Niceni (1561)", in CR 23, pp. 197–346.
——, "Disputatio, quare fide iustificemur, non dilectione", printed in *Abhandlungen Alexander von Oettingen zum siebenzigsten Geburstag*, C. H. Beck'sche Verlagsbuchhandlung, München 1898, pp. 251–255.

Musculus, Andreas, *Responsio ad virulentumacmaledicum scriptum, ex meris calumnijs & mendacijs conflatum, Friderici Staphylij. De adoranda unitione duarum naturarum Christi inseparabili, in unam personam*, 1558.

Mörlin, Joachim, *Historia Welcher gestalt sich die Osiandrische schwermerey im lande zu Preussen erhaben / und wie dieselbige verhandelt ist / mit allen actis / durch Joachim Mörlin*, 1554.

——, *Apologia Auff die vermeinte Widerlegung des Osiandrischen Schwermers in Preussen, M. Vogels. Sampt gründlichen kurtzen bericht, Was der Hauptstreit und die Lere Osiandri gewesen sey*,... Magdeburg 1557.

——, *Antwort auff das Buch des Osiandrischen schwermers in Preussen, M. Vogels*,... Madgeburg 1557.

——, *Disputatio D. Iochimi Morlini, De Communicatione idiomatum*... N.p., 1571.

——, *Repetitio Corporis Doctrinae ecclesiasticae Oder Widerholung der Summa und inhalt der rechten, allgemeinen christlichen Kirchen Lehre wie diesselbige aus Gottes Wort, in der Augspurgischen Confession, Apologia, und Schmalkaldischen Artickeln begriffen*... Eisleben 1567.

——, *Wieder die Antwort des Osiandrischen Schwermers in Preussen, M. Vogels, Auff meine Apologiam. Sampt gründlichen bericht, das zwischen uns und Osiandro kein grammaticale, sondern reale certamen gewesen sey*, Magdeburg 1559.

Osiander, Andreae, d. Ä., "*[Der Grosse Nürnberger] Ratschlag* (1524/1525)", in AO 1, pp. 299–386.

——, "Disputatio de justificatione", in AO 9, pp. 422–447.

——, "Beweisung, dass ich dreissig Jahre immer einerlei Lehre von der Gerechtigkeit des Glaubens gelehrt habe", in AO 10, pp. 421–449.

——, "[Von dem Einigen] Mittler Jhesu Christo und Rechtfertigung des Glaubens", in AO 10, pp. 78–300.

——, "[Wider den lichtflüchtigen] Nachtraben", in AO 10, pp. 398–413.

——, "Gutachten zu einem Gutachten der Gräfin Elisabeth von Henneberg", in AO 10, pp. 463–483.

——, "Widerlegung der Antwort Philipp Melanchtons", in AO 10, pp. 561–670.

Selnecker, Nicolaus, *In acta apostolorum annotatio grammatica, indicatis figuris orationis, & praecipuis quibusdam locis, qui in illorum lectione considerandi occurrunt*, Ienae, Ex Officina Thomae Rebarti MDLXVII.

——, *Paedagogia Christiana. Secunda pars*, 1568. (Latin)

——, *Paedagogia Christiana. pars secunda*, 1569. (German)

——, *Catechesis D. Martini Lutheri minor, graecolatina*, Lipsiae 1575.

——, *Institutionis Christianae religionis* 1–2, 1579.

——, *Notatio Nicolai Selnecceri De studio sacrae Theologiae, & rationali discendi doctrinam coelestem*, Lipsiae MDLXXIX.

——, *Repetitio doctrina de idiomatum communicatione, & humanae in Christo naturae exaltatione, gloria, & maiestate*, Lipsiae 1581.

——, [*Christliche und Sehr* Schöne] *Trostsprüche vor engstige betrübte und verfolgte Christen*, Leipzig 1594.

Trutvetter, Jodocus, *Summa in totam physicem: hoc est philosophiam naturalem conformiter siquidem vere sophie: que est theologia per Judocum Jsennachcensis*, Erffordie, Maler 1514.

Wigand Johannes & Mathaeus Judex, Σύνταγμα, *seu Corpus doctrinae Christi, ex novo Testamento tantum, Methodica ratione, singulari fide & diligentia congestum*, Basileae ex officiana Oporiana.

Wigand Johannes, Johannes Frid & Timotheus Kirchner, *Bekentnis Von der Eechtfertigung* (!) *für Gott und von guten wercken*, 1569.

Wigand, Johannes, *In S. Pauli ad Ephesios epistolam, annotationes D. Johannes Vuigandi*, Erphordiae 1581.

——, *De Osiandrismo: Dogmata et argumenta, studiose ac fideliter collecta*, Ienae 1586.

——, *In S. Pauli ad Colossenses epistolam, annotationes D. Johannes Vuigandi*, Witebergae 1586.

——, *De Ubiquitate seu omnipreasentia Dei*, Regiomonti 1588.

Documents

The Papal Confutation

Ficker, J., *Die Konfutation des Augsburgischen Bekenntnisses. Ihre Gestalt und ihre Geschichte*, Leipzig 1891.

Immenkötter, Herbert, *Die Confutatio der Confessio Augustana vom* 3. *August* 1530, *bearbeitet von Herbert Immenkötter*, Corpus Catholicorum 33, München 1979.

The Maulbronn Formula

Pressel, Theodor, "Zwei Actenstücke zur Genesis der Concordienformel, aus den Originalie des Dresdener K. Archivs mitgetheilt von Dr. Th. Pressel", *Jahrbüch für Deutsche Theologie* (1866), pp. 640–742.

The Swabian Confession

Hachfeld, H., "Die Schwäbische Confession", *Zeitschrift für historische Theologie* 36 (1866), pp. 230–301.

The Swabian-Saxon Confession

Pfaffius, Christopher Matthaeus, *Acta et scripta publica Ecclesiae Wirtembergicae*, Tubingae 1720, pp. 381–511.

The Book of Torgau

Heppe, Heinrich (hrsgb.), *Der Text der Bergischen Concordienformel verglichen mit dem Text der schwäbischen Concordie, der schwäbisch-sächsischen Concordie und des Torgauer Buches*, Zweite Ausgabe, Koch & Sipmann, Marburg 1860.

Literature

Aquinas, St. Thomas, [*Sancti Thomae Aquinatis Doctoris Angelici Ordinis Praedicatorum*] *Summa Theologiae*, Biblioteca de Autores Cristianos, Matriti 1955.

Aristotle, *De anima*, recognovit brevique adnotatione instruxit W. D. Ross, Clarendon, Oxford 1956.

——, *Nicomachean ethics*, Focus Publishing, Newburyport, MA 2002.

Asendorf, Ulrich, "Rechtfertigung und Vergottung als Thema in Luthers Theologie und als Brücke zur Orthodoxie", *Ökumenische Rundschau* 41 (1992).

Ambrosius, "Epistolae in duas classes distributae", in MPL 16.

Athanasios, "Oratio de Incartione Verbi", in MPG 25.

——, "Orationes adversus Arianos", in MPG 26.

Aulén, Gustaf, *Den kristna försoningstanken: huvudtyper och brytningar*, Svenska kyrkans diakonistyrelse, Stockholm 1931.

Barnes, Michel R., "The background and use of Eunomius' causal language", in *Arianism after Arius*, ed. M. Barnes et al., T&T Clark, Edinburgh 1993.

Barton, Peter F., *Um Luthers Erbe. Studien und Texte zur Spätreformation. Tilemann Hesshusius* (1527–1559), Luther-Verlag, Witten 1972.

——, "Matthias Flacius Illyricus", in *Gestalten der Kirchengeschichte*, Band 6, hrsgb. Martin Greschat, Verlag W. Kohlhammer, Stuttgart 1981.

——, "David Chytraeus", in TRE VIII (1981), pp. 88–90.

——, "Hesshusius, Tilemann", in TRE XV (1986), pp. 256–270.

Baur, Jörg, *Salus Christiana. Die Rechtfertigungslehre in der Geschichte des christlichen Heilsverständnisses*, Band 1, Gütersloher Verlagshaus Gerhard Mohn, Gütersloh 1968.

——, "Martin Chemnitz", in *Einsicht und Glaube. Aufsätze*, Vandenhoeck & Ruprecht, Göttingen 1978, pp. 154–72.

——, "Flacius—Radikale Theologe", in *Einsicht und Glaube. Aufsätze*, Vandenhoeck & Ruprecht, Göttingen 1978, pp. 173–188.

——, "Christologie und Subjektivität. Geschichtlicher Ort und dogmatischer Rang der Christologie der Konkordienformel", in *Einsicht und Glaube. Aufsätze*, Vandenhoeck & Ruprecht, Göttingen 1978, pp. 189–205.

——, *Luther und seine klassichen Erben. Theologische Aufsätze und Forschungen*, Mohr Siebeck, Tübingen 1993.

Beck, Nestor, *The Doctrine of Faith. A Study of the Augsburg Confession and Contemporary Ecumenical Documents*, Concordia Publishing House, St. Louis 1987.

Bellucci, Dino, *Science de la Nature et Réformation. La physique au service de la Réforme dans l'enseignement de Philippe Mélanchthon*, Edizioni Vivere, Roma 1998.

Bente, F., *Historical Introductions to the Book of Concord*, Concordia Publishing House, St. Louis 1965.

Beutel, Albrecht, "Antwort und Wort", in *Luther und Ontologie. Das Sein Christi im Glauben als Strukturiendes Prinzip der Theologie Luthers*, Schriften der Luther-Agricola-Gesellschaft 31, Helsinki 1993, pp. 70–93.

Beyreuther, Erich et al., *Nikolaus Selneccer* 1530–1592. *Herausgeben im Gedenkjahr zum* 450. *Geburtstag* 6.12.1980, Karl Pfeiffer's Buchdruckerei und Verlag, Hersbruck 1979.

Bielfeldt, Dennis, "Ontology of Deification", in *Caritas Dei. Beiträge zum Verständnis Luthers und der gegenwärtige Ökumene*, Festschrift für Tuomo Mannermaa zum 60. Geburtstag, ed. Oswald Bayer et al, Schriften der Luther-Agricola-Gesellschaft 39, Helsinki 1997, pp. 90–113.

Bizer, Ernst, "Reformationsgeschichte 1532 bis 1555", in *Reformationsgeschichte Deutschlands bis* 1555, ed. Franz Lau und Ernst Bizer, Die Kirche in ihrer Geschichte, Ein Handbuch, Vandenhoeck & Ruprecht, Göttingen 1964.

——, *Theologie der Verheissung. Studien zur Theologie des jüngen Melanchthon* 1519–1524, Neukirchener Verlag des Erziehungsvereins Gmbh, Neukirchen-Vluyn 1964.

Karin Bornkamm, *Luthers Auslegung des Galaterbriefs von* 1519 *und* 1531, Walter de Gruyter, Berlin 1963.

Brandy, Hans Christian, "Jacob Andreaes Fünf Artikel von 1568/69", in *Zeitschrift für Kirchengeschichte* 98 (1987), pp. 338–351.

——, *Die späte Christologie des Johannes Brenz*, J. C. B. Mohr, Tübingen 1992.

Brecht, Martin, *Die Frühe Theologie des Johannes Brenz*, J. C. B. Mohr, Tübingen 1966.

——, *Martin Luther*, Band 2, Ordnung und Abgrenzung der Reformation 1521–1532, Calwer, Stuttgart 1986.

Brecht, Martin und Schwarz, Reinhard (hrsgb), *Bekenntnis und Einheit der Kirche, Studien zum Konkordienbuch im Auftrag der Sektion Kirchengeschichte der Wissenschaftlichen Gesellschaft für Theologie*, Calwer Verlag, Stuttgart 1980.

Brown, Francis, *The Brown—Driver—Briggs Hebrew and English Lexicon*, Hendrickson Publishers, Massachusetts 1999.

BSELK, *Die Bekenntnisskriften der evangelisch-lutherischen Kirche*, 11. Auflage, Vandenhoeck & Ruprecht, Göttingen 1992.

Buchrucker, Armin-Ernst, "Einheit im Bekenntis de Wahrheit. Von Sinn, Ziel und Problematik der Konkordienformel", in *Bekenntnis zur Wahrheit. Aufsätze über die Konkordienformel*, hrsgb. von Jobst Schöne, Martin Luther—Verlag, Erlangen 1978, pp. 11–24.

Cyril of Alexandria, "In Joannis evangelium", in MPG 73–74.

——, "Adversus Nestorium Lib I.", in MPG 76.

——, "Homilia Paschalis", in MPG 77.

Czaika, Otfried, *David Chytraeus und die Universität Rostock in ihren Beziehungen zum schwedischen Reich*, Schriften der Luther-Agricola-Gesellschaft 51, Helsinki 2002.

Damascenus, "De haeresis", in MPG 94.

Denzinger, Heinrich, *Kompendium der Glaubensbekenntnisse und kirchlichen Lehrentscheidungen*, 37. Auflage, Herder, Freiburg im Bresgau 1991.

Diener, Ronald E., "Johann Wigand", in *Shapers of Religious Traditions in Germany, Switzerland and Poland* 1560–1600, ed. Jill Rait, Yale University Press, New Haven and London 1981, pp. 12–38.

Dieter, Theodor, *Der Junge Luther und Aristoteles. Eine historisch-systematische Untersuchung zum Verhältnis von Theologie und Philosophie*, Walter der Gruyter, Berlin 2001.

Dingel, Irene, *Concordia controversa. Die öffentlichen Diskussionen um das lutherische Konkordienwerk am Ende des* 16. *Jahrhunderts*, Quellen und Forschungen zur Reformationsgeschichte 63, Gütersloher Verlagshaus, Gütersloh 1996.

Ebel, Jobst Christian, "Jacob Andreae (1528–1590) als Verfasser der Konkordienformel", in Zeitschrift für Kirchengeschichte 89 (1978), pp. 78–119.

——, "Die Herkunft des Konzeptes der Konkordienformel", in *Zeitschrift für Kirchengeschichte* 91 (1980), pp. 237–282.

——, *Wort und Geist bei den Verfassern der Konkordienformel. Eine historisch-systematische Untersuchung*, Beiträge zur evangelischen Theologie 89, Chr. Kaiser Verlag, München 1981.

Ebeling, Gerhard, *Disputatio de homine. Dritter Teil. Die Theologische Definition des Menschen. Kommentar zu These* 20–40, J. C. B. Mohr, Tübingen 1989.

Elert, Werner, *Morphologie des Luthertums. Erster Band: Theologie und Weltanschauung des Luthertums hauptsächlich im* 16. *und* 17. *Jahrhundert*, München 1952.

——, *Der Christliche Glaube. Grundlinien der Lutherischen Dogmatik*, Sechste Auflage, Martin Luther–Verlag, Erlangen 1988.

Erikson, Leif, *Inhabitatio—illuminatio—unio. En studie i Luthers och den äldre lutherdomens teologi*, Meddelanden från stiftelsens för Åbo akademi forskningsinstitut nr 166, Åbo Akademi, Åbo 1986.

Estes, James M., *Peace, Order and the Glory of God. Secular Authority and the Church in the Thought of Luther and Melanchthon* 1518–1559, Studies in Medieval and Reformation Traditions CXI, Brill, Leiden 2005.

Flogaus, Reinhard, "Luther versus Melanchthon? Zur Frage der Einheit der Wittenberger Reformation in der Rechtfertigungslehre", in *Archiv für Reformationsgeschichte*, Vol. 91 (2000), pp. 6–46.

Forsberg, Juhani, *Das Abrahambild in der Theologie Luthers. Pater Fidei Sanctissimus*, Veröffentlichungen des Instituts für Europäische Geschichte Mainz 117, Franz Steiner Verlag Wiesbaden GmbH, Stuttgart 1984.

——, "Der finnische Beitrag zum Dokument Gemeinsame Erklärung zur Rechtfertigungslehre", in *Caritas Dei. Beiträge zum Verständnis Luthers und der gegenwärtige Ökumene*, Festschrift für Tuomo Mannermaa zum 60. Geburtstag, ed. Oswald Bayer et al., Schriften der Luther-Agricola-Gesellschaft 39, Helsinki 1997, pp. 152–169.

Frank, Günter, *Theologische philosophie Philip Melanchthons* (1497–1560), Erfurter Theologische Studien 67, Benno, Leipzig 1995.

——, "Melanchthons 'Liber de anima' und die Etablierung der frühneuzeitlichen Anthropologie", in *Humanismus und Wittenberger Reformation. Festgabe anlässlich des* 500. *Geburtstages des Praeceptor Germaniae*, Philipp Melanchthon, am 16. Februar 1997, hrsgb. Michael Beyer et al., Evangelische Verlagsanstalt, Leipzig 1996, pp. 313–326.

Gebremedhin, Ezra, *Life—Giving Blessing. An Inquiry into the Eucharistic Doctrine of Cyril of Alexandria*, Acta Universitas Upsaliensis 17, Uppsala 1977.

Geyer, Hans-Georg, *Von der Geburt des Wahren Menschen. Probleme aus den Anfängen der Theologie Melanchthons*, Neukirchener Verlag des Erziehungvereins Gmbh., Neukirchen-Vluyn 1965.

Glaser, Karl-Heinz et al. (hrsgb), *David und Nathan Chytraeus. Humanismus im Konfessionellen Zeitalter*, Ubstadt–Weiher 1993.
Gollwitzer, Helmut, *Coena Domini. Die altlutherische Abendmahlslehre in ihrer Auseinandersetsung mit dem Calvinismus dargestellt an der lutherischen Frühortodoxie*, Chr. Kaiser Verlag, München 1937.
Gozdek, Frank-Georg, "Der Beitrag des Martin Chemnitz zur lutherischen Abendmalslehre—dargestellt anhand seiner Schrift 'Repetitio sanae doctrinae de vera praesentia corporis et sanguinis Donini in coena'", in *Der zweite Martin der Lutherischen Kirche. Festschrift zum* 400. Todestag von Martin Chemnitz, hrsgb. W. A. Jünke, Ev.-luth. Stadtkirchenband und Propstei Braunschweig, Braunschweig 1986, pp. 9–47.
Grane, Leif, *Contra Gabrielem. Luthers Auseinandersetzung mit Gabriel Biel in der Disputatio Contra Scholasticam Theologiam* 1517, Acta theologica Danica IV, Gyldendal 1962.
——, *The Augsburg Confession. A Commentary.* Augsburg Publishing House, Minneapolis 1987.
——, *Reformationsstudien. Beiträge zu Luther und zur dänischen Reformation*, VIAG Beiheft 49, Mainz 1999.
Green, Lowell C., *How Melanchthon helped Luther find the Gospel. The Doctrine of Justification in the Reformation*, The Attic Press Inc., Greenwood 1980.
——, "The Three Causes of Conversion in Philipp Melanchthon, Martin Chemnitz, David Chytraeus, and the 'Formula of Concord'", in *Lutherjahrbuch* 47, Vandenhoeck & Ruprecht, Göttingen 1980, pp. 89–115.
St. Gregory of Nazianzus, *"Epistola 101"*, in MPG 37.
St. Gregory of Nyssa, "Oratio Catechetica", in MPG 45.
Greschat, Martin, *Melanchthon neben Luther. Studien zur Gestalt der Rechtfertigungslehre zwischen* 1528 *und* 1537, Untersuchungen zur Kirchengeschichte, Bd.1, Luther-Verlag, Witten 1965.
Haikola, Lauri, *Gesetz und Evangelium bei Matthias Flacius Illyricus. Eine Untersuchung zur lutherischen Theologie vor der Kondordienformel*, Studia Theologica Lundensia, CWK Cleerup, Lund 1952.
——, *Studien zu Luther und Luthertum*, Otto Harrassowitz, Wiesbaden 1958.
——, "A comparison of Melanchthon's and Luther's doctrine of Justification, transl. by Robert Schultz", in *Dialog* 2 (1963), pp. 32–39.
Hamann, Henry P., "Righteousness of Faith before God", in *Contemporary look at the Formula of Concord*, Concordia Publishing House, St. Louis 1978.
Hardt, Tom G. A., *Venerabilis & adorabilis Eucharistia. En studie i den lutherska nattvardsläran under* 1500-*talet*, Studia doctrinae christianae Upsaliensia 9, Stockholm 1971.
Hardy, Edward R., *Christology of the Later Fathers*, Philadelphia, Westminster Press 1954.
Harvey, Ruth E., *The inward wits. Psychological theory in the middle ages and the renaissance*, Warburg Institute Surveys VI, The Warburg Institute, London 1975.
Hauke, Rainer, *Gott—Haben—um Gottes Willen. Andreas Osianders Theosisgedanke und die Diskussion um die Grundlagen der evangelisch verstandenen Rechtfertigung*, Kontexte, Neue Beiträge zur historischen und Systematischen Theologie 30, Peter Lang, Frankfurt am Main 1999.
Haussleiter, Johannes, "Melanchthons Loci praecipui und Thesen über die Rechtfertigung aus dem Jahre 1531", in *Abhandlungen Alexander von Oettingen zum siebenzigsten Geburstag*, C. H. Beck'sche Verlagsbuchhandlung, München 1898, pp. 245–262.
Hirsch, Emanuel, *Die Theologie des Andreas Osiander und ihre geschichtlichen Voraussetzungen*, Vandenhoeck & Ruprecht, Göttingen 1919.
——, *Hilfsbuch zum Studium der Dogmatik*, Walter der Gryuter, Berlin 1937.
Hirvonen, Vesa, *Passions in William Ockhams's philosophical psychology*, Kluwer Academic Publishers, Boston, Dordrecht 2004.
Hoffman, Gottfried, "*Die Rechtfertigung des Sünders vor Gott nach dem Examen Concilii Tridentinii von Martin Chemnitz*", in *Der zweite Martin der Lutherischen Kirche*, Festschrift zum 400.

Todestag von Martin Chemnitz, hrsgb. W. A. Jünke, Ev.-luth. Stadtkirchenband und Propstei Braunschweig, Braunschweig 1986, pp. 60–92.

Højlund, Asger, *Ved gaven helbreder han naturen. Helbredelsetanken i Luthers retfaerdiggørelselaere*, Menighedsfakultetets Videnskabelige Serie 4, Århus 1992.

——, "Forsoningen i Luthers teologi", in *Forsoningen. Udvalget for Konvent for Kirke og Theologi* (1995), pp. 59–75.

Holl, Karl, *Gesammelte Aufsätze zur Kirchengeschichte*, Band 1, Mohr, Tübingen 1932.

Holfelder, Hans Hermann, *Tentatio et consolatio. Studien zu Bugenhagens "Interpretatio in librorum Psalmorum"*, Arbeiten zur Kirchengeschichte 45, Berlin/New York 1974.

——, *Solus Christus. Die Ausbildung von Bugenhagens Rechtfertigungslehre in der Paulusauslegung (1524/25) und ihre Bedeutung für die theologische Argumentation im Sendbrief "Von dem Christlichen Glauben"* (1526), *Eine Untersuchung zur Genese von Bugenhagens Theologie*, J. C. B. Mohr, Tübingen 1981.

Huovinen, Eero, *Fides infantium. Martin Luthers Lhre vom Kinderglauben*, Veröffentlichungen des Instituts für europäische Geschichte 159, Philipp von Zabern, Mainz 1991.

Hägglund, Bengt, "Rechtfertigung—Wiedergeburt—Erneuerung in der nachreformatorischen Theologie", in *Kerygma und Dogma* (1959), pp. 318–337.

——, "'Majestas homini Christi'. Wie hat Martin Chemnitz die Christologie Luthers gedeutet?", in *Lutherjahrbuch* 47. Vandenhoeck & Ruprecht, Göttingen 1980, pp. 71–89.

——, "Die Rezeption Luthers in der Konkordienformel", in *Luther und die Bekenntnisschriften. Veröffentlichungen der Luther-Akademie Ratzeburg*, Band 2, Erlangen 1981, pp. 107–120.

Immenkötter, Herbert, *Die Konfutatio der Confessio Augustana vom* 3. *August* 1530, bearbeitet von Herbert Immenkötter, Corpus Catholicorum 33, München 1979.

Jacob, Friedrich, "Von Christi Tat und unserem Tun. Zur Interpretation von Artikel III und IV der Konkordienformel", in *Bekenntnis zur Wahrheit. Aufsätze über die Konkordienformel*, hrsgb. von Jobst Schöne, Martin Luther–Verlag, Erlangen 1978, pp. 49–64.

Joest, Wilfrid, *Ontologie der Person bei Luther*, Vandenhoeck & Ruprecht, Göttingen 1967.

Johansson, Torbjörn, *Reformationens huvudfrågor och arvet från Augustinus. En studie i Martin Chemnitz' Augustinusreception*, Församlingsfakultetets skriftserie nr 3., Församlingförlaget, Göteborg 1999.

Johnson, J. F., "Justification According to the Apology of the Augsburg Confession and the Formula of Concord", in *Justification by faith. Lutherans and Catholics in dialogue*, 7. ed., Hugh George Anderson, Minneapolis 1985, pp. 185–199.

Jungkuntz, Theodor, *Formulators of the Formula of Concord. Four Architects of Lutheran Unity*, Concordia Publishing House, St. Louis 1977.

Juntunen, Sammeli, *Der Begriff des Nichts bei Luther in den Jahren von* 1510 *bis* 1523, Schriften der Luther-Agricola-Gesellschaft 36, Helsinki 1996.

Järveläinen, Petri, *A study on religious emotions*, Schriften der Luther-Agricola-Gesellschaft, Helsinki 2000.

Eberhard Jüngel, *Das Evangelium von der Rechtfertigung des Gottlosen als Zentrum des christlichen Glaubens: eine theologische Studie in ökumenischer Absicht*, Mohr, Tübingen 1998.

Kaufmann, Thomas, "Die Brüder David und Nathan Chytraeus in Rostock", in David und Nathan Chytraeus—Humanismus im konfessionellen Zeitalter, hrsgb. Glaser, Karl Heinz et al., Ubstadt–Weiher 1993, pp. 103–116.

——, "Martin Chemnitz (1522–1586). Zur Wirkungsgeschichte der theologischen Loci", in *Melanchthon in seinen Schülern*, Scheible, Heinz (hrsgb.), Harrassowitz Verlag, Wiesbaden 1997.

——, "Die 'Kriteriologische Function' der Rechtfertigungslehre in den lutherischen Bekenntnisschriften", in *Die Zeitschrift fuer Theologie und Kirche Beiheft* (1998), p. 10.

Keller, Rudolf, "Der Beitrag von David Chytraeus zur Einigung des Luthertums", in *Humanismus im konfessionellen Zeitalter*. Glaser, Karl-Heinz et al. (hrsgb.), Ubstadt-Weiher 1993, pp. 117–128.

——, *Die Confessio Augustana im theologischen Wirken des Rostocker Professors David Chyträus* (1530–1600), Forschungen zur Kirchen- und Dogmengeschichte 60, Vandenhoeck & Ruprecht, Göttingen 1994.

——, "*David Chytraeus* (1530–1600). *Melanchthons Geist im Luthertum*", in *Melanchthon in seinen Schülern*, hrsgb. Heinz Scheible, Wolfenbütteler Forschungen 73, Wiesbaden 1997, pp. 361–371.

Kimme August, *Rechtfertigung und Heiligung in christologischer sicht. Eine dogmatische Untersuchung*, Martin-Luther-Verlag, Erlangen 1989.

Kirjavainen, Heikki, "'Minä' ja mystiikka", in *Elevatis oculis*, Studia mystica in honorem Seppo A. Teinonen, ed. Pauli Annala, Missiologian ja ekumeniikan seuran julkaisuja 42, Helsinki 1984, pp. 107–114.

Klatt, Detloff, *Chyträus als Geschichtslehrer und Geschichtsschreiber*, Beiträge zur Geschichte der Stadt Rostock, Band V, Heft 1 & 2, Rostock 1909.

Hermann Kleinknecht, *Gemeinschaft ihne Bedingungen: Kirche und Rechtfertigung in Luthers grosser Galaterbrief-Vorlesung von* 1531, Calwer Verlag, Stuttgart 1981.

Klän, Werner, "Der 'vierte Mann'. Auf den Spuren von Nikolaus Selneckers (1530–1592) Beitrag zu Entstehung und Verbreitung der Konkordienformel", in *Lutherische Theologie und Kirche* 17 (1993), pp. 145–174.

Koen, Lars, *The Saving Passion. Incarnational and Soteriological Thought in Cyril of Alexandria's Commentary on the Gospel according to St. John*. Acta Universitas Upsaliensis 31, Uppsala 1991.

Kolb, Robert, *Andreae and The Formula of Concord. Six sermons on the way to Lutheran Unity*. transl. R. Kolb, Concordia Publishing House, St. Louis 1977.

——, "Martin Chemnitz—Gnesiolutheraner", in *Der zweite Martin der Lutherischen Kirche*, Festschrift zum 400. Todestag von Martin Chemnitz, Hrsgb. W. A. Jünke, Ev.-luth. Stadtkirchenband und Propstei Braunschweig, Braunschweig 1986, pp. 115–129.

——, *Confessing the Faith. Reformers define the Church* 1530–1580, Concordia Publishing House, St. Louis 1991.

——, *Luther's Heirs define His legacy. Studies on Lutheran Confessionalization*, Collected studies series C539, Variorum, Norfolk 1996, pp. VIII, 136–156.

——, "'A Hammer of God against Free Choice'. Johannes Wigand's Interpretation of Luther's *De servo arbitrio*", in *Vanha ja nuori*, Juhlakirja Simo Heinisen täyttäessä 60 vuotta, ed. Kaisamari Hintikka et al., Studia missiologica et oecumenica Fennica 60, Luther-Agricola-Gesellschaft, Helsinki 2003, pp. 131–146.

Kolb, Robert & Nestingen, James A. (ed.), *Sources and Contexts of The Book of Concord*, Fortress Press, Minneapolis 2001.

Kramer, Fred, "Biografical sketch of Martin Chemnitz", in Martin Chemnitz: *Examination of Council of Trent*, Part I, Transl. Fred Kramer, Concordia Publishing House, St. Louis 1971.

——, "Martin Chemnitz", in *Shapers of religious traditions in Germany, Switzerland and Poland* 1560–1600, ed. Jill Raitt, Yale University Press, New Haven 1981, pp. 39–51.

Kusukawa, Sachiko, *The Transformation of Natural Philosophy. The Case of Philip Melanchthon*, Cambridge University Press, Cambridge 1995.

Kärkkäinen, Pekka, *Luther trinitarische Theologie des Heiliges Geistes*, Philip von Zabern, Mainz 2005.

Kötter, Ralf, *Johannes Bugenhagens Rechtfertigungslehre und der Römische Katholizismus. Studien zum Sendbrief an die Hamburger*, Forschungen zur Kirchen- und Dogmengeschichte 59, Vandenhoeck & Ruprecht, Göttingen 1994.

Lawrenz, Carl J., "On Justification, Osiander's Doctrine of the Indwelling Christ (FC, III)", in *No other Gospel. Essays in Commemoration of the* 400th *Anniversary of the Formula of Concord* 1580–1980, ed. Arnold J. Koelpin, Northwestern Publishing House, Milwaukee 1980, pp. 149–174.

Lehmann, K. & Pannenberg, W., *Lehrverurteilungen—Kirchentrennend? Rechtfertigung, Sakramente und Amt im Zeitalter der Reformation und heute*, Herder, Freiburg im Breisgau 1988.

Lehmkühler, Karsten, *Inhabitatio. Die Einwohnung Gottes im Menschen*, Forschungen zur systematischen und ökumenischen theologie 104, Vandenhoeck & Ruprecht, Göttingen 2004.

Lehtonen, Tommi, *Punishment, Atonement and Merit in Modern Philosophy of Religion*, Schriften der Luther-Agricola-Gesellschaft 44, Helsinki 1999.

Letham, Robert, *The Work of Christ. Contours of Christian Theology*, IVP, Downer's Grove 1993.

Lexutt, Athina, *Rechtfertigung im Gespräch: das Rechtfertigungsverständnis in den Religionsgesprächen von Hagenau, Worms und Regensburg* 1540/41, Vandenhoech & Ruprecht, Göttingen 1996.

Lienhard, Marc, *Martin Luthers christologisches Zeugnis*, Evangelische Verlanganstalt, Berlin 1980.

Locher, Gottfried, *Die Theologie Huldrich Zwinglis im Lichte seiner Christologie*, Zwingli-Verlag, Zürich 1952.

Loewenich, Walther von, *Duplex iustitia. Luthers stellung zu einer unionsformel des* 16. *Jahrhunderts*, Franz Steiner Verlag GmbH, Wiesbaden 1972.

Lohff, Wenzel & Spitz, Lewis W (eds.), *Widerspruch, Dialog und Einigung. Studien zur Konkordienformel der Lutherischen Reformation*, Calwer Verlag, Stuttgart 1977.

Lohse, Bernhard, *Ratio und Fides. Eine Untersuchung über die RATIO in der Theologie Luthers*, Vandenhoeck & Ruprecht, Göttingen 1958.

——, "Dogma und Bekenntnis in der Reformation: Von Luther bis zum Konkordienbuch", in *Handbuch der Dogmen- und Theologiegeschichte*, hrsgb. Carl Andresen, Band 2, Die Lehrentwicklung im Rahmen der Konfessionalität, Ungekürtze Studienausgabe, Göttingen 1980, pp. 1–164.

——, "Philipp Melanchthon in seinen Beziehungen zur Luther", in *Martin Luther: Ein Einführung ein sein Leben und sein Werk*, Beck, München 1983.

Lombardus, Petrus, *Sententiae in IV Libris distinctae*, Tomus II, Liber III et IV, Grottaferrata, Romae 1981.

Lutz, Jürgen, *Unio und communio. Zum Verhältnis von Rechtfertigungslehre und Kirchenverständnis bei Martin Luther. Eine Untersuchung zu ekklesiologischen relevanten Texten der Jahre* 1519–1528, Konfessionskundliche und kontroverstheologische Studien 55, Bonifatius, Paderborn vuosi 1990.

Mager, Inge, "Jacob Andreäs lateinische Unionsartikel von 1568", in *Zeitschrift für Kirchengeschichte* 98 (1987), pp. 70–86.

——, "Das Testament des Braunschweiger Stadtssuperindenten Martin Chemnitz (1522–1586)", in *Braunschweigisches Jb.* 68 (1987b), pp. 121–132.

Mahlmann, Theodor, *Das Neue Dogma der lutherischen Christologie. Problem und Geschichte seiner Begründung*, Gütersloher Verlagshaus Mohn, Gütersloh 1969.

——, "Martin Chemnitz", in TRE VIII, Walter de Gruyter, Berlin 1981, pp. 714–721.

——, "Jacob Andreä im Lichte neuerer Forschung", in *Lutherische Theologie und Kirche* 14 (1990), pp. 139–153.

——, "Zur Geschichte der Formel 'Articulus stantis et cadentis ecclesiae'", in *Lutherische Theologie und Kirche* 17 (1993), pp. 187–194.

——, "Die Stellung der unio cum Christo in der lutherischen Theologie des 17. Jahrhunderts", in *Unio. Gott und Mensch in der nachreformatorischen Theologie*, hrsgb. M. Repo und R. Vinke, Schriften der Luther-Agricola-Gesellschaft A 31, Helsinki 1996. pp. 72–200.

Mannermaa, Tuomo

——, "Einig in Sachen Rechtfertigung? Eine lutherische und eine katholische Stellungnahme zu Jörg Baur", in *Theologische Rundschau* 55 (1990), pp. 325–335.

——, "Hat Luther eine trinitarische Ontologie?", in *Luther und Ontologie. Das Sein Christi im Glauben als structuriendes Prinzip der Theologie Luthers*, hrsgb. Anja Ghiselli, Kari Kopperi & Rainer Vinke, Schriften der Luther-Agricola-Gesellschaft A 31, Vammala 1993, pp. 9–27.

——, "Über die Unmöglichkeit, gegen die texte Luthers zu sysmatisieren. Antwort an Gunther Wenz", in *Unio. Gott und Mensch in der nachreformatorischen Theologie*, hrsgb. Matti Repo und Rainer Vinke, Schriften der Luther-Agricola-Gesellschaft A 31, Helsinki 1996, pp. 381–391.

——, *Christ Present in Faith. Luther's View of Justification*, Fortress Press, Minneapolis 2005.

Manns, Peter, "Fides absoluta—fides incarnata", in *Reformata reformanda*, Teil 1, Festgabe für Hubert Jedin zum 17. Juni 1965. Hrsgb. Erwin Iserloh & Konrad Repgen, Münster 1965, pp. 265–312.

Marquart, Kurt, "Contemporary Significance of the Formula of Concord", in *No other Gospel. Essays in Commemoration of the* 400th *Anniversary of the Formula of Concord* 1580–1980, ed. Arnold J. Koelpin, Northwestern Publishing House, Milwaukee 1980, pp. 11–44.

Martens, Gottfried, *Die Rechtfertigung des Sünders—Rettungshandeln Gotter oder historisches Interpretament? Grundentscheidungen lutherischer Theologie und Kirche bei der Behandlung des Themas 'Rechtfertigung' im ökumenischen Kontext*, FSÖTh 64, Vandenhoeck & Ruprecht, Göttingen 1992.

——, "Christusgemeinschaft als Erkenntnisgrund. Anmerkungen zu einem bemerkenswerten Tagungsbericht," in *LutherischeTheologie und Kirche* 19 (1995), pp. 173–177.

Martikainen, Eeva, *Doctrina: Studien zu Luthers Begriff der Lehre*, Schriften der Luther-Agricola-Gesellschaft 26, Helsinki 1992.

Matz, Wolfgang, *Der befreite Mensch. Die Willenslehre in der Theologie Philipp Melanchthons*, Vandenhoeck & Ruprecht, Göttingen 2001.

Maurer, Wilhelm, *Der Junge Melanchthon zwischen Humanismus und Reformation*, Band 2, Der Theologe, Vandenhoeck & Ruprecht, Göttingen 1969.

——, "Lex spiritualis bei Melanchthon bis 1521", in *Gedenkschrift für Werner Elert*, hrsgb. Hübner et al, Lutherisches Verlagshaus, Berlin 1955.

——, *Historischer Kommentar zur Confessio Augustana*, Bd. 2, Theologische Probleme, Gütersloher Verlagshaus Mohn, Gütersloh 1978.

McGrath, A. E., *Iustitia Dei. A History of the Christian Doctrine of Justification*, Second Edition, Cambridge University Press, Cambridge 1998.

McKinion, S. A., *Words, Imagery and the Mystery of Christ. A Reconstruction of Cyril of Alexandria's Christology*, Supplements to Vigiliae Christianae LV, Brill, Leiden 2000.

Megivern, James J., "The Catholic Rejoinder", in *Discord, Dialogue and Concord. Studies in the Lutheran Reformation's Formula of Concord*, ed. L. Spitz & W. Lohff, Fortress Press, Philadelphia 1977, pp. 191–207.

Meijering, E. P., *Melanchthon and Patristic Thought. The Doctrines of Christ and Grace, the Trinity and the Creation*, E. J. Brill, Leiden 1983.

Meyer, Harding et al. (hrsgb.), *Confessio Augustana. Bekenntnis des einen Glaubens. Gemeinsame untersuchung Lutherischer und Katholischer Theologen*. Verlag Otto Lembeck, Frankfurt am Main 1980.

Moldaenke, Günter, *Matthias Flacius Illyricus. Schriftverständnis und Schriftauslegung im Zeitalter der Reformation*, teil I, Verlag von W. Kohlhammer, Stuttgart 1936.

Montgomery, John Warwick, *Chytraeus on Sacrifice. A Reformation treatise in Biblical Theology*, Concordia Publisching House, St. Louis 1962.

Muehlenberg, Ekkehard, "Synergia and Justification by Faith", in *Discord, Dialogue and Concord. Studies in the Lutheran Reformation's Formula of Concord*, ed. L. Spitz & W. Lohff, Fortress Press, Philadelphia 1977, pp. 15–37.

zur Mühlen, Karl-Heinz, "Melanchthons Auffassung vom Affekt in den Loci Communes von 1521", in *Humanismus und Wittenberger Reformation*, Festgabe anlässlich des 500.

Geburtstages des Praeceptor Germaniae, Philipp Melanchthon, am 16. Februar 1997, hrsgb. Michael Beyer et al., Evangelische Verlagsanstalt, Leipzig 1996, pp. 327–336.

Müller, R. A., *Dictionary of Latin and Greek Theological Terms. Drawn Principally from Protestant Scholastic Theology*, Baker Book House, Grand Rapids 1985.

Neuser, Wilhelm, "Haardenberg und Melanchthon. Der Haardenbergische Streit (1554–1560)", in *Jahrbuch der Gesellschaft für niedersächsische Kirchengeschichte* 65 (1967), pp. 142–186.

Nilsson, Kvell Ove, *Simul. Das Miteinander von Göttlichem und Mensclichem in Luthers Theologie*, FKDG 17, Göttingen 1966.

Noth, Gottfried, "Peccata contra conscientiam", in *Gedenkschrift für D. Werner Elert*, hrsgb. F. Hübner et al., Lutherisches Verlagshaus, Berlin 1955, pp. 211–219.

Nüssel, F., *Allein aus Glauben. Zur Entwicklung der Rechtfertigungslehre in der konkordistischen und frühen nachkonkordistischen Theologie*, Vandenhoeck & Ruprecht, Göttingen 2000.

Oberman, Heiko A., *Harvest of Medieval Theology. Gabriel Biel and Late Medieval Nominalism*, Harvard University Press, Cambridge 1963.

Ockham, Guillelmi de, *Scriptum in librum primum sententiarum ordinatio. Prologus et distinctio prima*, St. Bonaventure, N.Y. 1967.

——, Quodlibeta Septem, St. Bonaventure, N.Y. 1980.

Oftestad, Bernt Torvild, "Traditio und Norma. Hauptzüge der Schriftauffassung bei Martin Chemnitz", in *Der zweite Martin der Lutherischen Kirche*, Festschrift zum 400. Todestag von Martin Chemnitz, hrsgb. W. A. Jünke, Ev.-luth. Stadtkirchenband und Propstei Braunschweig, Braunschweig 1986, pp. 172–189.

——, "Lehre, die das Herz bewegt. Das Predigtparadigma bei Martin Chemnitz", in *Archiv für Reformationsgeschichte* 80 (1989), pp. 125–153.

Pannenberg, Wolfhart, *Systematische Theologie*, Band 3, Vandenhoeck & Ruprecht, Göttingen 1993.

——, *Hintergründe des Streites um die Rechtfertigungslehre in der evangelischen Theologie*, Bayerische Akademie der Wissenschaften, Sitzungsberichte, Heft 3. Verlag der Bayerischen Akademie der Wissenschaften, München 2000.

Pauck, W., "Luther und Melachthon", in *Luther und Melachthon. Referate und Berichte des Zweiten Internationalen Kongresses für Lutherforschung Münster*, 8.–13. August 1960, hrsgb. Vilmos Vajta. Vandenhoeck & Ruprecht, Göttingen 1961.

Pelikan, J., *From Luther to Kierkegaard. A Study in the History of Theology*, Concordia, St. Louis 1950.

Peters, Albrecht, *Realpräsenz. Luthers Zeugnis von Christi Gegenwart im Abendmal. Arbeiten zur Geschichte und Theologie des Luthertums*, Band V, Lutherisches Verlagshaus, Berlin und Hamburg 1966.

——, *Rechtfertigung. Handbuch Systematischer Theologie*, hrsgb. Carl Heinz Ratschow, Band 12, Verlaugshaus Gerd Mohn, Gütersloh 1984.

Peters, Christian, *Apologia Confessionis Augustanae. Untersuchungen zur Textgeschichte einer lutherischen Bekenntnisschrift* (1530–1584), Calwer Verlag, Stuttgart 1997.

Peura, Simo, "Der Vergöttlichungsgedanke in Luthers Theologie 1518–1519", in *Thesaurus Lutheri*, hrsgb. Tuomo Mannermaa et al., Veröffentlichungen der Finnischen Theologischen Literaturgesellschaft 153, Helsinki 1987.

——, Mehr als ein Mensch? Die Vergöttlichung als Thema der Theologie Martin Luthers von 1513–1519. Philip von Zabern, Mainz 1994.

——, "Gott und Mensch in der Unio. Die Unterschiede im Rechfertigungsverständnis bei Osiander und Luther", in *Unio. Gott und Mensch in der nachreformatorischen Theologie*, hrsgb. M. Repo und R. Vinke, Luther-Agricola-Gesellshaft, Helsinki 1996. pp. 33–61.

Pfnür, Vinzenz, *Einig in der Rechtfertigungslehre? Die Rechtfertigungslehre der Confessio Augustana* (1530) *und die Stellungnahme der katholischen Kontroverstheologie zwischen* 1530 *und* 1535, Abteilung Abendländische Religiongeschichte, Wiesbaden 1970.

Pihkala, J., *Gnadenmittel oder Gnadenangebot? Auslegungsgeschichte des Passus per baptismum offeratur gratia Dei im Taufartikel der Confessio Augustana im zietraum von* 1530–1930, Studien zur systematischen theologie und Ethik 34, Lit Verlag, Münster 2003.
Preger, W., *Matthias Flacius Illyricus und seine Zeit*, I–II, Verlag von Theodor Bläsing, Erlangen 1859.
Prenter, R., *Das Bekenntnis von Augsburg. Eine Auslegung*, Martin Luther Verlag, Erlangen 1980.
Pressel, Th., "David Chytraeus", in *Leben und ausgewaelte Schriften der Vaeter und Begruender der Lutherischen kirche*, VIII, R. L. Friderichs, Elberfeld 1862.
Preus, J. A. O., *The Second Martin. The Life and Theology of Martin Chemnitz*, Concordia Publishing House, St. Louis 1994.
Preus, Robert D., *The Theology of Post-reformation Lutheranism*, Volume I, A Study of Theological Prolegomena, Concordia Publishing House, St. Louis 1970.
——, "The Influence of the Formula of Concord on the Later Lutheran Orthodoxy", in *Discord, Dialogue and Concord. Studies in the Lutheran Reformation's Formula of Concord*, ed. L. Spitz & W. Lohff, Fortress Press, Philadelphia 1977, pp. 86–101.
——, "Historical Backround of the Formula of Concord", in *Contemporary look at the Formula of Concord*, ed. R. Preus, Concordia Publishing House, St. Louis 1978, pp. 12–87.
——, *Justification as Taught by Post-Reformation Lutheran Theologians*, Concordia Theological Seminary, Fort Wayne 1982.
Preuss, E., "Vita Martini Chemnicii", in Martin Chemnitz: *Examen concilii Tridentinii*, Wissenshaftliche Buchgesellshaft, Darmstadt 1972, pp. 925–958.
Pöhlmann, H. G., *Rechtfertigung. Die gegenwärtige kontroverstheologische Problematik der Rechtfertigungslehre zwischen der evangelisch-lutherischen und der römisch-katholischen Kirche*, Gütersloher Verlagshaus, Gütersloh 1971.
Quere, R. W., *Melanchthon's Christum cognoscere. Christ's efficacious Presence in the Eucharistic Theology of Melanchthon*, Bibliothece Humanistica & Reformatorica XXII, B. de Graaf, Nieuwkoop 1977.
Raeder, S., "Heerbrand, Jacob", in TRE XIV (1985), pp. 524–526.
Raunio, Antti, *Summe des Christlichen Lebens. Die "Goldene Regel" als Gesetz der Liebe in der Theologie Martin Luthers von* 1510 *bis* 1527, Veröffentlichungen dews Instituts für Europäische Geschichte Mainz 160, von Sabern, Mainz 2001.
——, "Divine and Natural Law in Luther and Melanchthon", in *Lutheran Reformation and Law*, ed. Virpi Mäkinen, Studies in Medieval and Reformation Traditions CXII, Brill, Leiden 2006.
Ritschl, Otto, *Dogmengeschichte des Protestantismus*, II Band, 1. Hälfte, J. C. Hinrichs'sche Buchhandlung, Leipzig 1912.
——, *Dogmengeschichte des Protestantismus*, IV Band, Orthodoxie und Synkretismus in der altprotestantischen Theologie. Das orthodoxe Luthertum im Gegensatz zu der reformierten Theologie und in der Auseinandersetzung mit dem Synkretismus, Vandenhoeck & Ruprecht, Göttingen 1927.
Rogness, Michael, *Philip Melanchthon. Reformer without Honor*, Augsburg Fortress, Minneapolis 1969.
Roth, Erich, "Ein Braunschweiger Theologe des 16. Jahrhunderts: Mörlin und seine Rechtfertigungslehre", *Jahrbuch der Gesellschaft für niedersächsische Kirchengeschichte* 50 (1952), pp. 59–81.
Saarinen, Risto, "Ipsa dilectio Deus est. Zur Wirkungsgeschichte von. 1. Sent. dist. 17 des Petrus Lombardus bei Martin Luther", in *Thesaurus Lutheri*. Hrsg. Tuomo Mannermaa et al., Veröffentlichungen der Finnischen Theologischen Literaturgesellschaft 153, Helsinki 1987, pp. 185–204.
——, *Gottes Wirken auf uns. Die transzendentale Deutung des Gegenwart—Christi—Motivs in der Lutherforschung*, Veröffentlichungen des Instituts für Europäische Geschichte Mainz, Band 137, Franz Steiner Verlag Wiesbaden GmbH, Stuttgart 1988.

——, "Die Teilhabe an Gott bei Luther und in der finnischen Lutherforschung", in *Luther und Ontologie. Das Sein Christi im Glauben als Strukturiendes Prinzip der Theologie Luthers*, Schriften der Luther-Agricola-Gesellschaft 31, Helsinki 1993, pp. 167–182.

——, "Melanchthons Ethik zwischen Tugend und Begabung", in Melanchthon, hrsgb. Walter Sparn, Erlanger Forschungen, Reihe A, Band 85, Erlangen 1998.

——, "Die Rechtfertigungslehre als Kriterium", in Kerygma und Dogma 44. (1998/2).

Scaer, D. P., *Christology. Confessional Lutheran Dogmatics*. Vol. VI, The International Foundation for Lutheran Confessional Research, Fort Wayne 1989.

Schlink, E., *Theologie der Lutherischen Bekenntnischriften*, Evangelischer Verlag Albert Lempp, München 1940.

——, *Ökumenische Dogmatik, Grundzüge*, Vandenhoeck & Ruprecht, Göttingen 1983.

Schurb, K., "The New Finnish School of Luther Research and Philip Melanchton", *Logia* XII/3 (2003), pp. 31–36.

Schäfer, R., *Christologie und Sittlichkeit in Melanchthons frühen loci*, Beiträge zur historische Theologie 29, J. C. B. Mohr, Tübingen 1961.

Seeberg, E., *Luthers Theologie in ihren Grundzügen*, Stuttgart 1950.

Seeberg, Reinhold, *Grundriss der Dogmengeschichte*, Leipzig 1934.

——, *Lehrbuch der Dogmengeschichte*, IV/2, Benno Schwabe & Co, Basel 1954.

Seils, M., *Glaube. Handbuch Systematischer Theologie*, Bd. 13, Gütersloher Verlagshaus, Gütersloh 1996.

Sparn, Walter, "Substanz oder Subjekt? Die Kontroverse um die anthropologischen Allgemeinbegriffe im Artikle von der Erbsünde", in *Widerspruch, Dialog und Einigung*, hrsgb. W. Lohff & E. Spitz, Calwer Verlag, Stuttgart 1977.

Spitz, Lewis J., "The Formula of Concord Then and Now", in *Discord, Dialogue and Concord. Studies in the Lutheran Reformation's Formula of Concord*, ed. L. Spitz & W. Lohff, Fortress Press, Philadelphia 1977, pp. 1–12.

Spruit, Leen, *Species Intelligibilis: From Perception to Knowledge*, I. Classical Roots and Medieval Discussions, E. J. Brill, Leiden 1994.

——, *Species Intelligibilis: From Perception to Knowledge*, II. Renaissance Controversies, Later Scholasticism, and The Elimination of the Intelligible Species in Modern Philosophy, E. J. Brill, Leiden 1995.

Strawn, Paul, "Kyrill von Alexandrien als eine Quelle der Christologie bei Martin Chemnitz. Ein überblick als Werkstattbericht", *Lutherische Theologie und Kirche* 19 (1995), pp. 61–88.

Stupperich, Martin, *Osiander in Preussen* 1549–1552, AKG 44, Walter de Gruyter, Berlin 1973.

——, "Lehrentscheidung und theologische Schematisierung. Die Sonderrolle Württembergs im Osianderischen Streit und ihre Konsequenzen für die Formulierung des dritten Artikels der Solida Declaratio", in *Widerspruch, Dialog und Einigung*, hrsgb. von W. Lohff et al., Stuttgart 1977, pp. 171–195.

Söderlund, Rune, "Der Unio-Gedanke in der Konkordienformel", in *Unio. Gott und Mensch in der nachreformatorischen Theologie*, hrsgb. M. Repo und R. Vinke, Luther-Agricola-Gesellshaft, Helsinki 1996, pp. 275–295.

Teigen, Bjarne W., *The Lord's Supper in the Theology of Martin Chemnitz*, Trinity Lutheran Press, Brewster 1986.

Tiililä, Osmo, *Das Strafleiden Christi. Beitrag zur Diskussion über die Typeneinteilung der Versöhnungsmotive*, Annales Academiae Scientiarum Fennicae B XLVIII, Helsinki 1941.

Työrinoja, Reijo, "Nova vocabula et nova lingua. Luther's conception of Doctrinal Formulas", in *Thesaurus Lutheri. Auf der Suche nach neuen Paradigmen der Luther-Forschung*, hrsgb. T. Mannermaa, A. Ghiselli und S. Peura, Luther-Agricola-Gesellschaft 24, Helsinki 1987, pp. 221–236.

Urban, Waclaw, "Francesco Stancaro d. Ä." in *TRE* 32 (2001), pp. 110–113.

Urmson, James O., *The Greek philosophical vocabulary*, Gerald Duckworth & Co., London 1990.

Vaahtoranta, Martti, *Restauratio imaginis divinae. Die Vereinigung von Gott und Mensch ihre Voraussetzungen und Implikationen bei Johann Gerhard*, Schriften der Luther-Agricola-Gesellshaft 41, Helsinki 1998.

Wengert, Timothy J., "Melanchthon and Luther / Luther and Melanchthon" in *Lutherjahrbuch* 1999, Vandenhoeck & Ruprecht, Göttingen.

Wenz, Günther, "Unio. Zur Differenzierung einer Leitkategorie finnischer Lutherforschung im Anschluss an CA I–VI", in *Unio. Gott und Mensch in der nachreformatorischen Theologie*, hrsgb. M. Repo und R. Vinke, Luther-Agricola-Gesellshaft, Helsinki 1996, pp. 333–380.

——, Theologie der Bekenntnischriften der evangelisch-lutherischen Kirche. Eine historische und systematische Einführung in das Konkordienbuch, Band 2, Walter de Gruyter, Berlin 1998.

White, Graham, *Luther as nominalist. A study of the logical methods used in Martin Luther's disputations in the light of their medieval background*, Schriften der Luther-Agricola-Gesellshaft, Helsinki 1992.

Wiles, M. F., *Soteriological Arguments in the Fathers*, Studia Patristica, Academie Verlag, Berlin 1966.

Williams, George, H., *The Radical Reformation*, Westminster Press, Philadelphia 1962.

Zimmerman, Gunter, "Die Thesen Osianders zur Disputation 'de iustificatione'", *Kerygma und Dogma* 33 (1987), pp. 224–244.

INDEX OF NAMES

INDEX OF SUBJECTS